180° 179° k

16°—

EVU

TAVEUNI 17°—

VANUA BALAVU

KORO

○MAGO

KORO SEA

'IKI

○CICIA

GAU ○NAYAU 18°—

OCEAN LAKEBA○

○MOALA

KABARA○ 19°—

TOTOYA

MATUKU 180° 179°

Cambridge Human Geography

ISLANDS, ISLANDERS AND THE WORLD

The colonial and post-colonial experience of Eastern Fiji

Cambridge Human Geography

ISLANDS, ISLANDERS AND THE WORLD

The colonial and post-colonial experience of eastern Fiji

TIM BAYLISS-SMITH
RICHARD BEDFORD
HAROLD BROOKFIELD
MARC LATHAM

with contributions from Muriel Brookfield

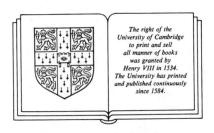

*The right of the
University of Cambridge
to print and sell
all manner of books
was granted by
Henry VIII in 1534.
The University has printed
and published continuously
since 1584.*

CAMBRIDGE UNIVERSITY PRESS

Cambridge

New York   New Rochelle   Melbourne   Sydney

Published by the Press Syndicate of the University of Cambridge
The Pitt Building, Trumpington Street, Cambridge CB2 1RP
32 East 57th Street, New York, NY 10022, USA
10 Stamford Road, Oakleigh, Melbourne 3166, Australia

First published 1988

Printed in Great Britain
at the University Press, Cambridge

British Library cataloguing in publication data

Islands, islanders and the world: the
colonial and post-colonial experience of
eastern Fiji. – (Cambridge human geography)
1. Eastern Fiji. Economic development, 1840–1987
I. Bayliss-Smith, Timothy P.
330.996′11

Library of Congress cataloguing in publication data

Islands, islanders, and the world: the
post-colonial experience of eastern Fiji /
Tim Bayliss-Smith . . . [et al.].
p. cm. – (Cambridge human geography)
Bibliography.
Includes index.
ISBN 0 521 26877 X
1. Fiji – History. 2. Fiji – Economic conditions.
I. Bayliss-Smith, Tim. II. Series.
DU600.I75 1988
996′.11 – dc19   88-1372

ISBN 0 521 26877 X

Contents

Illustrations

PLATES

FIGURES

Tables

Foreword
The MAB Programme and the Eastern Fiji Project

GISBERT GLASER

Division of Ecological Sciences, UNESCO, Paris

'Ecology and rational use of island ecosystems' is one of the main project areas included in UNESCO's Man and the Biosphere (MAB) Programme. MAB was launched in 1971 as a follow-up to the International Biological Programme (IBP) and in response to an increasing concern about serious man-induced environmental problems worldwide. MAB's overall aim is to contribute to the scientific basis for ecologically-sound development, and aims particularly at the sustained use and conservation of natural resources, training qualified personnel in this field, and helping to apply the knowledge acquired. As an international programme MAB's project areas cover virtually all of the world's major biomes and all of its major environmental management situations, including the conservation of natural areas and the genetic material they contain (Biosphere Reserve Action Plan). To meet its objectives the MAB Programme follows a problem-oriented interdisciplinary approach involving the social, human and natural sciences, an approach discussed at length elsewhere.

The authors of the present book were the key research workers in a MAB project on population/environment relationships in Eastern Fiji for which the field work was carried out from 1974 to 1976. Islands were considered to be appropriate sites for studying the complex systems relations among population dynamics, the availability and use of natural resources (mainly dependent on the state of agriculture), problems of the environment, and economic development in general, all under relatively controlled conditions. The Fiji study also dealt with the question of how to ensure that small isolated island systems do not lose their survival capacity, or, if they become integrated into larger systems, do not lose their capacity for self-reliance and endogenous development. The project's objectives were to develop a set of researched guidelines for planning and decision-making on population/environment problems in Fiji. It aimed as well at developing research methodologies which would also be useful outside Fiji for assessing population/resource/environment relationship situations at a micro-scale rather than at the global and regional scale of other models in this field.

The Eastern Fiji Project was a cooperative endeavour of the Government of Fiji, UNESCO and the United Nations Fund for Population Activities (UNFPA). The project's achievements and results have been published widely. A list of the formal technical reports including one synthesis report in UNESCO's MAB Technical Notes series, is given in the Appendix. Moreover, the project submitted to the Government of Fiji a comprehensive report containing detailed information for decision-making on population, resources and development in the eastern islands of Fiji.

The Fiji project is one of the few MAB pilot projects directed to the problems of man in relation to his environment rather than focussing on the problems of the environment in relation to man's activities. Both approaches are considered to be valid and necessary. As the present book demonstrates again, the first approach provides particular insights into the diversity of man's response to environment including the question of exploiting ecological diversity. It also demonstrates that *human use systems* are usually built on the interaction of sub-systems at different micro- and macro-scales, sub-systems 'in which men and women individually or collectively participate, ranging from household units and villages at the micro scale, to island ecosystems and core-periphery systems of regional interaction at the macro scale' (see chapter 11). The problem of the different spatial scales involved in man-environment studies is indeed one of the major challenges of an 'integrated' approach, and basically it is one that has not yet been solved. Another major methodological aspect highlighted by this book is the danger of applying a concept of 'standard' man. Individuals, small groups and societies need to be qualified with regard to their needs, perceptions, behaviour and cooperation in relation to their environment.

The initiative for this present publication was not taken by UNESCO and in fact the 1983 return visit to Eastern Fiji by the authors was, as described in the Editor's Note, independent of any official MAB activity. However, the idea to revisit the former study area seven years after completion of the field work of the MAB project was a commendable one. It enabled the team to analyse the changes which had occurred and to compare them with earlier findings and predictions as well as with the 'guidelines for decision-making on population/environment problems in the context of provincial and local development in the small islands of Fiji' which had been prepared at the end of the project. Longer term population/environment studies that allow the comparison of data over a ten-year period and more are all too rare.

Hence, we would like to express our gratitude to the editor of this book, Tim Bayliss-Smith, and to the other contributors, Harold Brookfield, Richard Bedford and Marc Latham for this excellent initiative. In addition to their specific role in the Fiji project, the authors have played an important role in the development of the MAB 'Island Project Area' in general, not least in the Caribbean region where a similar project was conducted in 1979/80. Moreover, they have reinforced the contribution of geography in its various dimensions, and of the social sciences, to the MAB Programme in general.

It goes without saying that the views expressed in this book, which is not to be considered part of the 'formal' reports of the 1974–6 Fiji project, are those of the authors and are their sole responsibility. These views are not necessarily shared by UNESCO and this publication does not in any event imply the expression of any opinion whatsoever on the part of UNESCO.

Editorial note

In most books it is the editor who writes the Introduction, but in this book he provides the Conclusion (chapter 11). The introductory first chapter is by Harold Brookfield, who was Team Leader of the UNESCO Project in eastern Fiji in 1974–6. The four authors of this book were core-members of the Project, which involved altogether sixteen people. Reporting was completed some years ago, and a list of formal Project publications is given in the Appendix. All four of us retained some contact with Fiji after 1976, and in 1982 two of us became involved in consulting work associated with development planning in the country. The idea of a return visit was thus born, and three of us, together with Muriel Brookfield, were able to revisit all our 1974–6 field sites in June–July 1983. We then decided to write a book about what has happened to eastern Fiji, and what this might add to the sum of knowledge about the colonial and post-colonial experience of the developing world. Because the book was to be published in Cambridge it was agreed that Tim Bayliss-Smith should undertake the work of editor.

Each of us first took responsibility for sections of the manuscript, and some substantial additions were then made by others to certain chapters. All of us have made some lesser contribution to all chapters as a result of correspondence, brief meetings and occasional frantic telephone calls. It remains true, however, that each chapter bears the stamp of a particular author. Not all of us necessarily agree with everything that has been written, though all have agreed not to disagree. Primary responsibility, and secondary responsibility where appropriate, is as follows:

Chapter 1   Harold Brookfield
Chapter 2   Marc Latham and Tim Bayliss-Smith
Chapter 3   Richard Bedford
Chapter 4   Harold Brookfield
Chapter 5   Harold Brookfield
Chapter 6   Richard Bedford
Chapter 7   Tim Bayliss-Smith and Richard Bedford

Chapter 8 Tim Bayliss-Smith
Chapter 9 Tim Bayliss-Smith, Richard Bedford, Harold Brook-
field and Muriel Brookfield
Chapter 10 Harold Brookfield
Chapter 11 Tim Bayliss-Smith

In addition to our own material, all of us have made use of data, ideas and writing generated by other members of the project, in particular Roger McLean, John Campbell and Muriel Brookfield. (See the Appendix.) Muriel made an important contribution to the 1983 field work and has provided new material used in chapters 9 and 10, as well as commenting on large parts of the manuscript. We thank all our UNESCO project colleagues, whose efforts contributed so much to our own understanding.

We would also like to thank the MAB Programme of UNESCO, and in particular Dr Gisbert Glaser, for their continuing interest in Fiji research. Financial help in 1983 came from St John's College, Cambridge, the Australian National University and the United Nations Fund for Population Activities. St John's College and the Australian National University have continued to provide logistic support during the writing-up stage. In particular, we thank Carol McKenzie and Pauline Falconer in Canberra, Anna Maloney and Linda Harrison in Christchurch, and Maria Constantinou in Cambridge for their work in typing (and retyping, and retyping ...) the manuscript, and Michael Young of the Geography Department, Cambridge and Keith Mitchell and Manilo Pancino of the Cartographic Office, Research School of Pacific Studies, in Canberra, for their expert work on the maps and diagrams. Helpful comments on the text were made by Rodney Cole, Derek Gregory, Patrick Nunn, Brian Robson and Matthew Spriggs.

Our acknowledgements to those who helped us in Fiji in 1974–6 have already appeared elsewhere. Several of the same people helped us again in 1983, but the crowded four weeks of this second visit could not possibly have been successful without the help of certain people, in particular Dr Isireli Lasaqa, CBE, then Cabinet Secretary and now Registrar of the University of the South Pacific. Also in Suva we are grateful to Suliana Siwatibau, Jim McMaster, Frank Ellis, John Cameron, Manfred Bienefeld, Daryll Tarte, Randy Thaman, Bill Clarke, and Sai who looked after us so well in the ANU flats. Elsewhere we particularly thank Ratu Tevita Uluilakeba, Inoke Taliai, Jone Taoba, Jone Toa, Rayasi Cakacaka and Dr Govind on Lakeba; Joeli Kaumaitotoya, Setariki Saiasa and Akaripa Tale on Kabara; Suliano Manakiwai on Koro; Moses Valaono on Batiki; the Tui Cakau, Taito Waqavakatoga, Master Jimilai, Mrs M.

Tukana, the staff of the Agriculture Department and several of the planters on Taveuni; Anare Boseniyasana in Levuka; and the Principal Agricultural Officer (Northern) Phil Hotchin. At sea, on the 'Vuniwai-ni-Lau' which was put at our disposal for ten days, we shall long remember Captain Akuila and his crew, both for their help and their herculean efforts to cope with repeated breakdowns without disrupting our schedule. Captain Akuila's navigational skills, both by day and night, remain as a remarkable memory of the high quality of Fijian seamanship. This list is of course incomplete, and does not begin to cover the many persons in eastern Fiji whose help we should particularly acknowledge: those islanders who were our informants and our friends; best critics and true benefactors. To them we say '*Vinaka vakalevu na veivukui kemudou a vakayacora vei keitou. Keitou masulaka mena sotavi kemudou na veivakalougatataki.*'

St John's College   Tim Bayliss-Smith
Cambridge
Midsummer Night 1987

I

On the study of islands, people and events

Prologue

In May 1987 the apparent calm of the Pacific island country of Fiji was suddenly shattered by a military *coup d'état*. In a general election held in April the long-ruling Alliance Party, which had controlled Fiji since Independence in 1970, and even for some years before that under self-government, was toppled from power and its place taken by a coalition formed between the Indo-Fijian-dominated National Federation Party and a multi-racial Labour Party formed less than two years earlier. The election was followed by a month of disquiet fomented by indigenous-Fijian nationalists, who saw dangers to Fijian hegemony from a new Government in which more than half the ministers were Indo-Fijian, even though the Prime Minister and all ministers concerned with mainly Fijian matters were indigenous Fijians. The new Government proposed an inquiry into the festering land problems of Fiji, and threatened also to expose corruption and cronyism under the Alliance. The third-ranking officer of the small Fijian army then led a coup which seized the whole government and – within a day – restored most of the former Alliance Party ministers to office in a *de facto* Council of Government. The press was stifled, the radio and telecommunications were censored, and arrests were made. Assertion of executive authority by the Governor-General, at first ignored, achieved the release of the deposed government but not its re-instatement. The Great Council of [Fijian] Chiefs, the supreme advisory body on Fijian affairs, then became a *de facto* parliament to resolve conflicting views among the ethnic Fijians. It confirmed the Governor-General in executive power, and later became judge of what sort of new constitution Fiji should have to ensure not only Fijian hegemony, but also the hegemony of traditional authority over the Fijians. The Pacific nations, and the Commonwealth, accepted these changes with minimal demur. Fiji thus joined that group of nations in which full democratic rights are denied to a large ethnically defined part of the population, and in which political opposition even among the indigenous people is stifled.

The strains which this event exposed go very deeply into the history and political economy of Fiji. When Fiji became a British colony in 1874 the islands had already endured more than half a century of warfare among a group of 'sea-states' around the shores of Koro Sea in the east of Fiji, and some twenty years of rapacious land alienation at the hands of planters who came mainly from Australia. The new colonial government sought to 'conserve' rather than 'dissolve': it first regularised the land situation, then set up a system of administration which effectively separated the Fijian people from the economic currents of the world around them. The Great Council of Chiefs was part of it. These actions deprived the planters of labour, so from 1880 to 1916 large numbers of Indian workers were recruited to grow sugar cane and other crops. By the end of the Second World War the Indo-Fijian descendants of these immigrants slightly outnumbered the indigenous Fijians, which they still do though by a declining margin. Yet over four-fifths of the land still remains under Fijian ownership, registered in the main by descent groups (*mataqali*) rather than individually.

As we show below, not all indigenous Fijians remained on the land and since early in this century they have moved in growing numbers into towns and into rural employment away from home. A high proportion of Indo-Fijians remained on the land as tenant farmers, but many are in the towns and they include a strong professional and business component. The Indo-Fijian share of the commercial economy has increased significantly since 1980, when Australian companies which once controlled most of the large-scale businesses began a significant withdrawal, shifting their interests elsewhere. Many of the wealthier Indo-Fijians have worked closely with the Alliance party, which is itself dominated by an aristocratic class of chiefly Fijians though it drew its main support from the mass of rural Fijians and, until 1987, also from middle-class and working-class Fijians in the towns. Under the Independence constitution most of Parliament has been elected on communal rolls, but with a small proportion of members elected by cross-voting. It was a shift of allegiance by considerable numbers of ethnic Fijians who felt that their interests had been neglected under the Alliance Government, as well as of an important part of the intelligentsia, which gave the new Labour Party strong support and determined the outcome of the April 1987 election.

By their control over land, by the constitution, and by a policy begun by the British and continued after Independence of recruiting the armed forces mainly from among indigenous Fijians, the Fijian people had their interests well protected. None the less, the Indo-Fijian domination of business and the professions had disquieted them, and increasingly so in recent years as Indo-Fijian enterprise had replaced European business enterprise in an increasing range of economic sectors. A sense of vulnerability has been enhanced by the failure of the Kanaks of New Caledonia to make headway against the immigrant French – 'les Caldoches'. A French visitor to Fiji in 1986 perceptively remarked that the 'Caldoches' of Fiji are all brown-skinned. Vocal discontent among the minority Maori of New Zealand and the Aborigines of Australia has also made ethnic Fijians fear, however unrealistically, a similar loss of control in their own country.

The coup therefore had considerable support among indigenous Fijians, both among supporters of the Alliance and among a heterogeneous but powerful racially nationalist movement that sprang up shortly after the election and, on the later statement of one of its leaders (*Fiji Sun*, 19 July 1987: 1), had plans for arson and murder against Indo-Fijians, plans that were pre-empted by the coup. This *Taukei* (sons of the soil) movement has both chiefly and commoner leadership, and after the coup it came out with simplistic demands for wholly Fijian rule and even expulsion of the Indo-Fijians and other foreigners. Faced with this very popular new force that had been unleashed the Governor-General and his advisers first called on the (indigenous) Fijian Provincial Councils for their views then hastily re-convened the Great Council of Chiefs in July to present an authoritative view on new constitutional arrangements. Predictably the Council proposed a new constitution which would give Fijians certain control of the legislature, but by Fijian members who would not be elected by vote, but nominated.

With the economy in disarray there were moves toward reconciliation and restoration of civilian rule. However, a compromise reached in September between the Alliance and Labour leaders was at once overturned by a second coup, after which the army shared power with the then-strong *Taukei* movement. A Republic was declared. Then in December the coup leader, promoted Brigadier-General in command of the enlarged army, ousted the *Taukei* leaders and restored the traditional chiefs and their Alliance supporters to nominal power in a third post-coup Government, with the former Governor-General as President of the Alliance leader as *de facto* Prime Minister. The old leadership rules, but only with army support. Moves to restore *Taukei* dominance have been suppressed. The new constitution is delayed indefinitely in this tense situation. Many of the wealthy and skilled, Fijians as well as Indo-Fijians, have left Fiji. In mid-1988 no end is in sight; an uneasy new Fiji has been created.

The eastern islands

The islands with which this book is concerned comprise only a part of Fiji, and exclude the main island of Viti Levu where the capital, Suva, is situated and where the events of April and May 1987 principally took place. None the less, they have an important role in the national story. The eastern island region is part of the historical heartland of Fiji, the area in which the 'sea-states' of Bau, Rewa, Verata, Bua, Cakaudrove and Lau struggled for power in the nineteenth century, and in which the settlers backing the victorious ruler of Bau established the first national capital, at Levuka on Ovalau. A high proportion of the Alliance Party leadership is drawn from this region, and especially from its high-ranking chiefs and members of high-ranking descent groups. The Prime Minister, the President (formerly Governor-General) and his predecessor have all been from this region. The coup leader, though a commoner, is a member of a high-ranking descent group living within it. Most of those men and women whose demonstrations through Suva after the April 1987 election provided the excuse for the coup were people from the east, especially from the Lau islands, and much of the crowd that vociferously supported the coup was also made up of Lauans. Though the eastern region itself now houses only a small share of the national population, many of its native people are in and around Suva, and they include a wide spectrum from the unemployed to people firmly established in the corridors of national power. There are few Indo-Fijians in the east, and this region is politically the most important of the three main areas of little-diluted indigenous-Fijian rural hegemony, the others being the south of Vanua Levu and the rugged interior of Viti Levu.

Paradoxically, it was largely the fact that the eastern islands represented a region of Fijian rural people that took us to the east when we embarked on the UNESCO/UNFPA Project on Population and Environment in Fiji in 1974–6. The project which we set up in 1974 was part of that section of the international Man and the Biosphere Programme of UNESCO that was concerned with islands, and principally with small islands. The conventional wisdom of the day had it that islands and their people could be studied in isolation, as a microcosm of the larger world. Eastern Fiji was not our own first choice, but in the early 1970s Fiji was the only fully independent country with an archipelago of small islands in the south Pacific, and UNESCO could itself mount a pilot project only in such a country. When sent to Fiji by the decision of our masters in Paris, we laboured under no illusions about studying islands 'in isolation', a matter to which we return again in our concluding chapter. We recognised from the outset that no island is truly an island in the modern world. We went there to study islands in the periphery of a nation itself part of the world periphery, and our team was formed with this perspective in mind. But we at first saw the eastern region as a wholly dependent periphery, and it was only after we arrived that we began to appreciate the importance of the 'other island population' in Suva and in the corridors of power.

Issues of land, and of national policy toward a region perceived both as 'core' and as 'periphery' in different contexts, thus formed important elements in our research, and because of this idiosyncratic – though not unique – interrelation of core and periphery we found much of the economic literature on islands and on core-periphery relations, whether neo-classical or Marxist, of rather limited value in our work. Our search for a relevant literature is discussed in some detail in our second major report for UNESCO (Brookfield 1980), where we found reason to question not only the utility of the island literature but also of dependency theory, in particular because of the failure of the latter to take full account of adaptation and resistance to external forces in the periphery. In longer retrospect, we would now add that the island economic literature has stagnated since the 1970s for want of adequate consideration of all those essentially political forces which introduce 'distortions' into the market for factors of production and goods. Later in this book, in chapter 10, we take up this point in the specific context of these islands.

Allowing the peculiarity of islands that they are isolated from the systems of land transport, and the further peculiarity of limited and skewed resources, we found it more helpful to draw on the literature of rural development as a whole, and again to draw out contrasts between theoretical expectation and reality. Peripheral rural Fiji, islands though it be, shares many of the same problems as peripheral rural anywhere else, but it also exhibits many of the positive characteristics of other areas of rural periphery. It experienced a period of heavy capitalist penetration during the later stages of which the rural village population, though exploited, were able to enjoy higher living standards than were people in other parts of rural Fiji. Locational disadvantage grew as capitalist enterprise entered a withdrawal stage, much as Crotty (1979) describes for Ireland. But throughout, the people of the eastern islands resisted efforts to convert them wholly into cash-crop producers, and clung stubbornly to control over the means of subsistence, while selecting among the alternatives available to them for earning money in a rational manner. We discuss this in detail in the case studies which form chapters 6, 7, 8 and 9.

When we went back to Fiji in 1983, for a period only a fraction of the length of our 1974–6 field work, we encountered a number of surprises. Cyclones and a collapse in the prices of all Fiji's products after 1980 had greatly reduced producer incomes and the national economy was perceived as still in crisis. Unemployment was for the first time since Independence a serious issue; real incomes of cane growers had been almost halved, and the economic differentials between a salaried middle class and the self-employed and the lower-paid workers were sharpened.

This was the environment in which the formation of the Labour Party was first mooted in the following year. Yet in the eastern islands a recent rise in the price of copra, their main economic product, generated a spirit of optimism and it was possible for much of 1983 that a new major initiative to revitalise the industry might be undertaken with World Bank support. It was, moreover, a time of innovation as we describe below. These circumstances dulled our perception of the deeper stresses that had emerged in the islands as well as in all of Fiji during the hard times after 1980. We certainly became aware of a widening gulf between the more arrogant of the aristocracy and the common people among the Fijians, perceptibly wider than in the mid-1970s, but we did not become aware of a hardening of attitudes toward the Indo-Fijians. The greater stress that we give to class than to ethnicity in the chapters which follow reflects this perception.

A question to ourselves

Today, after the May 1987 events in Suva and in the sugar-cane regions, those who 'know' Fiji all say that a Fijian coup against an elected Indo-Fijian majority government was inevitable. We feared it, being aware that the Fijian Military Forces have in effect for years been undergoing a form of training, through their assignment to UN Peace-keeping Forces in Sinai and Lebanon, for the role within Fiji they were most likely to be called on to perform. But we were not sure, having believed optimistically that the emergence of a multi-ethnic political party heralded the emergence of a new form of politics, and being aware also of the widespread mutterings about the high chiefs and their dominance among the commoner Fijians, not least Fijians in the east. We hoped, with many others, that a commitment to democracy had become established at the popular level, as well as in law. The fact that we were wrong, and had not perceived (or allowed ourselves to perceive) that communal fears and hatreds lay so near the surface, quickly able to muster so many ethnic Fijians behind the chiefly leadership, throws into question all our interpretations in this book. It is some years now since a Fijian colleague, writing in a book edited by one of us in which we claimed to be seeking understanding as well as explanation, questioned our ability to achieve understanding of a society not our own. Among other perceptive comments he wrote of

a measure of pride [among Melanesians] in the knowledge that the expatriate cannot really grasp the inner workings and nuances of indigenous societies. This leads in many cases to a patterned and artificial set of behaviour by many Melanesians in the presence of most expatriates, in contrast to the more casual and more real responses in the company of familiar local people. This is not dishonest behaviour: it is simply a natural reaction to a colonial [or recently colonial] status which contains little that encourages and preserves self-respect among islanders. This is the sort of feeling and situation that is not likely to be immediately apparent to expatriate observers, thus missing study and analysis. (Lasaqa, 1973: 309–10)

Expatriate researchers such as ourselves, and some indigenous social scientists too, are often further drawn away from the phenomenological search for real understanding by the academic imperative of seeking theoretical meaning in their findings. Human ecologists look for adaptive systems that can be set out in diagrammatic form; radicals seek to generalise modes of production articulated through the capitalist system; 'small-l' liberals seek behavioural interpretations in the theories of such writers as Chayanov, Schultz, Lipton and Sahlins. Explicitly or not, we seek models, and so inevitably select among our data. If we use case-study material there is often a measure of selection according to the system of explanation on which we have resolved, though this need not necessarily be so stark as the method of an earlier generation of anthropologists thus caricatured by Leach (1961: 11–12):

Case-history material ... seldom reflects objective description. What commonly happens is that the anthropologist propounds some rather preposterous hypo-thesis of a very general kind and then puts forward his cases to illustrate the argument ... Insight comes from the anthropologist's private intuition; the evidence is only put in by way of illustration.

Confronted by so dramatic a failure to predict – though far from alone in this failure – we are forced to ask ourselves just how much our interpretations also reflect 'private intuition', and – more importantly – what we wished to see. In an unusual book on explanation in behavioural science an exchange took place between Jarvie (1970a,b) and Winch (1970) which is highly germane to this question. Winch (1964) had earlier argued that the institutions of a 'primitive' society can only be understood if their internal rationale is first accepted within the whole context of the society concerned, and only afterwards and as a secondary task con-fronted with a 'western' standard of comparison. Jarvie, on the other hand, argued that cross-cultural value judgements, such as the use of the norms of one's own society as a measuring instrument or sounding board, are the principal way in which sociological understanding of alien societies is reached (Jarvie 1970a: 232). Winch hotly denied this claim, and in particular rejected Jarvie in denying that 'the almost universal success of western ways of life in ousting other "more primitive" ways shows anything about the superior rationality (or superior anything else, except persuasiveness) of western institutions' (Winch 1970: 259). Jarvie (1970b: 268–9) retorted that the success of western rationality lies in its scientific basis, and that its superiority is the reason why it has been able to displace other and more 'primitive' systems: 'action taken to gain scientific knowledge is at the heart of any idea of rationality.'

The chapters which follow were all written before the Fijian events of May 1987, and in editorial revision have not been changed greatly in content. This applies even to most of chapter 10, which is concerned with planning. It is therefore appropriate in this chapter, the last to be written, to consider where we seem to stand in relation to the Winch/Jarvie controversy, and in relation to Lasaqa's scepticism. If we look at what we have written we find that we explain farmers' behaviour in regard to an economic calculus, very much following the approach pioneered by Schultz (1964). We note the failure of attempts to solve modern problems by traditional methods. We seek evidence of the emergence of classes, and we note the way in which certain chiefs have used change in order to reinforce the position of their class. We conclude that survival of a 'Fijian way of life' in the outer islands is something of a *faute de mieux*, the product of an externally imposed political economy more than of conscious resistance. Notwithstanding our professed sympathies with the position taken by Winch, all this smacks rather heavily of Jarvie's point of view.

Yet could we have done differently? In our defence we can certainly point to the weight given to the heavy centralisation of decision-making in Fiji, an observation that would be hard for any researcher to miss. Perhaps more pertinently, we also made much of the importance of the eastern islands as a power-base for an aristocratic national leadership, and of the mutual interdependence of people in the rural periphery and a national leadership which transfers national resources to ensure that their marginalisation is muted. Though we made some attempts in 1976, not followed up in 1983, we did not, however, adequately examine the conditions of the large numbers of islander migrants in and around the capital, from whom some of the mass support for the 1987 coup was drawn. In 1975–6 we were constrained by our status in a project mounted by a United Nations agency from examining too closely, and more specifically from writing about, the relations between indigenous Fijians and Indo-Fijians in those islands where Indo-Fijians are found; perhaps, however, this should not have prevented us from making more use, in subsequent writing, of our own observation of a situation full of stress, jealousy and prejudice.

There is one way in which we might have been more prescient. We might have thought more about a daily contradiction in the behaviour of Fijian commoners toward their chiefs, and placed it in an historical context. All of us noted, and often, that the many Fijian commoners who revile certain chiefs behind their backs, and the smaller number who describe the whole chiefly system as a pernicious anachronism doomed to an early end, will humble themselves before chiefs in their presence. They will say, in effect, 'I am against chiefly privilege, but I owe allegiance to the Tui X [the high chief of one of the pre-colonial states]'. If, therefore, it is the decision of the chiefs that a supposed Indo-Fijian threat to their hegemony must be overthrown, the people will still rally behind them, at least in eastern Fiji where the chiefly system has deep historical roots. This is in contrast to the western regions, and it helps understanding to recall that the Labour Party Prime Minister elected in April 1987 is not only a commoner, but is also from the west.

Continuing in this vein, we might then have followed Sahlins (1983), who has rejected Marxist interpretations of Fijian history, and has turned instead to the Mediterranean classical writers for inspiration. In revising the history of a mid-nineteenth-century east Fijian war, he has stressed the importance of 'heroic kingship' and its divine right in Fijian affairs. Thinking along these lines, rule by the high chiefs of the east from Independence until April 1987 really meant that history could continue to 'unfold as the social extension of the heroic person' (Sahlins 1983: 521). The loss of power was the defeat of the sacred chief, and the stage was set for 'heroic action' by a Lieutenant Colonel whose family ranks high in one of the major old confederacies. And the people cheered him, as crowds composed mainly of eastern islanders living in Suva did during the May days. Following this reasoning further,

the pertinent historiography cannot be – as in the good Social Science tradition – a simple quantitative assessment of the people's opinions or circumstances … as if one were thus taking the pulse of generative *social tendencies*. Heroic history proceeds more like Fenimore Cooper Indians – to use Elman Service's characterization: each man, as he walks single-file along the trail, is careful to step in the footprints of the one ahead, so as to leave the impression of One Giant Indian. (Sahlins 1983: 519)

An indigenous Fijian historiography of the 1987 events might indeed follow such a path. But the issues are confused by elements of a more modern kind. Western Fiji, where political opposition to the Alliance had its own regional movement for some years before the formation of the Labour Party, is the sugar-growing and tourist-serving region whose people, both indigenous Fijians and Indo-Fijians, have produced the wealth that supports the national economy as a whole. The growth of a web of transfer payments to the poorer east, which we describe below, has been resented in the west, where a sense of being under-served in the national distribution of infra-structural investment and benefits has long been festering. Urban Fijians in Suva, whose votes swung the 1987 election, were protesting in a very modern way against the economic sovereignty of chiefs and their allies, and its exercise for very modern forms of gain.

Conclusion

With hindsight, it might have been better had we recognised more clearly that we were in the presence of a complex and changing play of contradictions, in which allegiance and rebellion, ethnic confrontation and cordial interdependence, traditionalism and modernity, clan and class, east and west within the nation, all had their parts. Fijians whose daily speech and behaviour reflect these unresolved contradictions could not themselves have predicted how they would respond to the pressures of April and May 1987, still less to tell us. Lasaqa's disregarded warning to us contained yet another, but unstated warning. Islanders in the modern island world are so beset by the conflicts and contradictions under which they labour that even their own perceptions are flawed. Our compounding failure was to over-simplify this complexity, to select within it, and to impose our perceptions on the analysis.

Even when a real effort is made to 'understand' the minds of a people being studied, social scientists inevitably find themselves asking questions which derive from their own disciplinary systems of theory, and moreover reasoning from the norms of their own society. When, as in Fiji, they are dealing with a people very many of whom speak fluent, idiomatic English, it is easy to be lulled into believing that an open one-to-one relationship of understanding is being achieved, and for Lasaqa's warning to be disregarded. By training, anthropologists are less likely to fall into this trap than are geographers or sociologists, and they in turn less likely than economists. None the less, all do fall into this trap, which even applies when undertaking social research within different classes in one's own society. Recently in reviewing some of the underpinning assumptions of behavioural geography one of us (Brookfield, forthcoming) wrote that

The behavioural environment that we need first to study, then, is our own as social scientists. Our own training, value systems, ideology and preferences impose themselves on any research inquiry. It is important that we recognize this, and that we are projecting our own behavioural environment onto the data.

He did not, however, expect so soon to have this lesson pressed so firmly home! Our confidence that we have correctly interpreted the 'colonial and post-colonial experience of the eastern islands of Fiji' is a very minor casualty among the much greater consequences of the events of May 1987 in Suva. But the realisation does mean that we must present the chapters which follow as no more than our own interpretation, blinkered, shaded through dark glasses and limited by selective hearing, and not as the whole 'truth'.

It is one of the 'iron laws' of observational research that hindsight is the least useful of tools; one cannot go back to observe a second time. We did get so far as to appreciate the dependence of the island periphery on the state of the national economy; we did not get so far as to appreciate the full measure of its dependence on the course of national politics. If the outcome of the 1987 coup is the firm intrenchment, for the foreseeable future, of the mainly eastern chiefly class in national power, then the eastern islands have probably little to fear for continuation of the mass of direct and indirect supports that they have enjoyed since Independence. If, on the other hand, the improbable happens and the anti-chiefly sentiments of April 1987 ultimately prevail, then the future for the islanders will become much more uncertain. The coup and its still unknown aftermath are thus a vital part of the context of the story we tell in this book. Unfortunately, however, the reader will seek in vain for any real premonition of this disaster for Fijian democracy, social harmony and economic progress in the pages that follow.

2

The island landscape

Reconstructing prehistoric geography

In order to justify its content this chapter must start with a simple assertion: that the contemporary configuration of population, economy and environment in eastern Fiji is incomprehensible without consideration of its historical roots. In the island world as elsewhere all geography is historical geography, not merely in the facile sense that every present soon becomes the past, but also because the context or structure within which human actions occur is slow to change, and is therefore not transformed as rapidly as are human intentions. To extend the metaphor proposed by Kirk (1952), we can regard this structure as the 'ecological theatre', not forgetting that it includes culture, artefacts and their location as well as the physical landscape. Present-day human actions are merely the latest episode in a long-running 'evolutionary play' that is happening within the ecological theatre. This play is one in which every scene necessarily takes place amid a scenery in part newly created, but in part inherited from past scenes, some of them quite remote from the actions taking place at any given moment.

This theatrical metaphor is perhaps more useful than the usual biological notion of 'cultural adaptation', as it suggests the existence of important lags and mismatches in the dynamic relationship between structure and human agency. To adequately comprehend what is happening now to the geography of eastern Fiji (or anywhere) therefore demands an explicit focus on what in the structure is inherited from the past, and how, and why. Kirk (1952: 15) pointed out that to follow the ancient academic convention that 'would limit the geographer to a description of the stage and the historian to the human drama played out on it' must destroy the essential unity of the whole, since 'stage and actors are in dynamic relationship both in space and time'. In this chapter, however, where we focus on the island landscape, we can only provide a partial account of this dynamic relationship. With reference to the emergent social and economic structure of colonial Fiji (chapter 3) a more complete explanation is attempted, but with the islands themselves we are not in this position.

One reason is that the physical environment is typically a very conservative part of the total structure, with some elements inherited from the remote past in an essentially pristine state, others bearing the imprint of human actions in the prehistoric (in Fiji, pre-colonial) past, and others inherited from the historical (colonial) period. The study of environmental change, or the lack of it, therefore requires the consideration of processes operating over thousands of years, with few data and much guesswork.

On the human side a more fundamental problem restricts our capacity to reconstruct the prehistoric geography of eastern Fiji, and that is our ignorance of what has variously been termed the 'behavioural', 'cognised' or 'perceived environments' of the past (Kirk 1952; Rappaport 1968; Brookfield 1969). Apart from ethnoarchaeology, which is essentially the imaginative use of ethnographic analogy to interpret sparse archaeological data, there is no means available to establish precisely what 'actors' were living on these islands during most of the period of landscape change, nor how, nor why their management practices lead to the (barely) observed effects. It is the familiar problem of much historical geography: necessarily our analysis 'ignores the dual problem of reconstructing the actor's and constructing the observer's view of the past' (Baker 1984: 18). Beyond potsherds, middens and a reconstructed core vocabulary, we have no secure means to establish the 'behavioural environment' of the Lapita colonists in Fiji; we have no mental maps of the 'perceived environment' of Fijians in the age of European expansion. Secure history starts in eastern Fiji around 1830, and the sources only become garrulous after Cession to the British Crown in 1874.

For these reasons this chapter examines the prehistoric geography of eastern Fiji primarily from the standpoint of the physical and biological sciences. We consider the status of the island landscape in terms of current geomorphological, pedological and botanical perceptions. We do not have the capacity to attempt cross-sectional reconstructions of the processes operating within pre-colonial landscapes, so we focus instead on three major 'vertical themes' of landscape change: the changing coastline, the retreating forests, and the accumulating swamps. These themes faintly echo Darby's (1951) well-known vertical themes in the historical geography of Europe (clearing the woodland, draining the marshland, reclaiming the heath, etc.), but they are not designed, as was his approach, to define what constitutes 'geography' as opposed to 'history' in the Fijian context. Rather, we are concerned simply to establish the broad nature of the relationships, past and present, of the Fiji islanders to the resources that they use.

Our underlying purpose is to scrutinise an inherited stereotype that until recently has dominated our ideas about Pacific islanders to an unacceptable degree. This is the notion invented by eighteenth-century romantics and sustained by twentieth-century prophets of ecological crisis, that the South Sea islands once represented models of optimal resource use, Gardens of Eden in a degraded world or biosphere. It is this aspect of the ecological relationship that we examine first, before discussing in turn the three vertical themes of landscape change.[1]

Island populations: stasis or crisis?

An interdisciplinary symposium was held at the Tenth Pacific Science Congress in 1961, where the theme of *Man's Place in the Island Ecosystem* was explored by a range of distinguished contributors. The publication that followed, edited by Fosberg (1963), can be taken as broadly representative of conventional academic opinion concerning human adaptations to islands. Indeed, many of the viewpoints quite tentatively expressed at the symposium were later presented in more extreme form, as problems of ecological adaptation, resource management and the limits to growth began to attract increasing attention in the 1960s and 1970s. At the symposium four major themes emerged, each of which can be illustrated without undue distortion by means of selective quotation.

(i) *Islands are worth studying*:
Islands ... have played a role, sometimes of remarkable subtlety, in leading to scientific truth and to hypotheses concerning man's place in the order of nature ... Sometimes men observing them have seen more than they could see in wider and less manageable regions; they could see, especially with repeated visits, the effects of human activities on the landscape (Glacken 1963: 76).

(ii) *On islands there is an accurate perception by the inhabitant of the possibilities and limitations of nature*:
One cannot help but suspect that small, insular populations are either consciously more aware of resource needs, or have developed necessarily good cultural adaptations to resource development ... The consequences of over-multiplication in such cases is immediate and clear. (Bates 1963: 111).

(iii) *We can expect to find on islands close ecological and social adaptations to environmental problems*:

---

[1] The data presented in this chapter are merely a summary of what is discussed in greater detail in some earlier publications of the UNESCO/UNFPA Project (Appendix), and in Brookfield (1981).

Before measures limiting the increase in population are instituted there will probably be a tendency for island people to utilise more fully the resources available within their limited territory. Efforts in this direction need not be confined to ... improvements in the technology and organisation of food production ... There may also be the development of certain social forms and usages that help to get people to resources and resources to people, for example in Polynesia (Vayda & Rappaport 1963: 137)

(iv) *Until recent times there is little evidence from the Pacific for disastrous mismanagement of island resources*:
The small tropical islands in the Pacific ... do not generally belong to the category of densely populated islands that are, for this reason, especially threatened with overutilization of resources (Gourou 1963: 207).

It would seem that on the high islands of Micronesia and Polynesia serious degradation of the ecosystem was not frequently or widely induced by human populations, despite their size and density, occupancy of one to three millennia, and removal of primary forest cover from large areas (Rappaport 1963: 165).

There is not space here for a detailed review of the ways in which these four viewpoints have been confirmed or modified in the years that have elapsed since the 1961 symposium (although it is worth noting that quite similar views were expressed in a plenary address to the Fifteenth Pacific Science Congress in 1983: Leach 1984). There is no question that islands have retained their appeal for the biological sciences, as the growing interest in island biogeography and conservation over the last twenty years has shown. In 1972 UNESCO decided to choose *The Ecology and Rational Use of Island Ecosystems* as one project within its Man and the Biosphere (MAB) Programme (UNESCO 1973), and it was MAB which enabled the authors of this book to become involved in interdisciplinary research in eastern Fiji.

The second theme, the perceived environment of islanders, also continues to be a focus of interest, and in the Pacific region it has been the subject of some remarkable monographs (e.g. Rappaport 1968; Gladwin 1970; Ross 1973; Christiansen 1975; Johannes 1981; Sillitoe 1983). Even so the links between insularity, perception, and a more rational use of resources remain hypothetical and difficult to test in this age of all-pervasive and externally induced social change. In a prehistoric context, Rhys Jones (1978) has claimed that a small and very isolated population may suffer from perceptual limitations, as in the case of Tasmania. On that island the disappearance of skills such as fishing suggested to him the possibility that 'events in Tasmania constitute a specific case within a general proposition, that the number of ideas in a cultural system is a function of the number of minds interacting within it' (Jones 1978: 47). It is unlikely, however, that Pacific island populations were as culturally isolated as were the Tasmanians. There is growing evidence for purposeful voyaging, trade and exchange in Pacific prehistory (e.g. Davidson 1977; Specht & White (eds.) 1978), suggesting that interaction rather than isolation might be more appropriate as a context for understanding islanders' adaptations.

The third theme, the extent of 'adaptation' by islanders, remains an area of debate in anthropology, with the evidence from Pacific island societies continuing to be influential (e.g. Harris 1968; Odum 1971; Ellen 1982; Carlstein 1982; Chapman & Prothero (eds.) 1985). As regards the effectiveness of ecological adaptation, theme 4, there is now a growing body of evidence from Pacific prehistory that emphasises change rather than harmonious static adjustment in environmental relationships (e.g. Golson 1977, 1982; Spriggs 1981, 1985, 1986; Kirch 1983; Kirch & Yen 1982). A dynamic relationship is suggested not only by changes in the cultural artefacts of Pacific populations, but also by change in the landscape and resources that these populations had under their control. If the symposium on *Man's Place in the Island Ecosystem* was reconvened in the mid-1980s, then for both past and present islands crisis not stasis would be the dominant emphasis.

Three thousand years of prehistoric geography

The ecological theatre

The island ecosystems that we are concerned with are situated in the Fiji group, almost one hundred populated islands and over two hundred uninhabited islets, all scattered across an expanse of the South Pacific Ocean equivalent in area to Turkey or Afghanistan. The total area of actual land in Fiji is much smaller, about 18,000 km², or about the same area as Wales. Two islands, Viti Levu and Vanua Levu, make up about 90 per cent of the land area and contain about the same percentage of the population, but we are concerned in this book with the outer islands, in particular those in eastern Fiji. This region includes Taveuni, the Lomaiviti Group and the Lau Group. *Taveuni* is Fiji's third largest island, with a land area somewhat larger than Barbados in the Caribbean but with only one twenty-fifth of Barbados' population. Southeast of Taveuni is the *Lau Group*, a chain of eighty islands which extends from north to south across 450 km of ocean. The *Lomaiviti Group* (Gau, Ovalau,

Koro, Wakaya, Nairai, Batiki, and Makogai) lies between Viti Levu and Lau.

On the whole, then, these are not large islands. As one geologist remarked, 'unlike more spacious continents, Fiji could not long survive the ravages of erosion if the energies of orogeny were stilled' (Dickinson 1967: 543). Geological uplift probably continues, although in the time scale during which human settlement has occurred it may be too gradual to be detected. All land in Fiji dates from the last 25 million years, with Viti Levu the oldest and most complex of the islands. The majority of the geological formations are only between twelve to two million years old, belonging to the late Tertiary era, but in the Lomaiviti islands and in Taveuni there is also evidence of Pleistocene vulcanicity, with successive basaltic flows and ash falls which, in Taveuni, continued into very recent times. Many craters are still remarkably fresh, and in one cinder cone in the south of the island vestiges of human occupation layers, dated at 2200 years Before Present (BP), are separated by volcanic ash and derived soil from a more recent occupation layer dated around 750 BP (Frost 1969). This is the most recent vulcanism in Fiji, but geothermal activity and continuing intermittent earthquakes are a reminder that the region is still an active zone close to the plate tectonic boundary. There was a major earthquake between Kadavu and Viti Levu in 1953, and there have been many minor shocks in this area, in the area north of Vanua Levu, and in 1977 also north of Taveuni; this last event appears to have affected ground water levels in the island.

All the smaller islands consist entirely of volcanic rocks and limestone, sometimes deeply weathered and in places mantled with the products of recent erosion. The limestone rocks date back to the late Miocene in the case of the Lau group, and have been uplifted to form impressive cliffs, several hundred metres above sea level in places. Honeycomb weathering and karst features testify to a long period of chemical weathering. During the Pleistocene coral reefs grew as fringes around both volcanic and older limestone islands, and in most of southern Lau these now form exposed structures a few metres above present sea level. Post-Pleistocene coral, most close to present mid-tide level, thinly veneers the earlier formations, including the large submerged reef systems which cover extensive areas especially in northeastern Lau. Reef growth had to match a rise in sea level which was most rapid from about 10,000 until 4–5,000 years ago, the sea reaching a maximum elevation that, in Fiji, was probably slightly above the present level. The coastal flats of reefal sands that fringe most islands have been formed mainly by storm-wave deposition during the past 4,000 years, as have the mangrove swamps that veneer some former reef flats (McLean 1980b).

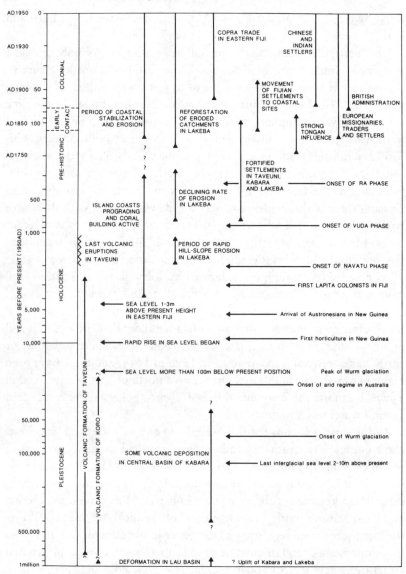

2.1 The last million years BP (Before Present) in eastern Fiji

The evolutionary play

The human response to this diverse physical landscape is difficult to reconstruct. The evidence so far available from archaeology, palaeo-environmental studies, linguistics, etc., cannot at present do much to compensate for the deficiencies of oral history. As the missionary Thomas Williams noted, the time depth of Fijian historical accounts is shallow: 'we seek in vain for a single ray of tradition of historical record to guide us through the darkness of a remote antiquity' (Williams 1868: 17). What accounts do exist must be interpreted with care. In Viti Levu, for example, there are several traditions which describe the arrival on the coast of important ancestral figures, according to genealogies about AD 1500–1600 or somewhat before, while in the Lau Group accounts of Tongan immigration correlate well with Captain Cook's observations of Fijian influence in Tonga. However, Peter France has pointed out:

> Even those carefully preserved tribal histories which are delivered solemnly around the *yaqona* bowl, and with every assurance of truth, need careful examination; for in Fiji, as elsewhere, the emergence of politically powerful units in the early nineteenth century led to the elevation of mythical theories of origin to the level of historical fact. (France 1969:10)

Genealogies in Fiji seldom extend beyond ten or twelve generations, so that earlier events can only be established by the indirect methods of archaeology or palaeo-environmental reconstruction.

In the light of this work, and with a knowledge of what was happening in other parts of Melanesia and Polynesia (Fig. 2.1), the archaeologists propose three main phases of settlement in Fiji (Groube 1971; Bellwood 1978; Frost 1979; Green 1979; Hunt 1986):

(i) *The Lapita colonists* These mobile, seafaring people were expanding rapidly through Melanesia three and a half thousand years ago, and colonised Polynesia soon after. On the coasts of Viti Levu colonists using Lapita pottery were established by 3200 years Before Present (BP), and their settlement of the entire Fiji group at this time is a reasonable assumption. The Lapita Cultural Complex is associated with the Austronesian languages and a strong emphasis on coastal settlement and marine resources, leading to the initial suggestion that these people had a 'strandlooper' adaptation. Evidence for horticulture has now emerged, but it is evidence of an indirect kind, such as the exotic land snails found in the early occupation levels at Yanuca island, and suspected of being 'hitch-hikers' that arrived unseen on economic plants (Hunt 1981).

(ii) *The Navatu phase* This phase is distinguished by impressed ceramics and started around 2,000 years ago. It is unclear whether the Navatu phase developed gradually out of the Lapita tradition, as suggested by Hunt (1986), or whether its appearance reflects influence from New Caledonia where a similar technology became established. Very little correlation can as yet be attempted between Navatu pottery and changes, if any, in other aspects of material culture.

(iii) *Vuda and Ra phases* These phases are distinguished by incised ceramics, which appear about 850 years ago. Once again there is no clear discontinuity in pottery styles between the impressed and the incised ware, but it may be significant that the Vuda phase (1100–1800 AD) corresponds to the appearance of fortifications, for example on Taveuni, Wakaya, Kabara and Lakeba, and that the ceramics have close parallels with pottery west of Fiji, especially in the New Hebrides (Vanuatu). This may have been a time of Melanesian population migration into Fiji, resulting in warfare, population movements, racial mixture and political realignments, an interpretation consistent with Fijian oral traditions and with the physical and linguistic patterns of the group (Smart 1965; Frost 1979; Rowland & Best 1980; Hunt 1986).

Continuity or immigration?

There are two ways of interpreting this sequence of phases, either continuous change or discontinuity. We might emphasise the apparent overlap in time between ceramic assemblages belonging to each phase, and thus infer continuity of settlement during a change in culture (or at least pottery tradition). Alternatively we could regard apparent overlap in ceramics as merely the product of post-depositional disturbance, as is known to have occurred in rockshelter deposits on Yanuca island, for example (Prescott et al. 1982). Definite breaks between phases of occupation would represent distinct periods of occupation of sites by different groups, some of them immigrants from beyond the Fiji group.

This latter interpretation would certainly correspond with the impression given by oral histories. France (1969) shows that out of a total of over 600 oral accounts of tribal origins recorded by the Native Lands Commission, only 21 tell of a tribe which claims to occupy a site on which the tribe was founded. The remainder indicate that in recent prehistory social upheaval, war and migration were more normal:

There is no period of calm and enduring settlement of land as far back as the traditions record ... Normal conditions ... were those of incessant inter-tribal skirmishing involving continuous migration and resettlement. (France 1969: 13)

Perhaps the smaller outer islands of the Fiji group were less subject to the constant upheavals of Viti Levu and Vanua Levu, but at the same time their dependent status in the chiefdoms of the nineteenth century indicates that even if they avoided internal dissent, the capacity of island societies in Lau and Lomaiviti to withstand the depredations of outside groups was extremely limited.

Lakeba – a case study

The island of Lakeba in the Lau group provides an interesting case study, because of the opportunity here to attempt to match the ethno-historical data and the archaeological evidence. The people of Lakeba provided the Lands Commission with accounts that begin with the arrival of Tui Lakeba and his followers from north-east Viti Levu. Tui Lakeba is said to have constructed the first hill fort on the island on the limestone ridge at Ulunikoro, an event dated by genealogies to the end of the sixteenth century AD (Reid 1977). Unfortunately, seven radiocarbon dates from early occupation levels on Ulunikoro hill fort give a secure average date of 960 BP, i.e. around 990 AD (Rowland & Best 1980). Only in the recent period are history and archaeology in agreement, both proposing a period of continuing political struggle and conflict leading to the construction of the major hill fort at Kedekede in the seventeenth century AD, a period of anarchy in the eighteenth century, and the installation of Tui Nayau as paramount chief in the nineteenth century. The greater stability of the period before the construction of Ulunikoro may be more apparent than real, in view of the evidence for a much earlier occupation of Kedekede and the evidence from coastal middens of the consumption of humans, both of which strongly suggest fighting and the need for defence (Rowland & Best 1980).

What is questionable in these interpretations is the extent to which the archaeological evidence for fortifications and the oral accounts of conflict and migration necessarily imply any lack of continuity in settlement or land use practices. France (1969) has pointed out that it is erroneous to suppose that the normal condition of a society is that described in its epic accounts, since the only reason for survival of those epics is that they describe conditions which deviate sufficiently from the normal to arouse the interest of the listeners. Moreover, Laura Thompson (1949) has argued strongly for a very different kind of history for southern Lau. She sees the relationship between population and resources as based on a balanced system of distribution of resources within and between islands, such that each household was guaranteed the means to obtain a balanced diet. Resource availability was further safeguarded by social controls to counteract overexploitation, to regulate harvesting, and to prevent over-population. She argues that the arrival on Kabara of conquering warriors from north-west Viti Levu fifteen generations before the 1930s did not unduly disturb the society, since the original population 'kept most of the land, their food-producing patterns, and their basic ecological adjust-ment' (Thompson 1949: 257).

We must conclude from this survey that in Fiji no clearcut answer yet emerges from archaeology or oral history concerning the adaptation of prehistoric populations to their island environment. Not much can be learnt about the nature or intensity of environmental exploitation from the available evidence, and to infer major changes in population or land use from subtle shifts in ceramic style might be quite unjustified. For a more complete (or less incomplete) picture, other forms of evidence must be brought into play. Data concerning landscape change, particularly from two islands where the UNESCO/UNFPA project concentrated its work, Lakeba and Kabara, show that important new insights can emerge through a more integrated treatment of man's place in the island ecosystem. This we shall demonstrate by reference to three components of the landscape, the coastline, the forested hills, and the swamps, but it is important first to establish how far ecosystem change might reflect sea level or climatic change, rather than the impact of human factors.

A stable ecosystem?

For most people in the outer islands of Fiji the coastal fringe represents the most important single component of the landscape. On the smaller islands virtually all settlement has been coastal since the nineteenth century, when the Fijian population abandoned defended sites inland to live in villages by the sea, where access to Church and trade was easiest and where there was land favourable for growing coconuts. The typical village is situated on the coral sand flats but often close to the freshwater back-swamps that are ideal for taro cultivation. There is easy access to reef flats, fringing reefs and mangrove swamps for fishing and the gathering of shellfish, crabs and firewood. These coastal habitats have the appearance of being stable and productive, but research now shows that in fact the coast is subject to continuous gradual change, and to sudden, often catastrophic, disturbance. Sea level, sediment sources, earthquakes and hurricanes are the main factors to consider, and of these sea level is undoubtedly the most fundamental.

Sea level change

Some detailed evidence for sea level change in eastern Fiji is presented below. The data suggest sea levels were considerably lower during the late Pleistocene, but that by 5,000 years BP the Holocene transgression had resulted in sea level reaching an elevation somewhat higher than the present one. It also seems likely that sea levels remained high during at least the first millennium of human settlement. Archaeological evidence from elsewhere in the South Pacific shows that the Lapita sites tend to be located on coastal landforms 1–3 m above their present-day equivalents, and some distance inland.[2] This relative emergence is usually ignored by the archaeologists or is attributed to local tectonic uplift, but for uplift to have occurred equally and simultaneously in such structurally separate islands seems very improbable. There is also an impressive accumulation of geomorphological evidence for higher sea level stands, from features such as high beachrock, small-scale solutional grooving and emersed fossil corals.[3] The regional pattern that is being proposed is reasonably consistent with the predictions of hydro-isostatic response models, which predict that during the last 5,000 years all of the southern part of the Pacific will have experienced a relative emergence of the land by 1.5–2.0 m (Clark 1980; Hopley 1982).

There are substantial implications of fluctuating sea levels both for coastal processes and for the cultural adaptation of communities, particularly on low-lying coasts and on coral islands wholly formed by wave action. For the atolls of the south Pacific it has even been claimed that settlement of any kind was not possible until well after the maximum transgression of the sea, which in Tuvalu and Kiribati is estimated as 2.4 m above present level 2,700 years ago (Schofield 1977b, 1979, 1980). Islands may not have formed at all on these reefs until some stage during the subsequent regression of sea level to its present height. Atolls are likely to exhibit in extreme form the geomorphological changes which all coastlines have experienced in this region. We must therefore conclude that coastal resources in Fiji have been subject to complex secular changes, interspersed with the episodic fluctuations associated with hurricane damage (see chapter 4). It is upon this shifting baseline that human impacts have been superimposed.

Climatic change

An equally fundamental control over the course of prehistory has been proposed by Bridgeman (1983) for Eastern Polynesia. He argues that the colonisation of more remote island groups was facilitated by the conditions of the Little Climatic Optimum (AD 75–1250), a period of persistent south-east trade winds and limited storminess. According to

[2] In the Reef Islands and Anuta (Santa Cruz group), in Futuna and Niuaafo'ou (Tonga outliers), in Tongatapu, and in Erromango sea levels were somewhat higher than at present during the time of early settlement (Green 1976; Kirch 1976, 1981, 1982b; Rogers 1974; Poulsen 1968; M. Spriggs, personal communication).

[3] The geomorphological evidence comes from New Caledonia, Tonga, Kiribati and Tuvalu, and the northern Great Barrier Reef (Fontes et al. 1977; Taylor & Bloom 1977; Schofield 1977a; McLean et al 1978). In eastern Polynesia the evidence from a number of islands that is reviewed by Stoddart et al. (1985: 136) suggests that 'a regional sea level stand at around + 1 m between 2000 and 6000 years BP seems likely'.

this model long-distance canoe voyaging came to an end in Polynesia because of the harsher conditions of the Little Ice Age that followed, between about AD 1400 and 1850. On the other hand, interchange between eastern Fiji and Tonga was at its height during this period (see chapter 3), possibly facilitated by the stronger westerlies. Finney (1985) has argued that Polynesian maritime technology was insufficient to enable long-distance voyages from west to east during periods of persistent trade winds. The weakening of the trade winds that occurs during an El Niño phenomenon, as in 1982–3 (see chapter 4), is suggested by Finney as a means whereby Polynesian colonisation eastwards would have been facilitated, perhaps on an involuntary basis because of the greater frequency of hurricanes that is associated with El Niño episodes.

Unfortunately direct evidence for such climatic change does not exist for the Pacific islands, where even the large-scale changes associated elsewhere with the Pleistocene–Holocene transition are difficult to demonstrate.[4] Phosphate deposits, formed under semi-arid conditions from the guano of sea birds, may in some cases date from drier phases in the Holocene (Aharon & Veeh 1984; Brookfield 1986b). Guano is not likely to have been produced on a large scale after human settlement, since almost everywhere (the uninhabited islet of Ogea Driki in southern Lau is an exception) the presence of man has lead to the elimination of large bird colonies.[5]

For the high altitude zone firm evidence for climatic changes comes from pollen analysis. Data from cores at Lake Tagimaucea in Taveuni span 14,300 years, and reveal that before 13,000 years ago the climate was cooler, supporting a forest assemblage not now encountered in Fiji and probably growing in semi-permanent cloud. Such cooler montane conditions imply less convection and lower rainfall, which in turn suggest semi-arid conditions for small islands and leeward coasts (Southern 1986). Thereafter conditions resembling those of the present day became established, and subsequent climatic variation cannot be determined. There probably has been such variation (Isdale 1984), but at present we can say little beyond the period of the historical record (see chapter 4).

[4] It can, however, be shown that certain landforms and soils, on islands like Lakeba or Aneityum in Vanuatu (Spriggs 1983), are more easily explained if we invoke a phase of aridity in the late Pleistocene. The likelihood of accelerated erosion during this period must be remembered if we are to make any balanced assessment of man's impact on geomorphic processes in more recent times.

[5] Phosphatisation of guano from sea birds has occurred on several islands now too wet for this process as well as lacking bird colonies, for example Ninigo and Purdy off northern New Guinea, Bellona in the Solomons, and Vanua Vatu in Fiji. More arid conditions in the late Pleistocene would have assisted this process, but most of these deposits are geologically much more ancient (Roe et al. 1983).

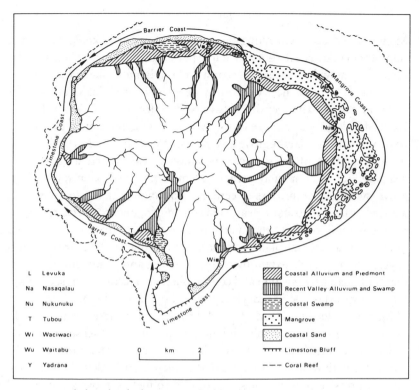

L   Levuka

Na   Nasaqalau

Nu   Nukunuku

T   Tubou

Wi   Waciwaci

Wu   Waitabu

Y   Yadrana

0   km   2

	Coastal Alluvium and Piedmont
	Recent Valley Alluvium and Swamp
	Coastal Swamp
	Mangrove
	Coastal Sand
	Limestone Bluff
	Coral Reef

2.2 Lakeba island, showing coastal landforms and valley alluviation

The changing coastline

In Fiji the chronology of the earlier high sea level has not been accurately established, but it is clear that many of the adjustments of landforms to the present, lower relative sea level have been occurring during the period of human settlement. We cannot, however, ignore the possibility that on some Fijian islands the effects of local tectonic movements are superimposed on the sea level changes (Bloom 1980).[6]

In the outer islands of Fiji there are three main types of coastline to be considered: mangrove coasts, barrier coasts, and limestone coasts (McLean 1979, 1983; Bedford et al. 1978). All three are well represented on the island of Lakeba (Fig. 2.2).

[6] Localised tilting may be more important in Lomaiviti than in Lau, since contemporary stability of the Lau Ridge can be inferred from the absence of seismicity there (Berryman 1979). The localised tilting that was suggested for Kabara island (Salvat et al. 1976), where the barrier reef on the east coast consists of dead corals emergent at low tide whereas the western barrier reef is submerged and partially living, could instead be due to differential subsidence or submarine karst collapses, or may be simply illusory (P. D. Nunn personal communication).

Mangrove coasts

Mangrove coasts occur along the eastern shores of Lakeba. The dense stands of mangrove are rooted in dark sticky mud, and form a belt of forest up to 1.5 km wide adjacent to a coastal plain. In most places the trees are growing on a thin veneer of recently deposited silt which overlies older reefal materials. The reef deposits must date from a time when the east coast of Lakeba was a more open, more exposed, and much less muddy environment. In the mangrove swamps at Waitabu a loose coral sample from 25 cm beneath the surface was radiometrically dated at 4470 ±155 years BP, but this date may predate the main phase of extension of mangrove swamp. The process is certainly continuing at the present time, assisted by new deposits of weathered volcanic fragments and clays derived from stream floods. On the landward side the mangrove backs on to a discontinuous coastal plain, consisting of old marine (mangrove) muds covered to a variable extent by recent alluvium and colluvium. It is clear that both mangrove swamp and coastal plain are recent features, developing during the last 4,000 years but particularly during the last 2,300 years of human settlement, a period which has seen huge increases in the sediment yield of streams draining inland catchments (see discussion below).

This accelerated rate of terrestrial input to coastal landforms can be paralleled with what has occurred in the Sigatoka river delta in Viti Levu. Here impressive coastal dunes rise to over 50 metres above sea level and cover an area of almost 3 sq. km. The dunes derive from sands that are deposited by the river at its mouth, accumulate on the beach, and are then blown inland (Dickenson 1968). Occupation debris belonging to the Lapita and Navatu cultural phases can be found in two horizons, dated to 2460 BP ±90 and 2180 BP ±80 respectively. These surfaces outcrop in the seaward face of the dunes at heights of only 1.7 and 5.8 m above high water mark (Birks 1973). There has clearly been a substantial development of dunes on this coast since then, suggesting there has been a rapid acceleration in the erosion of the Sigatoka catchment in the last two thousand years associated with the conversion of the forest cover to savanna grassland.

Barrier coasts

Barrier coasts are well illustrated by the northern side of Lakeba, and also occur in the south-west (see Figs. 2.2 and 2.3). There are four parallel zones: reef flats, sand barrier, swamp (not always present), and piedmont. The reef flat is wide and exposed at low water, and is subject to mangrove invasion in some places. Fields of dead micro-atolls, emergent with respect to present sea level, can be found along the inner half of the reef flat,

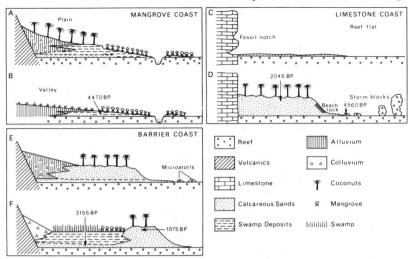

2.3 Coastal types on Lakeba

passing beneath the present beach in a few places. Similar features were noted at Wainiketei Bay on Batiki, partly mantled with terrigenous muds and undergoing colonisation by mangroves. On Lakeba McLean (1979) obtained a radiocarbon date from one elevated micro-atoll of 4560 ±70 years BP and there is archaeological evidence which suggests that the sea continued to be higher than at present in the early period of human settlement. Simon Best (personal communication 1977) suggests that stratigraphic evidence from rockshelters along the old cliffline of west Lakeba shows that sea level was about one metre higher at the time of the first Lapita settlements over 3,000 years ago.

On the north Lakeba coast the sand barrier itself provides further indirect evidence for continuing coastal change. The ridge consists of weathered coral sand and is currently undergoing erosion along the beach, suggesting it is effectively a fossil feature. Inland of the sand barrier is a series of coastal swamps at the edge of the main alluvial deposits, for example at Levuka and Nasaqalau. Here alluvial sedimentation is less dominant, and the stratigraphy enabled McLean (1979) to outline a successional sequence. The reef flat which is isolated behind the sand barrier is subject initially to washover deposits of reefal debris during storms; it then becomes a mangrove swamp; and finally, through alternate sediment deposition and organic accumulation, it is converted to a freshwater swamp which can be used for taro cultivation. This interpretation is supported by pits that were dug in the freshwater swamp at Levuka, 500 m landward of the present shore. These passed through clays and peat before reaching a basal layer of calcareous sand, molluscs and *in situ* corals 2 m below the surface. The coral was radiometrically dated at 3155

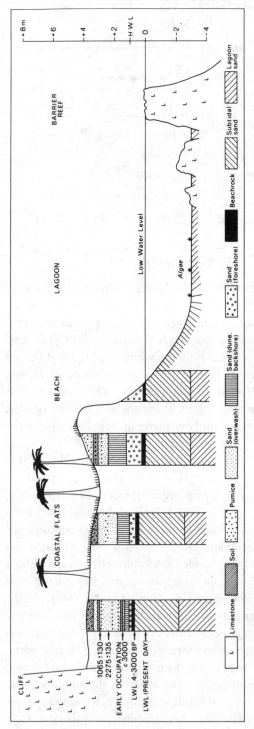

2.4 The limestone coast of Kabara

28

±140 years BP (McLean 1979). The implication is that the enormous coastal swamps, used for intensive taro cultivation in the nineteenth century and one factor in Lakeba's pivotal position in the Lauan political system, were not even in existence at the time of the island's initial settlement.

Landward of the coastal swamps is a piedmont which backs on to marine-faceted hillspurs, the fossil cliffline of circa 4500 BP. The whole appearance of the inner part of the barrier coastline of Lakeba suggests to McLean (1979: 73) that 'the last few millennia have been characterised by high stream sediment yield and very active mass movement on slopes'.

Limestone coasts

Limestone coasts on Lakeba are characterised by bold rocky promontories of limestone separated by low sand-filled embayments, and much of the coastline of Kabara is also of this character (Bedford et al. 1978). The sandy lowlands are usually 1–2 m above high water spring tides, and are generally planted with coconuts. The sands are all reef-derived carbonate materials, with occasional coral fragments and drift pumice interspersed, sometimes in thin layers (Fig. 2.4). Generally the soils thicken and darken with distance back from the shoreline, a reflection of the age of the deposit and the length of time of occupation and cultivation. On Lakeba, where stream valleys cut through the limestone cliffs, land-derived alluvial clays, muds and pebbles overlie the marine sands, an indication that large influxes of stream flood debris have occurred since the beach deposits accumulated (McLean 1979). As in Tikopia (eastern Solomons), Futuna and Niuatoputapu (Tongan outliers north of the Lau group), and Aneityum (Vanuatu), alluvial deposition has not only extended significantly the land area of the islands but has also created the most valuable areas of present-day agricultural land (Kirch & Yen 1982; Kirch 1981; Rogers 1974; Spriggs 1981, 1986).

For the sand flats, periods of stability with intermittent episodes of storm deposition are indicated by the stratigraphy, and by the fact that even today the coastal plain can be flooded by the sea during major hurricanes. At Waciwaci on Lakeba, for example, Hurricane Val flooded the village in 1975 by a surge which reached 0.7 m above high water spring tides 180 m inland; while on Kabara after a hurricane in 1938 the village headman reported that 'our village in Qaliqali is just like a long sandy beach, there is no soil', as a result of a storm surge which destroyed 56 houses and penetrated over 400 m inland to the foot of the limestone cliffs (McLean 1979, 1977).

In many cases, both in Fiji and elsewhere, coastal sand flats are no longer prograding, probably because the late Holocene fall in sea level, referred to above, has resulted in a decline in the productivity of coral reefs

Table 2.1 *Evidence for the age and development of coastal sand flats*

Location	Distance landward from beach	Depth from surface	Sample	Age (years BP)
a Lakeba (Levuka)	175 m	1.2 m	Wave-deposited reef sands	1875 ±125
b Lakeba (NW coast)	200 m	0.5 m	Wave-deposited reef sands	2045 ±130
c Kabara (Muimuila)	260 m	0.08 m	Charcoal in occupation layer	1065 ±130
d Kabara (Muimuila)	260 m	1.3 m	Wave-deposited reef sands	2275 ±135
e Kabara (Muimuila)	n.s.	2.3 m	Lowest occupation layer found (Lapita colonists?)	2–3,000 ?
f Viti Levu (Karobo)	n.s.	1.3 m	Occupation layer, same pottery as Sigatoka Lapita levels	2460 ±90 at Sigatoka Lapita level
g Taveuni (Vunivasa)	80 m	2.0 m	Wave-deposited reef sands, underlying Navatu/late Lapita phase occupation levels	1–2,600 ?

Sources: Bedford et al. 1978, McLean 1980a (a, b, c, d); Smart 1965 (e); Palmer 1965, Birks 1973 (f); Frost 1969 (g).

and reef flats, so that sediment supplies have become more restricted. Alternative explanations would attribute erosion to a small and very recent eustatic rise in sea level (McLean 1980b), or to the destructive role of man in replacing the natural vegetation of the littoral fringe with coconuts, which are certainly far less effective in resisting storm wave erosion and which fail to trap sediment during washover by big storms (Stoddart 1971). Whatever the reason, it seems likely from the radiometric dates obtained for samples within Lakeba's sand flats that progradation was indeed most rapid in the period from 1–2,000 years ago (Table 2.1), the process slowing down or becoming reversed in more recent times. At Tubou, Lakeba, one present-day consequence is the need to protect by a sea wall the sand flats on which the government station and village are located.

To summarise, it is very clear that on all the islands that have been examined the present coastal scenery has only developed in quite recent times. Sea level, rates of marine sediment production, and rates of terrestrial input have all changed significantly during the three thousand years that these islands have been inhabited, and human impact on vegetation and hence the rate of erosion has been an important contributory factor. The net result of these changes has been the creation of many hectares of new subaerial coastal land of quite variable character, much of which is vitally important to the agricultural economy but is still subject to the forces of environmental change. It is also clear that the unfortunate location of most villages on landforms that are subject to erosion and/or intermittent inundation during storms contributes greatly to the cost of counteracting the effects of natural hazards.

The retreating forests

It has long been recognised that 3,000 years of human settlement has had, in places, a substantial effect on the vegetation of the Fiji islands. On the dry, leeward sides of the larger islands, and on small islands which are drier and have vulnerable soils, the original forest cover has been largely replaced by a savanna formation of open grassland, fernland or dense thickets of *gasau* reeds (*Miscanthus floridulus*), with occasional stunted *nokonoko* trees (*Casuarina equisetifolia*), pandans or other fire-tolerant shrub species. On Viti Levu introduced species of grass, such as mission grass (*Pennisetum polystakyon*) have to a large extent replaced the native species (particularly *Miscanthus*), but in the outer islands the introduced species are less widespread.

This savanna formation is pyrophytic, in other words it is maintained by repeated fires. In former times the burning was carried out on a seasonal basis. In August 1860 a visitor to Kadavu noted that 'the gentle slopes covered with grass [were] at the time of our visit marked by many burnt patches, showing that the yam-planting season had commenced' (Smythe 1864: 45). Some years later, Horne noted during his agricultural survey that in the dry zone of Viti Levu 'the soil is not bad, but it has been much injured by the fires which periodically burn up the grass' (Horne 1881: 49). The Fijians call the poorest, most eroded areas *talasiga*, or sun-burnt lands. *Talasiga* generally has a very restricted plant cover dominated by bracken ferns (*Pteridium esculentum* and *Dicranopteris linearis*), and this vegetation dominates the interior of Lakeba island. Its origin formed a particular object of research in the 1974–6 UNESCO/UNFPA project (Latham 1979; Hughes et al. 1979; Latham & Brookfield (eds.) 1983). Different types of *talasiga* vegetation have been observed, varying in density and floristic richness, and the effects of deforestation must be viewed along a continuum according to the degree of degradation of the vegetation–soil complex and its capacity to regenerate back to forest. It is convenient to consider three steps in this evolution, which correlate with islands of recent, i.e. Pleistocene, volcanic formation (Koro, Taveuni), those of intermediate age (Batiki, Nairai), and those older islands that have volcanic rocks extending back to the upper Miocene (Lakeba and its neighbours).

Recent volcanic islands

On Taveuni, volcanic activity came to an end in very recent times. Between two and three hundred craters, mostly very fresh, lie along the main axis of the island, and archaeological evidence suggests that the latest eruptions took place between 2,000 and 1,200 years ago (Frost 1969). Along the precipitous east coast coral reefs are entirely absent, and elsewhere the fringing reefs and associated coral sand flats are restricted in development. The island's altitude and mass are sufficient to generate cloud and rain throughout the year, and the south-east coast has the highest recorded rainfall in Fiji (over 6 m per annum). The island is composed entirely of basic volcanic rocks, mostly olivine basalt overlaid in places by layers of recent volcanic ash. Although some deeply incised valleys have been formed, the soils are highly permeable and much of the runoff is subsurface. Despite the high rainfall and continuous leaching the soils, mostly andosols, are exceptionally fertile and will support permanent cultivation even of demanding crops like taro (*Colocasia esculenta*) without base minerals becoming depleted (Denis 1983). As a result, cleared areas will revert rapidly back to forest if cultivation is abandoned, and grassland is almost completely absent from the island.

The geology of Koro is less well known, but volcanic activity here appears to be somewhat less recent. Moreover the island is smaller and has a maximum altitude of only 560 m, compared to over 1,200 m on Taveuni, so that the foothills around the coast have a smaller total rainfall and a more pronounced dry season. It is in these areas that patches of grassland are found, especially on the ridges and hill tops where defended sites were maintained until the late nineteenth century. These open areas support a dense growth of tall *Miscanthus* reeds (*gasau*) invaded in places by thickets of the introduced tree species *Leucaena leucocephala*. The grassland also contains saplings of native secondary forest trees, and would rapidly revert to closed woodland if it were not occasionally burnt by accidental fires associated with the preparation of new yam gardens in the dry season. Mature *gasau* has a high biomass and provides (except after fires) a good protection for the ground surface. Deterioration in soil structures may not necessarily be associated with this vegetation change, and it is one that is by no means irreversible.

It would appear that these recent volcanic islands provide ecosystems that are favourable in agricultural terms and highly resilient despite long-term human disturbance. The soils are inherently fertile but also permeable and thus structurally stable. The rainfall is sufficient for continuous cropping, but not generally the cause of soil erosion or flooding. Only during cyclonic storms does rainfall become so torrential as to cause overland flow, landslips and floods, as occurred on Koro during Hurricane Tia in 1980 (see chapter 8).

Volcanic islands of intermediate age

Elsewhere in Lomaiviti a greater degree of weathering of the volcanic rocks testifies to the islands being of greater age, as does the development of fringing reefs around them. Such conditions prevail on Batiki and Nairai, and these are also low-lying islands that generate much less cloud and rainfall, and are therefore susceptible to seasonal drought. On Nairai the hill tops are still under forest, but on Batiki forest is restricted to a few steep slopes in parts of the island remote from settlement.

There is a close association between the vegetation pattern and soil types. Grasslands are associated with eutric cambisols (especially on Batiki) and ferrallic cambisols (especially western Nairai), the former supporting dense thickets of *Miscanthus*, the latter a poor *talasiga* with bracken (*Dicranopteris linearis*). The forest patches are associated with humic ferralsols, and these soils permit shifting cultivation, but in the savanna country cassava is the only feasible crop, and even it is restricted to sites under tall *Miscanthus* at the base of slopes, where the soils are deeper and more humid (Latham 1983a).

On Moala, an island in the Lau group that is wetter than Nairai but has forested areas with similar soils, land around defensive sites on the crest of the island was cleared and burned up until about 1880. These patches had degenerated to a *talasiga* fernland which has not significantly recovered in the period since these sites were abandoned. Twyford and Wright (1965: 479) comment that 'the persistence of this *talasiga* condition after burning has ceased for many years and in a climate which does not have more than a weak dry season shows how serious it is when *talasiga* conditions are allowed to develop irresponsibly'.

On Nairai and Batiki both cambisols and ferralsols show evidence of extensive erosion of the surface, and this is undoubtedly related to the regular burning to which the grasslands have been, and are, subject. Perhaps as a consequence of this erosion, colluvial and alluvial deposition in valleys and at the base of slopes appears to be well developed, and these soils (eutric fluvisols) support a wider range of subsistence crops as well as coconuts. No research has been directed towards the question of landscape change, but it would not be surprising if islands like Nairai and Batiki had not seen a substantial transformation in their soil resources during the last 3,000 years, but probably not on the scale that is proposed for the older volcanic islands such as Lakeba.

Older volcanic islands

Most islands in the Lau group are formed either of volcanic rocks (the Lau Volcanics), or of elevated limestone (the Futuna Limestone), or of both (Ladd & Hoffmeister 1945). The volcanics derive from the upper Miocene, six to nine million years ago, while the limestones are upper Miocene to lower Pliocene in age (Gill 1976). Under predominantly humid tropical conditions such a period is sufficient for the volcanic rocks to have become deeply weathered, and for the limestones to have become transformed by solution into a forbidding karst landscape such as that of Kabara, in which soil of any kind is restricted to small pockets of bauxitic ferralsols in amongst the limestone. The fertility of these soils is fragile since it depends on an organic content which is rapidly depleted by cultivation and can only be restored by a bush fallow (Latham 1983a). Agricultural possibilities on these predominantly limestone islands are therefore very limited: in the nineteenth century the population of Kabara supplemented its meagre agricultural resources by means of reciprocal trade with neighbouring volcanic islands (Thompson 1949). We concentrate in this section on the volcanic islands, where it can be shown that a substantial transformation has taken place in the prehistoric period in their soil resources.

Lakeba again provides a case study of this transformation. The island is predominantly of andesitic lavas, breccias and lapillaries, with elevated limestone restricted to the western side (see Fig. 2.2). An early description indicates that the appearance of Lakeba was as bare in 1860 as it was prior to pine afforestation in the early 1970s:

The island is composed of numerous low hills, of a poor-looking reddish soil, and generally covered with coarse grass, with here and there a screw pine or a few stunted trees. The valleys in between are, however, well wooded, and a thick belt of cocoa-nuts lines the beaches. (Smythe 1864: 124)

In the Fiji climate a bare landscape such as that described has hydrological consequences which are hinted at in the diary of David Cargill, who established the first mission station on Lakeba in Tubou village:

Sunday 22 November 1835: very heavy and constant rain prevented us from worshipping God under the canopy of heaven ... Thursday 26 November 1835: during the last three days we have had to endure one of the severest storms that I ever witnessed ... The rain fell in torrents, and literally deluged a great part of the

Mission premises ... Our premises were flooded with water, which rushed from the neighbouring hills in deep and rapid torrents ... (Schutz (ed.) 1977: 68)

The coastal flats at Tubou shows the effects of many such 'deep and rapid torrents', with alluvial flood deposits near the surface overlying coral reef sands that accumulated at an earlier stage during the last four thousand years. As already discussed, the mangrove swamps also show evidence of a recent deposition of terrigenous muds on top of the old reef flats (see Fig. 2.3). The main source of this material must be the deforested *talasiga* hill-slopes of the interior, and since the streams that drain the hills are normally trickles of clear water, we must consider the role of storm events in the whole process of soil erosion and sediment transport.

Observations in the Yadrana valley in 1975 showed that even a modest rain storm (average return period about 30 days) can cause flash floods when the catchment consists mainly of steep slopes under *talasiga* vegetation and truncated ferrallic soils with a low infiltration capacity (Bayliss-Smith 1977a, 1983a). After six hours of rainfall at an intensity of 4–5 mm per hour, the rate of discharge from the Yadrana catchment amounted to 34 per cent of the rate of rainfall input. These data match observations in small catchments in Kenya, where cleared areas experience flash floods comparable to the one monitored at Yadrana, whereas nearby areas still under rain forest experience peak runoff after such storms that amounts to only 1 per cent of the rate of rainfall input (Pereira 1973: 107).

Stream floods on Lakeba also carry substantial amounts of suspended sediment, derived mainly from lateral abrasion by the streams cutting into their banks. These banks are themselves formed out of the thick colluvial and alluvial infill of the valley floors. Towards the mouths of the main valleys this infill is mainly a very recent alluvial deposit (eutric fluvisols), but in other valleys there are soils showing evidence of pedogenesis and representing essentially fossil deposits (chromic luvisols). It is clear that the recent period of accelerated erosion of hill slopes by slopewash must be balanced against hundreds of thousands of years of more gradual landform development during the Pleistocene, when climatic conditions were often more arid than at present, and during millions of years in the late Tertiary.

It is therefore simplistic to say that the *talasiga* soil vegetation complex is entirely anthropogenic. It is true that on islands like Lakeba almost all the present vegetation is affected by clearing and burning, and it has been shown that degrees of impoverishment in *talasiga* plant associations do correspond to variations in the soil pattern (Twyford & Wright 1965; Garnock-Jones 1978; Leslie & Blakemore 1978). On the other hand Latham (1979, 1983b) has demonstrated that in certain respects man's influence is quite superficial and not necessarily irreversible, and moreover

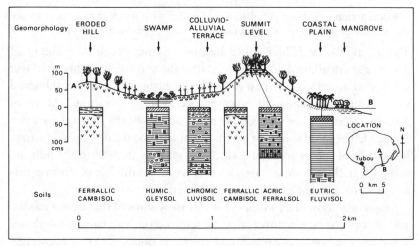

2.5 Landforms and soils on Lakeba

that it is superimposed on a landscape where both landforms and soils indicate a substantial inheritance from the past.

For example, there are two relict plateau surfaces with highly mature bauxitic soils, acric ferralsols with a high alumina content suggesting evolution under continuously hot, wet conditions in the Pliocene (Fig. 2.5). The older valley fill seems to correspond to a later phase during which these plateau surfaces were eroded, producing what is today the most common soil type on Lakeba, the ferrallic cambisols, which are truncated and exceptionally poor in nutrients. These are the soils supporting the most impoverished type of *talasiga* fernland. More recently, in the Pleistocene, denudation under a drier climate has produced some quite shallow soils rich in montmorillonite clays. These are the eutric cambisols of areas under *Miscanthus* grassland and the humic cambisols of relict forest patches, soils of somewhat greater fertility because of rejuvenation through truncation, a process tentatively ascribed to erosion during a phase of reduced vegetation cover, possibly natural fires, and intermittent but violent runoff. Subsequently the renewed incision of valleys can be ascribed to very low sea levels during the glacial maximum in the late Pleistocene (Latham 1979, 1983b).

Thus human influences are merely the last chapter in a long and complicated landscape history, which has produced a mosaic of soil and vegetation types of varying degrees of impoverishment and vulnerability. Latham (1983b: 140–1) concludes that 'man appears to have sustained and at times encouraged the extension of *talasiga* formations', but on the other hand 'the degraded state of the *talasiga* soils appears to owe more to inherited pedological characteristics than to a relatively recent defores-

1 The *talasiga* landscape of Lakeba (TBS photograph, 1975). The burnt area in the foreground is subject to slopewash during rain storms. The products of erosion have accumulated as colluvial infill in the valley bottom, in the zone planted with coconuts (middle distance), and as alluvium on coastal flats and mangrove swamps (far distance). The view is from the central plateau looking northeast towards Nukunuku.

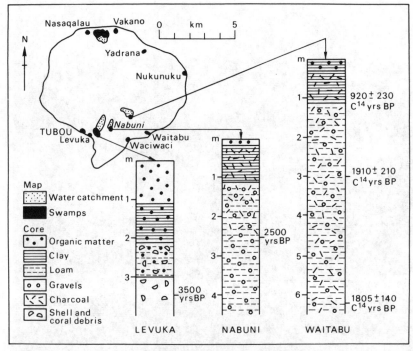

2.6 Swamp cores on Lakeba

tation'. Moreover, the recent plantations of pines (*Pinus caribaea*) have shown that this entire ecosystem can rapidly revert to evergreen, closed-canopy forest, with far-reaching implications for the island's soil fertility, erosion dynamics and water storage.

We can conclude that the older volcanic islands do constitute distinctly fragile ecosystems. Soils, vegetation, and probably the associated terrestrial fauna are not resilient in the face of human disturbance, but this vulnerability partly reflects an extended period of exposure to natural disturbance, through the effects of climatic change, fluctuating sea levels, natural forest fires, and hurricanes. It is very difficult in such a landscape to disentangle the respective roles of man and nature.

The accumulating swamps

It is in certain of the depositional environments, rather than in erosional ones, that the effects of human interference can be seen most clearly. The UNESCO/UNFPA project concentrated its efforts at four sites on Lakeba where it was hoped that swamp stratigraphy would reveal the extent of the effects of deforestation upon swamp deposition (Fig. 2.6). The two sub-coastal sites, at Levuka and at Nasaqalau, have already been discussed above in the context of coastal changes. Two small inland swamps are also examined, at Nabuni and at Waitabu (Hughes et al. 1979; Latham et al. 1983).

The origin of these swamps is not easy to explain without a human agency. At their downstream end there are no rock barriers preventing water flow. Hughes et al. (1979) and Latham et al. (1983) suggest that natural barriers produced by dams of tree trunks and branches may have been reinforced by human action, and that the groves which are today left intact at the downstream end of the swamps is another practice designed to slow down the flow of water and encourage sedimentation.

Nabuni swamp covers 1.9 ha and receives drainage from a gently sloping catchment of 27.4 ha. At the present time the catchment is mainly under a low *talasiga* vegetation. In the swamp 4.5 m of core was obtained before the substratum became too compact for further penetration. The lower horizons appear to predate the formation of the swamp as a waterlogged environment. At 2.4 m depth there is a sudden increase in carbonised particle density, which probably represents the arrival of people on the island and their use of fire for clearing vegetation. Charcoal is not, however, entirely lacking from the bottom two metres of the core, suggesting that a few natural fires accompanied the colluvio-alluvial deposition process in the late Pleistocene period. The upper levels of the core are not reliably dated, but from the accumulation rate in the upper 1.25 m, which was deposited over the last 800–2,400 years, a mean minimum erosion rate for the catchment of 4–10 cm per thousand years can be calculated. The density of carbonised particles is extremely high and increases right up to the surface, in a *talasiga* catchment that is still regularly burnt over at the present time.

Waitabu swamp covers 3.4 ha, and receives water from 45.6 ha of steeply sloping catchment, forested at the present time by a secondary growth dominated by *Geissois ternata*. At Waitabu 6.5 m of core were recovered, and further downward progress was only halted for lack of extension rods. The deposit was rather homogeneous throughout this depth, with very high concentrations of carbonised particles throughout. Six radiocarbon dates provided a good correlation between age and depth of deposits, and showed that the upper six metres of this swamp were deposited during the last 1,900 years. The bottom 3.4 m seems to have been deposited extremely rapidly between about 1900 and 1750 BP, suggesting a mean erosion rate for the catchment as a whole of at least 173 cm of soil per thousand years. This massive erosion rate occurred in the presence of repeated fires, and was already underway at 1900 BP, i.e. during the Navatu phase of Fiji's prehistory. Deposition slowed between

1750 and 900 BP, to a mean rate of erosion of 20 cm per thousand years, and then slowed again during the last 900 years to 7 cm per thousand years. The final part of this last period also saw a sharp decline in carbonised particles, which suggests fewer fires and the conditions which permitted the re-establishment of forest cover over much of the catchment.

Implications of swamp stratigraphy

At both sites the estimated erosion rates of the catchment must exceed the pace at which the weathering front advances even under humid tropical conditions, and they are of course minimum estimates because of the unknown amount of sediment not deposited in the swamps but instead lost downstream as suspended matter exported by stream floods or as solutes. Two features of the chronology are of particular interest:

(i) Erosion rates were extremely high at Waitabu two thousand years ago, but these rates were not sustained for long, either because more resistant sub-soil horizons were being uncovered or because of a declining intensity of human use. Prior to 2100 BP there is no archaeological evidence for occupation of hill top sites (Rowland & Best 1980), suggesting the possibility that the interior of the island only started to become the focus of intensive exploitation at around this time. It is tempting to associate this change in focus with the transition from Lapita to Navatu culture, and with the decline in the productivity of coastal ecosystems as a consequence of over-exploitation and a fall in sea level.

(ii) The sudden and recent decline in the prevalence of fire at Waitabu suggests a possible link with the historical evidence for a movement of population towards the coast in the nineteenth century. Alternatively it could reflect a change in agriculture, with the abandonment of swidden cultivation on eroded hill slopes and a concentration instead on intensive taro cultivation in the swamps.

If we accept that agricultural intensification leading to a food surplus is often associated with the development of stratified societies having centralised political control (Brookfield 1984a), then the recent ecological changes inferred from Waitabu can be linked to other evidence. The construction of large-scale hill forts on Lakeba seems to have occurred between *c.* AD 1500 to 1800 (Rowland & Best 1980), and can perhaps be regarded as another symptom of the same process of political centralisation (Spriggs 1981: 127).

The closest known parallel to Lakeba is the island of Aneityum in

Vanuatu, where landscape changes on an even larger scale have occurred during the period of human settlement. Agricultural intensification began on Aneityum 500–600 years ago, and is seen by Spriggs (1981, 1985, 1986) as being closely associated with the emergence of chiefdoms wielding political power over more than local areas, and as permitting the production of surplus food for competitive feasting. On both islands the use of productive swamp land could not begin until after this component of the landscape had itself been created, as an accidental side-effect of forest clearance, fire and dry-land farming activities on hill slopes vulnerable to catastrophic erosion.

The political economy of degraded landscapes

Further stratigraphic work is needed in the swamps on Lakeba and elsewhere, and a much greater degree of integration is needed with local evidence for cultural change, such as archaeological data (Best 1977). Even so, on Lakeba an outline is beginning to emerge which challenges very strongly the homeostatic model that proposes a harmonious adjustment of populations to their island ecosystems. Some ecosystems and some islands will be more vulnerable than others to disruption, but it is clear that on the older volcanic islands like Lakeba quite dramatic changes have occurred in both the quantity and quality of available land and marine resources. Prehistorians have speculated about the kinds of social change that might result from adaptation by colonists to a new environment, and about the effects of cultural diffusion. In addition we suggest that populations in the outer islands of Fiji have been under pressure to make two other kinds of adaptation: firstly, continuous adjustment to secular changes in the landscape and its productivity; and secondly, contingency measures for coping with the impact of occasional natural hazards: sudden storms and fires, droughts and floods.

As Kirch (1982a) and Spriggs (1981, 1985, 1986) have both pointed out, the erosion of some landforms and the loss of certain resources should not, in most cases, be regarded simply as ecosystem degradation, since in the process of transformation new landforms and new resources are created. These new opportunities may provide better prospects for agricultural intensification, political expansion and social stratification. Indeed, one could suggest that Sahlins' (1958) contrast, between the egalitarian social organisation of Polynesian atolls compared to the stratified societies found on high islands in Polynesia, might have a somewhat different ecological basis from that which he postulated. Despite the potential threat posed by hurricanes, droughts and overpopulation, atolls can offer a limited but dependable set of resources that are not easily degraded by overexploitation: abundant coral reef, lagoon and nearshore fishing resources, plentiful coconuts, and swamp taro (Bayliss-Smith 1974).

The ecosystems of high islands, on the other hand, although potentially more productive, are in some respects inherently less stable. Whether we view the changes that have occurred on islands such as Lakeba as representing overall a landscape degradation or a landscape enhancement, it is clear that in the process of ecological change some local groups will have been favoured and others disadvantaged. In particular, access to swamp land and a recognition of the potential benefits of managing water flow and sedimentation in such sites, would have provided a 'royal road' towards agricultural intensification. Fijian chiefs were perhaps not social engineers on the scale of Wittfogel's (1957) Oriental Despots, but the new opportunity for political control over production provided by emerging landforms such as the Rewa delta on Viti Levu or, on a smaller scale, Lakeba's swampland and coastal flats, is undeniable.

We might also speculate that in an environment that encourages agricultural intensification and so permits population growth, the processes (both ecological and social) which maintain the productivity of the economic system become more complex and so are more easily disrupted. In this situation the role of the chief as mediator between the laity and the supernatural is enhanced. Identifying the propitious moment for carrying out crucial tasks in the agricultural cycle becomes important. There is an increased need for spiritual leadership to provide protection against supernatural punishment in the shape of hurricanes, floods and droughts, as well as to form alliances against more conventional kinds of enemy.

Paradoxically, then, the degraded environments of the older volcanic islands proved to be fertile seed beds for the evolution of a form of 'archaic kingship', an institution through which a Fijian 'heroic history' could unfold (Sahlins 1983, 1985). A prominent feature of the pre-colonial social structure first observed by Europeans around 1800 was 'the presence of divinity among men' as in the person of the sacred king or the powers of the magical chief (Sahlins 1983: 518). William Lockerby, a castaway on Vanua Levu in 1808, found 'the lower class of the people ... under complete subjection to the different chiefs, particularly to the kings' (Lockerby 1925: 19). He recounts one instance of the paramount chief of Bua not enforcing a particular custom: 'by this act of indulgence and humanity towards his niece, the King told me he was afraid he had incurred the displeasure of his Callow [Kalou], or God, and the different chiefs of the surrounding islands'. In this political economy of absolute and divine power, infrastructural change can be wholly dependent on superstructural change. In Sahlins' words, history becomes intelligible 'only in the terms of a native theory that turned Marx on its head by its insistence that "in the final analysis" the economic base depended on the spiritual superstructure' (Sahlins 1983: 519).

We cannot possibly, from the evidence available, identify with confidence the prehistoric roots of this hierarchical society in Fiji, but we do suggest its emergence would in various ways have been fostered by the landscape changes that we have identified. The quite new challenges that were posed to this society by European contact in the nineteenth and twentieth centuries are the subject of chapter 3.

3

Capitalism and colonialism in the periphery

In this chapter we examine the historical geography of eastern Fiji in the colonial period, focussing on the uneven penetration of capitalism into this region, and its effects. The island landscapes that evolved under the pre-colonial political economy (see chapter 2) were transformed during this period in ways which still constrain the decisions and actions of islanders, but a total history of this process of transformation is not attempted here.[1] Nor do we examine in all its aspects the relationship between superstructure and infrastructure. The idiosyncrasies of the individual actors, whether Fijian chiefs, missionaries of colonial ideology, or commissars of capitalism, are presented here only in generalised form. Our primary concern is to examine the impact of capitalist relations and forces of production on the reproduction of labour in the small island periphery. One consequence of integration into a global capitalist economy for scattered groups of islands in the Pacific has been a radical modification of age-sex structure, ethnic composition and spatial distribution of the indigenous populations. These transformations have had, and continue to have, important implications for reproduction of labour in different parts of the social formation.

A conceptual note

The focus on reproduction of labour takes its inspiration from the writings of the French anthropologist, Claude Meillassoux (1972, 1975). It is acknowledged at the outset that there are some important ambiguities

---

[1] There is an extensive literature on the history of Fiji, and this is not the place to attempt a short review. Readers unfamiliar with this part of the world will find Scarr's (1984) short history of Fiji very informative. A very different interpretation, using a Marxist framework, has been written by an Indo-Fijian sociologist, Narayan (1984). Classical histories of Fiji include Derrick (1950), Legge (1958), France (1969), Gillion (1962) and the numerous publications by Scarr (1965, 1970, 1972, 1973a, 1973b, 1979, 1980a). Other recent publications which provide valuable insights into the complexity of interpreting colonial history include Ali (1980), Britton, (1980), Lal (1980, 1984a, 1984b), Lasaqa (1984), Knapman (1976a, 1976b, 1984, 1985), Macnaught (1974, 1979, 1982), Moynagh

in Meillassoux's conceptualisation of the relation between production and reproduction (O'Laughlin 1977), but these are not discussed here. Rather than debating issues of terminology and theory, our concern in this chapter is to throw into sharper relief than is possible using other traditions of analysis, the way in which economy and society in eastern Fiji were transformed by capitalist relations of production between 1800 and 1970.

Two related dimensions of labour and production are highlighted in this discussion. The first concerns the capacity of communities in eastern Fiji to generate sufficient population to ensure that the domestic village economy, as it was progressively restructured by capitalism, can replace itself. Until comparatively recently, the costs of reproducing and maintaining the Fijian labour force have been sustained by the village community despite substantial capitalist penetration of relations and forces of production. The process of 'freeing labour from the land' was discouraged in Fiji by a combination of economic, ideological and political forces which conserved the older relations of production (Bedford 1984). Another dimension to the conservation tendency is the role of labour migration as a process for restructuring production systems. A consistent characteristic of articulation of capitalist and non-capitalist modes of production in many parts of the Third World has been reliance on village socio-economic systems to reproduce cheap labour. Rather than destroying non-capitalist modes, the process of articulation, operating specifically through the mechanism of labour circulation, has conserved in villages the function of social security for the young, sick, unemployed, and elderly, along with the means for human reproduction – subsistence and women.

Through a focus on labour reproduction we seek to illuminate contradictory tendencies in the history of capitalist development in Fiji which both reflect Marx's (1867: xiv) view that 'the backward country suffers not only from the development of capitalist production, but also from the incompleteness of that development', and accommodate a long-standing sentiment among Fiji's indigenous leaders that 'any call for modification of the existing system, if it is to be of any lasting advantage, must come from within, from those whose lives are likely to be affected by it' (Sukuna in Scarr (ed.) 1983: 62). Our analysis commences with a short review of the initial stages of capitalist penetration in Fiji. This is followed by an analysis of production and reproduction in eastern Fiji between 1875 and 1970, with particular reference to transformation in the economic base. Some aspects of the ideological and political superstructure of colonial

(1981), Nation (1978), Nayacakalou (1978), Narsey (1979), and Subramani (ed.) (1979).

Fijian society are discussed briefly here, but the contributions of state ideology and practice, especially since Independence in 1970, to the process of preserving a neo-traditional order are examined in greater detail in chapter 6.

Capitalism in Fiji: origins

The process of capitalist penetration in the island Pacific had its origins in the fifteenth century with the voyages of exploration of the Spanish and Portuguese (Spate 1979). Some island groups north of the equator were colonised by Spaniards, and there were attempts to set up shore bases in parts of the western and eastern Pacific (Langdon 1975). These early forays by Europeans into the islands had an uneven spatial impact on the indigenous population, but the process of progressive restructuring of non-capitalist modes of production was to be delayed in most Pacific islands, given the irrelevance of their human and physical resource endowments for the development of commodity trade with Europe, until the nineteenth century.

In the history of the capitalist expansion outside of its European hearth, the Pacific has always been periphery. While the Ocean may have been destined to become the site of busy sea lanes across which were transported 'the silks of China, the spices of Ternate and Tidore, the silver of Zacatecas and Potosi' (Spate 1979: 291), the oceanic island societies were spared most of what Spate termed the 'blood and iron "and the sweete liues of multidues of men"' until the nineteenth century. By the end of the eighteenth century virtually every island and island group was located on the explorers' charts, but it remained the task of later explorers to find out what lay beyond the foam-fringed coastlines (Howe 1984: 83).

Commercial penetration of islands in the western Pacific, including Fiji, was initiated from Australia, not from Europe. In 1788 the British government established a penal colony at Botany Bay on Australia's east coast. The economic base for this colony was very tenuous, and the Pacific Ocean itself was the colony's first frontier. From the outset 'vessels radiated out from Sydney Harbour, travelling halfway across the ocean to Polynesia and beyond in search of food and other basic commodities for the colony as well as the luxury items – sandalwood, beche-de-mer, pearl shell, seal skins – for sale on the lucrative Chinese market' (Howe 1984: 92). In 1804 sandalwood stands in southwest Vanua Levu in Fiji were incorporated into this trading network, thus initiating the capitalist penetration of Fiji (see Fig. 3.1).

Fiji around 1800

Reconstructions of Fijian society in the late eighteenth and early nine-teenth centuries essentially chronicle a period of considerable political instability and social upheaval, especially in the small islands to the east and north of Viti Levu and Vanua Levu.[2] As the situation has been interpreted by expatriate researchers, Fijian society was in a state of often violent flux due to an on-going transition from a weakly hierarchical and diffusely connected chiefly system to larger more complex lineage aristo-cracies based on geographical suzerainty rather than purely kinship ties. While the domestic economy revolved around production of foods and material items to ensure reproduction of an essentially self-sufficient agrarian society, there was generation of surplus product for ceremonial prestations and trade. There was also considerable marital and martial mobility. Fijian communities in the small islands were not isolated self-sufficient cells, and by the time merchant capital began to extract value from the physical and human resources of Fiji, a complex system of political patronage, alliances and economic exchanges had evolved to exploit ecological diversity and to facilitate division of labour, centralisation of power and inter-island trade (Sahlins 1962).

We can characterise the economic basis of life in Fiji around 1800 as follows:

(i) The means of production were simple; land was the primary instru-ment of labour, and human strength was the major source of energy in agriculture and craft processes. There was no animal power, and apart from sailing canoes, machines to harness non-human sources of energy were not used.

(ii) Productive relations were characterised by labour processes organised on a basis of co-operation under the co-ordination of a hierarchical system of chiefly leadership and mutual obligations.

(iii) There was a fairly rigid division of labour, which varied in detail between groups, with adult men doing the heavy work of clearing the land for cultivation, going on expeditions and fighting, while the adult women did most of the manual work in the house and were often responsible for much of the cultivation of nearby subsistence gardens.

(iv) Social relations were marked by the appropriation of tribute derived

[2] One of the most skilful reconstructions of Fijian society and economy in the pre- and early colonial eras is Sahlins' (1962) study of Moala. Other useful studies include Calvert and Williams (1858), Derrick (1950), Geddes (1945), Henderson (1931), Hocart (1929 and 1952), Knapman (1976a), Quain (1948), Reid (1977, 1979, 1981, 1983), Roth (1953), Sayes (1984), Thompson (1940a and 1940b), Thomson (1908), and Young (1970 and 1982).

from, and simultaneously concealed by, the dynamics of economic co-operation, leadership, kinship and marriage customs (Sahlins 1962; Britton 1980).

At the level of the political and ideological superstructure the mode of production had five units of social organisation, termed in Fijian (from the bottom up) *i tokatoka*, *mataqali*, *yavusa*, *vanua* and *matanitu*. There were at least six categories of social status ranging from slaves and commoners to paramount chiefs, where status was defined primarily by birth and sex (Derrick 1950). The power of a chief depended on a combination of personal ability and, in places, an ideology of rule by prescribed right (Scarr (ed.) 1983; Sayes 1984; Sahlins 1983). It is important to appreciate at the outset that the emergence of powerful chiefs (*turaga*) in Fiji in the early nineteenth century was not the direct outcome of influence by European traders, nor did it stem directly from the efforts by Fijians to gain access to commodities and to a local labour force for their extraction and semi-processing. In a recent reconstruction of the political organisation of Cakaudrove, Sayes (1984) questions the emphasis which some writers have placed on the role of European weapons and the skilled assistance of Europeans themselves in the rise of complex political hierarchies. The confederations of chiefdoms (*matanitu*) which became typical of power configurations in north-east Viti Levu and Lomaiviti, Taveuni and eastern Vanua Levu, and the Lau islands during the nineteenth century had their origins in pre-capitalist Fijian society.

Within the social formation 'the face of the political sky was always changing' (Derrick 1950: 23); the major Fijian 'states' (the *matanitu* or loose confederations of chiefdoms) at the beginning of the nineteenth century were small – 'the largest the old men told of, Verata and Cakaudrove, were at most a few miles of coast with perhaps a conquered island or two'. Between 1800 and 1874, when certain chiefs of Fiji ceded political control to the Queen of England, and Fiji became part of the British Empire, there was substantial change in the political organisation of Fijian society. Three 'states', Bau, Cakaudrove and Lakeba, came to dominate all the small islands off the north and east coasts of Viti Levu and Vanua Levu, as well as much of these two islands (Fig 3.1).

Of major significance in this development was steel technology which diffused rapidly through eastern Fiji in the late eighteenth and nineteenth centuries. Indigenous trading networks and political alliances ensured that the introduction of implements, which were to transform agriculture, boat-building, house construction and weapons manufacture, often predated direct contact between Fijians and Europeans. This technology, discussed further below, had a major impact on the generation of surplus

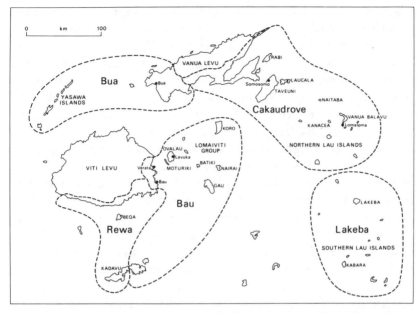

3.1 The major chiefdoms on the Fiji islands at the time of initial European settlement, *c.* 1840

labour and product in Fijian communities, and these changes in the economic base undoubtedly played an important role in centralisation of power among certain lineages in the political structure.

Also important was the build-up over at least two centuries of a powerful Tongan influence in the eastern islands. This was not the result of a major military conquest by Tongan forces; rather a process of long-term infiltration of immigrants into Fijian domestic communities had given them access to land and labour once the social relations which linked them to the local collectivity had been defined. Tongans were involved in the acquisition of hardwoods from islands in the southern Lau group (especially Kabara), sandalwood from Bua, and parakeet feathers on Taveuni (Thompson 1940b; Young 1982). All these items were of considerable value in the material life of Tonga and were very rare, even in Fiji. As we show later in this chapter, the Tongan presence was to be very important in the development of the economic base of the Lau islands in the mid-nineteenth century.

Contact networks, disease diffusion, and the new technology

In Bua the successful extraction of sandalwood for the China trade from 1804 was only accomplished with the co-operation of local chiefs. These chiefs were able to offer traders both a greater degree of security and a compliant labour force. Similar alliances between traders and co-operative chiefs permitted the exploitation of bêche-de-mer (a sea slug, also in demand in China) which was found on reefs throughout Fiji. There was a need for shore-based collecting and curing facilities in this trade, and between 1810 and 1840 trading activities were extended gradually along the coast of Viti Levu, to the Yasawa Islands in the west, and out to the Lau group in the east (Ward 1972).

The long-term significance of this trading activity for Fijian society and economy had three dimensions. On the one hand, traders' contact networks with local chiefs provided the framework for the next phase of European commercial activity, establishment of plantations and business enterprises in the islands. Another consequence of trading contacts was diffusion of alien diseases among the Fijian population. The short-term demographic effects of outbreaks of dysentery and a wide range of respiratory complaints among people who had never been exposed to such illness were devastating in small communities. McArthur (1967) has assessed the impact of alien diseases on the demography of Fiji's indigenous population in the first half of the nineteenth century; it is sufficient to note here that the capacity for biological reproduction of Fijian labour was greatly diminished in some parts of the group between 1800 and 1840.

A third influence, which partly compensated for and partly reinforced the reduced biological reproductive capacity of Fijian communities, was the on-going technological revolution accompanying more intensive involvement in commodity exchange with Europeans. As one of the first resident missionaries was to note in the 1840s:

Sheffield blades have long since taken ... place [of turtle shell knives], and hatchets, plane-irons, spades and butcher's knives have produced a great change, and given the present generation a vast superiority over those preceding it, in the facilities thus gained for producing food. (Calvert & Williams 1858: 64)

As in Tonga (Gailey 1987), these technological changes no doubt affected gender roles in the production process. In particular there was transferred to women an increasing part of direct productive labour, as men become more involved in the intrigue and warfare which facilitated and accompanied the development of centralised political authority.

The uneven spatial impact

The establishment of a permanent European settler population in Fiji from around 1840 has been described in detail in several histories.[3] From the point of view of Fijian society, the most critical changes accompanied the growing demand by Europeans for land, labour, and agricultural produce. As Britton (1980) has pointed out, the spatial pattern of planter settlement reflected the previous European contact network with Fijian chiefs, especially those whose territory embraced low-lying alluvial land or small offshore islands which could be alienated in their entirety. Taveuni, Lau and Lomaiviti are contrasting examples of the impact of this particular form of capitalist penetration.

Settlers and land alienation in Taveuni

Taveuni well illustrates the scale of transformation accomplished by a full-scale plantation economy. Land alienation was particularly extensive on this fertile island during the 1860s, initially because of the paramount chief's desire for revenge on some of his treacherous Taveuni subjects, whose land was sold from under them, and later because of the desire by Fijians for firearms and the protection provided by buffer zones of European settlement. By 1870 Taveuni was 'no longer a Fijian island except in name' (Brookfield 1978: 33).

Land alienation was also to result in the removal of population from several small islands around Taveuni and in northern Lau. Some came to Taveuni itself: the village of Kanacea in the south carries the name of the former home island in Lau. Others were either absorbed into communities where they had access to land and security through kinship ties, or were incorporated into the emerging plantation labour force. Some, no doubt, succumbed to the ravages of introduced disease. Despite this forced relocation, by the early 1880s, when a census was made of the indigenous and settler populations, numbers of Fijians on Taveuni were small (about 1,700 people). An English traveller noted in 1880: 'The visitor to Taveuni will observe how remarkably few Fijians there are upon the island ... There are not many Fijian settlements on Taveuni, nor do the planters feel the absence of them' (Anderson 1880: 41).

[3] Aspects of the initial phase of capitalist penetration and European settlement in Fiji have been described by Britton (1980), Brookfield (1978), Clammer (1975), Cumpston (1956), Derrick (1945), France (1969), Henderson (1931), Jarre (1955), Knapman (1976a, 1976b, 1985), Legge (1958), Lessin (1970), Narayan (1984), Narsey (1979), Scarr (1965, 1972, 1973a, 1973b, 1985), Stokes (1986), Thornley (1977), Ward (1969 and 1972), and Young (1970 and 1982).

2 Ma'afu, the most powerful chief in eastern Fiji, with his Tongan retinue (about 1876). Ma'afu is the seated figure in a white shirt. The photograph is from the collection of Baron von Hügel, and is reproduced by permission of the Museum of Archaeology and Anthropology, University of Cambridge.

Commodity production in Lau

Land alienation, labour recruiting, and depopulation had very uneven spatial impacts on the domestic economy. In some parts of eastern Fiji there was little direct interference by Europeans with the means of production; in southern Lau and many of the smaller islands in Lomaiviti land was not alienated and labour recruiting was minimal. In northern Lau, a change in the land tenure system, which accompanied settlement of the Tongan chief Ma'afu in Vanua Balavu in 1855, was to result in a significant increase in Fijian participation in surplus commodity production for the export trade. The oil of one locally grown tree crop, the coconut, was attracting increasing attention by European traders from the 1830s as the market for edible oils expanded in Europe. Lauans had been producing coconut oil for domestic consumption, as well as for their trade with Tongans, long before this commodity was in demand in Europe. By the mid-nineteenth century a barter-type exchange, whereby coconut oil (and other food products) were 'traded' by Fijians for pieces of iron, beads, cloth, and muskets supplied by European traders, was well-established in the eastern islands. This commodity trade took on a new dimension in the 1850s in northern Lau under the influence of Ma'afu.

Ma'afu instituted a system of land holding whereby all men over 16 years of age ('taxpayers') were given access to specified blocks of land (*magimagi*). The result, in France's (1969: 85–6) words, was that 'The commoner could cultivate his land with complete security, provided that he paid his tax. He was no longer subject to the unpredictable whims of a chief.' According to Knapman (1976a), Ma'afu's policy produced an immediate and sustained increase in Lauan production of coconut oil, often sold under Ma'afu's guidance, to meet the annual tax which could be paid either in kind or cash: 15 gallons of coconut oil or 24 shillings per adult male. While Ma'afu's taxation policy fostered an increase in the intensity of Lauan participation in the market economy, his land reform influenced the form which that participation took: 'by allocating to each taxpayer his own land, he provided institutional reinforcement of the Lauan preference for production for exchange as opposed to wage employment' (Knapman 1976a: 171). All the European settlers in northern Lau found it difficult to get local labour to work on their plantations, as the villages had no one to spare for the continuous work on plantations: 'instead of being regarded as a potential source of cheap labour for the planters, many of the Lauans were planters in their own right' (Derrick 1945: 6).

Dependency and development in Lomaiviti

In Lomaiviti the major development during the early nineteenth century was expansion of power of the chiefs of Bau and the incorporation of neighbouring islands into tributary status. Extensive quantities of tribute had to be supplied to Bau and the demand for produce such as coconut oil increased substantially from the 1850s as Cakobau, paramount chief of Bau, became heavily involved in trading with Europeans. For example, when Cakobau required a 30 ton schooner in 1869 he made payment with 400 casks of coconut oil from Koro, Gau, Batiki, Moturiki and Ovalau, and the gift of plantation land on Koro (Anon, 1880). Cakobau's increasing dependence on trade with Europeans to secure his power base as a paramount chief attracted many traders to Lomaiviti where they established a settlement at Levuka on Ovalau. Levuka and Lomaloma on Vanua Balavu (Ma'afu's headquarters in northern Lau) were Fiji's first urban centres. Levuka became more important, given its central location in relation to the main areas of settler production, its deep harbour and its political neutrality in the growing power contest between Cakobou and Ma'afu (Scarr 1970).

Although there was considerable interaction between Europeans and Fijians in Lomaiviti, a side-effect of this area's dependent status on Bau was that land alienation to Europeans was greatly restricted (Bayliss-Smith 1977b). Unlike the Tui Cakau, who in Cakaudrove sold off a lot of land belonging to groups in tributary status, Cakobau exerted rigid control over land sales in Lomaiviti, and thereby prevented large-scale European settlement except on Ovalau. An Australian journalist noted in 1870:

Cakobau guards his three islands [Koro, Nairai and Batiki] like the apple of his eye, and will not sell at any price . . . Koro possesses very great natural advantages, and when the old king dies there will, no doubt, be a scramble for the land. (Britton 1870: 24, 61)

Fortunately for the indigenous land owners on Koro and other islands in Lomaiviti, Cession in 1874 came before death of 'The old king' and the colonial government enforced a halt to further land alienation for several years.

Cession and foundations of an ideology

By the 1870s expansion of plantation agriculture, commodity trade, and progressive restructuring of the relations of production which dominated Fijian rural life were being constrained by an unwillingness on the part of many chiefs to sell land to Europeans, to make available men and women to work on plantations, and to extract from their communities ever increasing quantities of surplus product for trade. The demands of European traders and settlers (including the missionaries) for produce, land and labour were creating considerable tension between indigenous and capitalist interests in Fiji. The settler community was agitating for intervention by Britain to establish a colony run in the interests of Englishmen and Empire. Scarr (1965, 1973a, 1973b, 1979, 1984) has provided some vivid description of events and personalities in Fiji at this time. Fiji's paramount chiefs, however, were being advised by other Europeans to avoid the pattern of colonial domination which had occurred in New Zealand and Australia.

The end product of five years of intensive lobbying, political intrigue, economic pressure and continuing power struggles between Bau, Lau and Cakaudrove was formal cession of sovereignty to Queen Victoria on 10 October 1874.[4] According to a cherished Fijian myth, the country was ceded in loving trust (*loloma*) – a chiefly presentation which obliged the recipient, now Supreme Chief of Fiji, to redistribute power and privileges

---

4 The events leading up to establishment of British colonial rule in Fiji, and the policies and practices of the early governors and their advisers have been discussed in depth by Derrick (1950), France (1969), Heath (1974), Legge (1958), Macnaught (1974, 1982), Roth (1953), Routledge (1978), and especially Scarr (1965, 1970, 1972, 1973a, 1973b, 1979, 1980a, 1984).

to the original donors and to assume part of the responsibility for safeguarding the prosperity and rights of the people. In short, as Macnaught (1982: 1) points out, 'the Deed of Cession, far more effectively than the New Zealand Maoris' Treaty of Waitangi, came to be seen by Fijians as a solemn charter for a British–Fijian partnership premised on verbal assurances (the cession itself was unconditional) that colonial rule would respect and maintain the interests of Fijian society as paramount.'

The system of indirect rule in so far as Fijian village life was concerned, and the legislation which was enacted to protect Fijian society from the 'ravages of the free enterprise system', ensured that the transformation of the non-capitalist mode of production was slower and more uneven spatially and socially than in neighbouring New Caledonia, Vanuatu, New Zealand and Australia. The most significant developments which were to have a lasting impact on Fijian social and economic life, were the end of inter-group warfare, a prohibition of further land alienation, the introduction of regulations to restrict recruiting of Fijians for wage employment on plantations, imposition of a head tax which Fijians could pay in kind, and official sanction for a hierarchical social order and its associated relations of production, which Europeans identified as the 'traditional' system of organisation among Fijians throughout the country. The latter alliance between the agents of British colonial rule and Fiji's indigenous chiefs (especially those from Bau, Cakaudrove and Lau) ensured political stability, which was advantageous to the orderly functioning of foreign capital. It also essentially locked up Fijian land and labour within a non-capitalist mode of production (Britton 1980). This was to have very substantial implications for the development of the materialist base of Fijian society as well as for restructuring class relationships during the colonial and post-colonial periods.

Production and reproduction in the early colonial period

Taxation and trade

From the mid-1870s until around 1910 colonial policy ensured that Fijian involvement in the market economy was confined essentially to commodity production within the framework of communal use of labour and land. In order to meet the new administration's need for finances without forcing Fijians to seek wage employment, a system of tax gardens was set up. Communities were required to grow specified commercial crops, and to ensure that the necessary produce would be grown, regulations were passed decreeing the food-planting obligations of able-bodied men.

3 Levuka in 1879, soon after its role as capital of Fiji had been transferred to Suva. Levuka remained for another two decades the principal centre for European commerce serving the traders and planters of eastern Fiji. Photograph from the von Hügel collection, reproduced by permission of the Museum of Archaeology and Anthropology, University of Cambridge.

Knapman (1976a) has shown in the northern Lau islands that village work programmes made considerable demands on villagers' time, and thereby helped to keep levels of cash income, and hence the demand for trade goods, low. In Lau copra was required to pay the provincial tax, and a ban was often placed by the Fijian provincial administration on individual sale of coconuts to traders until the taxes had been paid. Surplus credits from the sale of produce for tax purposes were returned to the provinces and distributed by the chiefs among the growers' communities (Gordon 1879).

This system of taxation in kind had a variable impact on production. In Lau it seems that considerable tax returns were generated; a prominent Fijian chief, writing in the 1920s, recalled the successes of the communal production and marketing system which operated in the 1880s and 1890s (Scarr 1980b). This success in Lau was, in large part, due to the fact that a taxation system stimulating copra production had existed before 1874 under the direction of Ma'afu. In other parts of Fiji, where there had not been much exposure to commodity production for trade before Cession, the tax return from produce was low. Frazer (1973) reports that in Ra (on Viti Levu), for example, a high proportion of the provincial tax was accepted in cash originating from contract labour. In these areas the district administration officer (*Buli*) would permit some labour recruiting in the interests of meeting tax obligations.

The penetration of capitalist relations of production into Fijian community life was carefully regulated by the chiefs through their control over labour. In southern Lau, for example, Young (1982) argues that there was indifference to commodity trade with Europeans until late in the nineteenth century mainly because of involvement of the local inhabitants in production of large canoes (*drua*) which were in demand in Tonga and other parts of Fiji. The sheer size of the *drua*, and the scale of social organisation and specialisation involved in their construction, implied an economic significance extending far beyond the small island on which the timber happened to be located. The system of inter-island economic interdependence which evolved in southern Lau to support the shipbuilding industry goes far to explain the lack of interest by the paramount chiefs – especially the Tui Nayau based in Lakeba – in trade with Europeans. Many of the desired trade items were obtained from Tongans and other Fijians who wanted the *drua*.

In other parts of the eastern islands, chiefs became directly involved in plantation agriculture using members of their lineage as labour. Scarr (1973b) and Brookfield (1978) have recorded several important intra-Fijian land transfers in Taveuni which resulted in prominent chiefs gaining access to substantial freehold estates. Some of these are still run as 'commercial' coconut plantations in the 1980s. Other chiefs used their traditional authority, now given additional legitimacy by the colonial government's Native Regulations, to collect tribute in the form of commodities which could be sold to traders. For example, throughout the 1870s and 1880s Cakobau collected coconut oil as tribute from islands in Lomaiviti in order to finance his big projects (Bayliss-Smith 1977b).

Land and labour: aspects of demand and supply

The relations of production, whereby control of the allocation of Fijian labour remained with the class of chiefs, ensured that capital accumulation by Fijian 'commoners' was severely constrained. The most ardent critics of the native taxation system and its attendant labour regulations were not the Fijian villagers, however. It was the European settlers who found the system particularly irksome for, as Macnaught (1982: 8) points out: 'more than anything else it gave teeth to the government policy of insulating Fijians from the need to divert their labour resources to the plantations'. Had Fijians been granted the full personal liberty of British subjects, then they could have sold their lands and become a free-floating pool of labour.

In the early years of British administration the conflict between settlers and the government over access to Fijian land was contained by the fact that very extensive areas of the country's most productive agricultural land had been alienated before Cession. By 1874 approximately 20 per cent of the total land area of Fiji was claimed by Europeans. Continued ownership of this land was subject to determination by a Lands Claims Commission set up by the first British Governor (Sir Arthur Gordon) to establish that lands had been acquired 'fairly and at a fair price' (France 1969: 115), but in most cases the land alienated at the time of Cession remained in the hands of Europeans or the state.'

Much more critical for capitalist development in Fiji in the last quarter of the nineteenth century was the shortage of cheap labour. Under the Native Regulations introduced just after Cession, Fijian labour could not be recruited without the permission of local officials (almost always chiefs). Fijians were required, by regulation from the 1870s, to meet communal labour obligations in their villages, and to provide labour and produce for their chiefs. The demand for labour by settlers could only be met by bringing in workers from other countries. Before Cession plantation labour had been 'recruited' in the Solomon Islands, Vanuatu, Kiribati and Tuvalu, and this strategy was continued through the 1870s. The development of sugar cultivation in Fiji in the 1870s was compromised by insufficient and unreliable labour from the Pacific Islands, however, and in 1876 a scheme was introduced whereby indentured labour would be obtained from India. As Scarr (1967: 147) rather aptly noted, 'in Fiji, the imported islander [from other parts of the Pacific], like the indentured Indian, was a "human subsidy" to the government's native policy, the keystone of which was that the Fijians must not be forced to work on European plantations'.

Disease and depopulation

One of the major arguments used by Gordon and his immediate successors to justify settling on Fijians a communal system of land ownership and restricting their involvement in wage employment was that their survival as a race depended on retention of a viable village economy and society. The disruption to production and reproduction caused by 'freeing' land and labour from the control of indigenous chiefs was considered by Gordon and his senior advisers to be a primary cause of population decline in the colonies. The devastating impact on Fiji's indigenous population of a measles epidemic in 1875 strengthened the

Table 3.1: *Fijian population trends, 1874–1911*

| Year | Eastern Islands | | | Total |
	Cakaudrove	Lomaiviti	Lau	Fiji
a *Fijian population*				
1874 estimate	15,000	8,000	8,000	*c*.140,500
1881 census	?	7,700	7,300	*c*.115,000
1891 census	10,296	6,422	6,884	105,800
1901 census	8,691	6,414	6,784	94,397
1911 census	8,451	6,033	6,848	87,096
b *% change*				
1881–1891	?	(−17)	(−6)	(−8)
1891–1901	−15.6	−0.12	−1.5	−10.8
1901–1911	−2.8	−5.9	+0.9	−7.7

Sources: de Ricci (1875), Emberson (1881), Dods (1891), Sutherland (1901), Dods (1901), Boyd (1911).

resolve of those who favoured conservation of non-capitalist relations of production. It has been estimated that the introduction of measles by Fijians returning from Australia early in 1875, to a population without natural resistance and virtually no medical resources, killed around 30,000 people (McArthur 1967; Cliff & Haggett 1985). This represented at least one-fifth of the total Fijian population in the mid-1870s. In Gordon's words (cited in Heath 1974: 87), '"the more the native policy is retained, native agency employed, and changes avoided until naturally and spontaneously called for", the less likely was the Fijian "to perish off the face of the earth"'.

The decline of indigenous populations was seen to be an inevitable consequence of 'development' by many writers in the late nineteenth century (Bedford 1980b). In Fiji the first two reasonably complete enumerations of the population in 1881 and 1891 revealed that numbers of Fijians had fallen from around 115,000 to 105,800 – a drop of 8 per cent (Table 3.1). Ten years later, at the census in 1901, the Fijian total was 94,397 representing a decline by a further 11 per cent. The causes of this 'racial decay' in Fiji were the subject of a Royal Commission of Inquiry in the 1890s (Corney et al. 1896) whose report was to be a source of inspiration for many writers dealing with depopulation in the Pacific around the turn of the century.

The reality of population trends in Fiji in the late nineteenth and early twentieth centuries is much more complex than these aggregate statistics suggest. In the three provinces which comprise the eastern islands, for example, there were quite marked variations in trends over the period

1881 to 1911, the first two censuses for which island totals are available (see Table 3.1). Of the 27 islands with estimates for their Fijian populations in these two years, ten islands had larger numbers resident in 1911 than in 1881. Indeed, for Lau Province as a whole numbers of Fijians increased in the first decade of the twentieth century by almost 1 per cent, while the national total declined by a further 7.7 per cent. Explanations for the quite marked regional differences in growth rates vary. The hypothesis favoured by Thompson, who carried out ethnographic research in the southern Lau islands in the 1930s, was that the extent to which island populations had been disturbed by external influences (which also fostered internal political conflict) accounted for much of the variation (Thompson 1940b: 140). This hypothesis reflected the prevailing view of Fiji's colonial administrators in the first two decades of colonial rule. It was to be challenged seriously by policy makers after the death of Governor Thurston in 1897.

Redefining the rules, 1900–12

The argument that neither Fiji nor the Fijians could advance economically under the land, labour and taxation regulations which the colonial government had set in place after 1875 was favoured by successive governors in the twentieth century. The first serious challenge to the new orthodoxy came from Sir Everard im Thurn, whose administration seems to have been an exercise in applied anthropology founded on his assumption that 'nothing can save the Fijian race from dying out' (Scarr 1984; France 1969: 163). He found enthusiastic support from his senior staff for reform of a native policy which was failing to achieve the aim which constituted its major justification: reproduction of the demographic as well as economic basis of Fijian village life. Three major changes in government policy were proposed in the first decade of the twentieth century: the first concerned native land, the second payment of taxes and the third the employment of Fijians outside their village communities.

(i) *Land* Im Thurn's changes in land tenure policy in 1905 were a major departure from a policy originally devised by Sir Arthur Gordon, the first Governor, under instructions 'to disturb as little as possible existing tenures' (France 1969: 110). A Native Lands Commission was established, which sought in the 1880s and 1890s to determine the boundaries of the land belonging to the various *mataqali*, a *mataqali* being the social unit chosen, rather arbitrarily, as the primary land-holding unit for Fijian land. In the process of delineating *mataqali* boundaries the ownership of some of the land under cultivation by settlers was brought into question, and the activities of the Native Lands Commission were universally unpopular among the expatriate planters.

In the climate of opinion prevailing around 1900 it was not difficult for Im Thurn to get widespread support from Europeans for three major modifications to Gordon's land policy: further alienation of native land where this did not prejudice the economic activities of the Fijian population; leases of native land without limit of time; and an end to *mataqali* boundary registration by the Native Lands Commission. Im Thurn sold this proposal to the Council of Chiefs in 1905 in the wider context of a package of social reforms considered necessary to facilitate Fijian economic progress. He believed that Fijian development (material, social and spiritual) was being constrained by the communal agricultural system; Im Thurn, like his predecessor Sir George O'Brien, wished to foster an ethic of individualism in Fijian society.

Unfortunately for Im Thurn, for those settlers seeking access to large tracts of freehold land, and for some Fijians endeavouring to emulate Europeans in their capitalist enterprises, the Colonial Office would not accept his re-evaluation of land tenure in Fiji. Accordingly in 1908 acquisition ceased of unused land considered to be surplus to the requirements of Fijians, a race which many expatriates still believed was dying out. During the three years when land could be alienated a further 104,142 acres was freeholded, mostly on Viti Levu and Vanua Levu. However, there was little change in the pattern of land ownership in the eastern islands at this time. Of much greater significance, in terms of their impact on the transformation of relations of production in Fijian communities in the periphery, were attempts to promote the ethic of individualism through amendments to the taxation and labour regulations.

(ii) *Taxation* After 1900 the system of paying taxes in kind on a district or provincial basis, and receiving cash refunds for apportionment at this level of administration, came under continuous attack by Europeans and Fijians alike. As part of the drive to promote individualism, Governor O'Brien instructed district officials to divide the cash refund among individuals rather than communities, on the basis of the contribution each person made to the total amount of produce provided as tax (Macnaught 1982). Inevitably this strategy increased competition within villages for available copra (the tax crop in eastern Fiji) and, for the first time since the establishment of colonial rule, payment of taxes became a problem for those men with limited land suitable for, or planted in, coconuts.

Whereas previously a district had met its tax quota by pooling the resources of its landowners, and those who had no land in production made their contribution by helping their neighbours, now the owners began to demand payment in pigs or mats or cash to compensate for the diminution of their share of the refund. The problem was especially serious in the 'coconut provinces' of eastern Fiji, and in 1902 the Council of Chiefs asked that provinces be left to determine whether they paid the tax in kind or cash. Macnaught (1982) reports that in Lau, for instance, the absurd situation had arisen whereby villagers were selling produce such as mats, wooden bowls, fish and foods to storekeepers in order to raise the cash they needed to purchase the copra required to pay the tax in kind.

By 1912 few districts were paying tax in kind and government decided to make cash payments obligatory from 1913. The implications of this change in policy for relations of production in the periphery are summarised by Macnaught (1982: 27):

The mood of the government had changed. They knew full well that Fijians would mortgage their coconut groves to the nearest trader who would have the nuts collected and the copra cut, with the net result that the owners would receive less than half the value of their produce. They also knew that the loss of the central marketing organisation provided by the old scheme would relegate Fijians to the edges of an ever more alien-dominated colonial economy ... The changes were seen as the inevitable price of an ill-defined concept of general progress through the 'time of transition' to a more western way of life.

(iii) *Labour* This 'time of transition' was also to be hastened in 1912 by an amendment to the Native Labour ordinance which permitted Fijians to leave their districts to take up wage employment without the approval of the *Buli*. It was a period of increased interest within Fijian communities in periodic absences for wage employment, especially to accumulate money required to meet regular demands for taxes and levies from government officials and churches. From around 1910 the supply of Fijian contract labour, especially from Lau, for work on Taveuni increased substantially. For planters it was the only period when labour was no real constraint (Brookfield 1978).

The trend towards individual rather than communal endeavour, payment and reward, was not favoured by some Fijian chiefs. Ratu Sukuna, descendant of the paramount chiefs of Bau and Lau, Fiji's first Oxford graduate in law, and a senior civil servant in the colonial administration, summed up the situation as he saw it in 1917:

Up until two decades ago the autocracy and the communalism inherited by the Government thrived side by side, both unimpaired. But from that time Native Policy, with more democratic kindness than prudence, began to undermine the autocracy ... until it is now the shadow of its former self. This destructive policy was distinctly retrogressive because no effective substitute was created. (Sukuna in Scarr (ed.) 1983: 52)

Although the Council of Chiefs remained the recognised authority on Fijian custom and land, their influence on the colonial administration's social and economic policies was becoming less significant than it had been in the late nineteenth century. The structure of the Fijian administration and the associated regulations to conserve 'traditional' village life had been weakened considerably, basically because of a lack of commitment among European officials who now favoured individualism. Yet the opportunity for commoners to acquire individual title to land for cash cropping or to sell their labour as a commodity was not yet equated by many chiefs with progress or prosperity.

Establishment of a peasantry

Prosperity and its expropriation

The first two decades of the twentieth century have been interpreted as years of relative prosperity in the eastern islands of Fiji (Knapman 1985). According to Sukuna (then District Commissioner), on most islands in the Lau group the people 'included bread, rice, sugar, tea, coffee, tinned milk and tinned meat in their daily diet ... It was no uncommon sight to see two or more cutters in Levuka full of Lauans on holiday to the old capital, and all with money' (Sukuna in Scarr (ed.) 1983: 130). Extensive planting of coconuts during the latter half of the nineteenth century, partly in response to taxation policies pursued by Ma'afu and the colonial administration, and partly due to the annual contribution (*vakamisioneri*) for the support and expansion of the Wesleyan mission, provided the productive base on which Lauan participation in market exchange was founded. In addition to the expanding demands by individuals for trade goods, a greater expenditure on boats, church building and water supply systems had also become a necessary component of Lauan village life by the 1920s. The recurring expenditure on government taxation – payable in cash in Lau from 1907 at the Lauans' request – and mission collections accounted for a considerable percentage of total cash income generated by trade and, after 1912, by wage labour. It has been estimated that central taxes, provincial taxes, levies for schools, boats, village sanitation and drainage, and emergency relief funds, expropriated between one-quarter and one-third of Lauans cash income (Lessin & Lessin 1970). Estimates of contributions to the missions vary, but Knapman (1976a: 180) argues that at times these exceeded the government tax assessment.

What money remained was available for personal savings or expenditure. In addition to imported foods, cloth, tools, fuels and tobacco, which were all freely used by Lauan households from the 1890s onwards, house building and transport increasingly became items for individual expenditure. Before 1912 house building had been undertaken by the village community; it was an integral part of the communal system covered in the Native Regulations. In 1912, however, Lauans resolved 'that house building by the community be abolished and that it shall be the duty of the individual to arrange for the building of his own house' (Lau Provincial Council 1912).

The other major item of expenditure, usually at the level of the community but occasionally an individual enterprise, was on sailing boats to service the growing trade in commodities between the eastern islands and Levuka. The potential for control over transport made possible by the proliferation of Fijian-owned boats was seldom realised, however, because the boats ran at a loss. Indebtedness to traders was a major factor ensuring a continuing commitment to production of copra or temporary wage employment among Lauans, especially after wooden houses and plank-constructed boats became fashionable. As early as 1906 the Lau Provincial Council was reporting that the people of Lakeba 'were greatly pushed and many of them already in debt on account of the wooden houses they had gone in for. They also have their obligations to storekeepers. Besides only lately they had got an expensive Provincial vessel.'

This involvement in production of a surplus for trade was facilitated by the introduction of new subsistence food crops which could be cultivated with less labour input than traditional staples like yams and wet taro. For example, on Koro island in Lomaiviti important changes in the subsistence basis of life coincided in time with the first significant expansion in the area under coconuts. Between 1900 and 1912 dryland taro and cassava were introduced into subsistence gardens to supplement yams, plantains, breadfruit and wetland taro in the diet (Bayliss-Smith 1977b). These short-term food crops were all underplanted beneath coconut palms as the long-term tree crop. This integrated agroforestry system satisfied both economic, social and ecological requirements, and by this means Fijians quickly became, and were encouraged to remain, peasant producers.[5]

These farmers were operating on the fringes of an evolving capitalist system dominated by European and Indian enterprise and labour. The Fijian village economy subsidised the development of this capitalist economy by providing planters with a reserve of casual labour and traders with a variable supply of produce and a growing market for imported foods and material goods. However to term this a process of 'underdevelopment' is misleading: as Knapman (1985: 83) has argued

[5] The complex issue of the 'traditional' basis to Fijian land tenure is discussed by Belshaw (1964), Chapelle (1978), Fison (1981), France (1968, 1969), Groves (1963), Lloyd (1982), Nayacakalou (1971, 1975, 1978), Roth (1953), Sahlins (1962), Spate (1959), Walter (1978, 1983), Ward (1965), and Watters (1969).

recently, the colonial state's protective modification of Fiji's incorporation into world capitalism spared them the 'journey through hell' which the Indians in Fiji (Indo-Fijians) and many other Third World peoples had to experience, in their progress towards greater material well-being.

Continuity through change

Despite these substantial changes in the organisation of productive activity, in the distribution of population, in housing and in diet, at the level of relations of production little had changed. The new goods were simply presented for accumulation and redistribution alongside traditional goods. The traditional basis of inequality – descent group status, rank and control of manpower within a chiefly system of ceremonial exchange – persisted despite attempts by some Fijians to escape the perceived constraints of village life by absenteeism, and by others to emulate capitalist enterprises by forming local companies (Sahlins 1962; Knapman & Walter 1980). But few managed to break away from the communal life of the village: Sukuna was pleased to report in 1917 that only 150 Fijians had chosen to follow the path of individualism (Scarr 1980b: 47). At the time of the 1921 census over 90 per cent of Fijians were living in *koro* or nucleated villages and, in eastern Fiji at least, were allocating their labour to a range of subsistence, cash-earning and ceremony-related tasks in much the same way as they had since the 1880s.

The demographic turning point

During the 1920s the slow Fijian population decline was reversed and by 1936 the total (97,651) exceeded the number enumerated in 1901 (94,397). The decline in the eastern provinces had been arrested before 1921 – numbers of Fijians in Cakaudrove, Lomaiviti and Lau in 1921 were all larger than those enumerated in 1911 (Table 3.2). In fact, the period from 1905 to 1911 can be regarded as the turning point in so far as Fijian population replacement is concerned. As McArthur (1967) noted, from 1911 the Fijian birth rate exceeded the death rate in every year except 1918, the year of the influenza pandemic. Yet anxiety over high mortality rates continued, and fears of population decline were voiced as late as the 1940s (Hull & Hull 1973: 172). Throughout the 1920s and 1930s Fijians were exhorted to have large families and to care particularly for the welfare of their children.

To a very large extent the eastern islands remained a Fijian domain. In 1936 8 per cent of the population enumerated in Cakaudrove, Lomaiviti and Lau provinces was Indo-Fijian compared with 43 per cent for the

Table 3.2 *Population change in the eastern islands, 1921–46*

Year	Eastern Islands			Total
	Cakaudrove	Lomaiviti	Lau	Fiji
a *Fijian population*				
1921	8,720	6,452	7,693	84,475
1936	10,783	6,372	9,256	97,651
1946	12,063	7,428	10,360	117,488
Average annual rate of growth (%)[a]				
1921–36	1.4	−0.08[b]	1.2	0.97
1936–46	1.1	1.5	1.1	1.85
b *Indian population*				
1911	335	253	104	40,286
1921	1,585	1,164	244	60,634
1936	1,850	639	205	85,002
1946	2,548	775	161	120,063
Average annual rate of growth (%)				
1911–21	15.5	15.3	8.5	4.09
1921–36	1.0	−4.0	−1.1	2.25
1936–46	3.2	1.9	−2.4	3.45
c *Total population*				
1921	11,540	8,965	8,325	157,266
1936	14,334	8,208	9,671	198,379
1946	17,231	9,741	10,970	259,638
% Indian				
1921	13.7	12.9	2.9	38.5
1936	12.9	7.8	2.1	42.8
1946	14.8	7.9	1.5	46.2

[a] Average annual rates of growth were derived using the

$$\text{formula } r = \frac{\log_e\left(\dfrac{P_2}{P_1}\right)}{n} \times 100$$

[b] The absolute drop in Lomaiviti's population between 1921 and 1936 was due primarily to the declining significance of Levuka as an urban centre. Both its Fijian and Indian populations fell over the 15 years as urban employment opportunities grew in Suva.

Sources: Boyd (1911), Boyd and Stewart (1922), Burrows (1936), Gittins (1947).

country as a whole; in Lau Indo-Fijians comprised only 2 per cent of the population (see Table 3.2). The status of the eastern islands as one of the 'homes' of Fijian custom and tradition was therefore enhanced by continuity of a village-based Melanesian population, in a country where non-Melanesians living both in towns and in dispersed rural settlements were now in the majority (Lambert 1938).

A precarious continuity, 1930–60

Depression, disengagement and departure

Crisis in the global capitalist economy between 1929 and 1936 demonstrated convincingly that 120 years of exposure to capitalist relations of production had generated an enduring transformation in Fijian society and economy in the periphery. The Great Depression had a severe impact on Fiji's export trade. The market for copra collapsed quickly and poor prices for this commodity, coupled with hurricanes and a drought in Lau between 1929 and 1931, resulted in a substantial decline in production in the early 1930s. In 1932 the District Commissioner Sukuna reported that 'most of the people are back on native foods; there are families with just one change of clothes between them; others cannot even buy soap; houses are unlit at night' (Sukuna in Scarr (ed.) 1983: 130). The shortage of money in the eastern islands was a persistent theme in Sukuna's reports because one consequence was a shortfall in the payment of provincial rates and taxes. In 1934 the arrears were so substantial in Lomaiviti that a prohibition (*tabu*) on sales of copra to traders was imposed 'to ensure the payment of these dues and at the same time retrieve the financial position of the Province' (Sukuna in Scarr (ed.) 1983: 187).

Another consequence of the difficulty of obtaining money was a necessary revival in the non-capitalist sector, especially after a severe hurricane struck southern Lau in 1936. Thompson (1940b: 93–4) reported:

Neglected gardens were cleared and replanted, native crafts were revived, and inter-island trade was resumed. The southern [Lau] islands once more became the centre of canoe building, woodwork, barkcloth and mat making in Fiji. Involuntarily the natives regained most of their (former) economic independence.

Thompson was greatly impressed by the willingness of villagers at this time to revive subsistence production and revert to 'traditional' ways of resolving shortages in food and material produce on particular islands. She found 'a will to survive or zest for life, which grows out of a healthy and socially adjusted communal life' (Thompson 1940b: 140). Yet she also found that 'in at least 50 percent of the villages visited in Lau, practically all the young men between the ages of eighteen and thirty were away for a year on labour contracts, earning money' (Thompson 1940b: 80). The subsistence economy was being sustained by the labour of youths, women and older men; as Sukuna (in Scarr (ed.) 1983: 242) cynically observed in 1938: 'natives ... go out and labour on plantations and gold mines leaving their wives and children in the care of others, and for this Fijians will be counted as virtuous; their industry will be on men's lips as a sign of Fijian progress.'

When a population census was taken in 1936 approximately 800 Lauans were living outside of the Province and of these 150 were temporary absentees from Kabara and Komo, 'islands that have probably reached their limits of copra production'. Population growth was beginning to have an effect on the demand for productive land, but land shortage was not seen to be a major reason for migration away from the eastern islands in the 1930s. Perhaps more significant was 'the opposition of the rising generation ... [to] productive labour connected with the soil' (Sukuna in Scarr (ed.) 1983: 132). In Sukuna's view it was inevitable that increasing numbers of Fijians would leave the small islands to settle in urban areas on Viti Levu and Vanua Levu, especially those people with enough education to compete for places in the government and the church. His predictions were to prove realistic despite efforts by the government in the 1940s to shore up the neo-traditional order in the periphery.

The reinforcement of rural society

Economic uncertainty in the 1930s was replaced by a short era of unparalleled material prosperity for many Fijians in the 1940s. The military campaigns in the western Pacific during the Second World War were launched from forward bases in Fiji, Vanuatu and New Caledonia. Thousands of military personnel from the United States, New Zealand and Australia moved through these bases which provided substantial markets for produce (both food and handicrafts) and for unskilled labour. In addition to their direct contribution to the Allied war effort as soldiers, Fijians by their thousand, were involved in a hyper-ventilating capitalist economy after a decade of poor prices for their commodities and limited demand for their labour. As Brookfield (1972: 88) has argued, the reconquest of Melanesia after Japanese invasion in 1942 'had a major and lasting effect on the whole region: in a real sense it is the major event of modern Melanesian history'.

Withdrawal of the armed forces from the western Pacific was as swift, and in some ways as devastating, as their arrival. Suddenly the most lucrative markets for labour and produce were gone, and economic dislocation was severe. In Fiji the response of the Fijian administration was to advise Fijians to return to their villages, where a new era of prosperity was allegedly dawning under more enlightened government policy concerning rural development.

If piecemeal efforts by European administrators to 'liberate' Fijian villagers from the perceived bondage of communal economic endeavour in a society dominated by hereditary chiefs were to be a characteristic of British rule during the first three decades of the twentieth century, the next twenty were to see a substantial reinforcement of the neo-traditional order. There are several reasons for this, not the least of which was the growing political influence of Ratu Sukuna who, in 1937, left his post as District Commissioner in the eastern islands to become a member of the Legislative Council. Three years later he was appointed Commissioner of Lands and in 1943 became the Adviser (later Secretary) of Fijian Affairs, a post he held until 1954. Other reasons for a conservative response by Fiji's chiefs to socio-economic change at this time were competition from Indo-Fijians in commerce and their agitation for greater political representation in a country where they now comprised the largest single ethnic component of the total population. Through the 1930s this perceived challenge from the Indo-Fijians had resulted in reaffirmation of the alliance between Europeans and Fijians to 'safeguard the Fijian race'. Sukuna was to use this alliance to full advantage in the 1940s to obtain acceptance of a reconstituted Fijian administration which was, in essence, a revival of the nineteenth century structure (Scarr 1984: 153).[6]

The cornerstone of Sukuna's rural development programme was a more attractive village environment for work and leisure. Three basic requirements in this regard were removal of the drudgery of some repetitive time-consuming tasks, especially house building; promotion of a more disciplined approach to production for the market; and provision of a wider range of welfare services, education opportunities and entertainment facilities in places accessible to village residents. The emphasis was firmly on co-operative enterprise; village communities and kin-groups were the foundations for Fijian economic success; salvation did not lie 'in a parody of Western individualised economic man' (Scarr 1984: 154). Individual farmers (*galala*) were allowed to commute obligations to their village-based kin through payment of a tax in lieu of communal labour when they could convince local Fijian committees they had the crop, market and will to succeed. It was these villages, revitalised by the 5,000 to 6,000 returning servicemen, and with improved water supplies, housing, cash crops, and amenities such as travelling cinemas, that were supposed to counter the lure of towns.

The new colonialism: new wine in old bottles?

After the traumas of war, the ideological climate for colonialism became altered in irreversible ways. Everywhere in the Pacific the economic strategy of post-war governments became dominated by the desire 'to

[6] Reorganisation of the Fijian administration between 1944 and 1949 had a profound impact on Fijian development in the 1950s and 1960s. The objectives Ratu Sukuna had in mind, and the policies he persuaded the Council of Chiefs and the colonial government to introduce, are best articulated in his speeches and

Table 3.3 *Population change in eastern Fiji, 1946–66*

Year	Eastern Islands			Total
	Cakaudrove	Lomaiviti	Lau	Fiji
a) *Fijian population*				
1946	12,063	7,428	10,360	117,488
1956	16,088	8,835	12,954	148,134
1966	20,462	11,241	15,561	202,176
Average annual rate of growth (%)				
1946–56	2.9	1.7	2.2	2.3
1956–66	2.4	2.4	1.8	3.1
b) *Indo-Fijian population*				
1946	2,548	775	161	120,063
1956	3,633	834	237	169,403
1966	5,244	770	274	240,960
Average annual rate of growth (%)				
1946–56	3.5	0.7	3.9	3.4
1956–66	3.7	−0.8	1.5	3.5
c) *Total population*				
1946	17,231	9,741	10,970	259,638
1956	23,339	11,244	13,500	345,737
1966	30,053	13,264	15,988	476,727
% Fijian				
1946	70.0	76.2	94.4	45.3
1956	68.9	78.6	95.9	42.8
1966	68.0	84.7	97.3	42.4

Sources: Gittins (1947), McArthur (1958), Zwart (1968).

increase exports by all means possible ... a drive [which] has made the
policy conflict between equity and efficiency especially acute' (Brookfield
1972: 105). This 'new colonialism' was designed to assist in paying for a
rising value of imported goods and services, as a conscious prelude, at
least in British territories, to ultimate self-government. In Fiji, however,
the complications of Indo-Fijian domination in population, sugar production and, increasingly, urban commerce, meant that 'the equity versus
efficiency problem presented itself in an ethnic rather than an areal
dimension' (Brookfield 1972: 101). The periphery as such was unimpor-
tant by comparison with the overall need to boost Fijian participation in
the monetised sector.

Fortunately recovery in the price for copra was rapid during the late

reports which have been reprinted in Scarr (1983). Useful descriptions of the
structure of the post-war Fijian administration can be found in Lasaqa (1984),
Nayacakalou (1964, 1975 and 1978), Qalo (1984), Roth (1951 and 1953), Scarr
(1980b), Spate (1959 and 1961), Stanner (1953) and Watters (1969).

1940s. In 1938 the FOB price for a ton of copra at Suva had been £9; in 1945 it went above £20, climbing to over £41 by June 1947; and in January 1951 copra reached just under £60 per ton (Bedford 1978). Such prices brought a measure of immediate prosperity to the periphery, both for the village economy and for the commercial plantations on small islands in northern Lau and on Taveuni. Labour migration from Lau and Lomaiviti was also substantial; in the 1956 census, for example, over 1,000 Fijians from these provinces were enumerated on Taveuni (Bedford 1978: 97). The net result was a substantial return migration to rural areas after the war. Average annual rates of population growth in Cakaudrove and Lau provinces between 1946 and 1956 were much higher than they had been in the preceding decade, and migration as well as natural increase contributed to this growth (Tables 3.2 and 3.3).

During the post-war decade there was also considerable debate about, and experimentation with, strategies for promoting Fijian economic development within a set of institutions which built on the existing superstructure of Fijian society.[7] Schemes to amalgamate villages, administrative districts (*tikina*), and provinces to facilitate more rational provision of services and to create larger political and social organisations met with limited success: there was conflict with accepted views of tribal autonomy and prevailing notions of social obligations. There were also efforts to co-ordinate produce marketing through centralised authorities, to promote greater understanding of commercial practice (and, hopefully, cheaper consumer goods) through consumer-marketing co-operatives, and to create a fund through a cess on copra which could be used to support rural development projects. One outside observer felt that the new government ideology fell far short of the Fijian village reality: 'official economic development is wedded to a sort of semi-socialist agrarianism which meets with very little response from the people' (Spate 1960: 50).

Even so, there was a substantial growth in Fijian participation in cash cropping, and also a gradual transformation in village housing conditions made possible by loans from the Fiji Development Fund Board which administered the copra cess. In most of the periphery these changes occurred within untransformed village settings, very much as 'new wine in

---

[7] There is an extensive literature on social and economic change in Fiji in the late 1940s and 1950s. Several detailed village-level inquiries established the contradictions between the ideological and political aspirations of the Fijian administration and the economic and social aspirations of Fijians resident in rural and urban areas (Belshaw 1964; Geddes 1945 and 1956; Nayacakalou 1978; Quain 1948; Watters 1965 and 1969). Other studies of society and economy at national level emphasised repeatedly the need for a reduction in the regulation of Fijian labour and land use which the post-war administration continued to foster in the belief that a process of gradual transformation would safeguard the interests of Fijians (Burns et al. 1960; Spate 1959; Stanner 1953; Ward 1965).

old bottles', and did nothing to resolve 'the confusing incompatibility ... between the two official objectives of Tradition and Development' (Spate 1960: 50). The essence of some of these tensions was described as follows for Manava village, northern Lau:

> As the permanent coconut crop began to "eat up the land" and the population increase accelerated, a new phenomenon appeared in the village: land shortage. The group basis of production started to disintegrate ... Men now wished to control their own resources in land and coconut for their own purposes, and fragmentation of holdings was rapidly effected. The traditional redistributive system still operated but on a much reduced scale ... Ceremonial became largely divorced from the hard realities of the new economic life and diminished in social and cultural importance. Along with it diminished the raison d'être of the hierarchy of statuses and rank that it had supported. (Knapman & Walter 1980: 207)

A demographic response

On small islands where opportunities for generating a cash income were restricted essentially to agriculture, the combination of rapid population growth and aspirations for higher material standards of living led inevitably to conflict over land. In the eastern islands the source and nature of this conflict was not uniform; the restructuring of social relations of production had certain common elements but the historical experiences of communities in different parts of the periphery were quite varied, as we show in chapters 7, 8 and 9. Developments in the copra industry, which Brookfield (1985) has reviewed in depth elsewhere, and which are considered in the next chapter, also had a differential impact on enterprise in the periphery. One response by Fijians which was common throughout eastern Fiji, however, was the search for employment elsewhere.

All forms of population movement between islands were more intensive in the period of post-war prosperity than they had been in the depression years. But while short-term circulation of labour between villages and centres of wage employment (towns, coconut plantations and sugar estates) had become an integral part of the rhythm of rural residence in eastern Fiji, there was an accelerating net loss of population from small islands to larger islands, especially Viti Levu where the country's main towns were located. Both the diminishing overall growth rate and the increasingly distorted age–sex structure of the Fijian population in the eastern islands attest to this accelerating net loss in the period 1946–66 (Fig. 3.2). Some aspects of urbanisation in Fiji in the 1950s and 1960s are outlined below; it is sufficient to note here that migration as a regulator of demographic development in the periphery was assuming increasing

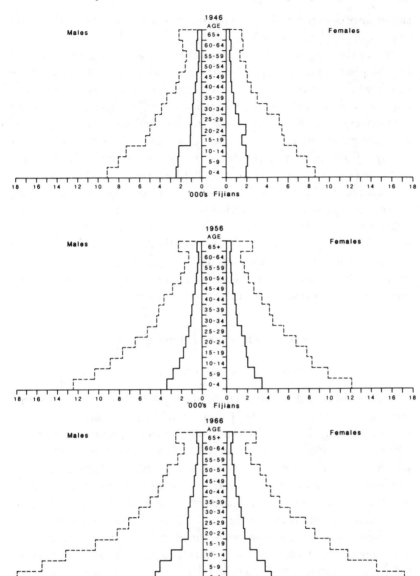

3.2 Fijian population structure, Fiji compared to eastern islands, 1946–66

significance despite high levels of natural increase in the Fijian population at this time (Bedford 1980b).

By the late 1950s the Fijian administration was being advised from several quarters that attempts to promote the economic and social welfare of Fijians through co-operative village-based enterprise were not achieving the desired ends. The trend towards individualism through wage employment (usually in town) or independent farming (*galala*) had attracted greater support from Fijians than expected, despite the absence of any official encouragement. Major studies of economic change in Fiji by Spate (1959), Burns et al. (1960), Belshaw (1964), and Ward (1965) stressed the need for radical change in rural development philosophy, strategy and action. Slow evolution from within, the design fostered by Sukuna from the 1920s until his death in 1958, was no longer appropriate. The 1960s, the last decade of colonial rule, saw a belated effort by colonial administrators, chiefs and commoners to break with the tradition of village-based co-operative economic endeavour in order to bring Fijians into the mainstream of capitalist development.

The late colonial period: freeing the land

Subdivision schemes in the 1960s

The dismantling of the communal system began in earnest in 1961 with a series of amendments to the Fijian Affairs Regulation of 1945: all communal obligations and the programme of work specified for Fijians in villages were removed. In the same year an ambitious land development scheme was initiated whereby potentially productive Fijian land under communal ownership could, with the approval of the *mataqali* members and the Native Lands Trust Board which administered the leasing of Fijian land, be subdivided for lease to Fijians seeking to establish their own farms. The stage was set for what many outsiders regarded as the right way for Fijians to modernise, namely to become part of a nation of independent farmers and so-called free agents within the capitalist economy (Macnaught 1982: 157). There was still considerable opposition within the Council of Chiefs to proposals by Spate (1959) and others to individualise land tenure, but concern within the colonial administration at the apparent lack of Fijian economic progress in the 1950s resulted in government moving 'with a speed and purpose unparalleled in Fiji before or since' (Brookfield 1984c: 9).

The activities of the Land Development Authority (LDA), which was set up in 1961 to provide the means of settling individual farmers, mainly Fijian, on managed re-settlement and land development schemes, have recently been reviewed by Brookfield (1984c). He points out that the LDA was involved in 38 schemes incorporating blocks for 2,407 farmers by 1967 – the equivalent of almost double the number of *galala* (around 1,300) registered in 1959 (Spate 1959: 89–90). Some of these *galala* were incorporated into the new schemes but most of the new blockholders were additional (Brookfield 1984c: 11). While there was considerable diversity in the nature of the schemes one trend was apparent from the outset: Fijians from the eastern islands, the hearth of 'traditional' village life, were heavily involved in the movement onto subdivided land.

There were two major reasons for this interest. The first was a genuine shortage of land for members of some *mataqali*, especially those on the smaller islands in Lau Province. Before the government-sponsored land development schemes were initiated Lauans had obtained access to land in south-east Viti Levu, and in 1956 a subdivision plan was drawn up to regularise their leases. When subdivision schemes, which were open to non-members of the *mataqali* who owned the land, were established after 1962 Lauans were invariably present in the new communities.

The second reason for interest in subdivision in the coconut provinces was that land development was linked to a coconut planting and re-planting subsidy in order to revitalise the ailing copra industry. There was a condition, however; only individual blockholders were eligible for the subsidy – it could not be paid for improvements to unsubdivided *mataqali* land. As a Fijian sociologist pointed out, it did not take Fijians long to find and exploit a loophole in this arrangement:

Men rushed to take out leases or agricultural licences over their own lands. The subsidies were duly paid on production of the relevant documents, but the rents [paid for leased Fijian land to the Native Lands Trust Board] were not, for the Fijians argued, why should they pay rent to themselves? ... The ultimate sanction available to [the Native Land Trust Board] was, of course, to cancel the lease, but this did not matter to people who had received their subsidies. (Nayacakalou 1971: 221)

Brookfield (1984c: 12–13) notes that the demand for subdivision in eastern Fiji 'quickly became enormous ... By 1967 the Divisional Development Commissioner, Eastern, could proudly inform his successor that 2,552 individual blocks had been established and that a further 10,000 blocks could be established in the near future.'

In fact these blocks were not created; the scale of subdivision demand in the coconut provinces, and elsewhere, overwhelmed the available human and financial resources of the LDA. Resource constraints, coupled with agricultural problems in LDA's show-piece scheme at Lomaivuna on Viti Levu resulted in a rapid decline in its activities from 1967. Brookfield (1984c: 15) suggested that factors other than purely economic ones were responsible for the winding up of the LDA in 1969 when he observed that the effect of coming independence was an important factor in the decline for the new Fijian leadership was drawn mainly from the conservative chiefs who had opposed the Spate and Burns recommendations: 'As the new Fijian leadership acquired power and influence, so the LDA was wound back.'

As we show in subsequent chapters, rural development policy after Fiji gained Independence in 1970 was characterised by ambivalence towards the independent farmer. In a book published 40 years after Sukuna introduced his plans to revitalise Fijian community life, Lasaqa (1984: 51) argued that in the 1980s 'It seems clear that the villager prefers to meet and shoulder all his responsibilities within the context of his village existence. He sees his village as the basis of his resource mobilisation and the crux of all this must rest on sound leadership, efficient organisation of effort and allocation of resources within the village.' The return to orthodoxy in Fijian rural development after 1970 is discussed further in chapter 6, but we can note here that the reality is much more complex than Lasaqa's words suggest. Just as the Second World War had revolutionised the material aspirations of many Fijians in the 1940s, the land development schemes of the 1960s had greatly stimulated a transformation in the nature of Fijian rural enterprise. Life in the *koro*, especially on islands like Taveuni, Koro and Lakeba has not been the same since (see chapters 7, 8 and 9).

Population growth, migration and urbanisation

The other process which was transforming village life in Fiji in the 1950s and 1960s was population growth. As noted earlier, rates of increase in the Fijian population had risen to over 3.0 per cent per annum by the mid-1950s, and an issue of considerable concern to some members of the colonial administration at this time was the long-term implications for Fiji's economic and social development of sustained population growth at this sort of rate (Hull & Hull 1973). Family planning programmes, as a strategy to reduce fertility, were being discussed publicly and informally in the administration, but official sponsorship of such programmes was complicated by the ethnic balance in Fiji's population. While Indo-Fijians remained the largest ethnic group numerically it was considered unlikely that 'the people of the land' would support a policy to reduce Fijian fertility. Besides, only 30 years previously government officials were exhorting them to have larger families in the interests of racial survival.

An important economic effect of rapid population growth in the small islands of eastern Fiji was to foster increased demand for productive land on which to grow cash and subsistence crops. Inequalities in access to land, either as a result of differential status within the social hierarchy, or because of membership of land-rich or land-poor *mataqali*, became more evident with a trend towards 'enclosure' of cash crop and subsistence holdings (Walter 1978, 1983). Problems over access to productive land intensified with rapid post-war population growth and contributed to an accelerating exodus from the eastern islands.

The difficulty of earning an acceptable income from cash cropping was not the only reason for the exodus, however. After the Second World War the colonial administration belatedly became much more involved in the financing of education in Fiji (Whitehead 1981). Recognition of the peripheral role which Fijians performed in the cash economy in general, and the urban public and private sectors in particular, prompted policies to improve schooling for Fijians in rural areas. In eastern Fiji the cost of providing anything but junior primary schools on the small islands was prohibitive. If villagers on most islands in Lau and Lomaiviti provinces wanted their children to attend advanced primary and secondary schools, they had to arrange for their residence on another island. In many cases the family decided to move to Viti Levu (especially Suva), find a job and accommodation there, and send the children to schools in town (Ward 1961; Bedford 1980a, 1985).

Although it was recognised that Fijians were highly mobile people, moving frequently within and between islands for a wide range of social and economic reasons, the significance of this movement for a substantial redistribution in the population after Cession was slow in coming. This is hardly surprising given the regulations that existed throughout the colonial period to discourage settlement outside of villages where Fijians had access to land through customary ties. However, data on Fijian population distribution contained in the censuses from 1921 onwards indicated that such a redistribution was occurring. Ward (1961: 260) notes, for example, that in 1921 just over 5 per cent of all Fijians were living away from their home villages; by 1946 the proportion had increased to 22 per cent. The sources of these 'migrants' could not be established and it was not until the 1956 census that a question was included in the decennial census to measure the extent of internal migration among Fijians.

In 1956 Fijians were asked to specify the province in which they were registered as landowners, and when this was compared with the province in which they were enumerated some crude assessments of magnitude and direction of migration flow could be made. These data must be treated with caution because there were several conceptual and administrative problems with the land ownership question (McArthur 1958: 35–8).

Table 3.4 *Internal migration of Fijians, 1956*

Province where enumerated in 1956	Province where had land rights			Total Fiji
	Lau	Lomaiviti	Cakaudrove	
Province where had land rights				
Persons	12,227	7,029	12,581	111,576
% of total	72.6	70.1	84.1	75.3
Rewa (incl. Suva)				
Persons	1,906	1,117	454	16,129
% of total	11.3	11.1	3.0	10.9
Other provinces (excl. Rewa)				
Persons	2,716	1,883	1,923	20,429
% of total	16.1	18.8	12.9	13.8
Total	16,849	10,029	14,958	148,134

Source: McArthur (1958: 166–7).

Even allowing for these problems, the census revealed that there had been more substantial emigration from certain provinces than expected. A quarter of all Fijians (26 per cent of the males and 23 per cent of the females) were enumerated outside those provinces where they had land rights; in the cases of Lau and Lomaiviti, the proportions were 27 per cent and 30 per cent respectively (McArthur 1958: 36). In Cakaudrove Province, with its much more substantial land area, the proportion of *mataqali* members resident at the time of the census was higher than the national average (Table 3.4).

Some important dimensions of rural–urban migration, already evident in the rapid post-war growth of Fiji's towns, were given sharper focus in the 1956 census tables. The largest migration streams from Lau and Lomaiviti had been in the direction of Suva and in 1956 11 per cent of Fijians with land rights in these two provinces were resident in the province (Rewa) containing this town (see Table 3.4). The largest inter-provincial flow from Cakaudrove had been to neighbouring Macuata where the major town in northern Fiji, Labasa, is located (see Fig. 3.1). Further analysis of these data by academics and others carrying out detailed community studies in the late 1950s helped to dispel a common myth that young Fijian men who left home to work in town or on plantations and in the gold mine returned to their villages after absences of a few months to one or two years. Ward (1961), reviewing research on internal migration in Fiji at this time, stressed that short-term labour circulation from a village base had become less significant, especially for Fijians who were able to get work in town. He went on to argue: 'as the contrast between urban and rural living has increased (especially in the post-war era), and as the number of Fijians in the towns has grown (thus making it easier for the new-comer to find friends), the migrant's desire to return home has grown progressively less' (Ward 1961: 265).

The results of the 1966 census confirmed that Fijian urbanisation was progressing apace. Almost one third of all Fijians (31 per cent) were enumerated in towns and their surrounding peri-urban areas in 1966; if the same urban boundaries are used for towns in 1956, the relevant proportion urbanised in that year was 24 per cent. Housing for migrants in town had become a major policy issue by the late 1940s and in 1959 a government agency, the Housing Authority, began constructing accommodation for low-income, but regularly employed, urban workers (Walsh 1978, 1984). High rates of natural increase in the urban populations, as well as extensive in-migration from the rural provinces were creating a new set of tensions in Fiji's capitalist and colonial transformation. Competition for jobs, services and accommodation in town between Fijians and Indo-Fijians brought people from many of the eastern islands into their first personal contact with the reality of life in a plural society. It was in the towns that Fijian villagers became aware of their marginal position in the market economy; the numerically very small European and Chinese (Sino-Fijian) population controlled all the larger organisations and enterprises and most of the dealings with the outside world while the Indians, with very limited access to land, were taking up jobs in the public and private sectors as soon as they became available. There were several conflicts of interest between Fijians and Indians, not the least important of which was intensifying competition for urban employment.

By 1966 over 40 per cent of Fijians aged 15 years or more, who had been born in Lau or Lomaiviti provinces, were living in other parts of Fiji (Table 3.5). Although populations in all the eastern provinces were larger in 1966 than they had been in 1956, average annual rates of growth in Lau and Lomaiviti especially were well below the national average (see Table 3.3). A family planning programme, which the government eventually sponsored in 1962 in response to pressures from several quarters (Hull & Hull 1973), was not responsible for this differential growth pattern; migration had become the major regulator of demographic development in many parts of eastern Fiji (Bedford 1980b). Relative depopulation of the periphery began to attract attention in the closing years of colonial rule; in this context it is interesting to note that several prominent Fijian civil servants who would assume leadership positions on independence were from the eastern islands.

Table 3.5 *Internal migration of Fijians aged 15 years and over, 1966*

Province where enumerated in 1966	Province of birth			Total Fiji
	Lau	Lomaiviti	Cakaudrove	
Province where born				
Persons	6,818	4,419	8,849	74,550
% of total	56.2	58.5	72.8	66.4
Rewa (incl. Suva)				
Persons	2,133	1,246	873	15,876
% of total	17.6	16.5	7.2	14.1
Other provinces (excl. Rewa)				
Persons	3,178	1,884	2,424	21,897
% of total	26.2	24.9	20.0	19.5
Total	12,129	7,549	12,146	112,323

Source: Zwart (1968: 145–6).

Reaffirming the village base

Almost exactly 100 years after the formal establishment of colonial rule, the reproduction of viable and vital village-based societies in the small islands was again a policy issue. In the 1970s rural development policy was to focus heavily on the village as home for Fijians, especially those resident in the eastern periphery. In his review of the political economy of Fiji on the eve of independence Fisk (1970: 43) observed, of the Fijian, that 'he believes, and many non-Fijians would agree, that the world would be a poorer place if the Fijian way of life is completely abandoned and lost'. Echoing Sukuna's basic philosophy about the security of village life in the face of economic and political uncertainty in a society where Fijians were on the fringes rather than part of the mainstream of capitalist development, Fisk went on to claim that unlike most people committed to capitalist relations of production,

the average Fijian who fails in commercial enterprise or in wage earning is not faced with abject poverty and hunger for himself and his family. He is merely faced with the need to abandon the bright lights and to move back to the subsistence sector, where a reasonably comfortable, secure and adequate living, with many fewer hours of work, remains accessible to almost all. (Fisk 1970: 45)

This view of the security of village life in the post-colonial era is a widely accepted one among Fiji's contemporary leaders. Two underlying assumptions of all development planning since 1970 have been that villages should 'continue to be recognised as the focal point of Fijian society' (Ravuvu 1983: 116), and that government leaders should 'continue to have their roots in the traditional rural social structure' (Ellis 1984: 44). Although there are many social and economic contradictions inherent in strategies endeavouring to shore up a semi-subsistent rural economy, contradictions which we endeavour to illuminate in subsequent chapters, such strategies are hardly surprising in the face of urbanisation without industrialisation, unemployment, marketing problems for the main export crops, and social tensions inherent in any multiracial society. The conclusion to Macnaught's (1982: 162–3) perceptive analysis of Fiji's colonial experience is apposite here: 'In a world that is running out of easy answers, no one will be surprised if the entire nation looks to its Fijian heritage for some of the arts of living well on islands.'

4

Physical and economic externalities and their impact

Small islands and their economies are more than ordinarily subject to external forces, as previous chapters have demonstrated for the historical experience of eastern Fiji. Larger events both in the atmosphere and in the economy can impinge dramatically on land masses of small size and population, limited natural resources and little economic diversification. This special 'vulnerability' of islands has been taken up in very different ways in the theory of biogeography and of economics, and to some degree also of demography. In this chapter we examine first the vulnerability of the Fiji periphery to external forces of physical origin, and then to events of economic and social origin. This leads in chapter 5 to an attempt to determine which groups in the island population and which parts of the economy are most vulnerable – an essay toward a 'political economy' – *sensu lato* – of vulnerability. The interrelated impact of physical and economic externalities is a major theme of argument.

External physical forces

McLean (1980b) has ably summarised the physical forces affecting small islands of the central Pacific, including tectonic forces and the sea-level changes of Pleistocene and Holocene time as well as the contemporary events with which we are concerned here. He points out that islands are affected by storm and wind from all points of the compass. In chapter 2 we have shown how these forces have brought about major changes in the very shape of landform of islands even during the limited time span of human settlement. Such change continues to this day.

With the exception of tsunamis which occasionally flood low-lying areas, and of earthquakes to which Fiji is also prone, all the physical events which have affected the islands within the more restricted time-span of the past 100 years arise in the atmosphere, or at least are expressed through the atmospheric side of the ocean–atmosphere coupling. Two types of event are of major importance: tropical storm and drought. We begin with a discussion of tropical storms and hurricanes, then stand back a little to look at events of larger scale causing major short-term variations in Fiji's climate and that of neighbouring island regions. We then turn to examine the incidence and effect of drought, a hazard which was insufficiently considered in our earlier publications under the UNESCO Fiji project.

Tropical storms and hurricanes

Over the 100 year period from 1875 to 1975 Fiji received on average just under one tropical storm or hurricane a year, and about 80 of these storms passed through the eastern islands (McLean 1977). The frequency, strength and size of the events are all, however, highly variable. In the South Pacific most tropical revolving storms travel meridionally, in contrast to the east-to-west path of most North Atlantic storms. While the majority recurve toward the east a proportion takes an opposite tack, and a few storms follow mainly latitudinal paths (Ward 1971). Storm tracks are highly unpredictable and winds may strike from any quarter. Normally, the winds in the left-forward quadrant of the storm are the most severe in southern hemisphere storms, and this sector is also most likely to contain tornado-like turbulence; storm-surges, in which the barometrically raised sea is driven forward by the wind, also normally peak in this sector (Simpson & Riehl 1981).

Figure 4.1 represents the approximate tracks of storms passing over or close to Fiji during the period 1970–83, and also indicates the approximate area over which sustained winds reached hurricane force. Storm-force winds outside this zone also do serious damage, and may contain hurricane-force gusts; their extent varies greatly from storm to storm, reaching up to 300 km from the central track in Val in 1975, but being far more restricted in the extremely violent Meli in 1979. Many of the storms failed to develop sustained winds of hurricane force, but still did localised severe damage where wind was funnelled over cols, down valleys and around headlands (Fig. 4.1).

It will be apparent that the eastern and western sides of Fiji have both suffered more than the central parts of the country around the western Koro Sea (Campbell 1984). This same contrast seems, in fact, to hold true over a much longer period (McLean 1977). This may not wholly be chance, for the size of the two main islands of Fiji, and their mountainous nature, may have some effect on the tracks of storms approaching from the north. The intensity of storms which do cross them is usually diminished in the course of passage, as happened in two hurricanes which crossed Fiji from north-west to south-east in 1985. Although severely impacting the west coast of Viti Levu, they degenerated to tropical storms

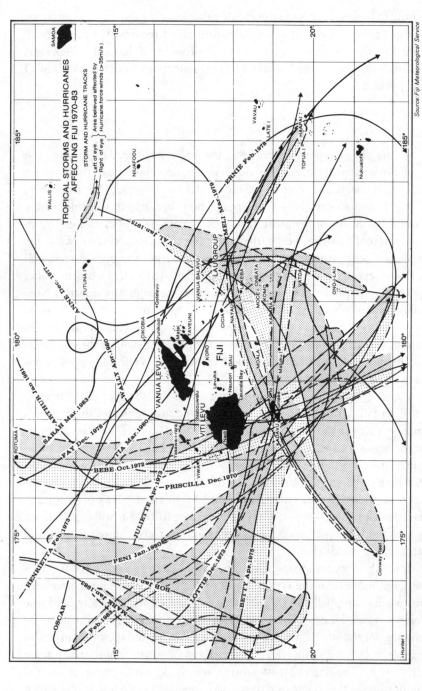

4.1 Storm tracks, and areas affected by winds of hurricane force, 1970–83 (Data from Fiji Meteorological Service, Nadi, *Reports*)

in their passage across the large island. One of these storms caused a ship to drag its anchor and capsize over the reef at Moala, but they did little damage on land in their passage across the eastern islands. Within the eastern island region this distribution creates a distinction between Lau and Kadavu, which have suffered on several occasions during the past decade, Taveuni where damage has been very variable, and Lomaiviti, which has suffered little.

The damage done by storms in which winds reach or approach hurricane force is considerable. Houses are damaged or destroyed and the flimsier separate kitchens and toilets suffer worse. The stems of cassava, now the main root crop in the islands, are easily broken by wind and the tuber then quickly rots; the trellis-work supporting yams is also destroyed, but these tubers, which are capable of long-term storage, are not now extensively grown, nor have the less vulnerable sweet potatoes been widely adopted except on a few drier islands. Taro is less readily damaged by wind, but irrigated taro is sometimes washed out by flood from rain associated with cyclonic storms, and salt spray blown across islands burns all field crops. Among longer-term crops, breadfruit and bananas are particularly vulnerable, though they recover if not blown down. *Yaqona* is subject to the same sort of damage as cassava, but since most *yaqona* areas are inland and often under the shelter of trees the damage is usually less.

It is the effect on the coconut crop which is economically the most serious, but also the most difficult to evaluate. In the highest winds trees may be broken, felled or canted at an angle. More widely they may be stripped of fronds, in which case new nut formation will not take place until after foliage has been re-established, in from two to four years. Still more widely, and requiring only a strong gale, young nuts fall prematurely, and continue to fall prematurely for some time after the storm. Every tropical storm or hurricane therefore brings about some loss of production, and the period before production is restored may vary from a few months to four years. The rate of recovery in turn depends on the age of trees, soil and weather conditions; it is, for example, severely delayed by long dry spells. But while all this is true, the total destruction of whole stands of established palms is a rare event; given time, the majority of wind-damaged older trees will recover.

The consequences of particular storms

Hurricane Val, which struck the Lau group on 31 January and 1 February 1975, is still recalled as the worst storm in living memory throughout the islands which it afflicted. A slow-moving storm of unusual size, Val inflicted little *total* devastation, perhaps mainly because the centre passed

4 Hurricane damage on Kabara (RBD photograph, 1983). The concrete sea wall (right) was destroyed by storm waves during the hurricanes of the mid-1970s, leaving Naikeleyaga Medical Centre (left) dangerously exposed. During the hurricanes the coastal sand flats were flooded by the storm surge, damaging those houses not destroyed by the wind.

a little east or south of all inhabited islands in its path, but it made up for this by doing unusually widespread damage. Close to the centre in Lakeba, where the impact of the event was reconstructed a year later by M. Brookfield (1977), many houses were blown down and others were further damaged by invasion of the sea, crops were wrecked and coconut palms widely damaged by wind stress so that copra production ceased for almost a year. Production over the full year 1975 was down by 51 per cent on 1974, and in 1976 by 60 per cent. However there was no wind-driven sea surge to sweep whole villages away, no lives were lost and few coconut palms were actually destroyed. All other islands in Lau also suffered but in most of them production recovered fully by 1977. The event caused widespread distress (Bayliss-Smith 1977a; Campbell 1977; M. Brookfield 1979).

M. Brookfield's reconstruction of the event (1977: 104–10) may usefully be quoted at length; obtained from interviews with villagers and from essays written for her by schoolchildren, it provides a graphic description of the storm experience:

On Friday morning, January 31, the sky was hazy and conditions were deteriorating ... By 10 a.m. the rain and wind were exerting real pressure ... By mid-day it was announced on the radio that all Eastern Division schools would be closed. The teachers at the Ratu Finau Primary School on a hillside above Tubou had already decided to close the school and send the children back to the comparative safety of their own homes; but these small children had to walk back through falling mango and coconut trees, and many were very afraid ... by late afternoon on Friday, the sky had become very dark and the winds had increased to Force 8 and Force 9; there was little doubt at the radio shack that worse was to come. Word began to spread; villagers at last realized that they might be in for more than an ordinary heavy storm, and began to take hurried precautionary measures. Those who had storm shutters put them up; those without nailed their windows shut or covered them with wood or corrugated iron. They made certain doors could be made secure and started to collect what food they could, clearing the compounds as far as possible of any loose material which might blow away or cause damage ... Some of the older children were sent to the store to buy extra rations, while some of the more experienced farmers who were lucky enough to have gardens near to the town worked hard to cut off the tops of the cassava plants ... By nightfall, conditions got very bad; according to the *Fiji Times*, Val first hit the island with full force at 6 p.m. on Friday evening, increasing in intensity throughout the night. The villagers were only too aware of the howl and force of the southeast winds, but did not know that the centre of the hurricane was already only a few kilometres from the north-northeast of the island, and would pass down the east coast during the night. Children reported hearing coconut trees, breadfruit trees, banana trees and mango trees falling down and striking objects, sometimes houses; all were deeply impressed, if not terrified, by the unceasing noise, thunder and lightning. Some mentioned feeling very cold and others could not sleep, but a few said they were excited by all that was happening ... As the wind rose, so did the sea, and since there was no wall between the lagoon and the village, the sea soon started flowing over the road, invading the cricket pitch, the Government compound, surrounding the Provincial office, and sucking at the houses, mounting in depth with increasing surges ... The water soon entered the Post Office. As one observant child said 'Waves were rolling up the road and broke the Post Office door down'. Shortly afterwards, he saw the Post Master come out with a big bag of money which he took to a safer place; the Post Master returned, to try to contact Suva, but was unable to do so as about 7 p.m. an aerial snapped. He then went out with a torch, in a very high wind, and climbed up and eventually mended the aerial; he was then able to transmit for a few hours longer. Villagers in similar positions at first tried to keep the water and sand and mud at bay by sweeping it out as it came in; but although many houses are on short poles to raise them above the ground, those in the southern half of the village were soon inundated. Families had to evacuate often by forming human chains to prevent being blown away in the wind and the dark ... Visibility was almost nil, with the wind and wall of rain, and already there was a great deal of debris to be dodged: floating oil drums, bottles, large branches and pieces of wood and iron where houses, copra driers and stores had already been blown apart. The water continued to rise as flash floods from the creeks were ponded back by the heavy seas and tidal surges.

The worst of the hurricane occurred during late Friday night and early Saturday morning; many mentioned the great roar made by the wind, waves, houses breaking apart, trees falling, and flying debris such as corrugated iron hitting the remaining houses. Also during this time as the eye of the hurricane passed, the wind changed and blew from completely the opposite direction, so that many houses received damage from two sides ... It was this wind shift, with all its ferocity, which gave the coup-de-grace to many of the older houses in western Tubou, some of which were third generation buildings and had been swaying alarmingly. It was a time of maximum damage in many places, particularly through the funnelling of down-winds in valleys which affected trees and crops very badly as well as houses.

In Waciwaci, the school teacher had tried to strengthen his Tonga type *bure*, after seeing his family to safety, and even tried to hold the roof on physically as it was being whipped from side to side but by 10 a.m. on Saturday he could fight the battering by the change of wind and the waves no longer. He stepped out of the house, which then caved in instantly, and the roof was immediately blown away ... One graphic story came from a man living out on the peninsula southeast of Tubou. He had not expected the hurricane to hit Lakeba; but by 2 a.m. his wooden house was shaking on its piles, and water and sand were blowing through it. Everything was wet inside, so he went out to check the copra drier. This had a cement floor, timber frame and flat iron walls and roof, and seemed of sturdier construction than the house; so he put the family in the drier. The sea had risen up to the window of the house, and was sucking back and forth with the waves. The family stayed in the drier until low tide then they walked, climbed over the fallen trees, often with water up to their waists and carrying the small children, to the Doctor's house in Tubou. The advice the father gave the family for the journey was 'look up, not down' because of the great risk of falling branches and coconuts ... The time of the Hospital's Doctor was largely taken up with the case of obstructed labour. The woman in question was the wife of the Secondary School's headmaster; in the last stages of obstructed labour, she had set out with one young companion to *walk* from the hill to the hospital (there are no telephones ... neither are there any private cars; nor were any of the very few official trucks in the neighbourhood); so without telling her husband, who was totally busy looking after the welfare of his 58 boarder students, she walked. Incredibly, in spite of the flying debris, the hazards across the road, the lack of visibility, she arrived safely at the hospital some two kms away, and after some hours of careful attention gave birth to a baby boy.

The picture in southern Lakeba on Saturday afternoon, when visibility had improved and the main fury of the storm had passed on further south, was one of almost total desolation. Let the children describe it. "I felt hopeless and very sad. All the houses were affected by the wind. Roofs of some houses were thrown into the sea, and into the bush. Toilets were flooded away, windows broken, houses fell down, and trees fell down on top of the houses. The roof of the church was blown off, and the roof of the old hospital; water came inside the houses". Many houses had no roofs, no walls, or poles, and some were leaning badly to one side and were cracked into pieces. The wind had blown sand and mud which had stuck to the walls of the houses, turning them brown and swept into the houses near the beach.

The long-term impact of this event on the village economy of Lakeba is reviewed in chapter 9.

Hurricane Meli in 1979 was smaller, faster-moving and also much more violent close to its centre than Val. Little wind damage was done further than 30 km from its central path, so that Lakeba, for example, escaped with minor effects, but in a very narrow band Meli achieved something close to total destruction. A particularly deadly aspect of this storm was the high wind-driven sea surge generated; when this surge struck the north coast of Nayau it was about 4–5 m high, and swept over two villages with severe loss of life. The nurse was so badly injured by debris while trying to care for the wounded and half-drowned that she later also died. The third village, on the lee of the island, was not flooded but an associated drop in sea level behind the surge exposed the lagoon to the wind so that the village was buried in sand. Damage to Nayau was so severe that the island was evacuated for more than two years, while copra production ceased entirely for almost four years. Major damage was also done to exposed parts of other islands but they escaped devastation.

Damage reports

Official damage reports on these modern events are far more detailed and informative than the reports on earlier events researched by McLean (1976, 1977). Unfortunately, however, the fact that reports have a purpose in assessing need for readily obtainable relief supplies and funds deprives them of objectivity. We discuss this aspect of modern life in the islands in some detail in chapter 6, since hurricane relief has almost become a part of a total structure of subsidy to the island economies in recent years. Very full detail on hurricane relief in Fiji since 1970 is provided by Campbell (1984).

Total destruction by the wind is in fact rare. Damage reports showing large numbers of houses, kitchens and toilets destroyed are built up from more detailed surveys, some of which we have seen, which describe lighter structures as simply thrown on their sides, and houses only partly destroyed. Often the houses that are destroyed are weaker structures: one recalls entering a village on Moce in 1983 and asking of a collapsed house if that were due to the recent hurricane, or to old age. 'Old age' came the ready answer, 'though the hurricane helped'. It takes a very major storm to achieve more total destruction, something of the order of the exceptional turbulent winds which passed over Dominica in the West Indies during Hurricane Frederic in 1979 and felled entire areas of forest and whole coconut plantations. There is a great deal of difference between the destructive effect of a 30–40 m/sec wind, and the rare wind of 60–80 m/sec. Winds of the latter force have been known to topple even masonry buildings. One such event destroyed a whole quarter of Port Louis in Mauritius in 1892. It seems probable that the only event in Fiji's recorded history that has approached this magnitude was the hurricane of 1886, in which widespread destruction of forests and even masonry buildings was reported; even in this event, however, the principal damage was done by surges of the sea (McLean 1977). Even a small sea surge can wreak very considerable destruction.

It was because the sea is the principal source of danger that the UNESCO Fiji project recommended that villages be re-located away from some very vulnerable sites as opportunity offered (UNESCO/UNFPA Project 1977). After the destruction of Nayau's villages in 1979 this was in fact done, and the new villages, of pre-fabricated houses, lie along narrow hillside terraces. This is not popular with the people of Nayau who would prefer to return to the shore. Given the starkness of the new villages one sympathises, but it is possible to re-create the charm of a Fijian village in an upland site; the people of one Taveuni village did it for themselves after their village was destroyed by a sea surge in 1912. This, however, was in the days before pre-fabricated houses, hurricane relief committees, UNESCO reports and planning.

Most discussions of hurricanes in Fiji describe their incidence as random, although it is clear that they do occur in clusters and that there have been periods of several years largely free of major storms. There were none between 1923 and 1929, and a long free period between 1931 and 1941 was broken only by two severe storms within weeks of one another in 1936. More recently there were none between 1959 and 1964, between 1967 and late 1972, and again between early 1975 and 1978. Since 1979 there have been more than a dozen of varying strength. Plots of hurricane tracks in the South Pacific as a whole show Fiji to lie close to the western edge of a large area in which tropical storms occur only infrequently, with marked clustering in particular short periods of time. Recent events, and recent research, have suggested some larger-scale causes of variation in Fiji's weather which are worth a brief examination. It will help us to link the discussion of storm to that of drought.

The effects of El Niño?

The unusual weather of 1982–3 in the Pacific as a whole has focussed attention on the interrelation between weather conditions all the way from India to South America, and even over the whole world, and the phenomenon known as El Niño – an east-Pacific warm episode. This interrelation has been explored in a number of ways since the 1960s, and it seems that the 1982–3 event was merely the strongest and most far-reaching in modern experience. The following brief summary is based on a range of literature that should be consulted by a reader seeking more detail.

The major regional controls of climate in Fiji are tentatively shown in Figures 4.2A and 4.2B (McAlpine et al. 1983; Heddinghaus & Krueger

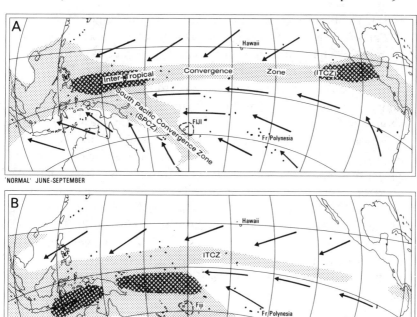

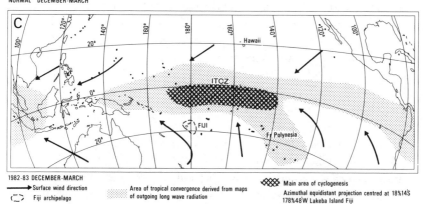

4.2 (A–C) An outline of the major regional controls of Fiji climate in the June–September and December–March periods in normal years (A, B) and in December–March 1982–3 at the time of a major El Niño/Southern Oscillation episode (C) (Data from Climate Analysis Center, National Office of Atmospheric Information, *Climate Analysis Bulletin* (various dates), also Falls, in McAlpine, Keigh & Falls (1983) and Heddinghaus & Kreuger (1981))

1981). The bifurcation of the Inter-Tropical Convergence Zone (ITCZ) east of New Guinea is seen as related to the equatorial easterlies and to the zone of upwelling cold water that extends eastward along the equator from South America about as far as the dateline. The cooled air over this stream is too heavy to be convected upward to join the 'Hadley circulation' in the South Pacific, in which air conveyed poleward aloft descends about 30° latitude to flow back equatorward on the surface as the South-east Trades (SET). Instead it flows westward along the equator toward the 'maritime continent' of Indonesia/New Guinea where there is a persistent zone of convection. This east-to-west flow is then balanced by westerlies aloft in what is termed the 'Walker circulation', linking persistent low pressure in the western equatorial Pacific to persistent high pressure in the eastern equatorial Pacific (Ramage 1968; Bjerknes 1969).

A southeastward trending branch of the ITCZ lies between the easterlies which feed into this circulation, and the southeasterlies of a normal Hadley cell in the southwestern Pacific. It represents a convergence zone between these two airstreams, and is nowadays termed the South Pacific Convergence Zone (SPCZ). The strength and position of the three elements – the SET, the equatorial easterlies, and the SPCZ – varies both between seasons and between years. Figures 4.2A and 4.2B represent the normal seasonal variation, in which the SPCZ weakens during the southern winter, exposing Fiji to the effect of the easterly/southeasterly airstream emanating from the Hadley cell in the southeast Pacific. Being far from the source area, this air is fairly humid and unstable, and gives rise to only a moderate dry season in Fiji except in the lee of the two main islands. During the southern summer the SPCZ is stronger and lies over Fiji, all of which then experiences rain.

From time to time, in association with variations in the balance of the Walker circulation known as the 'Southern Oscillation', the SET/easterly system as a whole becomes either stronger or weaker. Periods occur during which the equatorial easterlies fail, accompanying replacement of the cold upwelling water by much warmer water in the equatorial eastern Pacific. This is the phenomenon known as El Niño. A sudden weakening of the Walker circulation leads to a flow of water back along the equator. The dry zone along the equator is replaced by a zone of convection of normal ITCZ type which migrates eastward. The SPCZ migrates eastward with it.

Figure 4.2C, constructed from sundry sources relating to the major 1982–3 event, indicates in a very tentative manner the position that developed in late 1982 and early 1983. The Pacific ITCZ became completely separated from the ITCZ west of Indonesia, and the SPCZ extended as far east as French Polynesia. In the later stages, in 1983, a major drought developed in Fiji, and lasted until late in the year. It is believed that a similar but lesser sequence took place during other modern El Niño events (Wooster & Guillen 1974; Wyrtki 1975; Reiter 1978; Barnett 1981; Philander 1981; Rasmusson & Carpenter 1982; Rasmusson & Hall 1983; Climate Analysis Center 1982–3). The long-period record established by Quinn et al. (1978) provides a first basis for examining the climate of the western Pacific, in the context of this evolving theoretical system.

Figure 4.3 attempts a preliminary analysis of the incidence of drought and tropical storms or hurricanes in Fiji since 1951. Water balance calculations for five stations yield periods of drought sufficiently severe to deplete the water storage in the soil – periods which of course represent only the later stages of dry spells. Since the mid-year months are normally relatively dry in Fiji, the incidence of drought in the final months of each year represents no more than late onset of normal SPCZ conditions. However, when such droughts extend into the early months of the following year, or begin exceptionally early in a new year, they indicate a weakening of the SPCZ, or its removal from its normal warm season position. Such periods occurred in at least a part of Fiji, notably in Lau (Ono-i-Lau, Lakeba) in 1952, 1958, 1964, 1966, 1969, 1970, 1973, 1977–8, 1980 and 1983. All these periods except that of 1969 followed the onset of an El Niño, although there is no correlation with the reported strength of the event.

Drought

Four periods of widespread and prolonged drought are apparent in the record of Figure 4.3: 1950–3; 1957–9; 1965–70 and late-1976 to 1983, with breaks in 1978–9 and 1980–1. Humid periods intervene between the periods of widespread and prolonged drought. The longest period in the record without drought at any of the five stations runs from November 1973 to June 1975, while the longest periods without drought anywhere except Lautoka in the dry zone of western Viti Levu extend from December 1959 to September 1961 and from October 1973 to September 1976. Further analysis shows this period to represent the most marked positive anomaly of long duration in almost half a century. By chance, it extended through almost the whole field time of the UNESCO Fiji project in 1974–6. It is perhaps small wonder that the reporting of that project pays insufficient attention to the drought hazard!

The close-spaced droughts of the period after September 1976 therefore warrant some examination. They include the longest drought at any of these stations since at least 1951, an 11-month period of exhausted

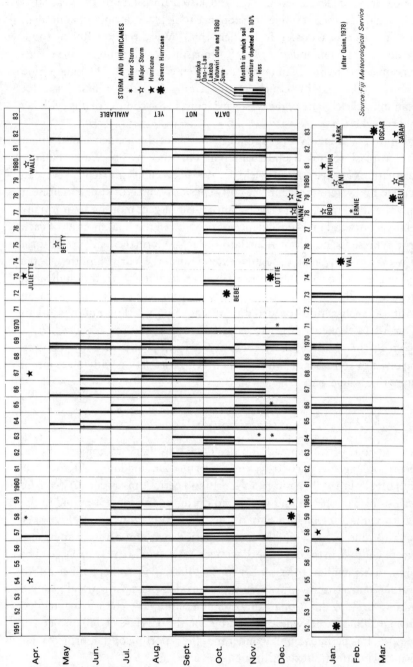

4.3 Incidence of drought sufficient to deplete soil moisture to 10 per cent or less at five stations, 1951–83 (Data from Fiji Meteorological Service, by method supplied by J. R. McAlpine)

STORM AND HURRICANES
* Minor Storm
☆ Major Storm
★ Hurricane
✳ Severe Hurricane

Lautoka
Ono-i-Lau
Lakeba
Vatuwiri data end 1980
Suva

Months in which soil moisture depleted to 10% or less

(after Quinn, 1978)

Source: Fiji Meteorological Service

soil-moisture storage at Ono-i-Lau from April 1977 to February 1978. This event, and its lesser precursor in late 1976, were widespread over at least southern Fiji.

The 1977 drought gave rise to considerable alarm. By the third quarter of 1977 the Agricultural Officer for Lau was reporting in terms of impending famine in the southern part of the group. Visiting the islands again in January 1978 to report on the effect of the two tropical storms Ann and Bob, his report concentrated mainly on the deteriorating situation due to the long drought, then affecting all islands southward of Lakeba and which the storms had failed to break. He found all crops in a poor way, and noted widespread fall of young coconuts which was probably due more to drought than to wind. The underground growth of tubers had ceased except where storm rains had fallen, but the effect of such rain had often been to cause decay of long-dormant roots, or else to cause the tubers to become fibrous and bitter. On Ono-i-Lau the few wet taro plots were completely dry and unusable. None the less, 'famine' was a large word to use, for crops remained alive and if water was short, coconuts were available for drinking. The officer's report led to relief supplies of flour, rice and sugar being sent to the affected areas, while water was supplied by ship, as in several dry periods during recent years. The drought ended in March 1978, and dry conditions did not return until late 1979.

When we re-visited Fiji in June–July 1983 drought was again a major problem. The worst afflicted area was in the west of Viti Levu, where the only significant rain had come from hurricane 'Oscar' under conditions which provided little benefit. Without this unwelcome contribution the March to June rainfall was only between 10 and 17 per cent of the mean in the western cane-growing districts. Around Nadi and Lautoka the combined effect of drought and hurricane produced a dismal scene in July, with brown stunted cane, much of it lodged, being harvested for what it would produce. Only in valleys where there was a reserve of soil moisture was cane green, and it was almost nowhere tall. The national sugar crop, the basis of Fiji's export income, was down by 46 per cent on the previous year's record production, and there was gloom which turned out to be unwarranted about prospects for the 1984 crop. Plans for rehabilitation and relief were being vigorously debated.

A much more varied situation obtained in the islands. On the windward sides of the larger islands, such as Taveuni and Koro, topographic forcing of the SET had produced persistent heavy rain, with even some torrential and damaging falls, as described at Nacamaki in chapter 8. But although the drought was everywhere less intense than in western Viti Levu it was becoming prolonged by June, and was visibly causing moisture stress in crops planted on open hillsides. In the swampland taro gardens of Lakeba the water level was as much as 30 cm below the levels of 1976, and it was possible to walk dryshod across swamps that had been deep mires during the wet period of the mid-1970s.

Food was not a problem for the people, as a March hurricane which did only limited damage had provided the basis for a further round of 'relief supplies' of rice, flour, sugar and some other foods. Most crops were, in any case, still growing and new planting was in progress. Water storages were, however, dry on many islands, and water was being supplied by ship throughout Lau and the Northern Division small islands from Lakeba and Taveuni, which still had good supplies of running water from groundwater sources. By mid-July, two Government vessels were continuously employed on water carriage.

Adaptation to drought

Although in terms respectively of length and severity, the droughts of 1977 and 1983 were remarkable events in Fiji, the record shows that there have been many previous periods of sub-normal rain. As in 1977 and 1983, such earlier periods of stress were punctuated by tropical storms and hurricanes with much the same effect as modern storms. Yet in earlier years there were no Government ships carrying water from island to island, nor any reserve of relief food supplies in Suva on which to draw in order to alleviate distress.

The island people had a considerable range of adaptive strategies in the past, of which one of the more important was a heavy dependence on yams as a major starch crop. Though yams suffer from both hurricane and drought they have the immeasurable advantage over other tubers that they can be stored, dry and sheltered, for periods of several months without loss of quality. On some islands water was conserved in hollow tree-trunks, into which it was fed from other trees by a network of bamboo tubes. On the remote island of Qelelevu in the Northern Division, where 'relief' was less easy to come by than in the more close-spaced islands of Lau, a few such systems were still in existence in 1976. Coconuts were in any case available to drink, and on islands with limestone or beach rock most villages had, and still have, hollows in which usually brackish water for washing remains in all but the severest drought.

In addition, a wide range of foods was used in times of shortage. On the small, drought-prone island of Batiki an aged informant provided Bayliss-Smith (1978a) with information on the former importance of famine foods, in particular wild yams (*Dioscorea bulbifera*) and cycads (*Cycas rumphii*), on an island where yams, taro, plantains, bananas and breadfruit were the main staples as late as the end of the nineteenth century. On more wooded islands *Dioscorea nummularia* occurs widely, and together with other wild fruits and aroids such as *Cyrtosperma chamissonis* provides an important reserve (Campbell 1977, 1984; M. Brookfield 1979). Marine resources were also of major importance at all times, but probably supplied only a small fraction of the normal diet except in a few islands with unusually good reef-lagoon resources. In Yadrana village on Lakeba, at the height of food scarcity in 1975, frequent trips for fishing and shellfish collection by large groups of women were still only producing food equivalent to about one-tenth of the daily diet (Bayliss-Smith 1977a).

As Thompson (1940a: 82) described it for Kabara, drought is a 'persistent menace' in the lower and smaller islands of Fiji. The 'traditional' trading networks that grew up in eastern Fiji in the century or two before the colonial period, had the role not only of exchanging food from the more fertile and better watered islands for handicrafts, perfumed coconut oil and other products of the smaller volcanic and limestone islands; they also had an important role in disaster insurance. It was not so in other parts of the Pacific, in the Cook Islands for example, where the weakening of an island population by storm-induced famine was treated as an opportunity for attack and massacre by unfriendly neighbours (McArthur 1967: 181). There are, moreover, accounts of more widespread events such as prolonged drought in the remote Marquesas in 1806–10 or thereabouts which was reported to have led to major mortality and even cannibalism, an event still traceable in the diminished size of age-cohorts many years later (McArthur 1967: 282; 294).

Long-term effects of storm and drought on production

Tropical storms and hurricanes are over in a day, but their effect continues to be felt for months and even years (Table 4.1). The effect of drought is more insidious, and less easy to establish. Coconut and copra production are influenced for long periods by events of both types. The relationship of drought to coconut production is not simple, and much depends on both the length and severity of the drought (Child 1974: 73–4). The initial effect of dry and sunny conditions is to increase nut production and this may continue for several months as in Fiji in 1977 and 1983. However, the diminution in available moisture delays the formation of leaves and inflorescences and slows their growth, thus leading to a subsequent drop in copra production which may continue for more than twelve months before recovery begins, and can depress yield for up to two years after severe dry periods. But while this may be true in the Asian data cited by

Table 4.1 *Copra production in Fiji, 1970–82*
('000 tonnes)

	1970	1971	1972	1973	1974	1975	1976	1977	1978	1979	1980	1981	1982
Lomaiviti Province	2.3	2.4	2.4	2.4	2.8	2.7	2.7	3.1	2.8	2.6	2.4	2.6	2.2
Koro	(0.9)	(1.0)	(1.1)	(1.3)	(1.5)	(1.2)	(1.2)	(1.4)	(1.4)	+	(0.7)	(0.9)	+
Lau Province	5.5	5.8	7.0	7.6	6.8	4.7	4.9	6.7	5.5	3.0	4.1	3.9	3.9
Lakeba	(0.8)	(0.8)	(0.9)	(1.0)	(1.1)	(0.6)	(0.5)	(0.7)	(0.6)	+	(0.8)	(0.8)	+
Kadavu Province	1.0	1.2	1.1	1.0	0.4	0.3	0.4	0.9	0.9	0.5	0.1	0.1	0.2
Rotuma Province	1.7	1.9	1.8	0.3	0.6	0.5	1.3	1.6	1.3	1.0	1.3	1.3	1.8
Northern Division	15.8	15.4	16.0	15.9	16.8	15.7	15.9	17.1	14.3	13.1	13.0	12.0	13.0
Mainland Cakaudrove	(6.6)	(6.6)	(6.9)	(7.0)	(6.7)	(6.4)	(6.5)	(7.2)	(6.3)	+	(5.7)	(5.5)	+
Island Cakaudrove	(6.3)	(6.3)	(7.0)	(6.5)	(7.2)	(6.9)	(6.9)	(7.7)	(6.2)	(4.5)	(4.8)	(4.8)	(5.4)
Bua	(1.5)	(1.2)	(1.0)	(1.0)	(1.3)	(1.1)	(1.2)	(1.2)	(1.0)	+	(1.4)	(1.0)	+
Central & Western Divisions	1.4	1.3	1.1	0.6	1.0	1.0	1.6	2.1	1.3	1.5	1.8	1.0	0.8
Total	27.9	28.0	29.4	27.9	28.5	25.0	26.8	31.6	26.3	21.7	22.7	20.7	22.0

+ Data unavailable

Source: Fiji Coconut Board, data by conversion from bag totals rounded to nearest hundred tonnes.

Child, Catala (1957: 30–44) presents data from Kiribati which show rapid recovery of production after a drought which extended through almost two years from late-1954. Within six months nut production had almost tripled from its low end-of-drought level when, at different sites, from 7,800 to 19,400 drought-starved nuts were required to make a long ton of copra, in place of a 'normal' 5,000 nuts. Catala also compares the performance of trees in different locations and attributes the differences mainly to soil-moisture conditions, together with availability of nutrient from wastes to palms grown in and around villages. Similar contrasts are certainly present in Fiji, and make generalisation difficult.

Whereas the effect of storms is almost immediate, that of drought is slow, and it is the combination of the two events which has the most durable effect on production. This applies not only to damage to coconuts, but also to the combined effect on food crops. Thus after the 1886 hurricane, the greatest need for relief was in drought-stricken southern Lau (Campbell 1984: 68). Figure 4.4 relates copra production at 14 places in northeastern Fiji to the area affected by storm force winds or stronger during the period 1977–82; three successive seasons were marked by tropical depressions affecting this part of Fiji, and drought then affected large areas in 1981 and 1982. Only three of the 14 places ended the series with a larger production in 1982 than in 1977. No storm of the period reached hurricane strength within this area, yet the effect on production is substantial. Especially in the four easternmost localities recovery after the 1980 storm was delayed, and even reversed, by dry conditions.

When they occur in the sugar industry production losses of the order of almost 50 per cent are a national disaster, such is their effect on the balance of payments as well as on the growers. Production losses of a similar or greater order in the coconut industry have no such national impact. In interpreting Figure 4.4, it must be stressed that although 1977 was itself a dry year it followed a humid period without storms since early 1975, and because weather was dry it was also sunny; copra yields and production were exceptionally good. Some fall was therefore to be expected in 1978, but not one of the magnitude or duration of that which occurred. Decline in personal incomes and regional income has been substantial.

Unfortunately the loss of production in 1979 also deprived growers of the benefit of a year of high prices. The same happened in parts of the region in 1983–4 when prices rose to new heights while growers still suffered the effects of storm and drought. Yet these are not wholly coincidences, since the same El Niño event that brought drought to Fiji also brought a cluster of tropical storms and then an almost unprecedented

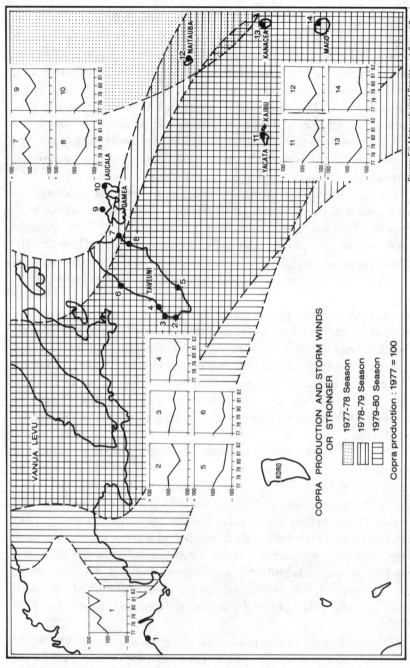

44 Copra production at 14 places 1977–82, and the area of incidence of storm winds or stronger during the same period

drought to the Philippines, and was possibly indirectly responsible for the United States drought of 1983 which reduced that country's soyabean crop. American soyabean oil production dominates world supply of vegetable oils, and the Philippines dominates the world's supply of copra, and it was the partial loss of these two crops that caused the world copra price to soar.

Such 'teleconnections' in weather and economy bring out the importance of relating local or regional events to the global hazards of economic cycles and great variations in the state of the market for primary products. The effect of inflation also, when it coincides with a fall in primary-product prices and the after-effects of a hurricane or a drought is further to depress incomes and purchasing power. We now turn, therefore, to events which impact the islands as severely as 'El Niño', but which have their origin even further afield.

External forces of economic origin

The significance of far-away events

The South Pacific region as a whole produces only about eight per cent of the copra reaching world markets and only about 3.5 per cent of the world's total of some 40 million tonnes of vegetable oil and fats. The prices ruling on the world market are not influenced by variations in the production of the South Pacific countries as a whole, let alone Fiji. The same applies even to Fiji's production of sugar, its principal export earner, while as a tourist destination Fiji enjoys a significant share only in the limited market offered by Australia and New Zealand. These two countries together supplied 57 per cent of Fiji's visitors in 1983, and the length of stay was from 30 to 40 per cent longer than that of tourists from other significant source-countries (Bureau of Statistics 1984). Everything that Fiji produces for or offers to external markets is subject to variations in price or market conditions over which the country exercises no influence.

The price of Fiji's copra during the period 1971–82 is represented in Figure 4.5. Very marked fluctuations have taken place. Global over-supply of copra and coconut oil was responsible for the low price period in 1971–3, and over-supply of all oils for that of 1975–7. In 1980–2 an over-supply of palm oil and of soyabean oil, coupled with the general recession, led to a very prolonged period of low prices. On the other hand, the price peaks of 1973–4 and 1978–9 were both due primarily to a drastic shortfall in the Philippine supply of copra, following cyclone damage to the region's major exporter. In 1982–3 events mentioned

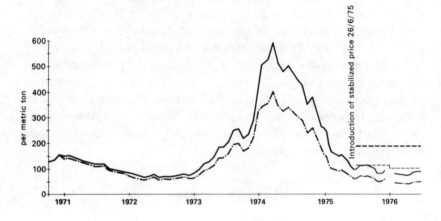

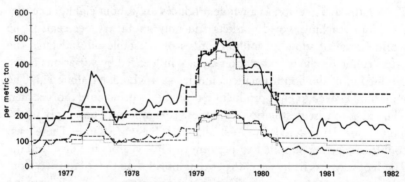

4.5 Copra prices at Suva and Lakeba, in Fiji dollars per tonne, 1971–82; actual prices and prices reduced by inflation following Ellis (personal communication) (Based on Fig. 3 in Brookfield (1985), by permission of the Department of Human Geography, Australian National University)

above produced a new boom, and the price did not begin to decline again until mid-1984, and was still above 1980–2 levels until 1986, despite a drop of over 50 per cent in a year.

These fluctuations are, however, superimposed on a generally unfavourable trend in the market position for copra and coconut oil. Previous periods of high prices have encouraged research into the substitutability of vegetable oils, and into the use of synthetics. While the latter trend, much feared in the 1960s (Roger Williams Technical Services

1966), was checked by the oil-price 'shocks' of 1973 and 1979, research into the modification of vegetable oils to improve substitutability has continued and has achieved impressive results. In soap and detergent manufacture, coconut oil has advantages over palm-kernel oil, and in the manufacture of margarine and shortening over soyabean and palm oil. But these advantages have been eroded, leaving coconut oil with a clear edge only in confectionery and bakery products. While new non-food uses have emerged through the development of vegetable-oil additives to diesel fuel and gasoline, these have yet to be introduced into Fiji, though a recent study has urged that the new uses of coconut oil be exploited (*Islands Business* 10(3) (1984): 10–13). We discuss this further in chapter 6. Meanwhile, however, the relative price of coconut oil, *vis-à-vis* other vegetable oils, declined right through the 1970s and continues to decline in the 1980s.

The effect of the copra price fluctuations

In order to understand the effect of the price fluctuations shown in Figure 4.5 we need first to know something about the cost of production. A survey by the 1974–6 UNESCO Project showed an average production cost for copra on a non-random sample of estates to be $160/tonne at 1975 prices, plus the cost of management. In 1983 one estate group gave its costs, without management, as only $110/tonne, but at around $300/tonne if an appropriate share of management costs were included. Villagers' costs are much harder to estimate. Two crude calculations based on Bayliss-Smith's (1977a) data on labour inputs gave $62 and $26/tonne at the 1983 agricultural wage, but this includes only nut collection, copra-cutting and a small amount of copra-drying, therefore comparable with estate costs ranging between $37 and $60 for the same operations in 1983. As noted in chapter 3, villagers' costs must also include a proportion of time spent on food production, house construction and other tasks needed for the reproduction of their own labour spent on copra production. It might therefore be more reasonable to calculate that if, say, one-third of a villager's working time is spent on copra production, one third of the balance of his working time is spent in reproduction of that labour, i.e. in all about half the total time would be spent on copra production. On such a basis villagers' costs approximate the range of total estate labour costs, if the same wage is applied (Brookfield 1985: 156–71).

The price of copra in Fiji in 1972, and again in 1975, fell to a level very close to the cost of labour used in its production. When the costs of delivery were added, even village growers were in fact making a 'loss' on copra production. Estates could not cover their management, fuel and overhead costs. The first time this happened, in 1972, growers had to bear the whole cost themselves, though at the end of 1972 a small element of assistance was introduced through a subsidy scheme on internal sea freight. When the same happened again in 1975 the first Lome agreement between the EEC and the APC (African, Pacific, Caribbean) countries had just been negotiated, and it made provision for a price stabilisation scheme. Anticipating the implementation of this scheme, the Government in Fiji intervened in June 1975 to create a supported price, the difference between which and the 'real' price was advanced as a loan to the growers. The support price, less the subsidised freight rate, offered a return about equal to the average cost of production on estates at that time (Fig. 4.5). It restored some profitability to the more efficient estates, and to the village producers. When the price rose again in 1977 only a small part of the improvement was passed on to the growers, so that the loan was recouped.

The price improvement that took place in 1979 was, by contrast, passed on in its entirety to the growers, and the opportunity for building up a stabilisation fund was lost. At this time, however, large parts of the copra producing areas were suffering the after-effects of both drought and storm so that many growers were unable to improve their production and gain full benefit of the short-lived period of higher prices. Production, shown in Table 4.1, actually fell by 17 per cent between 1978 and 1979, the sharpest single-year drop since the 1940s. When the copra price declined again in 1980 it did so very steeply, so that action similar to that of 1975 had to be taken in April, bringing the price in real terms back almost exactly to what it had been in 1975 (see Fig. 4.5). This 'loans scheme' support price was then maintained without change for more than three years, during which time it was eroded by further inflation, and also by an increase in sea freight costs, the subsidy on which remained unchanged. By the middle of 1983 when the copra price began a new increase to levels above the support price, more than $8 million had been 'lent' to growers in subsidy, and there seemed small hope that a sum of this size could ever fully be recovered, even though production increased by 17 per cent from its 1980 minimum reaching almost 24,000 tonnes in 1983. The prolonged nature of the 1983–5 price peak did, however, permit a substantial recovery of the advance to be achieved by the latter year.

The distribution of benefits within a 'successful national economy'

During the 1970s Fiji managed to maintain strong growth in its national economy despite the successive impacts of the 'oil-price shocks' of 1973 and 1979. Bienefeld (1984) argues that this was due to maintenance of a resource-based strategy inherited from the 1960s, to a strong growth in public investment associated with a high level of national savings, and to Fiji's good fortune in suffering no major adverse shift in the terms of trade. It was the resource-based policy of public investment that enabled Fiji to transfer its growth emphasis from tourism to sugar in the mid-1970s when the boom growth in tourism evaporated. In the new recession that began in 1979 conditions have grown suddenly worse, with a decline in the price of sugar and a consequent weakening of the terms of trade, coupled with a fall in the rate of international investment due to the recession and high interest rates. GDP per capita rose in every year except 1975 until 1979, then fell in 1980, 1982 and also 1983 (Bureau of Statistics 1984). None the less there was renewed improvement in 1986 and early 1987, before the coup.

Not only was growth in the economy well sustained in the 1970s, but there was important redistribution to a significant part of the workforce. Table 4.2 presents the movement in real terms of wages and salaries, and also the benefit received by cane cutters. Also shown is the real gross income of sugar and copra producers, given on the basis of the delivered price of their crops.

It is clear that different groups in the population have fared in very different ways. The real gross income of cane and copra growers both sank in the early 1970s but the copra growers suffered much worse. In the exceptional year 1974 the latter did better, but subsequently never again attained the real gross income obtained in 1970, and received less than half this in recent years despite subsidy. The cane growers, on the other hand, improved their real income substantially until 1980, after which their position declined close to the 1970 level in 1982 and certainly fell below it in 1983, 1984 and 1985. The real incomes of the mainly urban wage and salary earners underwent a more steady progression, though with a sharp upward movement in the mid-1970s, and a small decline in 1980.

For rural wages we can only use rates. Cane cutters' wages, based on a sample, showed a substantial improvement until the late 1970s. Since then they have declined in real terms while remaining static in money terms. Cane cutters enjoyed a particularly sharp improvement in their conditions in 1975. For coconut industry workers there is no standard wage, as we shall see below. On the basis of only scattered data we can say that except in 1974 their wage was consistently below the 1970 wage in real terms, and from 1975 until 1982 had an index value only between 60 and 70 where 1970 = 100.

Wage rates, however, are only part of the story, and a proper comparison requires supplementary information. Urban wage and salary

Table 4.2 *Selected economic indicators for Fiji, real indices,*
1970 = 100

	Consolidated consumer price index	Cane growers' real gross income	Copra producers' real gross income	Wage & salary real incomes (weighted average)	Cane cutters' real wage
1970	100.0	100.0	100.0	100.0	100.0
1971	106.5	86.7	73.1	105.6	93.9
1972	116.2	88.4	40.0	107.4	101.2
1973	129.2	87.1	68.9	114.6	100.2
1974	147.8	138.0	194.8	123.0	103.5
1975	167.2	183.0	55.8	129.4	211.1
1976	186.2	123.7	60.7	133.0	189.5
1977	199.3	148.4	76.0	138.7	236.1
1978	211.4	134.2	60.9	144.4	222.6
1979	227.7	156.7	96.5	145.5	206.7
1980	260.7	164.5	57.8	136.9	196.3
1981	289.9	126.8	45.0		176.5
1982		106.8	45.1		165.0

Source: Fiji Employment and Development Mission

earners generally depend entirely on their cash income, and so also do a proportion of the cane cutters, of whom about 5,000 are landless. The pay of cane cutters is fairly standard, but the amount of work that they can get is not. With a large increase in the number of cane cutters since 1975 gangs have become fragmented, leading to work sharing. A 1982 survey revealed an output of only 170 tonnes per man, yielding an annual income of only $700 (Ellis 1985). The disastrous effect of Hurricane Oscar and the subsequent drought in 1983 means that many of these seasonal workers, especially those who are landless, faced extreme poverty.

The mainly urban wage and salary workers appear comparatively well off, but there is a very wide range of wage rates. Taylor (1984) shows that while large companies in Suva pay award rates of between $1.20 and $1.80 per hour as their minimum, small Indo-Fijian companies pay far lower minimum wages, none over $1.00 per hour and some as low as $0.20 per hour. Even the more normal base rate of around $0.35 per hour an eight-hour day would yield only $2.80 per day, compared with at least $9.60 for workers in large companies.

The coconut industry workers are paid a variety of rates, some being paid by the day and some by the task. There is no standard. However, a 1982 normal wage around $3.00 per day was supplemented for most by free housing of very variable quality and the allocation of land on which to grow a proportion of household food requirements. Copra industry workers are poor, but are not the poorest workers in the country. There has, moreover, been an improvement in their position since 1982.

It is not easy to generalise about the progression through time of wage rates and incomes, since there is a wide range in the circumstances of workers. It can, however, be said that in general the lower-paid workers have suffered a depression of real incomes since the late 1970s, and this has also applied to cane growers and to copra producers until 1983. Only salary earners have continued to gain in real terms in this period, together with businessmen in the more prosperous sectors of the economy.

Moreover, inflation itself has borne more heavily on the poor than on the wealthy. That part of the Consumer Price Index which is made up of food items, the main purchase of the poor, has increased more sharply than the index as a whole. Analysing the effect of inflation on the expenditure patterns shown in the 1977 Household Income and Expenditure Survey (Bureau of Statistics 1981), Bienefeld (1982) has shown that over most of the period since 1970 the 'real' rate of inflation has been significantly higher for the lowest ten per cent of income earners than for the population as a whole, the departure from the national index reaching 11.9 per cent in 1981.

These areally aggregated data also conceal another important variable, which is the lower real incomes and higher cost of consumer goods received and paid for by those who live in areas where large internal freight costs must be subtracted from the received price of their produce and added to the shelf price of the goods they buy. This added burden applies to all people in the outer islands, wealthy or poor. Marine freight rates within Fiji (Fig. 4.6) increased by between 150 and 199 per cent between 1972 and 1982, even allowing for the effect of a subsidy introduced in 1973.

Geographical variations in the cost of living

The 1974–6 UNESCO/UNFPA Project carried out a survey of retail prices, covering all the commonly purchased food items such as rice, sugar, flour, milk, tinned fish, tea, etc. No attempt was made to weight these items according to their importance, but some interesting disparities were revealed in the cost of the total shopping list in various locations. In total, the 13 items cost $4.13 in shops in Suva, between $4.60 and $5.07 on Taveuni, $5.32–5.89 on Lakeba, and as much as $5.93 in one village on Koro. The comparison indicates clearly two things: the variations that exist locally in retail prices, reflecting differences between village stores in

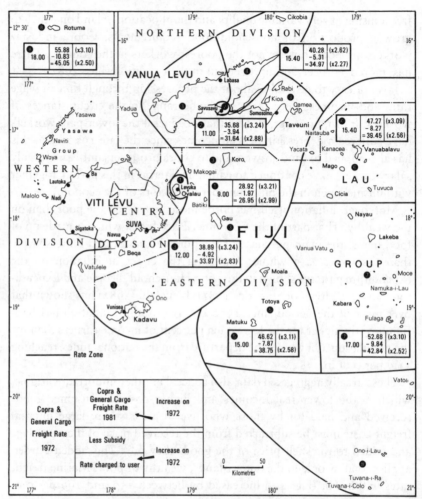

4.6 Changes in the copra and general cargo freight rates, 1972–81 (Reproduced from Fig. 4 in Brookfield (1985). By permission of the Department of Human Geography, Australian National University)

efficiency and profit margins; and, secondly, the overall picture of a 30–45 per cent penalty for consumers in the periphery, in terms of the prices they must pay for everyday store purchases.

In 1982–3 the same exercise was repeated, but on a larger scale. This time the various items in a more extensive shopping list were weighted according to their importance, this being determined by the proportion of consumer spending that was recorded for various categories of items in the Household Income and Expenditure Survey of 1977 (Bureau of Statistics 1981). The categories included in our survey constitute exactly 60 per cent of the total cash expenditure of villagers, as estimated by the

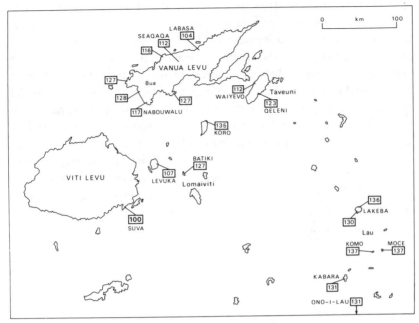

4.7 Variations in retail prices, Suva compared to the periphery, 1983 (Western Vanua Levu data from Atkins (1983). Eastern Fiji data from field notes)

government survey, so we are justified in regarding our data as broadly representative of the rural cost of living. Among the items included in our survey, one quarter is accounted for by carbohydrate foods (rice, flour, buscuit), and around one tenth is accounted for by each of the three categories tinned fish, cigarettes, and sugar and beverages. These items are therefore weighted far more heavily than infrequently purchased goods such as milk, butter and medicines (for details of weighting, see Atkins (1983)).

The results of this analysis are shown in Figure 4.7 with costs reduced to an index where Suva is 100. Although the data are not directly comparable to the 1976 shopping list, the results are broadly similar. The pattern reflects once again the high cost of transport from Suva to outer island destinations, and the high cost of the break of bulk that is involved in sending retail goods in small quantities to remote destinations, to village stores which are often inefficient and/or monopolistic in operation. In the towns (Labasa, Levuka, Waiyevo, Seaqaqa) the cost of living index stands at 104–112, only a few points above Suva's level of 100, but in the rural hinterland of these secondary centres it rises to 127–8 in remote parts of Bua province, 127–35 on islands in the Lomaiviti group, and 131–7 in southern Lau.

In industrialised countries the high cost of rent, travel and services in capital cities is often a justification for a cost-of-living allowance that is paid to city workers in compensation. In Fiji almost the reverse pattern of compensation appears to be justified, at least for the poorer sections of the community for whom the items covered by our survey usually represent more than the average 60 per cent of expenditure. In reality, of course, the rural poor in the periphery depend heavily on their own food production rather than on store-purchased food, and so avoid the poverty trap of low (often fluctuating) earnings relative to highly inflated retail prices. The persistent geographical disparity in the cost of living is merely another factor that discourages a complete dependence upon the market economy, and which therefore serves to restrict the penetration of capitalism into the rural sector, and even encourages some return to, or incorporation of pre-capitalist modes of organisation.

5

Vulnerability in a changing society

Toward a non-Marxist political economy of vulnerability

Class or ethnic group?

The unequal effect of imported inflation, wild fluctuations in the received prices for exports and weather-related events has become very clear in the preceding chapter. Geographical location is one important variable, and another is income level; it has also been suggested that landlessness can be a factor increasing vulnerability, and since most of the landless are Indo-Fijian this inevitably introduces the ethnic dimension. Ethnicity still divides all of Fiji's emergent classes and is still perceived as the most important divider of persons by a large majority. While it would force the evidence to undertake an analysis of Fiji's recent experience solely in class terms, to ignore class and follow the ethnic mode of most traditional analyses would be to disregard modern reality. Moreover, there are some structural elements in rural eastern Fiji which do not fit readily into the framework of either class or ethnic group.

A white planter and trader society established its hegemony over most of outer-island Fiji more firmly than over the rest of the country in the late nineteenth century, and the gradual erosion of its position in the present century must have an important place in any analysis. Moreover there is an important Indo-Fijian element in the population and workforce of Vanua Levu and Taveuni, yet in the coconut districts where they form only a minority of the population they differ from Indo-Fijians elsewhere in that many speak the Fijian language and operate in a very different social context from that of the cane districts and the large towns. The rural society of eastern Fiji and all parts of Vanua Levu except the sugar belt is everywhere dominated by Fijians, and it is with the changing structure of Fijian society that we must begin any analysis of the response of different population groups to external events.

Change in the structure of Fijian society in the islands

While colonialism and commercialisation of the economy have certainly had profound effects on Fijian society it is important to stress what was written in chapter 3 and avoid the trap of believing that pre-colonial Fiji was without classes, or that a well-oiled redistributive system operated benignly to assure an adequate living to all Fijians, whether chiefs or commoners. Rank of individuals and of groups has for centuries been important in Fijian society, and in the warfare that became endemic during the last centuries before colonial rule substantial surpluses were extracted from commoners and lesser chiefs in order to support the enterprises of the high chiefs. Life was insecure, as the amount of pre-colonial fortification still visible in the Fijian landscape bears abundant witness. Chapelle (1978) particularly notes the uncertain land tenure position of the large refugee populations and other supplicants, and their subordinate position in society. The subordinate position of women is symbolised in all aspects of traditional Fijian ceremony. The modern inequalities were not created *de novo* by colonialism.

None the less there have been major structural changes. Apart from the introduction of the planter and trader class, and of a whole new population of foreign workers most of whom have remained landless, there is abundant evidence that the advantages of rank and status have acquired a growing economic value, and moreover that Fijians with little land have found it increasingly hard to obtain land on usufruct from others (Ward 1985). Both trends were already recorded in the 1950s on the island of Moala where Sahlins (1962: 109) also remarks that 'an important trend of modern times has been the depression of status and power of all but the chiefly families ... At the same time there has been homogenization within the emergent lower stratum'. Subsequent observation confirms these trends, and their accentuation.

Land is very unequally distributed in the islands, the size of holdings in Taveuni having a Gini coefficient of 0.86; 85 per cent of the land was held by ten per cent of the people in 1975, the unoccupied central forests excluded. On Lakeba, if one landless *mataqali* is excluded, per-capita holdings of *mataqali* land ranged from 1.1 to 12.9 ha (M. Brookfield 1979). Cash incomes derived mainly from use of land are also very unequally distributed. The degree of inequality of cash incomes among Fijian villagers in Taveuni and Lakeba was one of the most striking findings of the 1974–6 UNESCO project from its detailed work in these two islands. Although Fijian villagers were under-represented among the poorest 20 per cent of the Taveuni population, and over-represented among the most affluent 20 per cent, there were very poor people among all groups, and the majority of such were either landless or short of land, or else were sick, disabled or old (Nankivell 1978). As one of us commented in an early report on our social surveys (Brookfield 1975b):

We met far too many elderly, sick or crippled people in houses bare of goods who gave their inability to work as the full and sufficient reason for their poverty. It becomes evident that in modern Taveuni society the worst hazards in life are crippling injuries and sickness, not those of natural disaster ... In one relatively affluent village no fewer than five out of 26 households reported age or sickness as the cause of their poverty.

This is not supposed to happen in Fijian society, where the mutual support system of the 'Fijian way of life' is supposed to take care of the disadvantaged and ensure distribution of basic needs (Lasaqa 1984). It is true that none of the people interviewed was starving, but the maldistribution of material goods and of the cash incomes needed to obtain clothing, tools, household equipment, simple furniture, schooling for children and to meet social obligations is now a striking aspect of rural society in Fiji.

More recently analysing the distribution of poverty in Fiji as a whole, and using data from the 1977 Household Income and Expenditure Survey (Bureau of Statistics 1981), Cameron (1983a) found that of 7,800 households in Fiji living below 'poverty line' levels 40 per cent, or 3,100 households, were in villages, where they comprised 13 per cent of the total of village households. The depth of poverty below the poverty line was, however, less in village households than in other poverty groups. Cameron concludes that among Fijians the redistributive mechanisms of the mutual aid system still operate, but only sufficiently to provide a floor of hardship.

Looking further at the results of a resurvey of ten villages (Siwatibau 1982), Cameron found that in the poorer six villages 39 per cent of households had per-capita cash incomes under $2.00/week, and hence must be regarded as 'vulnerable'; in wealthier villages the proportion was less. He hypothesises that weakening networks of support create a risk of passing from 'benign' to 'malign' neglect under stress, as after the natural disasters of 1983.

The evolution of vulnerability: the case of Taveuni

The creation of unequal access to the means of production

While island populations were at risk from natural hazards in the past, and while it seems highly probable that the land-poor and landless were especially vulnerable in pre-colonial times, the colonial impact with its

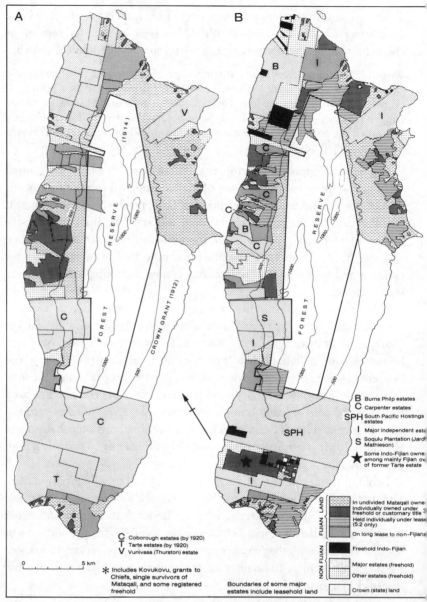

5.1A Principal elements of land tenure in Taveuni, around 1900 (Data from 'Regular' and 'Native Lands Commission' editions of Lands Department Plans at 1:12,672 adjusted to fit the 1:50,000 Directorate of Overseas Survey map of Taveuni (two sheets), and to ground features, plus a MS map of around 1900, showing all estates, made available by the District Officer, Taveuni (no authorship is indicated on this map)). Additional information from field work and archival sources. The map represents the approximate situation on the eve of Im Thurn reforms, but may include certain transfers of slightly later date. Some information from the Native Land Trust Board incorporated. 5.1B Principal elements of land 'triad of taxation, export commodity production and monetization' (Watts 1983: 249) has introduced the additional hazard of economic depression and has at the same time changed the nature of natural hazard by exposing cash incomes to its vagaries; it has also created a new social distribution of vulnerability. In most areas of eastern Fiji the transformation in the 'boundary conditions' of vulnerability was achieved rather rapidly in the second half of the nineteenth century.

We have reviewed the impact of colonialism on eastern Fiji above (chapter 3). In order to understand better how the inequalities discussed in the last section, and elsewhere in this book, came about, it will be helpful to use a specific example in order to trace a process which both deprived many Fijians of their land for the benefit of a new class of foreign planters, and at the same time reinforced the position of the chiefs. The island of Taveuni represents an extreme case of land alienation even within Fiji as a whole, and certainly within the island periphery (Brookfield 1979). Other than small islands which were wholly alienated, no other island has so large a proportion of its land in freehold. Yet as late as 1860, Seeman (1862) found only one small plantation on this island and commented on its unattractiveness to white settlers, already numerous elsewhere. Two years later, in 1862, the innumerable wars of the state of Cakaudrove reached a climax when a rebellion, supported by the Tongans who had established suzerainty over Lau, was decisively defeated at the 'battle' of Wairiki. This was a Pyrrhic victory, and only five years later Cakaudrove entered the Lauan confederation, or Tovata, under the Tongan ruler of Lau, Ma'afu. Meanwhile the Tui Cakau, ruler of Cakaudrove, sought to protect his position by the installation of a large number of white settlers.

The first wave of alienation affected the land of the defeated rebels, and it was then that whole islands such as Kanacea, Laucala and Rabi were sold from under their inhabitants who were forced to become refugees. However, arms were needed and more land was sold in order to obtain them. Thurston, the settlers' leader who became the effective ruler of Fiji in the early 1870s and later attained such power as to be dubbed the

Caption for fig. 5.1 (*cont.*)
tenure in Taveuni, 1975 partly updated to 1983 (Data sources as for Fig. 5.1A, with the addition of subdivision plans prepared on the 1:12,672 base, and located in various places including the Divisional Office, Labasa, the Land Titles Office, Suva, the Fiji National Archives (very few), and in files held in the District Office, Taveuni, by the Tui Vuna and in the hands of individuals on certain settlement schemes. Supplemented and corrected by field work 1975–6, with the assistance of the staff of the Department of Agriculture, Taveuni. Partial updating from field work in 1983. *Note*: Although all efforts have been made to maximise accuracy, both boundaries and attributions may contain errors, and this map does not necessarily represent any actual tenure or allocation of land.)

5 Captain Sewell's cotton plantation on Lomaloma island, northern Lau group, in 1876 or 1877. The thatched houses were to accommodate 'Polynesian' indentured labour, mainly Solomon Islanders. Photograph by Baron von Hügel, reproduced by permission of the Museum of Archaeology and Anthropology, University of Cambridge.

'Viceroy of the Pacific' by his biographer (Scarr 1973b), acquired a large and choice area in the north-east – recently offered for sale at $5,000,000 – for £130 together with some guns and ammunition. Thurston's acquisition, like almost all the others, belonged formerly to the Tui Cakau's vassals (Fig. 5.1A). Once the Tui Cakau had Thurston on his domain he used him as an adviser, and determined to sell no more land; indeed by this time, in 1870, he had little more to sell other than his own. The settlers' community at Vuna had become the main centre for Europeans in the northeast of Fiji and might well have gone on to become a significant town but for its total destruction by the hurricane of 1886. Taveuni became almost an experiment ground for cash crops; Fiji's first sugar mill was built there. Planters and their imported workers formed a plantation society and economy almost totally separate from that of the remaining Fijian villagers, whom they ignored.

Many of the settlers, and much of the capital with which to turn southern Taveuni into a core region for plantation development, came from Australia. Tarte, founder of a line still important in Taveuni, heard of the opportunities from a Wesleyan missionary he met in the Victorian town of Ballarat. Prospering, he made repeated visits to Melbourne in order to obtain finance with which to buy out his less successful neighbours (Tarte nd). The capital for this and many other land ventures in Fiji was generated on the Australian goldfields; the labour was drawn widely from other parts of the south Pacific.

By 1880 little coastal land remained to the Fijians except in the humid and rugged east and in the 'central-west' near the two old fortified villages of Somosomo and Wairiki. In this area the Somosomo chiefs quickly learned the 'freehold' concept, and acquired substantial areas from their vassals around Wairiki (see Fig. 5.1A). Early in the twentieth century, during the period of relaxation of land transfer under Governor Im Thurn (chapter 3), these areas were lost, being sold by Government instruction in order to pay debts (Wairiki Mission nd); the government station at Waiyevo was established on some of this land (Fig. 5.1B). Somosomo chiefs continued to be active in land acquisition; one claimed and was granted almost all the land around Qeleni village in the northeast from his maternal kin, while in 1926 a group of seventeen of them subdivided all the *mataqali* land immediately around Somosomo village among themselves, with rights of individual descent in the male line. The numerous smaller holdings granted to marrying women and their descendants as 'kovu-kovu' also came to be treated as *de facto* freehold, so that this form of grant ceased to be made. Other survivors of much-reduced *mataqali* claimed the community land as their own, and when some of the shorter leases began to fall in around 1950 some of this land was claimed by individual chiefs. The longer-term leases, mostly for 99 years and granted between 1880 and about 1915, were cultivated by European planters who attached them to their freehold properties.

The then unusable mountain land in the centre of the island, and the rugged east, were detached into state hands as a 'forest reserve' and a 'grant to the Crown' between 1912 and 1914, so that by the 1920s the *mataqali* domain was reduced to a fraction of the cultivable area of the island together with only a small inland fringe (see Fig. 5.1A). By this time there were only 1,700 Fijians on Taveuni by comparison with a pre-colonial population of about 7,000 (Bedford 1978) and they had become second-class citizens in their own land. When the process of acquisition began to be reversed in the late-1920s and 1930s, by the grant of small plots in estate backlands to estate workers, the beneficiaries were Indo-Fijians; the plots granted were too small and too rocky to offer a full subsistence, and the object was to keep the Indo-Fijians and their labour on the island at a time when many were leaving to go to Viti Levu.

There was indeed a class structure on colonial Taveuni. The planters dominated; and among them a minority soon emerged as great landholders (see Fig. 5.1A). The Fijian chiefs also became differentiated by land-holding, but this trend was checked by the forced sales of the Im Thurn period. For some years the largest population group on the island was the downtrodden estate workers, including a few remaining Melanesians from Vanuatu and the Solomons, a large number of Indo-Fijians and after 1910 a growing number of Fijian immigrants from regions with less economic opportunity in southern Lau and eastern Vanua Levu. They had their own stratification between sirdars, skilled men and unskilled workers, further subdivided by race. Even today they remain almost unseen by villagers who look over the fence separating their remaining land from that taken from them, and exclaim: 'Only one man, and he has all that, while there are so many of us on so little'. Over all of them, in theory, were the officers of Government, but the planters were powerful and Taveuni was a dangerous posting for a man with ideas. In 1944 a Medical Officer mounted a forceful campaign against the living conditions of the estate workers, but when he tried to translate complaint into action by use of his legal powers he was soon posted elsewhere and his 'orders' were disregarded (Brookfield 1978).

Subdivision and its consequences

The decline of the planter class was at first gradual. Many smaller planters took local wives or mistresses, and their land was subdivided among children into holdings too small to be economically viable as estates after their deaths. Others left the island, for Suva or overseas. During the 1950s and early 1960s a number of estates changed hands, some to individual newcomers but more to large companies which hitherto had little direct participation in production. Their managers and the new owners briefly created a new generation of European population, but in the subsequent years of depression management has increasingly been localised; the remaining European population, other than church personnel, now numbers fewer than thirty. The plantation workforce has declined, and many smaller estates now rely heavily on casual labour.

The major change since 1960 has been on Fijian land, where the land subdivision movement described in chapter 3 was taken up with great enthusiasm, so that by the mid-1970s as large a part of the usable land was held by block-holders, with or without formal leases, as remained in the hands of the *mataqali*. Of the 54 per cent of the island regarded, rather generously, as 'usable' by the UNESCO/UNFPA project, the following was the distribution around 1975 (Brookfield 1978: 58).

	Area (ha)	Per cent
Freehold, Europeans, part-Europeans and Companies	13,300	54.9
Crown land	187	0.8
Freehold, Indo-Fijian	605	2.5
'Freehold', Fijian	1,560	6.4
Fijian, leased to non-Fijians	1,940	8.0
Fijian, held individually on lease	3,292	13.6
Fijian, undivided *mataqali* land	3,379	13.9

Creation of this new class of individual blockholders, which we discuss in more detail below and in chapter 9, has done much to change Taveuni, but it is evident that it has reduced the 'reserve' available to Fijians in the future to quite small proportions, with only the unexpired leases to non-Fijians as a reasonably sure addition at a future time. As Figure 5.1B makes clear, most of the subdivision area is inland, and includes two large intrusions into the forest reserve, but there is little beyond it that is cultivable under present conditions.

Despite the low density of population, landlessness is a very real fact in Taveuni society, and the jealousies which arise from this situation are powerful. Though far more people now have direct access to the means of production than at the height of the colonial period, there is no way in which the contrast between the patterns exhibited in Figures 5.1A and 5.1B can be described as a 'reform'. One consequence, however, is that the power of the chiefs has waned significantly, even though everything can still be halted to produce a vast surplus for a visit by the President of Fiji who is a Taveuni high chief. It is perhaps fortunate that from Independence to 1987 the two highest titles in the island were held by unassuming and progressive men who have done much for their people. Given the degree to which the 'traditional' base of power has been eroded by land alienation, while so large a part of the population has wage employment of one kind or another, this has been important for tranquillity on Taveuni, for this is an island on which the values of urban rather than rural Fiji increasingly prevail.

Taveuni is unusual, but many of the same elements are present elsewhere. In particular, land is almost everywhere unequally distributed, while on many islands there are substantial chiefly estates (e.g. Lakeba, see M. Brookfield 1979). While few villages are as constrained for land as some of those on Taveuni, there are landless and near-landless on every island, and land qualities are distributed in a very uneven manner. Except at a local level, no one in authority is willing to grapple with this maldistribution of land, and almost no Fijians anywhere are prepared to see it altered to the benefit of their Indo-Fijian co-nationals. Freehold and quasi-freehold title, whether non-Fijian or Fijian, shelter behind this larger defensive barrier; protection of the remaining indigenous land also protects and preserves the appropriation of land – both in the past from Fijians as a whole, by one *mataqali* from another at a point of time around 1880, by chiefs from commoners, and today by Fijian lease-block holders from others in their *mataqali*. A very few Indo-Fijians have managed to find themselves bits and pieces through movements within and between these rigid 'tectonic plates' of Fijian society and polity.

Land and class

Land remains the basis of status in rural Fiji, and it is the peculiarities of the land-allocation system which have inhibited the development of a more straightforward class structure with a clear division between prole-tariat and bourgeoisie. In other respects the Fiji system, being so char-acterised by inequality, would seem to have all the ingredients for class-based alliance among the underprivileged against the strong. The effect of this segmentation of rural society according to its status in regard to land is more clearly seen in Taveuni than elsewhere except in southern Vanua Levu. In islands that are now wholly Fijian, however, the same adherence to legal land title plays a similar segmenting role. Villager may be against villager, but both are for the chief who is also a Fijian. Only rarely, as at Vuna in Taveuni (Lasaqa 1984: 43–5), has a wise chief used his authority to redistribute land between the *mataqali* under his control. The rights of one community more generally are upheld against the demands of another. Even at sea fishing rights are segmented, and are closely guarded.

In the discussion that follows, therefore, groups are distinguished on the basis of their status mainly in regard to land, rather than on the basis of class. Each of these groups is vertically stratified, and none is independent of the others. There are villagers who live a precarious existence just as there are freehold owners who can barely make ends meet. But a cross-group class system has not yet emerged. It may not emerge within the lifetime of anyone now living in rural Fiji unless the political events of 1987 lead ultimately to rejection of the chiefs, and to a more secure place for Indo-Fijians. As of 1988 the former is unlikely, the latter impossible. The appropriate political economy for rural Fiji still depends, at base, on access to land.

Which groups are most vulnerable?

The profound changes that have taken place in the society of outer-island Fiji have, however, re-sorted people between groups in a variety of ways. Some of the poorest of the villagers long ago joined landless Indo-Fijians to form the present estate workforce, and many of the Fijian workers living permanently on estates now have no other home and some cannot even recall the name of their *mataqali*. Some more recent migrants find life on the estate more secure than in the villages they have left. Others have found a new security on the leasehold settlement blocks. At the other end of the range, the break-up of the white planter-trader society has left behind a significant group of part-European small planters, whose pathos is accentuated by their attempts to live an impoverished version of their grandfathers' lifestyle in decaying houses backed, in some instances, by the overgrown tennis courts of their forefathers.

Even among newer elements in the system there is distress. The Indo-Fijian and Sino-Fijian traders who replaced the former white traders two generations ago have only rarely succeeded in building up secure and substantial businesses, except in the quasi-urban society of central-western Taveuni and at Savasavu and a few other central places. Many small stores have perished, or eke out a parlous existence on the small business available from a region of declining real incomes, with occasional periods of severe financial stringency. Even the Co-operative Societies, whose establishment and acquisition of a monopoly of copra buying in the 1960s drove out a significant proportion of the Indo-Fijian and Sino-Fijian traders, are often themselves in deep financial trouble. All Societies are members of the Fiji Co-operative Association which listed a substantial number of them as 'closed accounts with bad debts' in late 1982. Seventy-five per cent of such societies, and 79 per cent of the individual customers of the Association in the 'bad debt' category had addresses in the coconut districts of the eastern islands and Vanua Levu. In the main coconut-growing Province of Cakaudrove 38 per cent of all accounts were closed for this reason, and in Lau the proportion was 26 per cent. Many others were in debt to the Association which was itself in a shaky financial condition.

It is instructive to consider the effect of external events, and of the structure of the system, on an unusual case. In 1971 a Californian family firm bought an estate in Taveuni and set about converting it into a prestigious subdivision, with 0.4 ha blocks for 'second homes', a hotel, club, golf course and other facilities. The site is magnificent, and the venture was initially supported by the banks and by Government. Unfortunately for the family-firm, the oil-price shock of 1973, subsequent escalation of costs and air fares and a temporary decline of tourism, cut off a large part of their market. Required by Fiji law to complete infra-structures before such sales as they had could be finalised, the family-firm made a desperate bid to complete this work in 1975 with a $100,000 loan from the Fiji National Provident Fund. They struck the wet period of the mid-1970s, and heavy rains during the 'dry' season washed away the work as fast as it could be carried out with their limited resources. In 1976 their funds were exhausted and the workforce was dismissed. The estate, and its plans, were then bought at an unknown price by a Suva company backed by Jardine Mathieson of Hong Kong, and with this large infusion of funds the infrastructure was completed. Over 500 blocks were reportedly sold to another Hong Kong syndicate allegedly linked to the 'Mr Asia' drug ring, which traded in them as a means of 'laundering' money (*The National Times*, Sydney, 10–16 June 1983: 42), but by 1983 fewer than 20 houses had been built. The internationally-backed company, however, was able to proceed with its development plans, and when the historical origin of Jardine Mathieson's wealth is recalled, there is some irony in this story of 'outer-island development'. It is not only the very poor who are at risk in this peripheral economy, and it requires assets as well as merely enterprise to survive.

Vulnerability extends across all land-holding groups, but for reasons discussed above it is best to organise discussion within them. Inequality in the village system is discussed in much greater detail below in chapters 7, 8 and 9. A review of the non-village groups will, however, more clearly distinguish who is more vulnerable and who is less so. The very poor in the villages may be as vulnerable as anyone outside the villages, but there remains the structure of support which Cameron (1983a) sought to assess. We shall see evidence of this below.

The rich and the powerful

Not much decision-making power now resides in outer-island Fiji. None the less, two very small groups of people who have homes in the outer islands are linked by the possession of comfortable affluence. One group is dominated by a small number of American and other millionaires who own land, mostly whole islands or large estates, and who reside there for some part of the year. It also includes less affluent executives of Suva-based companies who have small estates which, like the island homes of the expatriate wealthy are essentially 'hobby farms' to the owners' main activities and sources of income. The second group comprises a small number of Fijian high chiefs who constitute something of a landed aristocracy in the region and two of whom occupy the highest positions in the country. Together with some other high-ranking Fijians from the islands, they combine comfortable wealth with power at national level. Their island holdings are more than 'hobby farms' to them, but even though their power rests in large measure on their high rank and hence arises from the region, they spend little time in the islands. These two groups have in common a substantial degree of personal invulnerability to external events affecting the islands, both because of their large resources and of their other and principal sources of income.

While this much can be said about the rich and powerful as a whole, however, the ethnic division divides them sharply in other ways. The non-Fijians now have only limited political and social power, and the expatriates among them are all relative newcomers. They have bought freehold land, and this land has appreciated in value both among their own circle of 'second-home' buyers and also among developers seeking sites for subdivision and tourist development, catering to a less wealthy but still affluent market. They are thus able to sell their land if they wish at a profit measured in thousands or even millions of dollars. Island estates of this type, mostly bought for much smaller sums in the past, were on offer at prices ranging from $300,000 to $5,000,000 in 1983. Although buyers do not come quickly at these prices, all but the most over-priced estates do seem ultimately to be sold.

The powerful Fijian aristocracy does own some freehold land, but it is unlikely to be offered for sale. Together with land held in traditional title it is the base of their power. For the most part, and particularly in the case of Ratu Sir Kamisese Mara, they retain a profound sense of the responsibility that goes with power, and remain active in local affairs as well as on the national scene. Their influence, as well as their resources, are used to help their own people. They vary greatly in this respect, however, and there are those among the affluent chiefly Fijians whose leadership in local affairs is now rarely exercised except in matters of traditional ceremony.

Corporate groups

We have already seen that corporate groups own substantial areas in the islands and have an important role in commerce. The present corporate groups are again of two main types: those with only peripheral interests in Fiji, and those which either spring from, or have taken over and still operate local companies. External events in recent years have elicited a somewhat different response from the two groups. The former have either done nothing and simply accepted events or else have invested in their properties by new planting or by subdivision in a manner that seems almost unrelated to profitability; it might have a basis in company tax-reduction policy. The latter group, those companies with roots in Fiji, have been affected much more directly.

Events of recent years have led the two main island companies, both now owned in Australia, toward shedding or reducing their interests in the outer islands, offering estates for sale, ceasing unprofitable operations such as shipping and, more recently, provision of retail trading outlets. Their behaviour has seemed erratic, with surprising innovations standing out from the general pattern of contraction. Some of these innovations are quite specifically on a trial basis, such as Carpenters' coffee planting in Taveuni, in which they refused to adopt a continuing role as nucleus estate for surrounding smallholders; the possibility of withdrawal remained open. Others have been more for demonstration purposes, such as Burns Philp's introduction of coconut husking machines which they hoped to market widely in the Pacific. But there is also another element: having historical roots in Fiji and retaining large and profitable areas of operation in the central national economy, these companies are concerned to preserve their image.

This did not last however. Taylor (1984) analyses the manner in which these and other 'Australian colonial' companies are progressively peripheralising all their operations in the Pacific islands, eliminating whole sectors and shifting their emphasis more and more to Australia, and also to Asia. The further this disengagement proceeds, the more are adverse external events likely to bring about decisions to withdraw from an area fraught with such uncertainty. By 1988 all corporate operations in the islands had ceased, and most land was sold.

The struggling planter and entrepreneur

Except when they can sell their land or their businesses, the non-corporate planters and entrepreneurs who depend on the production and trade of the outer islands for their livelihood, or most of it, are in a very different position from that of the two groups discussed above. Although still numerically dominated by Europeans and part-Europeans, this group also includes Indo- and Sino-Fijians, and a significant and growing number of Fijians. With the exception of a very few immigrants who have bought estates or businesses since 1950, all are Fiji-born.

These are the people whose enterprises have been under the greatest stress since 1970. It is perhaps remarkable that there have been so few bankruptcies or failures among planters and businessmen. This is the product both of their own efforts at diversification, and of the substantial support given to the copra price during low-price periods after 1975. Since the price has been supported to a figure around the average plantation cost of production, it can reasonably be said that this whole sector has been kept above water by a temporary transfer of funds from other parts of the national economy. This support has permitted efficient planters, and most village producers, to make some profit and hence has also assisted the maintenance of employment and of businesses dependent on the multiplier effect of incomes in the coconut industry.

The loss of real income has, however, led to accelerated contraction of a social and economic sector which once dominated all parts of the eastern islands of Fiji from Lakeba northward. As an older generation disappeared the survivors have increasingly come to terms with their Fijian neighbours. Local managers on large estates and owners of small estates now often enter into mutual aid arrangements with these neighbours, although not to the extent to which such arrangements are practised by the few Fijian planters. The difficulties of recent years have accelerated this trend, and only a shadow of the former plantocracy now remains. Among those who remain are some few risk-taking innovators whose introductions into the system of production we discuss in chapter 10. It is remarkable that all these private innovations have taken place during the period of sharp contraction that set in after the mid-1970s.

The estate workers

Including families, about 5,000 people live permanently on estates in the eastern islands and in Vanua Levu. Rather more than half are now Fijians. We have seen earlier (see Table 4.2) that their remuneration has fallen behind the rate of inflation, and the fact that they have lost somewhat less in real terms than the copra producers themselves reflects a significant contraction that has taken place in their numbers. Their wages and conditions have been a source of complaint for many years, and have tended to improve only in spurts during periods of prosperity, as in the 1950s and more briefly in 1975, 1979 and again in 1983. They have no union, and there is no national wage which applies to them. Conditions are a matter for 'negotiation' between employer and employee, a 'negotiation' in which the worker's bargaining power rests only on his ability or willingness to move to another estate, or out of the industry.

One such spurt of rising wages was taking place during our return visit in 1983, as estates which had run down their workforces during the years of low production and low prices sought new workers in order to increase production in response to a sharp improvement in the market. Some months before the official price was increased, millers were already paying premium prices in order to obtain copra in competition with one another. Day workers, meaning those employed on any task other than copra cutting and some tasks let out to casuals, were paid only around $2.75–3.00 a day in 1982, but in 1983 the rate was already around $3.60 on most estates, and as much as $5.00 or even $6.00 on a few. Copra cutters, paid $0.80–1.00 for each 45 kg bag of 'green' copra cut in 1982, were receiving up to $1.10–1.50 in mid-1983. While the highest wages were unlikely to survive a further drop in price, it seemed probable that a new step in upward progression was taking place. Much the same had happened in 1974 and 1979. The difficulty of obtaining new labour forced wages upward.

The estate workers are vulnerable to hard times brought about by external events of both economic and physical origin in at least two ways. Wages may be reduced or held at a constant level despite inflation, and employment itself may contract, reducing the workers' bargaining power and sometimes depriving them of both work and home. In storm or drought they also suffer from shortage of food in their own gardens. However, some at least may acquire greater security. Many small estates have ceased to pay wages and instead offer a share in estate proceeds – usually 50 per cent – to their workers who thus acquire a stake in the business, and greater opportunity to use land for their own production. The first desire of most estate workers is to have land of their own, and as the size of the workforce has diminished the conditions under which land is made available to them have often eased. Thus their wages have been increasingly supplemented – or subsidised – by use-value production. These changes in the position of estate workers have tended to make estate employment less unattractive than it was a decade or more ago, and to improve their security. It is noteworthy that some modification of proletarianism is an important element in this amelioration.

The lease-block holders

The last group to be examined in this chapter has arisen mainly since the 1960s. They include among them an emergent new class of farmers, to some degree self-selected by motivation. Before the 1960s there was a small number of independent Fijian farmers, termed *galala*, who opted out of the village system and worked their own allocated land separately from the *mataqali* domain. After the reports of Spate (1959) and Burns et al. (1960) a national land-development scheme was instituted. Its object was to create a population of Fijian lease-block farmers living and working on their own land, by leasing undeveloped sections of *mataqali* land to individuals. In the island regions the farms were to be coconut/cocoa blocks, with food crops grown on a section of the land. The scheme was implemented in Vanua Levu, Lomaiviti, Kadavu and Taveuni, but not for Lau. Its history in Taveuni was reconstructed in some detail by Brookfield (1978, 1988) using scattered and fast-vanishing sources, one product of which research is summarised in Figure 5.1B. In that island, as elsewhere, the scheme quickly got out of hand, and the pace of subdivision far exceeded the capacity of the Administration to survey and grant leases. By the late 1960s it was apparent that many blocks had simply been planted with coconuts in order to obtain a planting subsidy that was then available, only to be abandoned once the subsidy had been collected. Some individuals persisted, however, growing root crops – mainly taro – and *yaqona* for the urban markets.

The Land Development Authority was wound up in 1969 after some spectacular failures on Viti Levu, and because of conflict with a village-based ethos of rural development that re-surfaced as independence approached (Brookfield 1988). The most spectacular failure was at Lomaivuna, a settlement scheme north of Suva occupied almost entirely by migrants from Lau. Bananas were the initial crop, but they failed as elsewhere in Fiji due to disease, inadequate marketing and quality-control problems. In 1967 the settlers were offered their fares home, but almost none accepted. They stayed to become vegetable farmers for the Suva market, and more recently cultivators of ginger for export. Other Lauans found land elsewhere in Viti Levu, some of them even before the 1961 scheme was initiated (Ward 1965: 182–3), and others acquired land on Ovalau. On Taveuni a few Lauans obtained blocks from *mataqali* heads who wished to see the land developed; some migrants from Vanua Levu also got land in this way, and by the mid-1970s a number of estate workers had also acquired their own lease-blocks.

In the mid-1970s Taveuni was one of the strongest lease-block areas outside Viti Levu. Former Taveuni villagers and migrants both held land, and there were also freehold subdivisions on former estate land where most of the landholders were former Indo-Fijian estate workers. There were 404 blocks, covering almost 42 km^2, but only 17 km^2 were developed, the mean developed area being 4.3 ha (SD 1.56 ha). Of the developed area 15 km^2 were on Fijian land and only 2 km^2 on freehold land where most holders were Indo-Fijian (Brookfield 1978). The developed area was probably about the same in 1983, for while there was substantial enlargement on some schemes, others had been largely abandoned by their holders who had returned to live in the villages. We examine such a case in chapter 9, through a detailed account of Qeleni village and its settlement-block area.

Most of the blocks abandoned between 1976 and 1983 belonged to local people, who had withdrawn into the greater security of the village economy and its system of support. Most of the still-productive blocks, on the other hand, belonged either to local people whose *mataqali* had little land, or else to migrants. One such group are Lauans, former estate workers settled at Delaivione in Taveuni (see Fig. 5.1B). They were almost unique in still growing taro in 1983 for the Suva market, sending one of their number with each shipment following failure of the formal marketing system. They found this regular income rewarding. Whereas in 1976 the settlers still lived in crude huts, in 1983 there were a number of substantial houses and a church had been built. There had been considerable turnover of leases, however, at prices as high as $1,100 per hectare. This is about one third of the price being asked by expatriate holders of freehold island estates who hope to sell their land to other 'hobby farmers', or to developers.

The people who have persevered, overcome problems and innovated in order to increase their productivity are mostly people with no other opportunities and no other means of support. Most of those who have given up, at least temporarily, in the face of difficulties have alternatives on which to fall back. Some of the Lauans and others who have sold out have gone to Vanua Levu to take up sugar-cane blocks in the hope of higher income. Those who seek land of their own for cash-crop purposes, and who succeed in finding it, are as much affected by external events as are others; they are, on the other hand, the most likely to seek ways around their difficulties.

Although they are not well represented in the outer islands, except on Taveuni, this population of independent farmers has continued to grow in Fiji so that it now represents about 25 per cent of all Fijian farmers. In this respect, Fijian farming has gone further toward the 'modern' principle of farmers working and living on their own land than any other Pacific island country except Tonga. The remainder of Fijian farmers, however, still live in villages and work *mataqali* land, albeit with a greater degree of individual decision-making freedom than before the reforms of the 1960s. While there may have been continued net movement toward individualisation, there are other forces which have weakened the drive toward 'independence', as we shall see in chapters 7, 8 and 9.

Conclusion

The distribution of individual risk in the face of external events is thus highly complex. In a major disaster no one escapes its effects, but it is in lesser disasters such as the minor storm, drought, or economic depression that differentiation of risk emerges most clearly. It is evident that possession of a strong asset backing, and secure employment paid from outside the island periphery are in modern conditions the best defences.

What has also emerged from this discussion, however, is that the rural society of the eastern islands has not simply remained passive in the face of natural and economic adversity. Means of coping with natural disaster were well-developed in pre-colonial times, and we shall see below in chapter 6 what has happened to them in the modern context of dependency. Vulnerability to economic adversity has grown as more people have detached themselves from the securities of the village economy. Yet even in cash-crop production, or in trade, many have retained diversity, and thus have retained protection. They have done this by declining full commitment to the market economy, or by spreading that commitment in such a way that they retain the ability to move the factors of production under their control between enterprises.

This retention of diversity is strongest in the village economy. Most of the groups we have discussed above are those who have either placed themselves at greater risk, or who have been so placed by forces that they were unable to control. Inequality, especially in monetary terms, is an inevitable consequence of risk-taking. It is also, however, an inevitable consequence of involuntary deprivation of decision-making control, that is by the intrenchment of low rank, and by proletarianisation.

The effect of colonial economic development in eastern Fiji has been to enrich a few, to place many more at risk, and to increase the risk for almost all. Eastern Fiji has been only partly transformed by colonialism and development. By 'commercialisation of the soil' the early planters certainly set out to dissolve 'the body economic into its elements so that each element could fit into that part of the system where it was most useful' for themselves (Polanyi 1944: 179). But the state intervened on behalf of the Fijian chiefs who sought the protection of their remaining land and rights through the Act of Cession. One effect was the creation through immigration of a population of true proletarians; another was to permit the chiefs to engross land while, however, restricting their other demands for surplus production and service. A longer term effect was, however, to remove most land from the 'free market' and by so doing to retain the opportunity for subsequent transformation in the conditions of access. At the same time, the development of a class system has been inhibited by segmentation of the land on group lines, and by the antagonism between the two main ethnic groups to which the segmentation of land has powerfully contributed.

The brief colonial period in eastern Fiji witnessed dramatic changes the full effect of which has not yet worked through the whole production and social system. During a phase of capitalist advance a large part of the region became dominated by estates and all of it by a trading economy which fell into non-local hands; notwithstanding legal protection of the village system, the remoter areas assumed the role of labour reservoir. During a more recent period the estate system has contracted rapidly, and local enterprise has resurfaced both through individualisation of farming and by some recapture of trade at island level; this same period, however, has witnessed much greater national centralisation of decision-making and heavy emigration to other parts of the country. Vulnerability to natural hazard has in one sense increased, while on the other hand the state has assumed an important role in the relief of distress. A system of subsidy that has grown up since 1970 has also moderated growing vulnerability to economic hazard, but only to a degree. Most of the remainder of the book is concerned with the contrasted responses to new conditions by government and villagers, and with the changes that have taken place between our field work in 1974–6 and our return visit in 1983. We encountered a number of surprises.

6

Pampered periphery?

The analysis so far of transformation in economy and society in the eastern islands has emphasised progressive loss of autonomy in response to ecological and economic variability, especially since 1945. It is not difficult to conjure up images of a region where material living standards are lower than in areas closer to the cores of modern capitalist development in Fiji; a region where it is no longer possible to obtain a livelihood which is perceived to be both adequate and desirable to Fijians raised in a world dominated by the 'consciousness industry of late capitalism' – the manufacture of dreams, fantasies and ideologies which comprise the all-pervasive cultural imperialism of the late twentieth century (Peet 1980). In addition to the false consciousness produced by diffusion of a consumption-oriented mentality in which preferences and aspirations are completely out of touch with the material reality of most locations, the language of development studies, especially as it relates to rural areas, is contributing to what Peet (1980: 96) calls 'geographical schizophrenia'. Repeated reference to regions as 'depressed', 'dependent', 'vulnerable', 'marginal' and 'underdeveloped' helps to foster a consciousness which is encouraging people all over the world to leave villages in order to avail themselves of the perceived advantages of an urban capitalist culture.

It is argued in this chapter that a region of villages in Fiji is not likely to become truly 'marginal' and 'depressed' when a dominant element in the state's political ideology is the desirability of village residence for Fijians. While it is true that not much decision-making power of national significance now resides in eastern Fiji, it is a fact that a great deal of decision-making power in the post-colonial state is in the hands of Fijians from the eastern islands. In a society where 'the villager enters the material life of the nation more frequently by way of the back door of bureaucracy than through the front door of the market mechanism' (Rutz 1982: 151) this combination of ideology and patronage has had a powerful impact on the material well-being of village-resident Fijians.

There are two distinct but related parts to this chapter. The first contains a brief review of the rhetoric of rural development in post-colonial Fiji, and a longer comment on state involvement in the rehabilitation of communities devastated by natural disasters. A question, which underlies much of the discussion in subsequent chapters, is introduced here: to what extent has the population of the small island periphery been pampered by planners and politicians in the interests of fostering the state's ideological commitment to preservation of a distinctively Fijian material culture?

The second part contains an assessment of recent population trends in Fiji and the eastern islands; initially in the context of the apparent turn-around in the country's widely recognised transition to lower rates of natural increase, and secondly with reference to the role of migration as a regulator of demographic trends in small islands. The trend towards absolute depopulation of parts of eastern Fiji, which has been used as a basis for regional population projections in the 1980s, is then assessed in the light of evidence from national and local-level inquiries in the early 1980s. Absolute depopulation seems to have been replaced again with the more normal condition for a pampered periphery of relative depopulation.

Manipulating consciousness: the contribution of planning rhetoric

In one of the few published studies of responses by rural populations in the Pacific to rationally planned public investment managed by bureaucrats, Rutz (1982) has argued that the extent to which government has become involved in rural development is one of the most important trends in the political economy of Fiji. In his view, 'on a gradient of government involvement in village life, Fiji has perhaps gone further than most Pacific Island societies' (Rutz 1982: 182). The legacy of this government involvement is a long one, although official development plans in Fiji post-date the Second World War. Since the attainment of political independence in 1970, rural development has become progressively more prominent in the articulation of national goals – goals which are having a powerful influence on options open to Fijians as they strive for a better material life. In chapter 10 we describe elements of the bureaucratic maze through which public goods flow from centre to periphery, and examine critically several of the government's policies to promote rural development. In this section our main concern is with the ideological underpinnings of Fiji's post-colonial development philosophy, particularly as these relate to the planners' rhetoric about rural development.

A legacy of colonialism

The efforts of Sir Arthur Gordon and the first colonial administration to protect Fijian village life from the ravages of capitalism laid the foundations of the ideology which has dominated official thinking about Fijian development for more than a century. A belief that the pre-capitalist mode of production should be preserved was enshrined in the political superstructure of Fiji through establishment of a system of dual administration and enactment of a set of Native Regulations which applied exclusively to one race in the colonial state. France (1969: 126–7) captured the essence of the relevant learning process which entrenched this ideology when he wrote:

The orthodoxy gradually evolved, dedicated to the preservation of the ancient Fijian traditions against the inroads of an alien culture ... When the Fijians who had received a mission education left their villages and took minor government positions, they too respected ... the clear outline of the Fijian society presented by the orthodoxy as the true and ancient tradition of the land ... The educated members of Fijian society were urged to join their European mentors in their efforts to preserve the foundations of that society. This involved stressing the subservience of the individual to his community as part of the 'communal system'; preserving the outward show of respect to the chiefs...; insistence on the communal ownership of land; and, above all, the maintenance of respect for customs which were held to be ancient, hallowed and unchanging.

As we demonstrated in chapter 3, there were challenges to this orthodoxy, especially in the 1910s and 1960s, and by the time independence was granted in 1970 substantial modifications had been made to the administrative system through which Fijian villagers participated in government at the local, regional and national levels. The essential ideological commitment remained, however, to a rural-based Fijian society, secure in their ownership of most of the country's land. Writing in the late 1970s about his people before and after Independence, Lasaqa (1984: 30) felt that it was still appropriate to stress that 'the village is at once the core and foundation of Fijian life; upon it is focused the Fijians' desire and attempt to demonstrate their separate identity and their urge to carve a better place for themselves now and in the future.'

Rural development as community self-help

Although by Pacific standards there is a long tradition of development planning in Fiji, it was not until the final years of colonial rule that explicit reference was made in an official development plan to the need for 'a more balanced and integrated development of the archipelago' (Central Planning Office 1966: 5). Widening disparities in opportunity, welfare and incomes between the core areas of development on Viti Levu and Vanua Levu on the one hand, and the small island periphery on the other, had been recognised at an official level for some decades, and were the subject of much public comment in the 1960s following publication of the Spate (1959) and Burns (1960) reports. But it was not until 1969 that a government-sponsored integrated rural development programme was initiated to probe problems and propose projects at village level.

The rural development programme, as detailed in Fiji's first post-colonial development plan, had two major aims. In the words of the planners, these were:

firstly, to increase the productive capacity and standard of life of the rural people by measures designed to promote the principle of community self-help; secondly to provide a framework for representative leaders of all communities to share in the preparation, co-ordination and execution of a diverse range of projects ... [which] may be entirely self-help in character or entirely Government-executed and financed. (Central Planning Office 1970: 82)

The emphasis on self-help, whereby communities seek their own improvement, express their own needs and find ways to meet these by their own efforts and resources (Central Planning Office 1975: 225) has persisted through the 15 years of development planning since Independence. The content of policies to stimulate rural community development has changed over this period, and we review some of the most important government initiatives in subsequent chapters. But the fundamental assumption that there is a great willingness among Fijians in particular to remain in a rural environment 'because of their traditions and culture' (Central Planning Office 1980b: 10) has not changed. Migration trends since the 1940s notwithstanding, village communalism is still considered by many prominent Fijian leaders to be both the most favoured and the most appropriate socio-economic foundation to secure a satisfactory livelihood, especially in peripheral islands with their limited land resources and small populations.

Reactions to the rhetoric

There is little doubt that the self-help philosophy of rural development has generated considerable frustration in the periphery. On the one hand, widespread discussion of the 'felt needs' of villagers in the early 1970s, at meetings called by administrative staff in rural communities, raised aspirations for action by government to assist villagers achieve a higher standard of living. The process by which these 'felt needs' were articulated at some meetings is recalled by Rutz (1982: 185) when he writes that the response was 'a question by the village as to what these [needs] might be and a listing, in order of the projects suggested as example by the representative, as those requested by the village'. While Rutz goes on to observe that no one believed the government was prepared to deliver on any of these requests, the fact that there was official interest in assessing needs more systematically had the effect of raising both the villagers' consciousness about possible inadequacies of rural life, and their hopes that something might actually be done to improve the situation.

When the UNESCO team commenced field work in Lau Province in 1975 the government's rural development programme was a topical issue in the villages. As part of the process of compiling information on rural resources, the Eastern Division administration had conducted a resource base survey in 1974 (Bedford & Brookfield 1974). The survey was organised on a household basis and, in addition to collecting information on population composition, economic activities, and standards of housing, there was also a question seeking the villagers' views on 'obstacles holding you back from raising your income'. It was not surprising to find a lengthy list of 'obstacles' spanning all dimensions of rural life. One of the questions we were frequently asked in the villages a year later was 'what is the government doing with the information they collected, because nothing seems to be happening'.

An obvious problem in this regard was a difference in perception of the intentions behind activities such as village meetings to determine 'felt needs' and government-sponsored surveys to obtain information on villagers' problems. To many villagers the rationale for such activities seemed clear: the post-colonial government was genuinely concerned to improve living conditions in rural areas. After all, Fijian leaders were in control of the bureaucracy and in a position to determine the allocation of public resources available for investment in development projects. The rationale for the debates and data gathering exercises was perceived rather differently in the administration. The two prime objectives were firstly to obtain information at local and regional levels which would facilitate formulation of development strategy, and secondly to involve rural communities in a more meaningful way than had occurred in the past in the rural development process. It was not long before villagers were observing cynically that while the debate about rural development had certainly intensified after Independence, the self-help philosophy basically meant they had to solve their own problems using their own resources.

Evidence of investment

In fact, there is plenty of evidence in villages in the periphery of a quite substantial influx of public goods and services since Independence in

Table 6.1 *Per capita allocation of proposed public investment in development, 1980 and 1985*

Investment & population	Region				
	Eastern	Central	Western	Northern	Fiji
a) *Total public investment allocations ($F million)*					
1980	1.7	38.1	29.8	12.2	81.8
1985	9.8	46.6	43.1	23.4	122.9
b) *Population estimates*[a]					
1981	38,100	240,250	259,350	112,350	650,050
1986	36,900	280,450	281,150	122,450	720,950
c) *Per capita allocations*[b] *($F)*					
1980	44.62	158.58	114.90	108.59	125.84
1985	265.58	166.16	153.29	191.09	170.47

[a] Central Planning Office projections.
[b] 1980 and 1985 investment allocations related to 1981 and 1986 population estimates.
Source: Central Planning Office (1980b)

1970. How much this is due on the one hand to action to match the rhetoric of rural development, or on the other to the substantial material aid supplied to communities devastated by natural disasters, is difficult to determine. The nature of government assistance with village rehabilitation after hurricanes is examined in the next section, but we can note here that in the proposed allocation of funds to development projects in Fiji's four administrative divisions between 1980 and 1985, the two divisions containing most of the small islands (Eastern and Northern) were scheduled to receive the highest per capita allocations by 1985 (Table 6.1).

In a sense it might be argued that the outer islands were being 'pampered' in order to increase the attractiveness to Fijians of continued residence in the periphery. While this acknowledges the long-established trend towards net-emigration from eastern Fiji to Viti Levu, the high per capita allocation to the Eastern Division in 1985 also recognises the cost of providing a range of public and private services in an archipelagic environment where there has recently been absolute population decline

Table 6.2 *Population change in Fiji, 1966–76*

Region/Division	Census population 1966	Census population 1976	Average annual growth rate (%) 1966–76
Eastern	41,248	39,524	−0.43
Central	154,429	206,875	2.92
Western	195,760	238,547	1.98
Northern	84,244	103,122	2.02
Fiji	476,727	588,063	2.10

Source: Zwart (1968), Lodhia (1978).

(Table 6.2). The Central Planning Office (1980b: 185) considered that a trend to depopulation 'could possibly continue, should no specific Government intervention be implemented, whether it be rural development, provision of social amenities, opportunities for some form of economic activity, or other policy measures.' Regional development in the periphery is the subject of detailed analysis in chapter 10 but it should be pointed out here that in devising its strategy for the Eastern Division the Fiji Government was determined to ensure that 'local customs and traditions were not traded off for commercialisation for its own sake' (Central Planning Office 1980b: 207). From the perspective of urban-based planners, one of the advantages of being located on the periphery of the nation's space economy was seen to be retention of a relatively simple life in unpolluted surroundings.

Another perspective

A very different perspective on the rhetoric of planners and politicians in the context of rural development in the Pacific is contained in Hau'ofa's (1985) analysis of development ideology in the Pacific region. He stresses that while it is the élites in government and business (the 'privileged') who decide on the needs of their communities, and determine the directions of development, 'increasingly the privileged and the poor observe different traditions, each adhering to those that serve their interests best' (Hau'ofa 1985: 17). The critical difference in these traditions, as Hau'ofa sees it, 'is that the poor merely live by their preferred traditions, while the privileged often try and force certain other traditions on the poor in order to maintain social stability'. As part of their strategy to maintain control over both national and regional resources that can be used to underwrite a high material standard of living, Hau'ofa suggests that ruling élites in the

Pacific are forcing onto their rural populations the 'tradition' of security in village residence and participation in a rural economy based on small-holder agriculture.

Hau'ofa's argument, which is part of a very vigorous debate about development and underdevelopment in the Pacific, is supported by many Fijians who cannot fail to see the ever-widening disparities in levels of material well-being and consumer consumption between senior civil servants on the one hand and villagers on the other. In his review of Fijian development since independence, Lasaqa (1984) frequently refers to the Fijian population as the 'handicapped' group in contemporary Fiji society. In his view there is a need to 'redistribute the fruits of development, in both the rural and urban areas, so that the poor, of whom the Fijians see themselves as the majority, are rescued from their present predicament and given a better place in life' (Lasaqa 1984: 195). While Lasaqa was not questioning seriously whether the village was an appropriate unit within which to foster Fijian development, he was very concerned at the weak position of the Fijian people in the commercial life of the country.

The debate about the relevance for Fijian economic advancement of village-based communal enterprise, as opposed to a rural society of independent farmers, is explored in depth in other chapters. It is apparent from the writings by Fijians on development issues in the 1970s and 1980s that the ideology of preserving a village-based society with its attendant systems of communal land tenure and kinship reciprocity is being attacked again increasingly from within. In the mid-1970s, for example, Goneyali (1975: 62) argued that 'we must discourage the continuance of villages. The village is the greatest stumbling block to farming develop-ment.' A decade later, Vusoniwailala (1985: 7) came to the conclusion that kinship reciprocity and communalism were becoming increasingly expensive for Fijians and that 'there is a danger that the rising cost of communalism will contribute to a widening gap between native Fijians and other ethnic groups'. As we show in chapter 5 and in village case studies in subsequent chapters, the political economy of 'vulnerability' in Fijian rural communities is much more complex than the stereotype which is conveyed in most accounts of the 'Fijian way of life'.

Response to disaster

Rehabilitation of communities devastated by natural disaster in the 1970s probably did more to translate some of the rhetoric of rural development into reality in eastern Fiji, than implementation of the development plans. This is especially the case with regard to up-grading village housing stock, diversifying cash and subsistence crops, modernising local schools and improving telecommunication links with Suva. The only development project which has had an equivalent impact on village livelihood in many parts of the periphery has been the construction of airstrips on several islands in Lau and Lomaiviti Provinces. As we argue later in this chapter and in chapter 10, improved linkage with the centres of development in Fiji is perceived by many residents to be one of the keys to a better quality of life in the periphery.

The 1970s and 1980s appear to have been particularly hazardous years for Fiji, and an impression one gains from reports on the country's post-colonial development is that natural disaster has been a continuous constraint to the achievement of rural and national development objectives. As we show in chapter 4, however, when the time frame for analysis is extended back for a century there is nothing particularly exceptional about either the magnitude or incidence of physical events during the 1970s and 1980s. What is exceptional is the cost of rehabilitation after these events for the communities concerned, the Fiji government and the international agencies which have responded to requests for financial and material assistance.

Another legacy of colonialism

The response of Fijian communities to natural disaster has been discussed at length in publications produced by the UNESCO MAB team.[1] In these studies it is stressed that before colonial intrusion Fijians were much more self-reliant in their strategies for coping with natural disaster than they are today. While there are many dimensions to the destruction of this self-reliance in the face of disaster, one of the most important is considered to be government intervention during the colonial period in the rehabilitation of communities affected by extreme events.

The first recorded instance of government relief for Fijians affected by a hurricane was in the mid-1880s (McLean 1977). In the following century the amount of post-disaster assistance to victims of hurricanes, floods and droughts increased steadily. In large measure this occurred because the administration perceived that a change had occurred in the capacity of communities to cope with the impact of disaster as relations of production were transformed by capitalism. This was not necessarily the Fijians' perception, as was demonstrated at times when Fijian administrators differed quite markedly from their European counterparts in the assess-

---

[1] Publications on responses to the hurricane hazard in eastern Fiji by members of the UNESCO team include Bayliss-Smith (1977a), M. Brookfield (1977), Campbell (1977 and 1984), and McLean (1977 and 1980a). Campbell's (1984) book, *Dealing with disaster: hurricane response in Fiji* contains the most detailed assessment of the role of the state in disaster relief in Fiji.

ment of post-disaster damage and need for assistance. In fact the provision of relief by central government became, in itself, a major factor in the destruction of community self-reliance in the face of hazard. By the time the colonial era came to a close the expectation of assistance by the state had become institutionalised as a 'coping strategy' throughout Fiji.

Before examining more closely this colonial legacy of increased vulnerability to natural hazards, it is necessary to describe briefly certain features of disaster mitigation and relief systems in the pre-colonial and colonial periods. In the 1980s the Government of Fiji is placing emphasis on greater community self-reliance in the face of disaster, and belated efforts are being made to re-introduce some elements of the 'traditional' response to natural hazards. Severe hurricanes undoubtedly caused great hardship at times for particular communities, but ethnographic reconstructions of Fijian society and economy in the eighteenth and nineteenth centuries suggest that many of the storms which caused serious damage to private property and public infrastructure in the 1970s would only have been a nuisance value in the pre-colonial period.

Aspects of pre-colonial coping strategies

The nature of pre-colonial coping strategies can be illustrated with reference to Kabara in the southern Lau group. We use this island as a case study in chapter 7; it is of relevance here because Campbell (1977) attempted to integrate into Thompson's (1938, 1940a, b, 1949) ethnographic reconstructions an assessment of the impact hurricanes would have had on 'traditional' Kabaran economy and society. Thompson and Campbell trace changes in population–resources relationships through several phases in the pre-colonial period and in this brief summary attention is focussed on the situation around 1800. By this stage Kabara's population was linked into an extensive network of exchange relationships throughout the Lau group and with Tonga to the east and the main islands of the Fiji group to the west. Kabarans were subject to demands for respect and tribute by chiefs on Lakeba, and their domestic economy had been influenced substantially by prolonged contact with Tongans seeking access to the stands of hardwood for which this island is renowned (see chapter 7).

Although yams and taro, the main subsistence crops of other parts of Fiji, do not grow well in Kabara, horticulture became increasingly important following the introduction by Tongans of the sweet potato. This was the staple root crop in the diet around 1800, supplemented with wild fruits, nuts, tubers, roots and leaves from the local forest, and imported yams and other cultivated crops from neighbouring volcanic islands. Thompson (1938 and 1949) has argued that there was a lively inter-island trade between coral limestone islands like Kabara and those of volcanic formation like Komo, Moala and Lakeba. The latter islands exchanged food for manufactured articles such as canoes and ceremonial bowls from Kabara. These linkages between islands with complementary resource endowments were of considerable importance in the context of pre-colonial disaster relief in the Lau islands. If food shortages on Kabara did result from extensive damage by hurricanes (or drought) to local subsistence gardens, supplies could be obtained from neighbouring islands if they had not been severely affected by the same extreme event. In the case of Kabara, there was also the permanent emergency supply of edible foods in the forest, although the taste for wild plants seems to have been lost as cultivated crops assumed increasing significance in the diet.

As far as material culture is concerned, Kabarans around 1800 were living in quite elaborate houses, the construction of which required specialised carpenters and large groups of people. Many were built following Tongan styles and there was a trend towards residence in closer proximity to the seashore than had been the case before extensive contact with Tongans. Both the structure and location of many houses lent themselves to damage from strong winds and storm surges. But the highly organised communal social structure, coupled with a ready supply of building materials in the forest, meant that reconstruction of damaged dwellings was carried out quickly.

In summary, although there was potential for hurricane damage to gardens and houses in pre-colonial Kabara, food stress was not necessarily great and losses were shared. Intra- and inter-community co-operation were clearly key factors in the rehabilitation of areas affected by extreme physical events. Complex chains of dependency relationships linked communities and islands throughout pre-colonial Fiji; relationships which could be exploited in different ways depending on circumstances.

The establishment of a centralised colonial administration in the 1870s did not change these relationships substantially until an attempt was made to restrict inter-island canoe traffic and to control large-scale ceremonial exchange of goods (*solevu*) (Sahlins 1962). As well as direct government intervention to discourage this interdependence, inter-island trade was also compromised by the dietary revolution accompanying introduction by Europeans of new crops (especially cassava) and imported foods. Another factor which was to play a significant role in the re-orientation of inter-island trade links was the demand for coconut oil and later copra for export to Europe. The former trading relationships between islands in the Lau group fell away as efforts were directed towards cash production, and outward links were re-oriented towards Levuka.

The effect of these innovations, together with the re-siting of villages on more readily accessible coastal flats, was to weaken Kabaran resilience in the face of hurricanes. It is true that cultural adjustments of previous times could be recalled, community effort was still available for village rebuilding, and it was still possible to get food from other islands to supplement the pickings from the forest. But, as Campbell (1977: 172) has suggested, 'The new way of life was based increasingly on dependence, and hardship, at least perceived, was greater than in the past.'

Creating new precedents

The hurricane of 3–4 March 1886 was considered by one contemporary European resident to rank 'first in importance of all storms experienced in the group for very many years' (Holmes 1887: 38). Approximately 60 people were reported killed, about 50 vessels were wrecked or damaged, and property on several islands in the eastern periphery was destroyed. The observations of colonial government officials who inspected the areas affected by this hurricane indicated that many of the traditional strategies for coping with disaster were in operation. Food shortages in Taveuni, Lomaiviti, Kadavu and parts of Lau were resolved by local residents 'in their own fashion'. In the case of certain Lau islands rations were provided where the hurricane followed a two year drought, and food scarcity was considered by the administration to be particularly severe.

In fact the colonial government did not make a practice of providing food relief after tropical storms until well into the twentieth century. The major problems of coping with post-disaster food scarcity, house reconstruction and long-term agricultural rehabilitation were left in the hands of rural residents, especially in the more isolated areas. During the first forty years of colonial rule the costs to the administration of providing relief were very small; by far the greatest contributions of food and planting materials came from Fijian communities unaffected by hurricanes or drought. There was also a practice in the nineteenth century anyway of charging the costs of any government relief programme against the tax refunds for the provinces that benefited from the assistance. In this regard, Campbell (1984: 74) reports that in the case of hurricane relief provided in 1886 the charge against provincial tax refunds included a sizeable sum for yams received by the government free of charge from non-affected areas!

There was considerable diversity in response to hurricanes in different parts of Fiji. In the small outlying islands, where the great majority of the population remained village-resident, it seems that traditional responses to disaster remained relatively intact through to the 1940s. When a highly localised but very severe storm struck Kabara, Komo, Oneata and Moce in 1936 the Fijian District Commissioner for Lau, Ratu Sukuna, advised the central government that food relief was unnecessary: 'The people affected are about the hardiest in Fiji and no distress is anticipated.' (cited in McLean 1977: 45). As McLean points out, however, there is evidence to suggest that on Kabara at least, there was serious food shortage and local officials on the island specifically requested relief food supplies. In the event some food was sent at government expense but an observer of post-hurricane rehabilitation on Kabara in 1936 marvelled at the speed with which traditional coping mechanisms were implemented (Thompson 1940a).

The 1936 hurricane in Lau, and a subsequent event in 1948 posed a question which was to become particularly significant in the 1970s – how is 'need' for relief best assessed? In the case of events in the 1930s and 1940s the government assumed communities would need assistance if a severe storm struck their island. McLean (1977) reports in his detailed review of the 1948 hurricane relief programme that a committee under the chairmanship of the Governor decided to despatch emergency rations to the affected islands immediately using an RNZAF Catalina flying boat. But while the 'Lauan airlift' was a successful operation in logistical terms, McLean (1977: 54) questions whether it was ever necessary in southern Lau; it appears there was sufficient food on hand to last until supplies could be dispatched by boat. By this time, however, food relief had become institutionalised as a response to disaster in all parts of Fiji.

Hurricane relief after Independence

After almost a decade of comparatively tranquil weather, Fiji experienced one of the worst tropical storms in living memory in October 1972. In addition to its severity as a climatic event, Cyclone Bebe proved to be particularly traumatic for two reasons. It was the first major disaster to test the resources and resourcefulness of Fiji's post-colonial administration and this test was made all the more demanding both for the residents and the government by the long gap since the last serious hurricane. Secondly the physical impact of Cyclone Bebe was not confined to a particular part of Fiji – it devastated communities in all regions. The government's response to Bebe established several new precedents in post-disaster relief in Fiji. Three of the most important from the point of view of village residents were the scale of food relief, assistance with house rehabilitation, and the reconstruction of schools.

The international response to Cyclone Bebe was unprecedented in Fiji's experience and the volume of aid in both cash and materials far exceeded that supplied by external donors during the entire colonial period. In part this reflected the scale of damage and personal hardship caused by this storm in a small country which was no longer the 'responsibility' of a particular colonial power; in part it was due to prompt action by the Fiji government in setting up a high-level committee, chaired by the Prime Minister, to co-ordinate relief operations. The Prime Minister's Hurricane Relief Committee (PMHRC), whose policies and programmes have been described at length by Campbell (1984), co-ordinated disaster relief operations in Fiji for a decade after Cyclone Bebe and played a very major role in the post-colonial development of areas, like the eastern islands, which were frequently in the paths of tropical storms.

Village housing

State-organised disaster relief contributed to the material development of peripheral areas in several ways. Probably the most conspicuous legacy of hurricane relief in eastern Fiji is to be found in village housing. During the 1970s the housing stock of entire communities was replaced, largely at government expense. Although the PMHRC was unable to assume responsibility for rehabilitation of all housing damaged in hurricanes in Fiji (it simply did not have the resources available to do this, especially in the first few years of its operations), Campbell (1984: 113) argues that 'the Committee became committed to financing extremely soft loans to those who had no fixed or guaranteed cash incomes.' The largest group in this category were Fijian villagers participating in the mixed cash-subsistence rural economy. Regions like the eastern periphery, where the great majority of residents are Fijians living in villages, were thus in a good position to receive financial assistance to rehabilitate housing.

Building programmes in villages covered by our initial field inquiries in the southern Lau islands in the mid-1970s demonstrated clearly that this government assistance was certainly exploited. On Kabara, for example, between 1972 and 1976 the proportion of housing stock that was classed as 'modern' increased from 5 per cent to 40 per cent. The cost of materials supplied by the PMHRC totalled approximately $14,000 and the expectation was that this money would be eventually refunded. In fact most of the PMHRC's loans for house reconstruction and repair have never been repaid either on Kabara or elsewhere in Fiji. The loans scheme was abandoned in the late 1970s when the Committee received substantial aid from the EEC to fund reconstruction of housing damaged by hurricanes. One stipulation of the EEC aid was that all buildings be constructed free of charge, with transport costs of materials being covered by the government, and the labour and other costs by the PMHRC (Campbell 1984: 121).

6 Hurricane-proof housing (right) in Naikeleyaga village, Kabara (RBD photograph, 1983). This design is less vulnerable than either traditional thatched houses or locally-designed corrugated iron buildings (for example, left).

Economic activities

Another legacy of hurricane relief programmes is to be found in some subsistence gardens. In an endeavour to reduce the need to continue supplying rations for several months after a storm that destroyed the staple root crops of cassava and sweet potato, a range of quick-growing vegetables was supplied to villagers along with schedules for garden rehabilitation. However, this attempt to diversify the subsistence crop base, and to encourage cultivation of indigenous plants such as yams which were more resistant to wind and water damage, has met with limited success. Use of imported foods in the diet has increased dramatically in rural Fiji over the past 20 years, and the tendency to supply such foods in the ration allowances after natural disasters has discouraged more self-reliant strategies. After the hurricanes which devastated the rural economy of eastern Fiji in the early 1970s (see chapters 4 and 7 for further details) the PMHRC made available food relief on a very generous scale. It could afford to do this because overseas aid covered most of the costs. By the 1980s, however, the Committee was endeavouring to reduce this dependence on imported food relief after natural disasters, much to the annoyance of many villagers who could recall the more generous allowances of the early 1970s.

An essential ingredient of the house reconstruction and garden rehabilitation programmes were tools which remained on the island and usually ended up as the personal property of particular villagers. Some of these tools, such as chain saws, contributed substantially to household economic activities. On Kabara, for example, chain saws made a substantial contribution to the cash-earning activities of those households which specialised in carving the large ceremonial kava drinking bowls (*tanoa*) (Bedford et al. 1978). They have also stimulated interest in a more concerted effort to exploit the forest resources by establishing a handicraft manufacturing factory on the island. This was one of the enterprises being considered by villagers when we returned to Kabara briefly in 1983.

The cost of hurricane damage

In concluding this overview of hurricane relief in the post-colonial period, reference should be made to the PMHRC's school reconstruction programme. Most primary schools in Fiji have been heavily subsidised by the communities which supply the pupils. The PMHRC recognised early in its deliberations on hurricane relief that in areas devastated by natural disaster there would be considerable delays in getting school buildings back to working condition if this task was left to the residents. The Committee undertook to fund school reconstruction entirely from its resources and, according to Campbell (1984: 129), 'in the ten years from Cyclone Bebe through Cyclone Arthur the Committee never wavered from that early decision.' The reconstruction of school buildings between 1972 and 1982 accounted for just over half of the total expenditure incurred by the Committee (Table 6.3).

It is impossible to quantify precisely the cost in dollar equivalents of the damage to people and their property and prospects caused by natural disaster. In the case of hurricanes in Fiji between 1972 and 1982, Campbell (1984: 105) has hazarded a guess at the cost of damage to private and public property and he suggests that it could be in the region of $70 million. This includes estimates for damage to infrastructure provided by the State, the costs borne by the victims themselves either directly from insurance claims or through assistance from relatives and friends, the value of international aid in cash and kind, and the expenditure on rehabilitation programmes by the PMHRC. While the magnitude of this estimated total is subject to much debate, the important point which emerges about disaster relief during this period is that the PMHRC, which incurred expenditure of $2.5 million, was directly responsible for covering a very small share of the total cost. Of course its role in co-ordinating the relief efforts ensured the real impact of the Committee's activities was much greater.

Table 6.3 *Expenditure of the Prime Minister's Relief fund, 1972–82*

Item	Expenditure	
	$ Fijian	% of total
Reconstruction	1,324,258	51.5
Wages	504,990	19.6
Transport hire & fuel	346,827	13.5
Equipment, plant, tools	218,266	8.5
Food relief and rehabilitation	98,502	3.8
Miscellaneous	78,410	3.1
Total	2,571,253	100.0

Source: Campbell (1984: 100).

An impression that can be gained from the popular press and public reports on hurricane relief in Fiji is that this Committee had substantial resources at its disposal and was actually responsible for incurring most of the expenditure to mitigate the effects of natural disaster. It probably covered a higher proportion of costs of rehabilitating communities on small islands, where the population is mainly village-based and the extent of government infrastructure exposed to damage is relatively limited, than it did in rural areas on the main islands. This certainly seems to be the case with housing relief.

The community response

In eastern Fiji, as elsewhere, residents had to bear substantial costs themselves, especially in terms of loss of cash earnings when coconut groves were devastated, fishing boats wrecked, and small business enterprises destroyed. A common response to this dimension of natural disaster was the migration of adult men in particular in search of work in other parts of the country. The Department of Labour has endeavoured to assist such migrants, either by finding them temporary work in state-run enterprises (such as the Fiji Pine Scheme on Viti Levu) or by giving men from devastated areas priority in the queue for the limited number of work permits issued for short-term employment in New Zealand.

This sort of government assistance was certainly instrumental in the reconstruction of Kabara's shattered villages and rural economy in the mid-1970s (Bedford 1976; Bedford et al. 1978; Campbell 1977). Along with food aid, the provision of building materials, and the reconstruction of community institutions such as schools, help in obtaining wage employment has generated responses among villagers which reflect a deepening dependence on the government in times of crisis. These responses also reflect an active exploitation of the government's ideological commitment to sustaining a viable village-based society in the small islands, a point we return to in the Kabara case study in chapter 7. In this sense there are positive dimensions to dependent development from the perspective of some villagers, especially those who know their way into the maze of bureaucracy and who can use the planner's rhetoric to further their aspirations for a higher material standard of living in the islands.

Depopulation and repopulation

The coincidence in time and space of severe hurricanes between 1973 and 1975 and the major research phase of the UNESCO project ensured that migration was a very topical issue in communities selected as sites for intensive field inquiry. As we show in the next three chapters, household surveys in several villages in Lau, Lomaiviti and Taveuni in 1974 and 1975 revealed the extent to which young adults especially were absent from their communities working elsewhere. The impression gained in some places was of an accelerating exodus of productive and reproductive men and women; an exodus which was perceived by some of those left behind as threatening the very fabric of community life in the small islands (Bedford 1980a).

This gloomy perspective on the demographic future for many small islands in Fiji was also held by members of a UNDP regional planning team. In a discussion paper on the future population carrying capacity of the smaller islands, it was noted that extensive emigration was a clear indication of dissatisfaction with living conditions in the periphery (Titley 1976). The team stressed that levels of public investment required to diversify the rural economy and provide an adequate service infrastructure to satisfy local aspirations in many of the eastern islands would be neither equitable nor politically expedient given the small proportion of the national population that lived in this part of Fiji. They concluded that natural increase in the population had to be offset continually by emigration if undue pressure of numbers on limited resources was to be avoided in the eastern islands.

The UNESCO team, while agreeing that heavy investment in social facilities and employment opportunities in all islands was not feasible, were unable to accept the assumption that the eastern region did not have the resources to support a larger population at a higher standard of living. To assume as a basis for development planning in the 1980s and 1990s that such a large proportion of the region's projected population growth must inevitably be lost to other areas through out-migration seemed to us to be unnecessarily wasteful of both natural and human resources. In the mid-1970s we argued that in this part of Fiji there was quite serious under-population, and that lack of people was a major constraint limiting development of resources on most of the larger islands (UNESCO/ UNFPA Project 1977).

These different perspectives on prospects for the periphery, which are explored in much greater depth in the next four chapters, provide a useful point of departure for an examination of processes affecting the size, structure and projected growth of eastern Fiji's population. Although internal migration is now the major regulator of population numbers and age–sex structures in this region, we begin with some observations on fertility. An apparent turn-around in the late 1970s in Fiji's internationally recognised transition towards lower birth rates since 1960 had had an impact on both the perceptions and the reality of population trends in the periphery as well as for the country as a whole. This is followed by a brief review of the role of migration in the population dynamics of eastern Fiji since 1966. The migration process received considerable attention in our research in the mid-1970s, and some behavioural aspects are examined in greater detail in chapters containing the village case studies. A brief comment on some implications of the trend towards absolute population decline in parts of the periphery between 1966 and 1976 for regional population projections and development planning concludes this overview of population dynamics.

Population trends since 1960: a national perspective

According to one recent analysis of population growth in Fiji, two quite distinctive periods can be identified since the early 1960s (Bienefeld 1984). The first of these, between 1960 and 1975, was characterised by a significant decline in the rate of growth. This was caused by a substantial drop in birth rates, especially between 1960 and 1970, and a sharp increase in the level of non-Fijian net emigration in the early 1970s (Table 6.4). These two processes effectively reduced the overall rate of growth in Fiji's population from around 3.3 per cent per annum in 1960 to 1.9 per cent per annum in 1976. An indication of the implications of these changes for the size of Fiji's population in the early 1980s was given by the Fiji Employment and Development Mission, when they observed that if there had been no reduction in population growth rates after 1960, the population of the country would have been at least 870,000 in December 1983 compared with an estimated total for the end of that year of around 690,000 (Bienefeld 1984: 1).

There is some uncertainty about actual levels of fertility in Fiji during

Table 6.4 *Estimates of fertility, mortality and international migration,*
1962–76

Measure	Population		
	Fijians	Indo-Fijians	Total
Crude birth rate (o/oo)			
Bureau of Statistics[a]			
1962	37.8	42.6	39.6
1966	36.9	34.6	34.9
1972	28.3 (30.4)	27.9 (28.5)	28.0 (29.3)
1976	27.0 (31.2)	29.4 (30.0)	29.0 (30.2)
Zwart (1979)[b]			
1966	39.3	39.9	N.A.
1976	31.6	30.9	N.A.
Total fertility rate			
(per woman)			
Zwart (1979)			
1966	5.58	5.51	N.A.
1976	4.26	3.47	N.A.
Crude death rate (o/oo)			
Bureau of Statistics			
1962	7.4	5.5	6.3
1966	5.0	5.4	5.2
1972	4.8 (5.5)	4.9 (5.3)	4.9 (5.3)
1976	3.9 (5.9)	4.7 (5.5)	4.4 (5.7)
Life expectancy at birth			
(years)			
Zwart (1979)			
1976	62.3	61.0	N.A.
Net migration			
Connell (1985)[c]			
1962–9	+820	−1,971	−4,173
1970–6	−532	−12,208	−25,331

[a] Estimates prepared by the Bureau of Statistics are based on data supplied by the Registrar General's Department which administers Fiji's birth and death registration. The figures for 1972 and 1976 in parenthesis are estimates by the Health Department based on data compiled by nurses throughout the country. These are generally believed to be better estimates than those based on the registration data (see Note 2).

[b] Zwart's estimates are based on data collected on fertility in the censuses in 1966 and 1976.

[c] Connell's data come from Jones (1976) and Central Planning Office (1980b). In both sources there are inconsistencies in the data and the estimates of net migration gains/losses between 1962 and 1969 especially should be treated with caution.

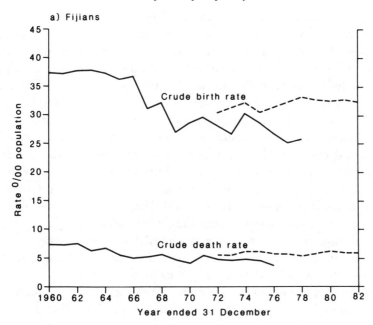

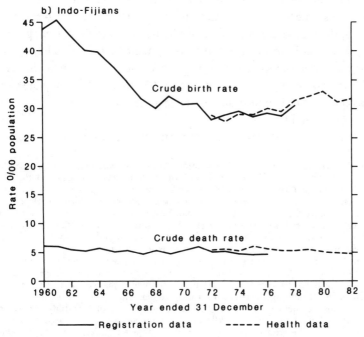

6.1 Fijian and Indo-Fijian populations, crude birth and death rates, 1960–82

the 1960s and early 1970s because of inadequacies with the birth registration data,[2] but it is generally accepted that the government-sponsored family planning programme played an important role in the decline of Fijian birth rates in particular.[3] Although evidence of a decline in Fijian fertility between the censuses in 1966 and 1976 is incontestable, it is apparent from records maintained by the Ministry of Health that between 1973 and 1976 crude birth rates had plateaued, rather than continued to decline as suggested in the vital registration data (Fig. 6.1). It was found during field surveys in rural communities on Taveuni and Kabara in 1974 and 1975 that there was little interest in family planning; the government's programme has lost considerable impetus after Independence (Bedford 1978; Bedford et al. 1978). The government's position on family planning shifted significantly during the 1970s, and by 1980 there was little official interest in a campaign aimed directly at reducing fertility levels. Family planning was seen to be part of the domain of maternal and child health care rather than a policy issue in its own right.

The gradual rise in crude birth rates, during the late 1970s, and their current fluctuation around levels reminiscent of those found in the mid-1960s, can be ascribed in part to progressive changes in the age–sex composition of the Fijian and Indo-Fijian populations. The proportion of fertile women in both populations has been increasing steadily since the mid-1960s and it was not anticipated that this would stabilise until the early 1980s. The higher birth rates since the mid-1970s are also a response to the shift in government policy on the issue of family planning. In the view of the Fiji Employment and Development Mission this has been an unfortunate demographic development because it will have 'a vital effect on the scale of the labour absorption problem that will face Fiji at the end of this century, and on the number of dependents to be provided for by the interim' (Bienefeld 1984: 2).

Trends in natural increase, international migration and population

---

[2] The deficiencies of Fiji's vital registration data have been explained in depth in McArthur (1967), and Zwart (1968 and 1979). It is generally accepted that more reliable data on births and deaths, especially among the Fijian population, can be obtained from records maintained by nursing staff in the Medical Department. There are also deficiencies with these data, especially when birth and death rates are calculated at a sub-national level. The reason for this is that the effects of internal migration in the various medical areas are not taken into account in the derivation of base populations used in the calculation of the rates.

[3] Zwart (1979: 123) estimated from census data that 84 per cent of the decline in the total fertility rate for Fijians between 1966 and 1976 was due to changes in marital fertility (such as decisions to limit family size) while changes in marital structure (such as age at marriage) accounted for only 16 per cent of the decline. In the case of Indo-Fijians, a higher proportion of the change in total fertility came from structural shifts (25 per cent) reflecting a trend since the mid-1940s towards a higher age at marriage among Indo-Fijian women (McArthur 1971; World Fertility Survey 1976; Zwart 1979).

Table 6.5 *Natural increase, net emigration and population growth,*
1976–82

Year ended 31 December	Natural increase (per 100 people)		Net emigration (numbers)		Population growth (per 100 people)	
	F	I–F	F	I–F	F	I–F
1976	2.53	2.45	−520	−2,151	2.33	1.70
1977	2.67	2.43	−253	−1,418	2.58	1.95
1978	2.79	2.63	−261	−1,683	2.69	2.08
1979	2.69	2.67	−161	−1,443	2.63	2.20
1980	2.62	2.79	−289	−1,517	2.52	2.32
1981	2.66	2.68	−224	−2,364	2.59	1.87
1982	2.65	2.69	−266	−2,350	2.56	1.97

F   – Fijians
I–F – Indo-Fijians
Source: Bienefeld (1984: 541–2).

growth for Fijians and Indo-Fijians since 1976 are summarised in Table 6.5. The estimates of natural increase suggest that differences which emerged between the two ethnic groups in the late 1960s and early 1970s had narrowed considerably by the early 1980s (see Fig. 6.1). However, substantial differences between Fijians and Indo-Fijians in the balance of resident arrivals over departures have persisted with much larger net losses to the latter population. This has had the effect of keeping the annual rate of growth in the Indo-Fijian component close to 2.0 per cent per annum since 1976. In the case of the Fijians, however, population growth has consistently been above 2.5 per cent per annum since 1977. In fact the real rates of natural increase and population growth for the Fijian population are likely to be higher than those shown in Table 6.5. The figures for annual births and deaths supplied by the Ministry of Health are known to understate Fijian vital events.

Fertility and natural increase in the periphery

The most significant implication of these national demographic trends for population change in the small island periphery relates to the Fijian rate of natural increase. Fertility and international migration tends, among Indo-Fijians, to have little direct impact on population trends outside of Viti Levu and Vanua Levu, although as we indicated in chapter 5, highly localised concentrations of Indo-Fijians can be found in parts of the eastern region (for example in Levuka town on Ovalau, in some settle-

Table 6.6 *Crude birth rates in eastern Fiji, 1972–4*

Area[a]	Year		
	1972	1973	1974
Lakeba Medical Area	20.4	20.0	23.0
Lakeba Subdivision	20.7	17.0	19.7
Lau Province	21.3	15.3	20.4
Lomaiviti Province	23.4	21.1	22.9
Eastern Division	22.0	18.3	22.7
Fiji (Fijians)	28.2	26.8	30.1
Corrected estimates[b]	30.4	31.2	30.8

[a] Derived from medical records, Headquarters of the Eastern Division, Levuka.
[b] Corrected estimates, based on revised mid-year populations and up-dated birth records, are published in Bureau of Statistics (1977) and used in Figure 6.1.

ments and estates on Taveuni, and in certain parts of the northern Lau group where they comprise a significant component of the workforce on 'island estates' such as Mago and Kanacea). Over the eastern islands as a whole, however, Indo-Fijians and other non-Fijians comprised less than 15 per cent of the total enumerated population in 1976.

The suggestion in the national estimates for Fijian crude birth and death rates that the real decline in fertility in the 1960s had been arrested by the early 1970s confirms findings in local village surveys carried out by members of the UNESCO team between 1974 and 1976 (Bedford 1978; Bedford et al. 1978; Bedford & Brookfield 1979). Although estimates of crude birth rates prepared by the Ministry of Health for medical districts in Fiji suggested that fertility in the eastern islands was lower than the national average at this time (Table 6.6), it was evident from the results of our local surveys and the 1976 census that this was not the case in reality. The Ministry of Health's subnational estimates of vital rates are based on mid-year populations which are not corrected for internal migration. In a region like eastern Fiji, which has experienced continuous net emigration for many years, the Ministry's population estimates are invariably too high. This has the arithmetic effect of reducing the magnitude of the crude rates.

A much more reliable indicator of differential fertility levels over time is the mean number of live births per woman in each age group, or average parities. Zwart (1979) found that at all ages women in the Eastern Division had higher average parities than Fijians in the other Divisions, and substantially higher parities than Fijian women enumerated in urban centres (Fig. 6.2).

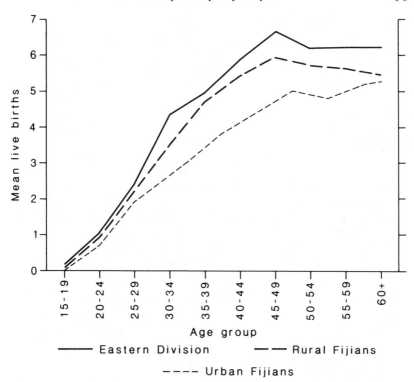

6.2 Mean live births per Fijian woman, by age group, 1976

The significance of this higher fertility in the mid-1970s for more recent population trends is that if the differential has persisted, then the rate of natural increase for Fijians in the periphery in the early 1980s will be higher than that estimated for the national population. Evidence obtained in some of our village surveys in 1983 suggested that fertility had increased, although an aggregate crude birth rate for the period since our initial surveys in the mid-1970s was lower than the national average for these years (see chapter 7 for a discussion of the village population data). The Ministry of Health's estimates of crude birth rates continue to suggest that fertility is lower in the Eastern Division than elsewhere in Fiji, even though this region now has the lowest incidence of contraceptive usage according to statistics compiled by medical staff responsible for administering the family planning programme (Table 6.7).

In the mid-1970s it seemed as if Lakeba had taken a lead in the dissemination and use of contraceptives for family planning (Bedford & Brookfield 1979), but by 1982 the region as a whole was very much a laggard in a flagging programme. Indeed, medical personnel went so far as to state in their annual report for the Eastern Division in 1982: 'It is too

Table 6.7 *Birth rates and family planning, 1983*

Division	Crude birth rate (all ethnic groups)	Fertility protection[a] (all ethnic groups)
Eastern	22.5	19.6
Central	33.6	33.0
Northern	31.2	26.7
Western	31.4	31.2
Fiji	31.6	30.2

[a] Percentage of women aged between 15 and 44 years using the pill or loop, together with those who had a tubal ligation, and those whose husbands were using condoms.
Source: Ministry of Health, unpublished tables on population, family planning, births and deaths for the year ended 31 December 1983.

obvious that the concept of family planning has not yet attained a serious place in the minds of people in this Division ... They don't face the problems they would if they lived in the rural and urban areas of Viti Levu. With this state of mind they do not think seriously about family planning'. Various reasons for an apparent lack of interest in family planning were expressed by residents during our village surveys in the mid-1970s and in 1983. One of the most common was that in populations which were being 'thinned' continuously of their younger and more dynamic members by migration to other parts of Fiji there needed to be high fertility if rural communities as viable social entities were to survive in the small islands. In eastern Fiji, as in many other parts of the Third World, the social and economic benefits to be gained from having several children are still perceived to outweigh the costs – especially by men.

In the light of these observations it seems realistic to assume that natural increase in the Eastern Division remains at least as high as the national average for the Fijian population. An overall Fijian average of 2.4 per cent annual growth was estimated for 1987 by the Bureau of Statistics (1987). However, as we noted in chapter 3, for many decades the rates of population growth have been much lower in eastern Fiji than among the Fijian population as a whole. The explanation for this lies in migration flows rather than fertility trends.

Migration and depopulation, 1966–86

In 1986 the eastern islands of Fiji were still the place of residence for almost 12 per cent of the total Fijian population (Table 6.8). However, the

Table 6.8 *Fijian population of eastern Fiji, 1966–86*

Census year	Province			
	Kadavu	Lau	Lomaiviti	E. Fiji
Population				
1966	8,426	15,561	11,241	35,228
1976	8,537	14,159	12,093	34,789
1986	9,630	13,894	14,592	38,116
AAGR 1966–76[a]	0.13	−0.94	0.73	−0.13
AAGR 1976–86	0.12	−0.19	1.88	0.91
% total Fijian population				
1966	4.2	7.7	5.6	17.4
1976	3.3	5.4	4.7	13.4
1986	2.9	4.2	4.4	11.6

[a] AAGR – average annual rate of population growth (per cent).
Sources: Zwart (1968), Lodhia (1978), Bureau of Statistics (1987).

eastern islands' contribution to the national total has been falling sharply since 1966, mainly as a result of absolute population decline in Lau Province. Between 1966 and 1986 the population of the Lau islands fell by 11 per cent, the only province in rural Fiji to experience absolute depopulation over this period.

Elsewhere in the eastern region the effects of migration were less dramatic, but everywhere it has left its mark. Between 1976 and 1986 the provinces of Kadavu, Lau and Lomaiviti together lost the equivalent of 22 per cent of their population aged between 5 and 49 in 1976 (Table 6.9). This rate of loss is three times the comparable figure (7 per cent) estimated for the total Fijian rural population. The emigration process is age selective – both the male and the female populations aged between 15 and 29 years in 1986 were more than 2,000 fewer than the expected number of survivors from those who had been enumerated in 1976 (see Table 6.9).

This heavy out-migration of young Fijian men and women is not a recent phenomenon. As we demonstrated in chapter 3, net emigration has been a fact of life for most of this century, and to those resident in the region migration is essential for the future well-being of small-island societies. None of the residents we interviewed in our village surveys wanted all those absentees with rights to land to return – in some villages they represented over 70 per cent of the total registered *mataqali* members (Bedford 1976; Bayliss-Smith 1978a). On the other hand, residents did not want migration to depopulate the islands to the extent that an active community life was no longer viable. For this reason the trend towards absolute population decline in some parts of the periphery during the last

Table 6.9 *Net migration losses between 1976 and 1986: estimates for Kadavu, Lau and Lomaiviti*

(a) *Numbers*			
Age group (1986 ages)	Differences between expected and enumerated populations, 1986		
	Males	Females	Total
Fijians			
15–29	−2,700	−2,200	−4,900
30–59	− 200	− 500	− 800
15–59	−2,900	−2,800	−5,700

(b) *Proportions*			
Age group (1976 ages)	Proportion of enumerated population in 1976 lost through emigration		
	Males	Females	Total
Fijians			
5–19	−35.5	−30.8	−33.2
20–49	− 3.7	−10.7	− 7.2
5–49	−22.2	−21.9	−22.1

Source: Estimates based on age-sex distributions of Fijians and Indians enumerated in the 1976 and 1986 censuses and life table survivorship ratios obtained from Zwart (1979, 143–6).

twenty years has caused some concern, both among community leaders in the islands and among some politicians and planners in Suva.

Lomaiviti and Lau: satellites of Suva?

Calculations of net migration gains and losses have been made for Lau and Lomaiviti for the three intercensal periods between 1956 and 1986 (Table 6.10). These calculations show that net losses in the last decade were somewhat smaller than they were between 1966 and 1976 for most age groups. It would seem that the ten years spanning Independence saw much heavier emigration for both Lau and Lomaiviti than was the case either before or since. Employment in the towns and in tourist hotels along the southern coast of Viti Levu expanded greatly in the late 1960s and early 1970s, and Fijians from the eastern islands were well placed to take advantage of new employment opportunities. In each of the three decades between 1956 and 1986 over 75 per cent of the net migration loss was represented by people, especially men, in the 15 to 29 years age group.

Table 6.10 *Fijian net migration gains and losses in Lau and Lomaiviti provinces, 1956–86*

Age group at end of census period	Province					
	Lau			Lomaiviti		
	Males	Females	Total	Males	Females	Total
15–29						
1956–66	−780	−580	−1,360	−350	−180	−530
1966–76	−1,500	−1,430	−2,930	−790	−630	−1,420
1976–86	−1,620	−1,190	−2,810	−650	−550	−1,200
30–59						
1956–66	−190	−280	−470	−40	−70	−110
1966–76	−390	−600	−990	−160	−200	−360
1976–86	−250	−390	−640	+80	−60	+20
15–59						
1956–66	−970	−860	−1,830	−390	−250	−640
1966–76	−1,890	−2,030	−3,920	−950	−830	−1,780
1976–86	−1,870	−1,580	−3,450	−570	−610	−1,180

Sources: Calculations using 1956, 1966, 1976 and 1986 age–sex distributions for the two provinces, and life table survivorship ratios obtained from UNESCO/UNFPA (1977, 126) and Zwart (1979, 143–6).

During the peak period of out-migration, which was the six years between Fiji's Independence and the 1976 census, 25 per cent of all the Fijians in Lau and 24 per cent of those in Lomaiviti in 1970 moved to another province.

The main destinations for these eastern islanders were the provinces containing Fiji's towns. In 1976 over 80 per cent of the Lau- and Lomaiviti-born absentees, including those who moved in the six years before the census, were resident in 'urban' provinces. More than half were enumerated in Suva itself. It is impossible to discuss many aspects of society and economy in these islands today without taking into consideration the communities from Lau and Lomaitivi in Suva; almost a quarter of the Fijians present in this city in 1976 had been born in the two eastern provinces (Bedford 1980a).

Taveuni: a more complex community

The situation in Taveuni District is rather different (Bedford 1978). On this island there were marked variations in population trends between the Fijian and the smaller Indo-Fijian populations, as well as between residents in the three types of rural community: nucleated village,

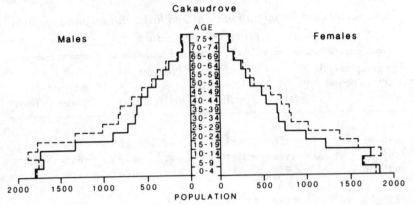

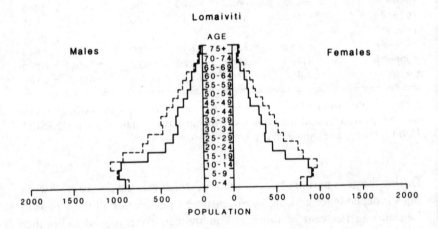

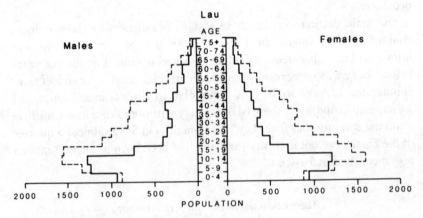

——————— Population enumerated in Province

- - - - - - - Population born in Province

6.3 Enumerated and natal populations, eastern Fiji 1976, by province

dispersed settlement and commercial plantation or estate. While the district as a whole did not experience such heavy net emigration as Lau and Lomaiviti Provinces, at the level of the individual community migration continues to have a profound impact on population dynamics, social life and economic activity. We demonstrate this impact in chapter 9 in a case study of a village in northeast Taveuni.

Although it is not possible to isolate Taveuni District in the published census tables on place of birth and place of usual residence in 1970, estimates of net migration by age group suggest that between 1966 and 1976 this area lost the equivalent of 10 per cent of its 1966 population. In the case of Lomaiviti the equivalent loss was almost 20 per cent, while in Lau it was 32 per cent. In all three cases the sex ratios and age composition of the net migration losses indicate that women and children were well represented in the population flows. Another dimension to these age–sex characteristics of inter-provincial migration in eastern Fiji is given in Figure 6.3. The pyramids indicate clearly the much greater effect that migration had on population structure in Lau Province. Whereas 80 per cent of the 'productive' men and women (aged 15 to 49 years) who had been born in Cakaudrove Province were still in residence in 1976, only 43 per cent of the relevant population born in Lau were living in the province in the mid-1970s (Fig. 6.3).

Migration, circulation and accessibility

The spatial patterns of inter-provincial migration in Fiji, and the age–sex characteristics of migrant populations have been discussed at length elsewhere and it is not proposed to review the detail of this analysis here.[4] Two points that should be noted are that family or household relocation has become much more common in recent years, and this suggests long-term rather than temporary movement from the eastern islands. Secondly, while the macro-level statistics contained in the census tables suggest the migration streams are heavily dominated by movement from the eastern islands to other parts of Fiji, there are important counter-streams. These can be detected at two levels. On the one hand there are the Fijians who had been born in other parts of Fiji who were enumerated in the region in 1976; in the case of Lau and Lomaiviti this group totalled around 4,000 and represented a quarter of the 16,000 locally born Fijians

---

[4] Some recent reviews of macro-dimensions to internal migration in Fiji include Bedford (1980a), Chandra (1981 & 1986), Connell (1985), Frazer (1982), UNESCO/UNFPA Project (1977), and Walsh (1982). There is also a chapter on internal migration in the Eighth Development Plan; the first of Fiji's official plans to include a comprehensive statement on migration trends and issues (Central Planning Office 1980b).

who had left. At another level, and one which cannot be detected in the aggregate census statistics, there is a very substantial circulation of population between rural communities in the periphery and the towns especially on Viti Levu.[5] This mobility can only be identified through field surveys, and in all the community studies carried out by the UNESCO team, circular migration was found to be a vital dimension to rural life in the 1970s.

As a result of extensive net out-migration from eastern Fiji (and, indeed from all parts of rural Fiji), there are now two components to any island's population – one resident in rural communities and the other in towns. Interaction between the two is fostered, in large measure, by villagers who periodically come to town seeking short-term employment or medical treatment, selling handicrafts and food, purchasing supplies or visiting friends and relatives. In addition children from the islands who are receiving their secondary education in schools located in the towns periodically return to their villages during vacations. This circular migration not only ensures that contact is maintained between different groups comprising an island's *de jure* population, but is also a most important process underlying contemporary social and economic change in the periphery. As we show in the village case studies, infusions of money earned outside the island provide a large part of the income to pay for food imports, houses built of permanent materials, school fees and so on. In addition, this intensive rural–urban interaction has led to the discovery of new marketing opportunities for certain kinds of produce and this, in turn, has stimulated both some diversification in rural economies as well as some return migration by Fijians with skills that can be used to exploit these opportunities.

As part of our policy recommendations in the mid-1970s for the development of the eastern islands, we argued that encouragement of population circulation, and its concomitant retention of a rural base, should be an integral component of development planning in Fiji (Brookfield & Bedford 1980). For certain parts of the rural Pacific, a relatively stable population, having ready access to local commercial centres and a range of employment opportunities in as well as outside of agriculture, is not a feasible policy option. Rather than attempting to provide jobs and other attractions to hold the populations on very small islands, a more

[5] Population circulation has only recently received explicit attention in the literature on migration in Fiji. Studies by three residents in Fiji are of particular relevance in this regard – Nair (1980 & 1985), Racule (1985) and Tubuna (1985). Several publications arising from research under the auspices of the UNESCO project also deal with this dimension to population movement in Fiji (Bedford 1978, 1980a, 1981, 1985; Bedford & Brookfield 1979; Bedford et al. 1978).

appropriate policy objective would be to promote active circular migration between local villages and urban centres on the larger islands.

The key to this strategy is obviously accessibility, and we discuss the critical importance of transport services in island development at length in chapter 10. Proposals to improve transport services to the small islands have been an integral component of the planner's rhetoric since the mid-1960s and in 1972 a major innovation for eastern Fiji was extension of the internal air network to Lakeba. Between 1976 and 1980 three more airstrips were opened in Lau Province (Vanua Balavu, Ono-i-Lau and Cicia) and four were opened in Lomaiviti (Ovalau, Koro, Gau and Wakaya). As part of the Development Plan Eight (DP8) strategy for the eastern islands, airstrips on Kadavu, Rotuma and Moala were brought into operation between 1980 and 1983, and it was planned to open another on Kabara before 1985.

In developing this network, the planners claim that 'air services in the Division will be closely monitored to ensure that the cost of air travel does not become beyond the means of the islanders themselves' (Central Planning Office 1980b: 201). While it is very doubtful whether the services to all these islands can be 'economical' in terms of fares covering operating costs, one likely consequence of the improved accessibility to the outer islands is that Fijians from these islands, who are in regular employment in town, will now find it easier to return to their villages for short periods. In turn, villagers requiring urgent access to urban services (or kin) will have a means of reaching their destination promptly as long as the air service is not co-opted by government officials merely to facilitate administration. If the experience of Lakeba is repeated in other parts of the eastern islands, then improved accessibility will not necessarily accelerate emigration to Viti Levu (Bedford & Brookfield 1979). Rather it will facilitate circulation of people between town and village, and assist those Fijians who wish to remain in a rural environment to satisfy their periodic demands for access to a wider range of social services and economic activities than can be found or provided on small islands.

After the coup d'état

As we have shown, one interesting feature of eastern Fiji in the period since Independence has been a conscious attempt on most islands to retain a 'traditional' socio-economic structure. The model that has been retained is the one established by the neo-traditional order during the first fifty years of colonial rule. As one of the objectives of the recent military coup is to reassert this neo-traditional order, especially in rural areas, it is reasonable to assume that communities in eastern Fiji will not be unduly alarmed by the rhetoric of General Rabuka and his supporters.

The economic effects of the coup, on the other hand, must add significantly to the region's 'hinterland penalty'. Devaluation of the Fijian dollar by 30 per cent between May and October 1987 will have a profound impact on fuel costs which, in turn, will affect freight rates and passenger fares. The price of imported foods and the market for handicrafts will also be affected.

The provision of services to the periphery will be influenced in indirect ways by the disruption to sugar and tourist industries. A substantial reduction in export receipts and income from tourism will make it impossible for the government to sustain its rural development programmes, despite their prominence in national development plans since the mid-1970s. Cuts in development assistance from neighbouring countries, particularly Australia and New Zealand, will also have an impact on rural Fiji. A large part of this external aid has been directed towards projects designed to diversify the rural economy and improve living standards in villages.[6]

Finally, the political upheaval could stimulate a return migration of Fijians who can no longer find work in the towns, tourist resorts and cane-cutting districts of Viti Levu and Vanua Levu. A limited return migration is sure to be appreciated in rural communities, especially those places where the numbers of young men and women are few in relation to children and elderly people. Elsewhere the capacity of small islands to absorb a sizable influx of migrants would be severely strained. The villages of the periphery may be perceived by Fijians as useful and desirable places for weathering post-coup recession and repression, but their long-term attraction depends on job opportunities not neo-traditional rhetoric. None of the fundamental relationships between centre and periphery that this chapter has identified have therefore been changed by the coup of April 1987; indeed, the 'hinterland penalty' seems in many ways to have multiplied.

[6] The long-term impact of the military coup upon external aid may be less negative than origianlly predicted. Once Ratu Sir Kamisese Mara was restored to office as Prime Minister in December 1987, France sent a special mission to Fiji whose activity produced a US$13m aid programme with a US$5m direct grant component – substantial sums for a country of 715 000 people. France official said at the time that their explicit aim was to nudge Australia and New Zealand into similar action, and such an outcome does now seem probable. From Malaysia and Indonesia too there are signs of an interest in trade agreements with Fiji. One year after the coup *The Economist* (London) commented: 'Since last year's military coups in Fiji, the South Pacific has begun to look disturbingly like the Balkans of a century ago: a region of small states whose very weakness helps them to enmesh stronger ones in their affairs and play these patrons off against one another' (307 (7545), 9 April 1988). Perhaps we can see this geopolitical position of islands as further evidence of a 'pampered periphery', albeit at the international rather than the subnational scale.

Conclusion

Exploiting dependence

At a macro-level, part of the explanation for the recent ebb and flow of population in eastern Fiji must lie in shifts and changes in the effectiveness of efforts by a government increasingly concerned to prevent a region of Fijian villages becoming completely marginalised within the country's evolving capitalist economy. Since 1970 residents in eastern Fiji have certainly witnessed quite a substantial flow of public goods and services into parts of the periphery, especially in the wake of natural disaster. For reasons which will become more apparent in chapter 10 patronage has been, and remains, an important element in the development of the eastern islands.

An explanation of recent population trends couched in terms of state intervention and subsidy is too simplistic. While this may be a pampered periphery in terms of its place in the ideological superstructure of Fiji's post-colonial state, it is also an area of considerable diversity in terms of opportunity for productive and rewarding endeavour. Residents have not been slow to perceive new opportunities, including the chance to exploit the various avenues of state subsidy and support for Fijian village society. In this regard a claim by Bertram and Watters (1985: 501), that development and dependence can 'go hand in hand and are not alternatives' in many small island societies in the Pacific, is relevant to eastern Fiji. As we show in subsequent chapters, these islands have many of the attributes of what Bertram and Watters have called MIRAB economies – economies in which the development process is now dominated by migration, remittances, aid and bureaucracy. But this is not the whole story, as we demonstrate in our village case studies and review of regional development.

7

Villages of adaptation: Batiki and Kabara

In this chapter the focus shifts to the individual islands in Eastern Fiji, and within those islands to particular village communities. In Fiji most of the indigenous population has lived in nucleated settlements since at least the early nineteenth century, and until about thirty years ago village life and Fijian life were regarded as virtually synonymous. In the post-war period the continuing influence of Ratu Sukuna (see chapter 3) upon a colonial administration already predisposed to 'economic development ... wedded to a sort of semi-socialist agrarianism' (Spate 1961: 50), ensured that for most Fijians the village remained the primary unit for social, economic and political activity. At the 1956 census over three-quarters of the Fijian population still lived in over a thousand villages, yet as Spate (1959) demonstrated, in some of these communities the symptoms of social disintegration could already be detected. This chapter and chapters 8 and 9 are concerned with the current status of about half of these thousand villages, those located in the eastern Fiji periphery.

We shall be drawing a distinction between villages where *adaptation* to the problems of island life has enabled the community to cope with fluctuating circumstances without undergoing radical change, and secondly villages where the alternative response of *structural transformation* has begun to take place. The costs and benefits of these alternative strategies will be reviewed with reference to village case studies on five different islands. In this chapter and the next we focus on villages on three islands within the Lau and Lomaiviti groups (Batiki, Kabara and Koro), in a part of Fiji still perceived as a stronghold of traditional village life. Despite this image, one hundred years of peripheral economic status within a nation state centred on Viti Levu has led to growing pressures for a compromise between the traditional ideology and the margin reality. The contradictions have been particularly hard to resolve on the small islands other than through the drastic solution of migration. We review the various manifestations of village adaptation on these 'traditional' islands, before considering in chapter 9 the more radically

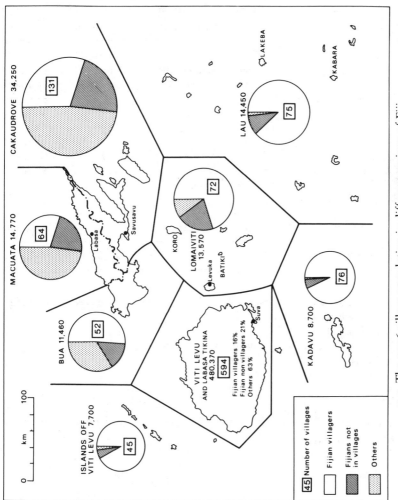

CAKAUDROVE 34,250 131

MACUATA 14,770 64

BUA 11,460 52

ISLANDS OFF VITI LEVU 7,700 45

LAU 14,450 75

LOMAIVITI 13,570 72

KADAVU 8,700 76

VITI LEVU AND LABASA TIKINA 480,370 594
Fijian villagers 16%
Fijian non villagers 21%
Others 63%

LAKEBA
KABARA
Savusavu
Labasa
KORO
Levuka
BATIKI
Suva

km 100
0

45 Number of villages

Fijian villagers

Fijians not in villages

Others

7.1 The 1976 village population in different regions of Fiji

Table 7.1 *The Fijian population living in villages, 1976*

Province or Region	Fijians enumerated in 'villages'[a]			
	Number	Average number per village	As % of total Fijian population	As % of total population
Macuata[b]	4,469	70	58%	30%
Cakaudrove	14,574	111	61%	43%
Bua	5,788	111	77%	51%
Lomaiviti	9,423	131	78%	70%
Kadavu	7,620	100	89%	88%
Lau	12,747	170	90%	88%
Islands off Viti Levu[c]	7,088	158	94%	92%
Fiji periphery	61,709	120	76%	59%
Fiji centre[d]	77,209	130	43%	16%

Notes:
[a] 'Villages' are all places described as villages in the 1976 census, but excluding places with only 1–2 households.
[b] excluding Labasa tikina.
[c] Yasawa group, Mamanuca group, Vatulele and Beqa.
[d] Viti Levu mainland and Labasa tikina.
Source: Lodhia (1978).

transformed village communities that are emerging on the islands of Lakeba and Taveuni.

Five hundred villages

The islands of the Fiji periphery contain over 500 villages, according to the 1976 census (Fig. 7.1). If we exclude places described as villages but consisting of only one or two households, we are left with 515 nucleated settlements containing 76 per cent of all the Fijians resident in the periphery. The proportion of Fijians living in villages rises to 90 per cent or more in Kadavu, Lau, most of Lomaiviti, and the offshore islands of Viti Levu. Everywhere the villages are overwhelmingly (over 97 per cent) Fijian in racial composition. They are very variable in size and the 1976 census indicates that in this respect there has been no change since G. K. Roth's time, when he wrote 'there is no such thing as a typical Fijian village: the population may vary from one with only twenty inhabitants to another of five hundred' (Roth 1953: 7). The population per village averages 130 in Lomaiviti and 170 in Lau, somewhat larger than those elsewhere in Fiji (Table 7.1).

Some of the large villages are becoming quasi-urban in character. On Lakeba, for example, Tubou (624 people) is an emerging local centre with traditional village functions, as well as a government station, boarding schools and an adjacent village suburb, Levuka. Other examples are Nasau (365) on Koro, Somosomo (339) on Taveuni, Nabouwalu (353) on Bua, and Vunisea (277) on Kadavu. These places are perhaps a modern equivalent of the 'towns' of early nineteenth century accounts: focal centres for local exchange networks, transport and administration, but with limited hinterlands. It is this limitation, together with their largely Fijian composition, which means we are still justified in treating these larger places as villages, rather than towns.

In fact, apart from Levuka and Savusavu, towns do not really exist in the Fiji periphery. Somosomo on Taveuni is a partial exception: if we take the village and a physically adjacent Indo-Fijian commercial settlement, together with the nearby government station and suburb of Waiyevo, then the collective, quasi-urban population amounts to over 1,500 people. At the other end of the eastern chain, on Lakeba, Tubou with the adjacent settlements mentioned above musters almost 1,000 people. Levuka and Savusavu are genuine small towns, but the urban population of both places is revealed as small and relatively stagnant if we exclude the Fijian villages which are included for statistical purposes within the urban areas. Savusavu, with 4,847 population in 1976 (but only 1,754 not living in the urban villages), grew at 1.1 per cent per annum during the preceding decade, well below the national average rate of population growth of 2.3 per cent. Levuka, total population 2,764 (but 1,367 not in villages), actually declined over the period 1966–76 by 0.8 per cent per annum, despite employment provided by a fish cannery and some tourism. In view of this history of very slow urbanisation in the periphery, it is hard to envisage any rapid transformation of even the 'quasi-urban' villages in the future.

Other forms of rural settlement are not well distinguished by the census, but they include dispersed Indo-Fijian farms ('settlements'), estate labour lines, and isolated farmsteads belonging to Fijians living on land holdings often remote from existing villages. Land settlement policies have encouraged independent farmers in this last category through loans and leasehold arrangements, but this growing component of the rural Fijian community is not represented in the more 'traditional' communities

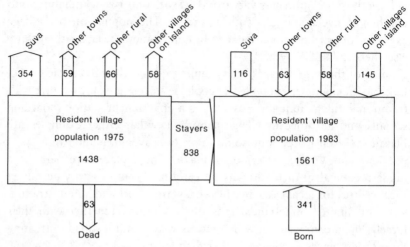

Aggregate population : 2161 persons

7.2 Aggregate population of selected villages in Taveuni, Koro, Batiki, Lakeba and Kabara: change, 1975–83

discussed in this chapter and the next. A summary account is given above in chapter 5, and the recent history of a settlement associated with a village in Taveuni is examined in chapter 9.

Villages on five islands

Village population change

A statistical analysis of population change in the 500 villages of the Fiji periphery would have to depend on census data. No doubt such an exercise would reveal a variable pattern of decline, stability and slow growth in village populations, as against the more steady growth that has occurred in other types of rural settlement and the more rapid growth of population in the central towns, particularly Suva. But national census data cannot reveal adequately the full range of processes that underlie population change in rural Fiji. Our own population censuses in 1975, which we repeated in 1983, covered selected villages on five islands: Taveuni, Koro, Batiki, Lakeba and Kabara. These data reveal that both male and female populations have undergone high turnover rates, as a result of mobility patterns of the kind already discussed in chapter 6.

We analyse these islands individually and in more detail later on, to determine what variations exist in the response of village communities to the opportunities and constraints of recent years. At this point we assume

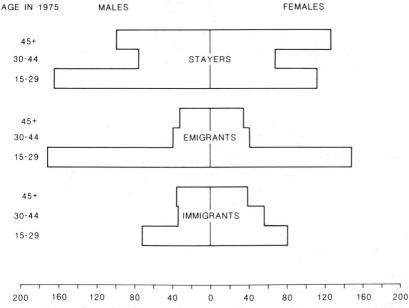

7.3 Age and sex distribution of stayers, emigrants and immigrants in the aggregate village population, 1975–83

that taken together the villages are broadly representative of their region, so that their aggregate population can be used to reveal some general patterns. Our surveys revealed that the aggregate village population had grown from 1,438 persons in 1975 to 1,561 in 1983, an average annual growth rate of 1.0 per cent (Fig. 7.2). But when we looked more closely at the names recorded on these two occasions, we found that only 58 per cent of the 1975 population was still present in the village eight years later. Out-migration rather than death accounts for the majority of these missing names. For migrants Suva is by far the main place of destination, although perhaps its importance is somewhat overstated by its role as the first port of call, but not necessarily the ultimate destination, of most persons leaving the islands. Nevertheless 77 per cent of emigrants in 1983 were reported as living in towns, mainly in Suva which accounted for 66 per cent of moves, with rural destinations accounting for only 23 per cent of moves.

The replacements in the 1983 population (i.e. those not present at the previous census) result almost as much from births (47 per cent of new names) as from in-migration (53 per cent), and it is significant that almost half of the immigrants are from rural rather than urban places. Migration removes more of the population aged 15–29 than other age groups. For every 100 persons aged 15–29 in 1975, 54 left the village in the following eight years to be replaced by only 26 newcomers (Fig. 7.3).

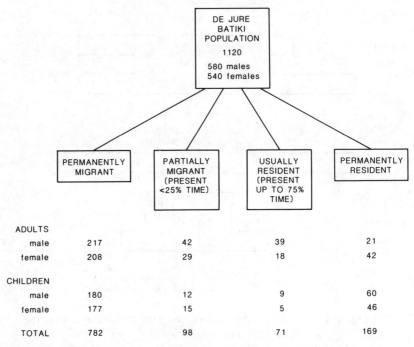

	PERMANENTLY MIGRANT	PARTIALLY MIGRANT (PRESENT <25% TIME)	USUALLY RESIDENT (PRESENT UP TO 75% TIME)	PERMANENTLY RESIDENT
ADULTS				
male	217	42	39	21
female	208	29	18	42
CHILDREN				
male	180	12	9	60
female	177	15	5	46
TOTAL	782	98	71	169

(DE JURE BATIKI POPULATION 1120, 580 males, 540 females)

7.4 Migration status of the *de jure* Batiki population in 1973–5

The mobility of the adult population is particularly marked on the smaller islands lacking in resources and employment opportunities, such as Batiki. For the two year period 1973–5, a record of all persons visiting the island showed that despite high copra prices 70 per cent of the *de jure* population (those with registered land rights) neither lived on the island nor visited it during this time (Fig. 7.4). Two-thirds of the Batiki population is now town-based, and those who appear to be permanent residents of the island represent only about 15 per cent of those who could live there. Yet the census eight years later showed that a number of the long-term absentees had ultimately returned, particularly men or women who had divorced or separated, unmarried mothers, and retired people.

Most of the village populations in the eastern islands therefore represent only a fraction of a larger dispersed population of migrants who retain tenurial rights and sentimental ties. For the *de jure* population the home village can fulfil a number of useful functions. For adults it is a place for holidays, it can be a refuge in time of trouble, and it is sometimes the retirement home. For their children it may provide a secure environment in which to grow up, a place where housing is cheap, where subsistence is reliably available, and where a congenial social life can be enjoyed. Young mothers gain support from the extended family, the elderly enjoy a position of some respect, and young children obtain easy access to primary schools, at the same time safeguarding their ultimate rights to the use of *mataqali* land. The village cannot usually provide secondary schools, well-paid jobs, or the social freedom of town life, but particularly for those who have grown up with it, it remains a cherished source of security, recreation, and, in times of need, a basic subsistence livelihood. Natural hazards or low commodity prices are both factors that can transform this expectation. Normally, however, villagers regard rural life as predictable and secure to the point of monotony. This is in contrast to the towns, which can be attractive in ways that small islands cannot be, but which also tend to be risky places where the unemployed become marginalised and increasingly demoralised by their dependent status.

In this situation, where the balance of advantage shifts with changes within the individual's life cycle, with changing job prospects in the centre, and with hurricanes, drought and attempts at 'rural development' in the periphery, it is not surprising that circular mobility patterns still predominate. Although in this chapter we focus on the village stage and the play that is unfolding there, we should not forget that village actors are part of a much larger cast which is performing more than one play simultaneously. Some scenes are played by some individuals on the village stage, but to understand much of what happens to people for long periods in their lives we must shift our attention to a different and larger theatre.

The village economy

The five sets of villages that we shall analyse were initially selected by the UNESCO/UNFPA project as geographically contrasted and hence likely to encompass some of the variability in environments and life styles in eastern Fiji. The islands concerned are Taveuni, Koro, Batiki, Lakeba and Kabara (see Fig. 7.1). Our expectation in the mid-1970s was that village populations on *Koro* ought to be among the most prosperous in the region, having plentiful land, a benign climate, fertile soils, and good shipping links to markets in Levuka and Suva. Nacamaki village on the north coast of Koro was chosen for detailed study because of baseline data available from the work of Watters (1969). *Batiki* possesses the same advantages of relative proximity to Viti Levu, but the island is smaller and drier and soils are less fertile. Our surveys covered the entire population of the island's four small villages. *Lakeba* in the Lau group has plentiful land but mostly of poor quality, and it suffers also from drought. Agricultural land is divided rather unequally between *mataqali*. Moreover in January 1975 the north of the island was badly damaged by Hurricane Val, at a

Table 7.2 *Summary statistics on the status of villages on five islands in eastern Fiji*

Island	Villages	Cash income per capita in 1974–6 ($)	Population growth 1975–83 (AAGR)
Koro	Nacamaki	158–174	+3.0%
Batiki	Mua, Yavu Naigani, Manuku	126–159	+0.6%
Lakeba	Yadrana, Nasaqalau	82–107	−0.4%
	Levuka	264–345	0.0%
Taveuni	Qeleni, Qeleni Road	101	+0.4%
Kabara	Naikeleyaga, Tokalau, Lomati, Udu	23–79	−0.4%

Note: Kabara income statistics exclude remittances, and population data refer to Naikeleyaga village only.

AAGR: average annual growth rate

Sources: Bayliss-Smith, 1977b, 1978a, 1977a; Bedford, 1978; Bedford et al. 1978; M. Brookfield 1977, 1979; and field notes.

time of falling copra prices and retail price inflation. Yadrana was selected as a typical traditional village in north Lakeba, while Levuka in the south provided a contrast as a virtually landless village much influenced by its proximity to the quasi-urban centre of Tubou. On *Taveuni* Qeleni village was chosen as representative of the Fijian population on an island where many have moved away from the village sector to become individual farmers on *mataqali* land, while those who prefer to remain in the village have limited access to land suitable for cash crops. Finally *Kabara* was chosen as one of the many islands in southern Lau that are remote, lacking in resources, and suffering in the early 1970s from repeated hurricane damage.

Summary statistics for these villages are shown in Table 7.2. The per capita income data obscure large variations between households, but on an average basis and excluding the special case of Levuka on Lakeba, it would appear that Nacamaki village on Koro was the most prosperous community in the mid-1970s, and Kabara the poorest. Events since that period have not greatly altered the relative rankings of these five islands, but the population data suggest that only on Koro and in Qeleni has the village been able to retain most of its population growth. What can we infer from this variable pattern of growth, stability and decline? Is it the case that the more prosperous communities are those which retain their

7 Village of Naigani, Batiki (TBS photograph, 1974). The survival of traditional thatched houses on Batiki is one indication of its marginal status relative to the copra economy, which is the main source of investment finance for modern housing materials.

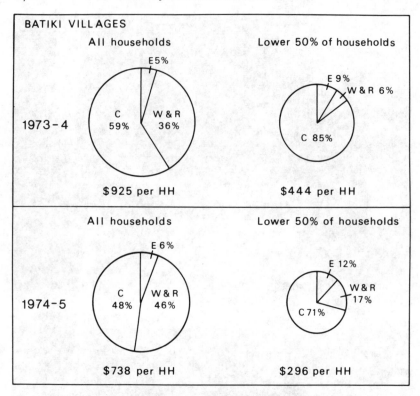

BATIKI VILLAGES

7.5 Income sources of households on Batiki, mid-1970s

expanding populations? A closer examination of the social and economic structure of these villages will show the form of rural development that is perceived by the people as providing opportunities superior to those that the outside world can offer. We consider first the islands of adaptation, Batiki and Kabara, small islands with a restricted resource base and few people.

Batiki

How small is beautiful?

Batiki is one of the smaller inhabited islands in the Fiji group. In eastern Fiji today fifteen of the forty or so inhabited islands have less land and support fewer people than Batiki, but many of these very small islands are either freehold property of foreigners (e.g. Wakaya, Mago) or they are coconut plantations managed effectively as outstations from neighbouring islands (e.g. Yanuca and Qelelevu, in Taveuni district). The problems of smallness are psychological as well as social and economic, and indeed the experience of Batiki would suggest that intangible factors are at least as important as material ones in determining whether or not a small Pacific island can sustain a viable community in the modern world.

There is nothing new about the resource problems of islands like Batiki. A visiting trader reported in 1834 that 'the island is small and nearly destitute of trees, it is not well watered so that they have no taro, yams are not very plenty,... at some seasons they must find grub scarce' (Anon. 1834). Batiki's 10 sq km may have supported as many as 500 people in 1840, when Captain Wilkes' expedition visited the island (Wilkes 1852). A reconstruction of the pre-colonial economy of the island shows that such a population could have achieved a subsistence livelihood and a 20 per cent production surplus by means of labour inputs quite similar to those of today (Bayliss-Smith 1980). By the time the first census was conducted in 1881, the population had fallen to 359, and despite improved health conditions and higher birth rates in the 1950s and 1960s, the general trend since the nineteenth century has been one of gradual decline to the present population of 245 persons. This resident population is outnumbered by the thousand or more people of Batiki origin who live elsewhere, predominantly in Suva but in some cases as far away as Australia.

Why has Batiki failed to maintain its population over the last few decades? Surveys covering the island's four villages in September 1974 indicated that household incomes on the island for the preceding 12 months averaged $925, of which copra contributed 59 per cent of the total. These figures imply an adequate welfare level and a not excessive dependence on copra, but there was growing polarisation between rich and poor households, and in poorer households copra provided a much higher proportion of the total (Fig. 7.5). If we take the 22 households on the island with annual incomes below the median level, then we find that copra earnings constitute 85 per cent of their total income (and 100 per cent in some cases). Twelve months later, in September 1975, the collapse in the copra price resulted in a fall in copra earnings. Whereas on some islands, for example Koro, villagers could shift back to *yaqona* as an alternative source of income, on Batiki no such alternative existed. Average earnings per household fell back to $738, and the decline was relatively more severe for the poorer half of the population: their incomes fell to $296 per household or $59 per capita, a level comparable to average incomes on the hurricane-damaged island of Kabara (see Table 7.2).

Table 7.3 *Household incomes in the mid-1970s: data for villages in Eastern Fiji*

Village and year	Number of households in sample	Cash income per household		Proportion of total income		Mean income per capita
				Upper quartile of house-holds	Lower quartile of house-holds	
		Mean	Median			
Nacamaki (KORO)						
9.73–8.74	41	$1,034	$866	46%	6%	$182
Mua, Yavu, Manuku and Naigani (BATIKI)						
10.73–9.74	44	$967	$704	55%	8%	$159
10.74–9.75	42	$773	$432	57%	4%	$126
Yadrana (LAKEBA)						
7.74–6.75	46	$848	$626	51%	7%	$124

Sources: Koro – Bayliss-Smith (1977b) and field notes; Batiki – Bayliss-Smith (1978a) and field notes; Lakeba – field data.

Inequalities between households

One reason for dissatisfaction with island life is the emergence of relative deprivation, an endemic feature of town life but something which also exists in the village setting, where it is now more clearly perceived than a generation ago. There are various reasons for this change, including increased population mobility and the presence in the village of government salary-earners who now form a privileged group enjoying a greater measure of security and prosperity than agriculture or fishing can provide. These income disparities have become noticeable only in the last decade, accentuated by government policy since Independence. Mass circular migration is also quite a recent phenomenon. There is evidence for considerable population circulation in the late nineteenth century, but colonial policies succeeded in discouraging Fijian mobility between islands (Bedford 1984). In 1958, Watters (1969) found on Koro that only 16 per cent of the population of Nacamaki village had ever travelled away from the island, whereas in 1974 75 per cent of the population had

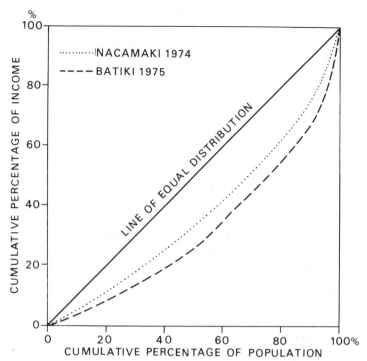

7.6 Lorenz curves showing income distribution between households, Nacamaki village, Koro, compared to villages on Batiki

migration experience, and only young children and a few very old people had never left the island. On Batiki, the process of circular migration may have begun at a somewhat earlier date, and the current situation of frequent contact between Suva and the island community (see Fig. 7.4) means that a knowledge of urban opportunities and non-village life styles is very widely shared.

The role of government salaries in the perception of relative deprivation is harder to assess. Even so, comments that were made to us on a number of occasions suggest that villagers in the Fiji periphery are well aware of the contrast between their irregular cash incomes and the financial security and relative affluence of the teachers, nurses, public works department employees, wireless operators, and even ministers of American or Australian-funded religious sects, who now reside in their midst. The inclusion of these salary earners in the village surveys that were done on Koro, Batiki and Lakeba means that average income per household or per capita is a rather inadequate indication of the situation of the majority of households. The upper quartile, or top 25 per cent of households, accounts for over half of the total income of the village, whereas the bottom quartile accounts for only 4–8 per cent of the total (Table 7.3). Batiki is distinctly more polarised in this respect than Nacamaki village on Koro (Fig. 7.6), and on Batiki the gap between rich and poor households widened somewhat during the mid-1970s. This factor certainly contributed to growing feelings of relative deprivation, encouraging out-migration and the search for alternative sources of income.

Satellite of Suva

Detailed surveys were not carried out on Batiki in 1983, but our observations suggest that little has changed. Its satellite status in relation to Suva seems to have become even more firmly established. The island's narrowly-based population pyramid implies that the resident population is no longer replacing itself in a demographic sense, and this is confirmed by the slow decline in total numbers. A high proportion of the children now living on Batiki were born in Suva and afterwards were transferred to the island, often for adoption by relatives. Island life still offers many advantages to the child, if not always to the mother. Many of the older people now living on the island have retired there after a working life spent living away.

These demographic trends can be contrasted with a striking lack of change in the economic basis of island life. In the early 1970s the emergence on Batiki of two commercial fishing boat schemes was a hopeful sign of greater autonomy and a reduced dependence on copra. The boats were seen as a means whereby the islanders could regain control over their links with the outside world, and exploit local reefs commercially for fish and trochus shell. The schemes were financed and operated partly by islanders themselves and partly by the Batiki community in Suva. In practice, however, although the fishing boats were useful for passenger trips to Suva and for shipping copra, they proved to be a disappointment as sources of income from fish, shellfish, and bêche-de-mer.[1] These items supplied a mere 2 per cent of total income in 1973–74,

---

[1] The larger boat, the *Marama-ni-Wai*, was acquired by Yavu and Manuku villages in 1971 with $15,000 in savings and a $11,000 loan from the Fiji Development Bank. Technical and financial expertise was supplied largely from the Batiki expatriate community in Suva, but labour was supplied by the villages concerned. By the end of 1976 the scheme was in trouble with loan repayments, and it would have become bankrupt but for free maintenance supplied by the Fisheries Division in Suva. In that year *Marama-ni-Wai* made 19 trips from Batiki to Suva carrying copra, which by then had emerged (along with passenger fares) as the principal source of revenue for the scheme. In 1983 the boat was still in existence, but it was laid up with engine trouble. On Batiki $1,800 out of the $3,000 needed for repairs had already been collected, but commercial fishing is now such a small part of the scheme that assistance from FDB or the Fisheries Division can no longer be counted upon.

and despite copra's collapse only 4 per cent in the following year (see Fig. 7.5). Wage employment in Suva or, on a temporary basis, in New Zealand, was considered to be a much more attractive option, particularly for young men and women without family responsibilities.

The efforts of Batiki villagers to gain control over transport links between their island and the capital are matched by numerous similar examples from elsewhere in Fiji and the Pacific islands (Couper 1973). If considered in relation to commercial shipping criteria, these village-based schemes are usually judged to be hopeless failures, since they seldom persist beyond the lifetime of one particular boat, a lifetime which itself may be terminated prematurely by shipwreck or bankruptcy. Commercial expansion in order to mount a sustained challenge to existing shipping interests is generally not envisaged by the organisers, but anyway it does not happen. Yet judged from the perspective of villagers the profit and loss account seems much more evenly balanced.

On Batiki the very small scale of cash benefits from fish, shellfish and bêche-de-mer was a disappointment, particularly in 1975 when an alternative to copra was so urgently needed. On the other hand the improved passenger service, cheaper freight rates, employment opportunities for islanders, better social links between the Suva community and the island, and perhaps above all the feeling of community involvement towards achieving some freedom from dependency upon existing trading companies, have all been major benefits, albeit intangible ones to some extent. Where social benefits outweigh financial costs in this way, then the methodology of commercial accountancy seems quite inappropriate. In the absence of alternative development options or other pressing needs (e.g. housing), shipping seems a reasonable investment for the savings of people on small islands. It may be cheaper for a government to subsidise these efforts in various ways than for it to provide itself the frequent shipping service which small islanders desire.

Alternatives for the future

There seems little immediate likelihood of Batiki becoming altogether

---

A second boat, the *Tomitomi*, was purchased in 1972 by the other two Batiki villages, but this scheme was never as successful. Persistent engine trouble led to the bankruptcy of the scheme in the later 1970s, and the sale of the boat to a Chinese trader on the neighbouring island of Gau. The same boat is now running successfully under a new name, and in 1982 it visited Batiki on six occasions for copra and freight. In the same year *Marama-ni-Wai* made 17 visits, but whereas in the mid-1970s the islanders were able to rely almost entirely on their own two boats (there were 41 copra-collecting trips in 1974, 40 in 1976), in 1982 *Marama-ni-Wai* accounted for only half of the 34 copra-collecting trips that were made to the island in that year.

depopulated. Its proximity to Levuka and Suva, its continuing social and symbolic role for the expatriate community, and its dependable resources of copra, cassava and fish, mean that for the foreseeable future Batiki will be the preferred place of residence for some individuals, and for others at some stages in their life cycle. But any more positive role for Batiki will depend upon what commercial opportunities can be exploited in addition to the rather modest subsistence base.

Copra production remains steady at around 140 tonnes per year, of which about 100 tonnes is shipped to Suva and the rest to Levuka. Maintenance of coconut groves is negligible and productivity per tree must suffer, but at present prices there is little incentive to intensify production. Most of the best flat land is already under coconuts, to the detriment of food crops which often have to be underplanted. It is not realistic to envisage any new cash crops emerging despite the efforts of extension workers from the Department of Agriculture to interest the farmers in peanuts and chillies. Without irrigation and fertiliser *yaqona* cultivation would be virtually impossible, and taro would require clearance of coconuts which have encroached on to the best areas of gley soils.

Livestock and handicrafts would appear to provide more promising possibilities for diversifying the economy. Two-thirds of the island's land area consists of inland slopes under dense *Miscanthus* reed thickets and light scrub, with poor soils (eutric cambisols). This land at present has no economic value, and it would probably revert to dry woodland if it were not burnt every few years (Latham 1983b). Efforts to fence off tracts of unused *mataqali* land for stock grazing would require agreement within the land-owning group, and perhaps more to the point would require a large investment in fencing. These factors have so far deterred any attempt at utilisation of the hills, but in 1983 one Manuku man had successfully converted his coconut groves into a goat farm. An initial investment of $1,000 purchased thirteen animals and enough fencing to keep them enclosed at night. Despite steady sales to other villagers and to the Indo-Fijian planter at Wainiketei (a leased plantation on Batiki), the herd has more than doubled in size. Cattle are also becoming important at Manuku, and sales have been made to visiting copra boats. With unreliable shipping but abundant low grade land, animal husbandry could provide a more appropriate source of livelihood for the islanders than agriculture.

A second development on Batiki is the increasing involvement by women in commercial handicrafts production. Nairai and Batiki, both dry, deforested islands unable to produce yams, taro or timber in any quantity, were famous in the pre-capitalist economy of Lomaiviti for their

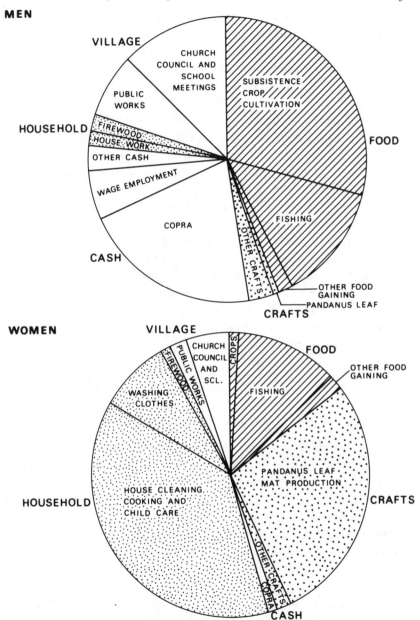

MEN

VILLAGE

CHURCH COUNCIL AND SCHOOL MEETINGS

PUBLIC WORKS

SUBSISTENCE CROP CULTIVATION

HOUSEHOLD

FIREWOOD

HOUSE WORK

OTHER CASH

FOOD

WAGE EMPLOYMENT

COPRA

CASH

FISHING

OTHER CRAFTS

OTHER FOOD GAINING

PANDANUS LEAF

CRAFTS

WOMEN

VILLAGE

CHURCH COUNCIL AND SCL.

PUBLIC WORKS

FIREWOOD

WASHING CLOTHES

CROPS

FISHING

FOOD

OTHER FOOD GAINING

PANDANUS LEAF MAT PRODUCTION

HOUSEHOLD

HOUSE CLEANING, COOKING AND CHILD CARE

CRAFTS

OTHER CRAFTS

COPRA

CASH

7.7 Allocation of working time on Batiki between different activities in September 1975; the activities shown occupied 38.8 and 44.9 hours per week for men and women respectively surplus production of labour-intensive handicrafts such as mats, baskets, sinnet and coconut oil (Jackson 1835; Eagleston 1831; Wilkes 1852). These skills are still maintained today, as indicated by the important position of handicrafts in the subsistence economy of the mid-1970s. Surveys were carried out on Batiki covering 65 person-weeks of daily activities in two villages (Bayliss-Smith 1978a). The results showed that processing pandanus leaves (*voivoi*) and weaving them into mats on average occupied every adult woman each for about 15 hours per week (Fig. 7.7). Sales of pandanus leaf or finished mats were still small-scale in the 1970s, but by 1983 both output and income were becoming much more substantial.[2] With a growing urban population in Fiji still using traditional mats but unable now to produce them themselves, and with demand for handicrafts swollen by tourist purchases, there appears to be a secure long-term market for such products. It is a market which could provide a useful means for mobilising reserves of female labour and initiative that in the village setting are often under-employed. Ironically surplus production of handicrafts is the same solution to the same problem of marginal status that faced Batiki 150 years ago, even though market incentives rather than ceremonial prestation are today the driving force behind this adaptation.

Kabara

A hazardous world?

Kabara in southern Lau was not only the remotest island studied by the UNESCO/UNFPA Project in the mid-1970s, but its environment is also quite different to that of other areas. In contrast to the mainly volcanic islands of Taveuni, Koro, Lakeba and Batiki, Kabara is essentially of limestone formation and quite poor in natural resources. As such, it is representative of more than a dozen limestone islands in eastern Fiji, some of them no longer inhabited. Forty years ago Kabara was described as 'a hazardous world where the struggle for existence is keen, land is poor and

[2] In 1974 only one household reported sales of pandanus leaf rolled into coils, but the following year eight households were supplementing their diminished copra income by selling coiled leaf, mats or baskets, although the total earnings of $350 were still negligible. By 1982 production was on a much larger scale, with pandanus being grown in substantial quantities particularly on some of the well-watered alluvial land formally used for taro. In that year a group of twenty women travelled to Suva with mats, and with the help of a Suva contact they were able to make sales estimated at $300 each, of which perhaps $30 would have gone on travel expenses. A few women returned home with money, but most converted their earnings into goods, especially items unobtainable in the very meagre village stores on Batiki. This single sales trip netted about $5,000, yet it only accounted for a few months of production.

food is scarce' (Thompson 1940b: viii). With an area of 53 km² of rough forest-covered limestone, a small volcanic outcrop and narrow coastal flats, the island has a harsh natural environment. Except for tiny pockets, soils are everywhere thin and deficient in nutrients. Rainfall is extremely variable and drought a frequent hazard. Hurricanes are an ever-present seasonal possibility. Because of the porosity of the limestone fresh water is a scarce resource; there are no streams on Kabara. As a result of soil and water deficiencies the main subsistence crops in other parts of Fiji – yams, taro and different varieties of bananas – do not grow well. Marine resources in the reefs and waters surrounding Kabara are also poor, even in comparison with other islands in southern Lau. The only important local natural resource is a hardwood forest in the limestone interior – a forest which enabled Kabara to become the centre of an extensive trade in wooden products embracing much of Fiji and extending to Tonga in the pre-colonial period. These products continue to provide a major source of income in the 1980s. Here we focus on aspects of contemporary society and economy on Kabara, with particular reference to the main village of Naikeleyaga, in an endeavour to explain why this island has remained home in spite of hazards for over 500 Fijians.

During the last few months of 1975, when Kabara was the site of several field inquiries within the UNESCO/UNFPA Project, the resident population was coping with the combined effects of two devastating hurricanes and a serious slump in markets for their major exports, copra and handicrafts. Forty years earlier, when a somewhat similar situation existed with a violent hurricane in 1936 and simultaneously chaos in the exchange economy during the Great Depression, the local response had been a return to an earlier life style. In the 1970s the response was quite different. The well-integrated system of specialisation in resource use which linked the ecologically diverse islands in southern Lau had been largely abandoned, as Kabara and its neighbours became more dependent on decisions affecting their livelihood made in Suva and outside Fiji. Ecological and economic crises now stimulate migration to other parts of Fiji or overseas, not a return to 'the old life'.

Village censuses on Kabara in October 1975 revealed that there had been a significant decline in population since the national census in 1966. Between 1956 and 1966, years of relative prosperity in the exchange economy, and also a period with few major cyclonic storms, the number of Fijians resident on Kabara rose by 21 per cent. Over the next nine years they fell by 23 per cent to reach the lowest number recorded since the late 1940s. During the late 1970s numbers resident on the island fluctuated somewhat, and at the time of a brief re-survey of the major village, Naikeleyaga, in July 1983 the population was just below that enumerated

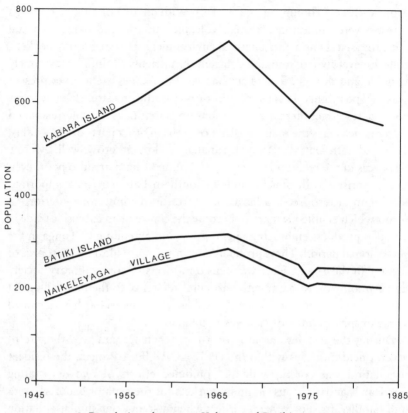

7.8 Population change on Kabara and Batiki, 1946–83

in October 1975 (Fig. 7.8). Between 1975 and 1983 the population increased quite rapidly as a result of natural increase, but net emigration held population growth in aggregate terms to around zero. Kabara, in common with Batiki and many other small islands in Fiji's eastern periphery, has been experiencing relative rather than absolute depopulation since the mid-1970s (see chapter 6).

While the extent of emigration is considerable (some indices of Kabaran emigration are given in Table 7.4), it is unexceptional in the context of developments in a region of small islands where opportunities for wage employment are very limited, and where the natural environment (among other factors) discourages diversification in agriculture. Of greater interest from the point of view of explaining contemporary socio-economic change in the periphery is the decision by a large number of Fijians to stay in places like Kabara, despite the 'costs'. It is the activities, aspirations and life style of these 'stayers' and of those who have chosen to return to Kabara from other parts of Fiji which require closer consideration.

Table 7.4 *Indicators of migration from Kabara, 1966–83*

Persons resident in village in 1966 and not there in 1975.	64%
Persons registered as members of Naikeleyaga mataqali and not resident in village in 1975.	73%
Households in 1975 with absentee heads in Suva.	30%
Households in 1975 with a son or daughter absent.	58%
Persons resident in villages in 1975 and not there in 1983.	47%

Source: Bedford 1976; Bedford et al. 1978; and field notes.

The village economy, 1973–83

Kabara's economy in the mid-1970s comprised five significant components: subsistence gardening and fishing, copra production, handicraft production, wages and remittance income obtained from outside the island, and assistance in cash and kind from the central government's hurricane relief programme. The local subsistence and cash economies were in a parlous state: root crops had been badly damaged by wind, rain and salt water; several fishing boats had been holed in the storms; copra production had fallen dramatically as a result of wind damage to the crowns of coconut palms, and exports of handicrafts had been compromised by a slump in Fiji's international tourist industry (Bedford 1976; Bedford et al. 1978). Cash incomes from sales of copra and handicrafts to local co-operative stores fell to less than $10 per capita during 1975, representing a derisory level of income from environmental sources by comparison with that available elsewhere in the region (see Table 7.2).

Household purchases from local co-operative society stores consistently exceeded the value of receipts from sales of copra and handicrafts to these stores. Kabara's population in 1975 was heavily dependent on savings and money earned mainly through wage employment on Viti Levu and in New Zealand. In October 1975 65 per cent of the households on the island had at least one of their members working in or seeking employment in Suva. Over half of these absentees had left during the previous eighteen months. Although no data on remittances are available, it is known that substantial sums of money (by local standards) came back to Kabara with men returning after three months work in New Zealand or a period of employment on Viti Levu.

The other important external input to the local economy in 1975 was hurricane relief supplied by the central government. The nature of hurricane relief in the 1970s has already been described in chapter 6, but it is worth recalling here that, in addition to emergency food supplies and temporary shelter, the hurricane relief committee also made available to

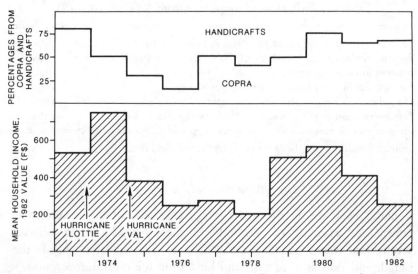

7.9 Household incomes (excluding remittances), showing proportion from copra and handicrafts, Naikeleyaga, Kabara, 1972–83

villagers materials for the construction of permanent houses (usually on a pay-later basis) including chain saws where local timber supplies were available for building purposes.

In 1983, according to informants who had been on Kabara for most of the period since 1975, the intervening years had been good ones in spite of the recurrence of cyclonic storms and a serious water shortage problem in several years (see chapter 4). The records of copra exports confirm that 1975 and 1976 were years of very low cash returns to local producers (Table 7.5). In 1977 production increased rapidly and during 1979, 1980 and 1981 the average income for 25 households in Naikeleyaga had almost reached the high level of the early 1970s. The mid-1970s were clearly exceptional years in the sense that over 70 per cent of income from sales of produce to the co-operative store came from handicrafts. By the early 1980s the situation was reversed: at least two-thirds of household income was obtained from sales of copra (Fig. 7.9).

Despite the changing contributions of handicraft sales and copra production to household incomes over the eight years, the structure of the village economy had not changed much. There had been no diversification in crop cultivation; indeed the limestone environment offers little prospect for innovation in this regard. The daily round of tasks for men and women was much the same as it had been in 1975, although certain individuals were endeavouring to promote more extensive development of the hardwood and fish resources. Production of surpluses for ceremonial

Table 7.5 *Exports of copra by Naikeleyaga and Tokalau Cooperative Societies, 1973–82*

Year	Tonnes exported	Income ($F)			Net return per tonne, 1982 value
		Gross receipts	Net receipts[a]	Net receipts, 1982 value	
1973	93	16,392	12,972	31,747	340
1974	20	10,562	9,637	20,617	1,010
1975	15	2,394	1,527	2,888	188
1976	14	2,652	1,855	3,150	220
1977	55	12,222	8,632	13,695	249
1978	35	7,714	5,002	7,482	213
1979	35	14,621	12,318	17,106	483
1980	98	27,918	21,533	26,117	265
1981	70	19,427	14,383	15,688	225
1982	49	13,619	9,731	9,731	200

Note: [a] After deductions for freight and cess.
Source: Data from Kabara Cooperative Society records, converted to 1982 value using Consumer Price Index of Cameron (1983b).

purposes remained an important dimension to economic activity especially in the late 1970s when the paramount chief of the Lau Islands, the Tui Nayau, made a *solevu* to his wife's people in Rewa (see Hooper 1982 for a detailed description of this presentation). In terms of the range of economic activities on Kabara in 1983, and the allocation of time to different tasks, adaptation rather than structural change had continued to be the dominant process. This was also evident in the continued dependence on external sources for income to finance the material standards of living which were regarded as basic to a satisfactory livelihood on the island in the latter part of the twentieth century.

Accompanying the increased value of locally generated cash incomes was a substantial growth in expenditure on consumer goods imported from other parts of Fiji and overseas. The heavy reliance on store-purchased goods, which was so characteristic of the mid-1970s when subsistence gardens were still recovering from hurricane damage, continued through the latter half of the decade and into the 1980s. The average expenditure in the Naikeleyaga co-operative by the 25 households in 1980 was $957 – in real terms almost double the expenditure level in the period 1973–6, and a reflection of the growing dependence on

Table 7.6 *Deposits, withdrawals and money order transfers, Kabara Post Office, 1979–82 ($ Fijian)*

Transaction	1979	1980	1981	1982
(a) Within Kabara				
Deposits	21,526	30,660	31,877	24,456
Withdrawals	29,805	42,388	47,538	26,827
Balance	−8,279	−11,728	−15,661	−2,371
(b) Between Kabara and rest of Fiji: (TMOs)				
Payments outward	20,423	26,592	37,602	38,953
Payments inward	17,571	25,156	32,680	34,460
Net flow outward	+2,852	+1,437	+4,922	+4,493

Source: Post Office records, Kabara, of (a) Savings Bank transactions, and (b) telegraphed money orders (TMOs).

cash generated outside the island for funding consumer expenditure. From 1979 onwards data on all post office savings accounts on Kabara show that withdrawals substantially exceeded the value of deposits (Table 7.6). This money not only subsidised household consumption of goods obtained from the local co-operative store, but also contributed towards the payment of school fees for children being educated off the island and to the purchase of goods direct from Suva. These and other transactions have resulted in a situation whereby more money leaves the island each year in the form of telegraph money orders than is received by the post office from external sources (Table 7.6). This is just another dimension of the dependency structures which have enabled Kabara to remain home in spite of hazards to a large proportion of Fijians born on the island. At the time of the 1976 national census it was established that of those people who had been born on Kabara, half were still in residence on the island.

The 'stayers'

Natural hazards and fluctuations in the exchange economy are not unusual occurrences on Kabara; both are enduring characteristics of life in villages throughout the southern Lau islands. That a significant proportion of Lauans who were brought up in the 'famine isles' (Thompson 1940b: 3) continue to reside in their natal communities is also not surprising given the deep attachments Fijians have for their land. The attitude was summarised by a woman from another island in Lau, when she said her island was 'where we have our relations, our home, our land: this represents something permanent' (Racule 1985). Residents on Kabara both in 1975 and 1983 had no difficulty in explaining why they were not living elsewhere; indeed, most found it strange to be asked to give reasons for staying.

Kabara's stayers in the mid-1970s were not representatives of an immobile population. A sample of 44 adult men living in three villages in October 1975 recounted migration and employment histories which indicated that the activities of residents span a wide spatial domain in which Kabara is only one, if still the most important, node. Forty per cent had worked in Suva at some stage over the previous five years, and a further 22 per cent had been employed in rural areas, mainly on Viti Levu. Of those who had moved, over 75 per cent returned directly to the village; their pattern of mobility corresponded to the circular migration which has been described for other parts of the rural Pacific (e.g. Chapman & Prothero 1985). Just under half of the men interviewed had been absent from Kabara at some stage within the previous 12 months, and almost all had spent at least two of the past five years living in the village. These summary statistics give some indication of the extent to which stayers are linked through inter-island mobility into the mainstream of Fiji's economy and society. Indeed, the opportunity to leave the island periodically, and to return with impunity when desired, is fundamental to the continued viability of small islands in the periphery as homes for Fijians in the 1980s and beyond.

Given the island's limited natural resources, wage employment prospects and service infrastructure, as well as its isolation and poor transport links with Suva and other parts of Fiji, we found it surprising in 1975 to find in Kabara's villages so many young men who had spent most of their formative years in Suva, and who had achieved good secondary education qualifications in town. Most of them could cite a specific reason for their presence, such as looking after elderly parents, providing for a widowed mother and younger kin, or helping to rebuild houses destroyed by hurricanes Val and Lottie. However, discussions with these young men around the *yaqona* bowl over several nights revealed that, in general, they also found village life deeply satisfying, and had no plans for returning to live in the city. These residence intentions were not just idle thoughts; in 1983 most of the same group of young men were still to the island, even though other young people of both sexes had been only too ready to leap at the first opportunity to leave Kabara and try their luck in town. The satisfaction of the returnees with village life, in Kabara and elsewhere, thus provides an intriguing dimension to the role of perception of the quality of life in the decision to move, return and perhaps stay.

On the other hand, readjustment to village life is not always easy, and it must not be forgotten that many who have left Kabara show no inclination to return.[3] When the residents were pressed to explain what made life on the island so satisfying, most could justify staying only in terms of a life style which in reality demands substantial subsidies of food, goods and money from other parts of Fiji. Hurricane relief, too, has helped many young adults to stay; if the contribution of government had been less generous many would have felt the need to leave Kabara and seek work and a new place of residence elsewhere.

Sustaining small societies

When reviewing the consequences of smallness for island societies in eastern Fiji in the 1960s, Ward (1967) suggested that very small islands could not fulfil the desires for more individualistic forms of socio-economic organisation, nor satisfy the growing demands among resident populations for more material goods and services. He concluded that:

> The general consequence of these changes is an increase in emigration from the smaller islands, whose ultimate role may be as sites for coconut plantations visited only occasionally from the larger islands. Such a development would take place gradually and in effect would mean the end of many small communities as separate entities. (Ward 1967: 95)

In Fiji's eastern periphery absolute depopulation of small islands has been extremely rare.[4] It seems unlikely that small islands like Kabara or Batiki will lose all their residents as a result of socio-economic changes in the

[3] Initially, at least, it has not been easy for the returned young men to adjust to the demanding physical work associated with gardening, fishing and repairing damaged buildings. The urban-raised and urban-educated Kabarans also found it hard to accept some of the restrictions which the village elders, and especially the elders of the church, placed on certain popular types of social activity. Only in one village – Naikeleyaga – was Western-type dancing, with its free style and possibility of body contact, permitted, at least to a minority, in 1975. In other villages only Fijian dancing was allowed. Home-brew parties, very popular with those accustomed to drinking alcohol in Suva or New Zealand, were also frowned upon by the church hierarchy, and in some villages were actively discouraged. Yet, in spite of a traumatic period of readjustment, these young men were repeatedly contrasting the virtues of freedom and variety in village life with the more regimented, clock-bound and costly way of life in Suva. The opportunity to choose whether and when to go fishing, visit the gardens, make handicrafts, or just sit around yarning, was highly valued by those who had experienced the 0800–1630 routine of hard labouring, office work or factory employment in the city.

[4] One very isolated island, Qelelevu, with a population of 20 Fijians in 1976, had become uninhabited by 1983. The residents had moved to north Taveuni, where they had access to land through customary connections, but occasionally some revisited their former home to cut copra. In some other cases there was forced displacement of small island communities following land deals in the 1850s and 1860s between Fijian chiefs and European settlers (see Brookfield 1978, for a description of the depopulation of certain islands in northern Lau as a result of this process). In general, however, developments over the century 1880–1980 caused fluctuations in the numbers resident on Fiji's smaller peripheral islands, rather than absolute depopulation and 'the end of many small communities as separate entities', as Ward (1967: 95) predicted.

1980s and beyond. As discussed in chapter 6, the Fijian-dominated Alliance Party has demonstrated since 1970 a commitment to preserving the eastern periphery as an area with a vital and viable Fijian rural community and cultural life. There has been substantial investment in strategies to ensure the periphery is not depopulated, and there is no reason to expect that the ideology underlying development planning in Fiji will change in the near future.

Conclusion

As on Batiki, there is continuing evidence on Kabara of attempts to diversify the island economy. In 1983 the most dynamic agents for potential change were two retired civil servants in Naikeleyaga who had come back to the island after more than twenty years in Suva. One, a qualified mechanic, was using his technical skills to promote the local fishing and handicraft industries. The other, a former radio inspector, was using his clerical skills and contacts in Suva to further development of wood processing on the island, both through roading projects to improve access to stands of useful timber, and through construction of a timber mill and associated craft workshop in Naikeleyaga. A Peace Corps volunteer had been recruited to assist with the saw milling project, amongst other ventures designed to improve employment prospects on the island. There was also the possibility that cruise ships might call periodically to enable tourists to experience an outer island environment and a 'traditional' Fijian community.

On the other hand similar initiatives have been talked about or attempted on almost every island in eastern Fiji over the last few decades. In very few cases have these proposals led to any lasting change in the material basis for island life, and what change has occurred has to a remarkable extent been grafted on to the existing agrarian structure. As a result, the capacity of island enterprise to compete successfully in the wider political economy of capitalist Fiji has been severely restricted.

Nevertheless, it has to be admitted that in various ways the communities on islands like Kabara and Batiki have achieved a continuing adaptation to their marginal status. It is ironic, however, that on these two islands the main element in diversification of the economy away from copra has been towards the production of handicrafts. Surplus production of handicrafts also occurred on these two islands in the pre-capitalist era, but then within a dependent-tribal rather than a marginalised-capitalist framework of external relations. That these relationships can be conducted without serious modification to the social structure of Batiki and Kabara itself is an indication of how successful a strategy adaptation can be in maintaining the *status quo*. What adaptation cannot do, however, is provide a satisfying livelihood for the wider population of island-born migrants and their sons and daughters. These absentees still retain rights on their home islands but their links are diminishing and in many cases their interest in the island has become merely symbolic and sentimental.

As in the case of the remaining peasant communities of western Europe, the economy and society of many small islands in the eastern periphery can only persist in fossilised form through government subsidy. Without a radical structural shift away from the continued dependence on copra-making, handicrafts and remittances, the small islands seem likely to become museums of traditional culture. This scenario conforms with the prevailing ideology of Fiji's leading politicians, but to retain such a population and to enable them to live a way of life which corresponds reasonably well to the neo-traditional stereotype requires an ever-increasing structure of state-directed subsidy. It is in exploiting their cultural role as guardians of the traditional Fijian village lifestyle that residents on small islands, with limited local alternatives for economic diversification, will ensure they retain some social and political status, even if the economic cost is increasing dependency on external forces and decision-makers.

8

Adaptation or stagnation? The case of Koro

The nature of the adaptation that we have described for small and relatively remote places like Kabara and Batiki, islands deficient in soils and vulnerable to hazards, would not be a surprise to environmental determinists of an earlier school of geographical thought. Elsewhere in the periphery, however, there are islands such as Taveuni, Koro, Gau and Moala that possess a much more promising resource base. A bigger land area, moderate slopes, fertile soils, dependable rainfall and a greater proximity to markets are all physical factors that should, if not determine, then at least make possible a more substantial set of changes than those that have occurred under more constrained conditions. To test this hypothesis the UNESCO/UNFPA project selected Koro, an island where good baseline data existed from 1958 surveys by Watters (1969), and where all the preconditions seemed to exist in the 1970s for a different approach to adaptation.

Koro: island of perpetual promise

'Magnificent but useless'?

Koro is situated some 50 km north of Batiki but unlike Batiki is partly of Pleistocene volcanic formation and has an upland plateau rising to over 500 m. Its land area of 113 km² makes it comparable in size with St Vincent or Grenada in the West Indies. In the mid-nineteenth century Koro was sheltered from European contact by its dependent status in the Bau chiefdom (see Fig. 3.1), but by 1870 a very different future seemed to be in prospect:

There is no settlement on Koro, which belongs to Thakobau ... The native inhabitants, as yet uncontaminated by association with white men, moved about the peaceful vales of this Eden ... Yet a few years, and their happy lazy lives ... will be changed to the laborious lot of the white man's plantation hand: for this rich soil, which has been gathering fertility from the repose of centuries, will not much longer be permitted to lavish its strength in magnificent but useless vegetation. (Britton 1870: 61)

Cession in 1874 prevented large-scale land alienation, but an embryo plantation economy did become established. In 1876 there were 'a good many planters, all poor, many of them having sunk quite large fortunes in their plantations when Fijian cotton was selling at very high prices' (Cumming-Gordon 1882: 158). As elsewhere, a variety of crops was attempted. On one estate, for example, cotton, maize and coconuts were all grown in 1876, the coconuts being processed on the spot into copra and coir, but the principal crop was red and white arrowroot. Given favourable markets and Solomon Islands labour the planters could at least survive, but by the 1880s it was clear that coconuts were the most viable crop, and they required a long-term commitment that was only attractive on freehold land. On Koro the hurricane of 1886 devastated many planters' hopes, and by the turn of the century the commercial part of the 'dual economy' had shrunk to one copra plantation and a handful of Chinese storekeepers. The future of commercial agriculture lay with the villagers, who by fortunate accident had retained almost all of their land.

Almost a hundred years later the economy of Koro appeared to be virtually unchanged. In the 1950s the Soil Survey found that most of the island was still covered by heavy forest, with only the seaward slopes being cleared for subsistence cropping (*teitei*) and coconuts. They concluded:

It is felt that Koro should be given very high priority, along with Taveuni and Gau, for agricultural development. Soils are generally fertile, the island is well watered and there are many easy slopes. Koro could be made to grow bananas and cocoa on a large scale on the slopes ... and the plateau ... is ideal for tea gardens, vegetables, citrus, rubber, coffee, oil palm, probably coconuts, all if fertiliser is provided, and for rich dairy pastures ... There seems little reason why, given road development and some increase in population, Koro should not become one of the richest islands in the Fiji Group. (Twyford & Wright 1965: 433)

Others shared this optimistic view. R. F. Watters, who undertook field surveys in Nacamaki village in 1958, felt that the easy attainment of subsistence affluence had been a conservative influence on Koro, despite 'unrivalled natural potentialities for economic development'. However, the adoption of co-operative societies was 'beginning to channel local production in promising directions' (Watters 1969: 110), a view shared by others (Boyan 1961; Silsoe 1963). R. G. Ward (1965: 243) felt that banana production could be revived on Ovalau and Gau as well as Koro, since all three islands were big enough to generate sufficient output to support regular shipping connections. On Koro itself he felt that market gardening was another possibility, given feeder roads and a jetty. It seemed unlikely that this 'peaceful Eden' could escape much longer from the impetus towards 'development'.

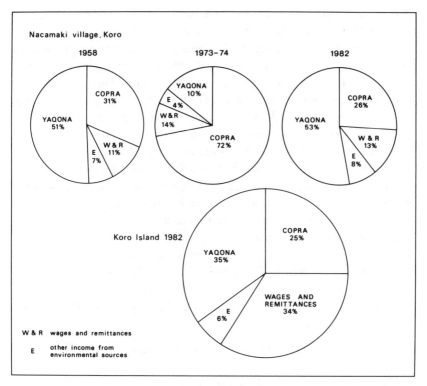

8.1 Sources of household income on Koro, 1958–82

Population and production

On Koro as elsewhere, the 1960s was a decade of belated colonial initiative. A number of roads were built, followed by a jetty and an airstrip. The population also increased to reach the present total of 3,500. It is significant, however, that population growth on Koro has been slower than the national average. From 1956 to 1966 the island population grew at 2.6 per cent per annum, but in the following decade this rate was halved, and for village populations a rate of only 1.2 per cent per annum was recorded for 1976–82 (Central Planning Office 1983). It is also significant that whereas in the nineteenth century a wide range of export crops was grown, by the 1950s only copra and bananas were being sold on a significant scale, plus *yaqona* for the domestic market. Banana exports to New Zealand ceased in 1962. Copra production, reported in 1929 as 'about 1,000 tons per annum' (Burns Philp 1929), was still at this level 40 years later, averaging 1,006 tonnes for the period 1969–71. Coconuts were planted extensively under the Coconut Subsidy Scheme in the 1960s, and this larger acreage made possible an increase in output to over 1,400 tonnes in 1974, 1977 and 1978, but after cyclone damage in 1980 production was down to 833 tonnes in 1980–82.

Stability rather than change is also suggested by statistics on the sources of cash income. In 1982 the Central Planning Office did a survey of 91 households from all fourteen villages on the island. This survey can be compared with surveys of Nacamaki village in 1958, 1974 and 1982 (Fig. 8.1). The comparison does not suggest that any radical process of structural change has occurred in the economy, in fact the reverse. Apart from an increased reliance upon salaries, wages and remittances, there appears to have been no basic change in the 1958 pattern of dependence on *yaqona* and copra, with copra challenging dominance of *yaqona* only in the mid-1970s, a time of unusually high copra prices.

We can conclude from this review that economic development on Koro has consistently failed to match the expectations of the resource planners, who have visualised various alternative roads to prosperity none of which the islanders have followed. To understand the reasons for this largely negative response to opportunities that others perceive as being available, we must examine the detailed workings of the economy at village scale.

The village economy: Nacamaki

An energy analysis

Fieldwork on Koro by the UNESCO/UNFPA project in 1974–6 was focussed on Nacamaki (population 309). This village was the location of a 1958 study by R. F. Watters (1969), and it was subsequently selected in 1977 by Suliana Siwatibau (1981), and in 1982 by the Fiji Employment and Development Mission (Siwatibau 1982), for follow-up studies. We therefore have data on this community that span a 25 year period, including a detailed analysis of the situation in July–August 1974 (Bayliss-Smith 1977b). It is to this period in the mid-1970s that we turn initially, and the surveys that were done at that time provide some basis for estimating the total pattern of energy flows within the village economy.

An energy analysis provides a highly generalised view of the economy, but it does at least highlight the strong degree of self-sufficiency that persisted in Nacamaki in the mid-1970s, over one hundred years after the introduction of plantation agriculture (Fig. 8.2). Two-thirds of the villagers' diet still comes from local subsistence sources. Human work is estimated as involving an expenditure of 182 gigajoules (GJ) of energy per year, still almost as important an input as fossil fuels (207 GJ). Imported foods contributed 336 GJ and subsistence foods 652 GJ. The great bulk of the fuel energy also derives from local sources, in particular the intro-

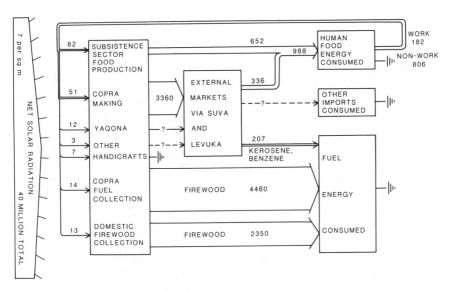

8.2 Energy flow model for Nacamaki village, 1974–5 (GJ per annum)

duced tree species *Leucaena leucocephala* (*vaivai*), which forms an understorey in neglected coconut plantations and is a major source of fuel for copra drying. From her surveys in Nacamaki, Siwatibau (1981: 37) estimated that domestic fuel requirements amounted each year to 369 kg of wood per capita, and that copra drying required in addition 332 kg per capita. For the village as a whole this amounts to 217 tonnes of wood (oven-dry weight) each year, amounting to about 6,800 GJ of energy. This is a substantial quantity, but one easily sustainable given that at least one-third of the village's 575 ha of landholdings is still under forest, and most of the rest is garden land which contains trees such as coconut, mango, *vaivai* and *Hibiscus tiliaceus*, all important fuel sources. Siwatibau suggests that eight times the present level of consumption could be sustained by natural regeneration of secondary woodlands alone, so that any 'energy crisis' in the subsistence sector seems to be a long way off.

Apart from subsistence foods, the major outputs of the agricultural system are copra and *yaqona*. *Yaqona* is a mild narcotic whose value cannot be assessed in energy terms, as any participant in a Fijian grog party would confirm! Copra on the other hand is a product rich in oil, but even so the energy value of exported copra (3,360 GJ) does not match the energy required to dry it (4,460 GJ), especially if we add in the labour costs of coconut collection, fuel collection, cutting and drying (65 GJ). Coconuts are grown mainly as a cash crop, and the unequal nature of the exchange relationship for copra becomes even more apparent when we

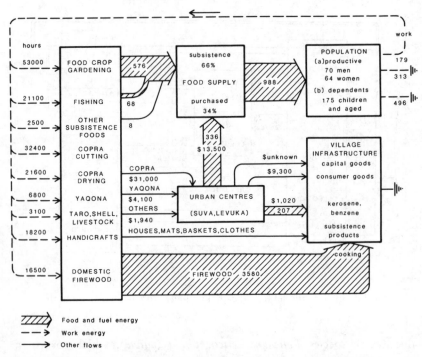

8.3 Input/output model of the Nacamaki economy: work, food and income,
1974–5

start to consider the *perceived* value of the product rather than its *de facto* energy value.

Money, work and productivity

An analysis of the village economy is needed in terms which correspond rather more closely to local perceptions than does the flow of energy. The value of copra, *yaqona* and other marketed products is perceived locally in relation to their monetary value, and in relation too to the price of the products which people want to buy with their income. In 1973–4, out of the total village income of around $43,220 (excluding two teachers' salaries), more than half was being spent in the local store, partly on food (33 per cent) and partly on fuel, cigarettes, hardware, soap and other consumer goods (67 per cent). The remainder of the money went on education, the church, community projects such as electrification, capital goods especially housing, and savings, this last only possible in a prosperous year such as the one in question. Despite this relative prosperity an estimated two-thirds of the diet still came from subsistence sources, in particular from food crop gardens. At this time 72 per cent of the cash income was derived from copra, but there were some supplementary cash crops, notably *yaqona* and taro, while pensions, wages and remittances accounted for 13 per cent of total income.

The major flows of work, money and products are shown in Figure 8.3. The work input amounts to an estimated 175,200 hours per year, from a 'productive' population (those aged 15–59 years) of 70 men and 64 women, who have in addition to themselves 175 dependants to support. When averaged out, the work input amounts to 25 hours per producer per week, which may not at first sight appear very substantial, even when disaggregated into men (about 32 hours per week) and women (about 19 hours). However, we should remember that apart from fishing, weaving and some copra work, the main practical contribution of women is within the home, cooking, cleaning and looking after children. This work was not covered in the Nacamaki survey. On Batiki, a survey which did ask questions about women's domestic work showed that about 21 hours per week were occupied in this way (see Fig. 7.7). If we assume that Koro villages are similar to those on Batiki, then we can suggest that total women's work occupies about 40 hours per week, no different from the West European norm for wage earners. For men also, we should remember that substantial variations exist according to age, family responsibilities and aspirations.

If we consider the village economy as a series of relationships between inputs and outputs, then at aggregate scale we can see that the various economic activities differ considerably in their productivity ratios. To make a fair comparison between different sectors of the economy, we must be able to convert the monetary value of the products sold into some form which is equivalent to the perceived value of the subsistence products. Alternatively, we could value the subsistence production according to some notional market price, but for islanders remote from any actual market such a procedure would be difficult and even more artificial than attempting the reverse. Since a high proportion of income is actually spent on food, especially sugar, rice, flour, biscuit and tinned fish, it seems a reasonable procedure to compute the amount of food capable of being purchased per average dollar spent in the village store, taking into account local prices and preferences, and to convert this food into its energy equivalent. This gives a measure of the value of money which is directly comparable to the value of subsistence production. This 'perceived energy value' is shown in Table 8.1 for the major sectors of the 1973–4 Nacamaki economy, alongside the hours of associated work input and their estimated energy value.

Table 8.1 *Input/output analysis of the Nacamaki economy for 1973–4*

	Subsistence sector			Market sector				
	Food crop gardens	Fishing	Livestock, hunting	Domestic firewood	Handicrafts	Green copra	Yaqona	Taro, shell, livestock
Inputs								
Work (hours)	53,000	21,100	2,500	16,500	18,200	32,400	6,800	3,100
Outputs								
Products	cassava, taro, yams	fish, shellfish	cattle, pigs, fowls, etc.	fuel	pandanus leaf, mats, baskets	co-op. copra, 214.5t worth $21,500	6,460 kg kava worth $6,870	miscellaneous sales worth $1,940
Energy								
Value (GJ)	575.5	67.6	8.4	2,349	n.c.	3,737[a]	n.c.	n.c.
Perceived energy value (GJ)	575.5	67.6	8.4	n.c.	n.c.	537.7[b]	171.4[b]	48.4[b]
Productivity								
Perceived energy per hour work (MJ)	10.9	3.2	3.4	n.c.	n.c.	16.6	25.2	15.6

Notes: n.c. not calculated or not calculable.

[a] assuming green coconut contains 17.3 MJ per kg, and with no consideration given to fuel energy expended in copra drying.

[b] monetary values are converted to perceived energy values using rate 24.95 MJ purchasable per $1 spent (Bayliss-Smith 1977b: 64).

Sources: Inputs: Bayliss-Smith 1977b: 85–6, adjusted to productive population of 73 men and 66 women. Outputs: Bayliss-Smith 1977b: 49–58.

Yaqona: output is partly consumed ($2,770 worth) and partly sold ($4,100 income). The data shown here differ from those in Tables 10 and 14 of Bayliss-Smith 1977b, which are incorrect. Labour input is calculated assuming 4,400 hours of work is needed per hectare of 2,300 plants, yielding 2 kg per plant (Watters 1969: 127; Hardaker 1976; Bayliss-Smith, field notes).

Yaqona versus copra

If we focus on the most dependable and most accessible sources of livelihood, we find from Table 8.1 that their productivity ratios, in megajoules (MJ) of food energy per hour of work, are ranked as follows:

Yaqona selling	25.2
Green copra selling	16.6
Food crops gardening	10.9
Animal husbandry etc.	3.4
Fishing	3.2

If Nacamaki villagers were economic maximisers, then their most rational course of action at this time would have been to concentrate all their efforts on *yaqona*, but for most this was not feasible. In the mid-1970s *yaqona* resources were depleted as a result of the events of two years previously. During the 1960s the price of green copra in the village stood at around $30 per tonne, but in 1972 it collapsed to only half this level (Table 8.2). Throughout the Fiji periphery the response of farmers was to switch from copra to *yaqona* wherever possible, with the result that *yaqona* prices also fell, although less steeply. Since the kava plant takes 3–5 years to reach a degree of maturity, when copra prices recovered in late 1973 farmers were very happy to keep their replanted *yaqona* in reserve, to allow it to mature. *Yaqona* prices doubled between 1972 and 1974, but this increase was modest by comparison with the extraordinary boom in copra, which at its peak had risen more than tenfold in price, and had become an even more rewarding crop than *yaqona*. For most farmers the comparison was hypothetical, since they had little *yaqona* ready for harvest whereas coconuts were lying in abundance in the neglected groves.

Moreover, in 1974 villagers were well aware that the boom in copra was likely to be short-lived. Subsequent events demonstrated the wisdom of exploiting copra to the full while the going was good. In 1975 the price subsided steeply (see chapter 4), and despite a brief boom in 1979 by 1983 green copra was worth only $70 per tonne. Since the buying power of money in 1983 was only a quarter of what it had been in 1958, the doubling of the copra price during this period represents a major decline in real terms (see Table 8.2). *Yaqona* prices, on the other hand, have more than kept pace with inflation, with the 1983 price more than five times its 1958 level.

In this situation of fluctuation and uncertainty in the market economy, complicated by the occasional emergence of alternative options – bananas, taro, cocoa, trochus shell – it is not surprising that strictly 'rational' decision-making is difficult for farmers. As the productivity

Table 8.2 *Prices and costs at Nacamaki, 1958–83*

Year[a]	Selling prices $ per tonne		Buying price MJ per $
	Green copra	Yaqona	Imported food
1958	32	640	52.76
1966	30	not known	47.52
1972	15	640	42.46
1973–4	100	1,150	24.95
	(50–154)[b]	(860–1,520)[c]	
1975–6	33	2,490–3,285[c]	24.16
1982–3	70	3,100–4,000[c]	12.64

Notes: [a] Calendar years 1958, 1966 and 1972, and 9/73–8/74, 7/75–6/76 and 7/82–6/83.
[b] Range of monthly prices during the year.
[c] Lower figure is average price at co-operative society store; higher one is that obtainable from merchants.
Sources: Bayliss-Smith 1977b, Table 11; and field notes.

ratios in Table 8.3 indicate, copra has only occasionally exceeded subsistence agriculture in its energy yield per hour of work. The optimum course of action would be to abandon copra and focus all efforts on *yaqona*, but this has not occurred for several reasons. Not all households have access to sufficient fertile land for large-scale *yaqona* production, and not all possess the male labour needed for initial clearance. The returns from *yaqona* tend to be in the form of large cash payments at infrequent intervals, whereas copra earnings are attractive in being available on an almost daily basis. There is also risk inherent in dependence on one source of livelihood, and a preference for maintaining a range of different activities. All these factors militate against a total concentration on one crop, however lucrative *yaqona* has been since the 1950.

Meanwhile subsistence agriculture and fishing continue to supply a high proportion of the energy and protein in the diet. The productivity of food crops, at about 11 MJ per person-hour, is typical of the staple crops of Third World farmers using hand labour (Bayliss-Smith 1982, 1984). Of course at particular sites and in particular years the return may not be as dependable as the data in Table 8.3 suggest. Root crops and *yaqona* are both susceptible to climatic extremes. Drought is not usually a problem on Koro, but in March 1980 torrential rainfall associated with Cyclone Tia caused considerable flooding and landslides, and also the deaths of two children buried by a mudflow. In Nacamaki six houses were swept away or destroyed by flood waters, but no one was drowned. A report by the

Table 8.3 *Perceived energy output per hour of work, Nacamaki,*
1958–83

	Food energy output (MJ) per person-hour of work input		
	Subsistence agriculture	Green copra	*Yaqona*
1958	10.9	11.2	32.2
1972	10.9	4.2	25.9
1973–4	10.9	16.6 (8.2–25.6)[a]	25.2
1975–6	10.9	5.3	57.3
1982–3	10.9	5.9[b]	37.3

Notes: [a] Range of monthly values.
[b] Dry copra in 1983 yielded 6.5 MJ per person-hour.
Source: Calculated using data in Tables 8.1 and 8.2.

Divisional Commissioner's office suggested that in this village 30 per cent of yams, 80 per cent of *yaqona* and 90 per cent of taro was destroyed, and that five months of relief supplies would be needed (Eastern Division 1980). Although these figures are probably exaggerated, and much *yaqona* was harvestable despite landslips, production was undoubtedly hit.

Fortunately on Koro these natural hazards are infrequent, and they are less important in decision-making than perturbations in the market economy. The long-term trend of gradual decline in the productivity of copra has been punctuated by years of severe depression (e.g. 1972) as well as brief periods of boom prices (e.g. 1974). *Yaqona* by comparison has been more dependable, and in general far more lucrative.

The response of farmers

We can therefore conclude that the response of farmers on Koro to these fluctuations and uncertainties has been both conservative and opportunistic. A strategy of risk avoidance is suggested by the reluctance to reduce the role of subsistence agriculture or to shift land use away from the two most dependable cash crops towards more speculative alternatives. Agriculture Department officials have at various times promoted bananas, cocoa, yams and taro as supplementary cash crops, and Koro farmers have willingly planted quite substantial areas with these crops, but markets have proved unreliable and prices disappointing. Both coconuts and *yaqona* have the advantage of being easily processed, and if properly dried can be stored for weeks or even months. *Yaqona* benefits from being left unharvested, or can be converted to subsistence use if marketing arrangements are unsatisfactory. Both crops are therefore particularly appropriate for the outer islands, where shipping can be erratic and prices fluctuate (Sofer 1985).

On the other hand, despite their basic reluctance to change the overall structure of land use, farmers have shown that given market incentives their response can be quite flexible. This flexibility is well demonstrated by the contrast between 1974 and 1976 (see Fig. 8.1). In 1974 high copra prices had led farmers to maximise output of copra and hold *yaqona* in reserve. Copra contributed 84 per cent of environmental income, *yaqona* only 11 per cent. Two years later, with a decline in copra prices and a further improvement in the returns from *yaqona*, the response was in most cases to maintain the output of copra, but because of much lower prices its contribution to income dropped to less than one-third of its previous value. To fill the gap, and to take advantage of rising prices, *yaqona* was exploited to the full, contributing 62 per cent of environmental income (similar to its 1958 contribution of 60 per cent). The situation had changed little in 1982, with any tendency for a decline in copra making checked by the severe damage to *yaqona* sustained in the 1980 cyclone, and the consequent need to exploit copra to the full.

Economic development or structural stagnation?

To what extent can we describe economic change in Nacamaki since the late 1950s, as constituting 'development'? The land use pattern remains the same, and apart from a small growth in the proportion of total income from wages (but this income is received by only a few individuals), the respective contributions of copra and *yaqona* to total income remain virtually unaltered. Farmers have not been unresponsive to price fluctuations in the mid-1970s and to occasional opportunities to sell bananas, taro, etc., but any changes have been short-lived. The vast majority of village producers do not seem to perceive any advantage in a commitment to greater dependence on any particular cash crop, let alone to the market sector as a whole.

If structural change has not occurred over this period, has there perhaps been economic growth within a stable structure? A glance at the population data is enough to suggest that this cannot be true in the demographic sense. The population enumerated in the village in sample years does not show any long-term growth in the number of persons that the village economy supports:

Table 8.4 *Total income in energy terms, Nacamaki, 1958–83 (villagers excluding salary-earning teachers)*

	1958	1973–4	1975–6	1982–3
Village income (GJ)				
Cash sector	647	1,079	930	744
Subsistence sector	854	653	590	738
Total	1,501	1,732	1,520	1,482
Income per capita (MJ)				
Copra	578	2,506	924	595
Yaqona	954	331	1,688	1,213
Other cash income	350	653	796	480
Subsistence	2,483	2,115	2,163	2,187
Total	4,365	5,605	5,571	4,475

Sources: 1958 and 1975–6: Bayliss-Smith (1977 b: Table 10)
1973–4: Bayliss-Smith (1977b: Tables 3, 4 and calculations)
1982–3: Central Planning Office (1983), Siwatibau (1982), and calculations.

	Population
1958	344
1966	302
1973–4	309
1974–6	274
1982	325
1983	331

These fluctuations suggest no trend, beyond the possibility that prosperity in 1974 financed circular migration which temporarily diminished the 1976 population.

Has the community become richer or poorer on a per capita basis? In real terms there has indeed been some growth in cash incomes over this period. The average income of $35 in 1958 would have purchased 1,880 MJ in food energy, using local food prices and preferences. In 1982 average incomes were estimated at $181, but the decline in purchasing power meant this money was only worth around 2,300 MJ in food energy, a rise of about 20 per cent. However, the 1982 incomes represented in real terms a considerable decline from the mid-1970s levels, when high prices for copra (1974) or *yaqona* (1976) lead to a more substantial improvement in income.

So far we have concentrated the analysis on cash incomes, which though important are clearly an incomplete index of welfare. Health, housing, and social amenities should all be considered. Moreover, the contribution of subsistence income to welfare must be assessed. At a national level a clear correlation has been shown among Fijians between high consumption of subsistence foods and low incidence of malnutrition measured in terms of either wasting and stunting in infants or of obesity in adults (Johnson & Lambert 1982). The substantial degree of food self-sufficiency on Koro island therefore suggests in itself that nutritional standards at least are being maintained.[1]

In order to take more account of subsistence production we must calculate the *total energy income*, which is the sum of subsistence-sector consumption and the perceived energy value of cash incomes. These data confirm the impression that significant economic growth has not been experienced in Nacamaki over this period (Table 8.4). Total energy incomes in 1958 were at a level of 4,365 MJ per capita when assessed in this way. By the mid-1970s a 28 per cent rise had occurred but it was not sustained, and the 1983 level was only 2.5 per cent above what it had been 25 years previously.

It would appear, therefore, that some comments made by Watters after his 1958 fieldwork remain almost as appropriate today:

In order for Nacamaki to satisfy its developing needs for Western goods it has not been necessary for the community to grow new crops that might have drastically altered the subsistence system and so speeded social change ... No major 'structural' alterations in the system have yet occurred, nor have significant new developments begun outside it. (Watters 1969: 120)

From the data presented here, we must conclude that despite the absence of any obvious constraints of land or labour, the village economy on Koro has not so much developed as stagnated over this period. Can marketing problems be seen as one factor that has contributed to this stagnation of the village economy? To answer this question requires a critical analysis of the role of the co-operative societies, which in recent decades have been the principal mediators between farmers on Koro and their urban markets.

---

1 Data from Nacamaki indicate that food self-sufficiency has been eroded somewhat during periods of prosperity. The proportion of the diet from local sources can be estimated from store records which show the volume of imported food purchased, converted to its energy value, combined with estimates of total energy consumption using per capita requirements and population data. For 1958 Watters (1969) provides approximate data, and more precise estimates are possible for the period of co-operative society store records (Bayliss-Smith 1977b). These data suggest that the proportion of the diet from subsistence sources has fluctuated as follows: 1958 73 per cent; 1973–4 59 per cent; 1975–6 60 per cent; 1982–3 70 per cent. Once again the mid-1970s period appears anomalous by comparison with the less prosperous and more self-sufficient years that both preceded and followed it.

The regulation of marketing

Role of the co-operatives

At first sight an important exception to the general impression of structural stagnation has been the growing role of co-operatives in copra marketing. In the 1950s it was generally felt that on largely Fijian islands like Koro co-operative societies could be an effective means of achieving sustained economic growth, and one that represented a viable alternative to the encouragement of individual enterprise. On Koro, as elsewhere in the Fiji periphery, co-operatives were popular because they 'seemed to express traditional collectivist sentiments that arise naturally from Fijian social structure' (Watters 1969: 129). Their arrival virtually ended Indo-Fijian and Chinese retail competition, but at the same time led to the voluntary curtailment of most of the activities of the existing Fijian entrepreneurs who were operating on a small scale in villages. Watters noted that since the co-operatives had been established on Koro most copra was being sold green to a co-operative for centralised drying. As a result surplus value was being denied to individual producers who might otherwise have processed their own crop and gained a higher price. Potentially the labour saved could have been applied by farmers to other activities, or to producing more green copra, but this effect was not noticeable. A further effect might have been better prices for consumers in store goods, but again not much price difference between co-operative stores and the former private stores could be detected.

In the 1950s the principal opposition to the co-operatives came from a few persons who in a full-blown peasant society would be termed as 'kulaks', and who were identified in Nacamaki as those 'individualistic and cash-conscious villagers' with 'healthy entrepreneurial tendencies' (Watters 1969: 132). At this time a proportion of the net value of copra was not paid to producers direct, but instead was retained by the Fiji Development Fund Board in the form of a 'copra cess'. Prior to the co-operatives this form of compulsory savings was levied on the production of individuals, and it was ultimately returned to them as a lump sum that was often used for new housing. It is clear that this system benefited those households with the land and labour to exploit copra to the full, whereas the levy on co-operative society output represents a substantial redistribution of income in favour of less productive households. This is another way in which the co-operatives acted as a disincentive to potential copra kulaks, and a further reason for the shift to individualistic *yaqona* production.

In general, the evidence does not seem to justify Watters' rather optimistic forecast:

Although the co-operatives have not increased production in the village they are most influential, and are gradually expanding the needs of the community for Western goods in their stores. Ultimately the "spread effect" of their influence must assist economic development in indirect ways while the new needs of the community should lead to direct increases in cash cropping. (Watters 1969: 133)

It is unfortunate that over the last 30 years the processing and marketing efforts of co-operative societies in the Fiji periphery have focussed so exclusively on copra. The long-term decline in the real returns from this crop has meant a continual squeeze on their profitability, exacerbated by the increase in freight rates and decline in shipping services in the last decade.

The regulation of copra marketing

Despite these unfavourable trends villagers on Koro do now receive a somewhat higher proportion of the Suva price for copra than was the case in the 1950s. In 1958 the price paid for copra at Nacamaki was equivalent to $15.7–$16.3 per tonne,[2] compared to the average Suva price of around $118 per tonne. This represents an extraordinary extraction of value by middle-men, amounting to 86 per cent of the Suva price. We should, however, add to the village price the $20 per tonne compulsory copra cess which is ultimately returned to the village, and this adjustment brings the proportion of extracted value down to 70 per cent.

In June 1983 the Suva assessed price plus subsidy had reached $290, by comparison to a green copra price in the village ranging from $66–$70 per tonne according to which store was used. This price is equivalent to about $138 per tonne in dry copra, to which $20 cess should again be added. The middlemen's share thus amounts to 52 per cent or 46 per cent of the Suva price, according to whether or not the cess is included. This relative improvement in the village price *vis-à-vis* the Suva price could be extended further if more Nacamaki producers were to dry their own copra and sell it direct to the Koro Co-operative Association depot at Namacu, 15 km away on the other side of the island. Despite freight rates of $1 per bag for the lorry trip and a $3 personal fare for the seller, amounting to at least $21 per tonne, and despite the copra cess which is forfeited, the net return per tonne marketed in this way is $208. This represents only a 28 per cent shortfall on the Suva price, a more satisfactory situation for the villagers and probably a very low profit margin for the Koro Co-operative

---

[2] Calculated from the range of green copra prices in the village of 1.73 to 1.80 pence per lb, and converted assuming 2,025 kg of green copra makes one tonne of dry.

Association (KCA), which could partly explain its fragile financial state. It is perhaps surprising, and reflects strongly on the continuing collectivist ideology of villagers, that in Nacamaki only four individuals bothered to market their copra direct to the KCA in Namacu in this way, accounting for only 9 per cent of Nacamaki output in 1982–3. The majority continued to depend on day-to-day cash handouts for green copra, sold to one of the two co-operatives (84 per cent of copra sold) or to a small private store (7 per cent).

For villagers the improvements in copra marketing have been facilitated by the development of the road network, which since the mid-1960s has provided connections between the Koro villages and has reduced their dependence on shipping. In the copra sector a smaller extraction of surplus value by middlemen has to some extent compensated villagers for the decline in the real price of the commodity. If, in the 1980s, villagers receive only 30 per cent of the Suva price for copra (which was the situation in the 1950s), then it is doubtful if much copra at all would still be produced. To receive 30 per cent of the Suva price would represent the equivalent of only 5 MJ food energy per hour of work, almost as bad as the actual productivity in 1972 when very low prices did persuade many producers on Koro to abandon copra production altogether.

The free trade in yaqona

For Koro, the improvement in copra marketing has occurred despite a general decline in Fiji in the quality of inter-island shipping services during the last 15 years. Between Koro and Suva a reasonably regular service has been maintained, partly because the island's copra output is sufficient to make the service commercially viable, but also because of Koro's importance in Fiji's *yaqona* trade. In the Eastern Division Kadavu, Ovalau, Koro and Moala are all major producers of *yaqona*, but reliable statistics on either production or marketing are very sparse (Sofer 1985). The trade in *yaqona* is largely in the hands of Indo-Fijians or Chinese, who account for 93 per cent of retail sales in urban markets according to recent surveys (Baxter 1980). Estimates suggest that in the Eastern Division as a whole production in 1982 amounted to 890 tonnes, worth just under $3 million to the farmers.[3] By contrast, the copra output of the Eastern Division was 7,250 tonnes in 1981, worth in Suva about $1.98 million, but earning substantially less for village producers (Brookfield 1985). Whereas the copra industry is organised by the Coconut Board and is supported by

[3] This estimate by the Ministry of Agriculture (Eastern Division 1983) is reasonably consistent with the total area under *yaqona* of 1,136 hectares, which was estimated for the Division in the agricultural census (Rothfield & Kumar 1980), if we assume yields of 4–5 tonnes per hectare and a period of 3–4 years from planting to harvest.

price support schemes, freight rate subsidies, copra grading stations and agricultural extension efforts, the *yaqona* industry merits not a single mention in the Eighth Development Plan for Fiji (1981–5), and costs the Government not one cent in intervention. These data suggest, however, that for the Fiji periphery it is in fact the more important cash crop.

Because *yaqona* as a cash crop arose from subsistence origins, because it involves mainly small-scale producers (although some estates have recently been established on Ovalau and Taveuni), and because the trade appears to be efficiently conducted, this lack of interest by government might seem to be justified. Apart from some experimental interventions in the early 1970s, the National Marketing Authority (NMA) has not attempted to enter the *yaqona* trade. Farmers have generally been able to expand output to match rising urban demands, and price regulation and restriction of consumption levels have never been seriously contemplated. In the major producing areas, such as Taveuni, Ovalau and the Suva hinterland, this may not matter. There is probably sufficient competition between middlemen to ensure that reasonable price levels are maintained. On Taveuni, for example, Hardaker (1976) found that:

The conduct of the *yaqona* trade appears to be quite efficient. Marketing costs and margins could not be fully investigated but no evidence of profiteering or of inefficiency was found on the part of middlemen. It is true that the fieldwork was carried out during a period of severe shortage of *yaqona*, so that it is possible that competition between trades was fiercer than usual. (Hardaker 1976: 12)

On this particular island entry to the trade seemed to require no more than a little capital and a modicum of entrepreneurial ability, so it is hard to see how the existing buyers could have maintained any effective cartel. The situation is different on the smaller islands. They lack a regular shipping connection to Suva, the major market, and the problems of entry into the trade become more substantial because a trader needs to operate his own boat. Moreover the opportunities for farmers to sell to traders are more intermittent, so that the competition factor is diminished.

On Koro *yaqona* was entirely a subsistence crop until the early 1930s, but by 1958 it had become the island's principal cash crop: 'the ease with which the crop can be grown as an intrinsic part of the subsistence intercropping system enables the island to corner a large part of the Suva market' (Watters 1969: 127). However, it is clear from Watters' data that any domination of this market was achieved more by merchants than by farmers. With merchants' selling prices far above their buying prices, and with the farmers having to organise and bear the costs of bags and shipping, the net price received by villagers was only 65 per cent of the Suva selling price. An opportunity clearly existed for the emerging network of co-operative societies to play a bigger role in *yaqona* market-

Table 8.5 Yaqona *prices, Koro compared to Suva*

| | Koro price per kg | | | |
Year	Nacamaki stores	Island merchants	Suva price per kg	Island price as % Suva price
1958	item not pur-chased	$0.64	$0.99	65%
7/1974	$1.52	price not known	$2.98	51%
7/1976	$2.49	$3.28	$5.00	50–66%
7/1983	$3.80	$4.00–$4.50	$8.00	48–56%

Sources: 1958 – Watters (1969); 1974–83 – Bayliss-Smith (1977b) and field notes.

ing, with potential benefit both for themselves and for farmers, but so far this opportunity has not been realised. The co-operatives do provide a useful service through their willingness to purchase *yaqona* at any time and in any quantity, but the prices they offer do not pose a serious threat to the Indo-Fijian traders (Table 8.5). These middlemen control both shipping and retail outlets in the major urban markets.

The result has been that the mercantile sector continues to attract a high proportion of *yaqona* output, offering prices superior to those in the local co-operative but only 56–66 per cent of those available in Suva. Since *yaqona* is transported in the same way as copra yet has a much higher value-to-weight ratio, excessive middlemen's profit seems to be the only explanation for the differences between *yaqona* and copra in the relative price that farmers receive. In 1983 these prices were, at best, 56 per cent of the Suva level for *yaqona* and 72 per cent for copra. On Taveuni, by contrast, the 1982 *yaqona* price to farmers was 75 per cent of that paid in Suva, a reflection of the closer approximation to free trade that can occur on a larger island supporting a number of middlemen engaged in genuine competition.

The dead hand of tradition?

Villagers on Koro are well aware of this particular problem of *yaqona* marketing, but the general feeling seems to be that the existing agrarian structure makes it difficult for any alternative marketing to be organised from a village base. As long ago as 1958 'some local [Koro] men were pressing the Administration to open a Fijian *yaqona* marketing agency in

Suva in order to ensure the grower a higher price' (Watters 1969: 129). In 1976 Tui Nasau, the hereditary chief of the island, organised about 300 young men to form a Koro Farmers Association. The short-term aim in this group was to fulfil a contract with the National Marketing Association to deliver 10 tonnes of taro to Suva each month, but in the long term Tui Nasau intended to by-pass the village co-operatives, the resident Indo-Fijian trader, and itinerant traders based in Suva and Levuka. The ultimate objective was to link up with similar groups already established in Gau, Moala, and Kadavu, in order to manipulate agricultural prices to the advantage of the farmer.

Changes in NMA policy towards the outer islands meant that even the short-term objective became unattainable, and the whole scheme collapsed, but it is a significant indicator in a number of ways. A wholly modern problem of organising agricultural production and ensuring efficient and equitable marketing arrangements was accurately diagnosed, but a wholly 'traditional' solution to this problem was attempted. With great enthusiasm a communal scheme was set in motion, relying on reciprocal labour, traditional leadership, and paternalistic state support for shipping and marketing arrangements. Similar schemes of 'community development' have occurred repeatedly in the last 100 years of Fiji's history, but despite the continuing strength of collectivist sentiments and continuing respect for the chiefs, without exception such schemes have failed to mount any sustained challenge to business enterprises operating in the same sector. R. G. Crocombe provides an apt summary of the failures of this model for rural development:

With some notable exceptions the hereditary [Fijian] aristocracy had neither skills nor motivation to maximise commercial agriculture; rather, their aim in maximising income was for consumption or distribution, i.e. for social rather than economic investments. Commoners, on the other hand, had two good reasons for not producing more than a limited surplus. (Crocombe 1971: 161)

According to Crocombe the two reasons for restricted production are the Fijian custom of *kerekere* whereby personal property is shared at the request of kinsmen (it being impolite to request the necessities of others, but common to request their surplus), and secondly the levies of the chiefs themselves. On most islands the entitlement of chiefs to a proportion of surpluses is now much diminished, but *kerekere* remains in force, as does the value system which legitimises it, whereby 'humility is virtue and attempting to rise above one's status is considered improper' (Crocombe 1971: 161).

Conclusion

In this light the role of the local co-operatives in eastern Fiji needs to be reassessed. The conformity of these institutions with traditional Fijian values is the reason for their repeated resuscitation at village scale, but as traders the co-operatives have proved inefficient both in providing cheap retail goods and in widening their marketing role beyond the protected realm of copra. Moreover the large measure of local support for co-operatives, even inefficient ones, makes the independent emergence of island-based Fijian entrepreneurs almost impossible. The question must be raised as to whether co-operative societies, as currently conceived, help or hinder the process whereby villagers can achieve an adequate livelihood from the resources of their own islands, rather than preferring migration to more secure and more lucrative urban jobs.

On Koro, with a generally benign climate and rich soil resources, the question is to some degree an academic one. Its population continues to enjoy a level of subsistence affluence that is envied by islanders elsewhere in eastern Fiji, and limited market participation even on unfavourable terms has been sufficient to satisfy most people's cash needs. Elsewhere in the periphery, however, the evidence points towards an inadequacy in the existing agrarian structure, which has become ineffective as a means whereby villagers can satisfy basic needs. The setbacks in attempts to diversify small-island economies on Batiki and Kabara have already been reviewed (chapter 7). To evaluate the success of more radical attempts to reform the agrarian structure we now consider the islands of Taveuni and Lakeba.

9

Villages of change: Taveuni and Lakeba

In chapters 7 and 8 we considered as case studies three islands where the main response to the internal contradictions and external pressures facing village communities has been *adaptation*. On the more prosperous islands (Koro) the success of this adaptive response, at least in maintaining the *status quo*, has meant that structural change has failed to occur despite the presence of abundant resources. On some smaller islands (Batiki, Kabara) the powerful constraints on resource development mean that radical change in the material basis of island life is anyway scarcely feasible. In either case land tenure systems can remain communal in ideology and basic organisation, even if in practice individual rights to the use of land have become more and more accepted. The social relations of production also retain many pre-capitalist elements, particularly in the fulfilment of domestic needs and in the sector of subsistence food production. The authority of traditional leadership within *mataqali*, village and island polities remains unchallenged, although increasingly evaded by the large absentee component of the population. Migration itself has been a means whereby pressures for social change have been postponed, and through which individuals have been able to satisfy modern needs without transformation of the rural base. This is not to imply that villages on islands like Batiki, Kabara and Koro are unchanged, nor to suggest that modifications in society and economy will not continue. Nevertheless the rate of change is slow by comparison with innovation in the capitalised rural and urban sectors of Fiji. In the case of such islands, arguably, the gap between centre and periphery continues to widen.

But villages are not everywhere preserving in fossil form the outward appearance of Fijian tradition. Elsewhere in the eastern islands can be found examples of more radical change, amounting to the beginnings of *structural transformation* in village society itself. Three further case studies will be considered in this chapter, one village on Taveuni and two on Lakeba. In each we can see the first halting steps towards two alternative futures for village society. If the processes glimpsed in embryonic form in these two islands become fully developed, then Fijian rural society will become either fully *peasantised*, or alternatively *proletarianised* in the service of a small-scale form of agri-business. Both kinds of change were possibilities foreseen during the colonial period, but they were prevented by the paternalistic interventions of colonial administration, and later by the Fijian leadership itself (see chapter 3), and secondly by the continuing viability of an adaptive version of the pre-colonial system of resource use.

In the future, however, if the Fiji state remains committed to a development strategy which attempts simultaneously to maximise the use of resources and to decentralise the pattern of growth, then the institutional constraints on land and labour which have encouraged adaptation rather than structural change will themselves come into question. In such circumstances the transformation of villagers into a peasantry or a proletariat may be seen as the price that must be paid for the achievement of planning targets. Taveuni and Lakeba are thus highly relevant case studies, indicating alternative pathways that the village sector as a whole might have to follow.

Taveuni

An unweeded garden island?

Taveuni, equal in area to Barbados in the West Indies, was by far the largest island studied by the UNESCO/UNFPA project. It was also the most complex in terms of its human use systems. On Koro, Lakeba, Batiki and Kabara the great majority of the residents live in villages, and the population/environment relationship has continued to be mediated in the context of a Fijian society and culture. On Taveuni, on the other hand, a distribution of land and authority created by colonialism has few parallels elsewhere in the eastern periphery, although it has many on Fiji's larger islands, as well as in other parts of the world. A historical review of this process is given in chapter 5.

Another factor which differentiates Taveuni from most other islands in the eastern periphery is its population composition. There are sizeable Indo-Fijian and part-European minorities living on estates, in small rural settlements, and in a dispersed quasi-urban area on the west coast of the island (Bedford 1978). In this section we focus on the Fijian population, particularly that resident in the village of Qeleni and its associated settlement along Qeleni Road. But, as shown in chapter 5, in the case of Taveuni the Fijian village experience gives insights into only one dimension of contemporary society and economy.

The villagers see an island in which – for example – the huge block of alienated land in the south-centre is a desert separating them from their fellows; estate owners and estate people alike move and relate between the estates, and know little of the villages; the settlement people know an inland frontier that belongs to neither estate nor village; the quasi-urban 'central-west' is the only place of common integration. (Brookfield 1978: 3)

Because of its fertile soils and productive land Taveuni is often termed Fiji's 'garden island', but it might be better described as a garden with many weeds and few flowers, even though a hundred years ago it was one of the main centres of concentrated 'development' activity in Fiji (see chapters 3 and 5).

Village and settlement: a Taveuni case study

The resident population of Taveuni's official villages has fluctuated considerably since 1911, the year of the first village-specific census (Fig. 9.1). Population change in the villages falls into three distinct phases: declining and/or slowly growing numbers until 1936; rapid growth between 1936 and 1956; very slow growth since 1956. Over the period 1956 to 1976, the rate of growth of village residents on Taveuni was much lower than for the Fijian population as a whole. Two kinds of migration were responsible for this deviation. The first was associated with land settlement schemes initiated in the early 1960s, when communities in the northeast and south of the island lost some residents to subdivided *mataqali* land. The second was net emigration of Fijians from Taveuni, a much more important factor underlying the slow growth of village populations than internal redistribution to settlement schemes.

Qeleni, the second largest village on Taveuni, was selected for more intensive inquiry into recent demographic and socio-economic change because it contains the two essential elements of a Fijian rural community on the island today, a nucleated village and a dispersed settlement on subdivided *mataqali* land. All but two of the major villages on Taveuni have established settlement schemes. During the early 1960s members of Qeleni's two *mataqali* agreed to subdivide a large tract of bush inland from the village as part of an agricultural development scheme sponsored by the newly-formed Land Development Authority, a bold late-colonial move to transform Fijian agriculture despite conservative opposition (see chapter 3). Most Qeleni households were allocated blocks in the subdivision and today a large proportion of the villagers' cash crops and subsistence gardens are located in the Qeleni Road area (Fig. 9.2). A sizable tract of land surrounding the village had earlier been alienated to a Fijian high chief, and this block is owned by his descendant Ratu Sir Penia

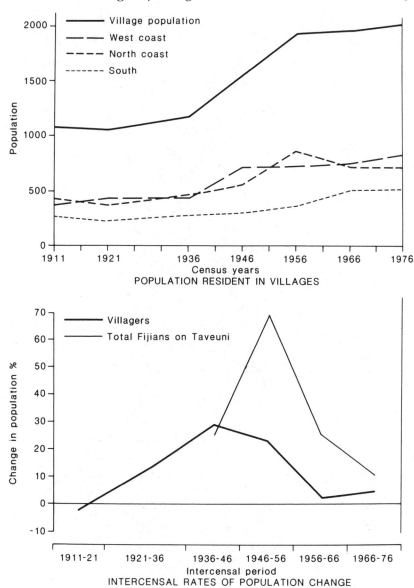

9.1 Population change on Taveuni, 1911–76

Ganilau, until 1987 Governor-General of Fiji. His estate comprises a large part of the best agricultural land near the village, but although little of it is planted in cash crops few villagers have sought permission to establish their main gardens in this area. Most prefer to use their remaining *mataqali* land and more recently their blocks along Qeleni Road. The Qeleni Road subdivision and its associated settlement are thus integral

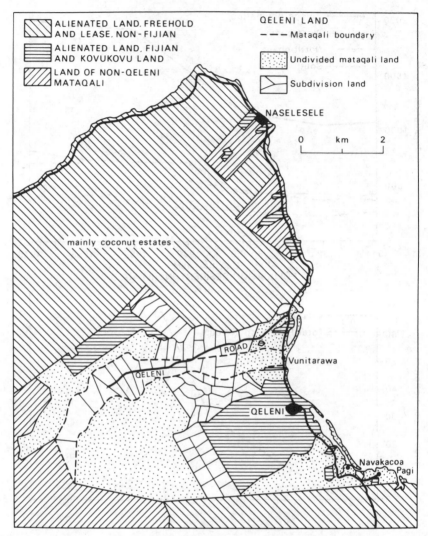

9.2 Land tenure at Qeleni

components of the modern village's socio-economic system, and can be seen as reflecting a more individualistic attitude to land and labour resources. In the mid-1970s many of the Qeleni Road blocks were managed as essentially independent peasant holdings, with much higher cash incomes than in the village (see Fig. 9.4 below).

A household survey in August 1975 revealed that there were 300 residents of Qeleni of whom almost one quarter were living in the new settlement. Whereas the numbers living in Qeleni Road had been growing rapidly since the census in 1966, the village population had been declining from the mid-1950s, but most of this decline occurred before the subdivision in Qeleni Road attracted many residents. Most emigrants from Qeleni between 1956 and 1975 left the island. Comparing the names of residents in the village in 1975 with those present at the time of the 1966 census, it was found that less than half of the 1966 residents were still living in the village in 1975, and of the 119 people who had left, 71 per cent were no longer on Taveuni (Bedford 1978).

Such a high rate of population loss is not unusual in the small islands of eastern Fiji, as we have shown in the preceding chapters. The Qeleni experience between 1966 and 1975 differs from that found on Kabara, however. In the case of Kabara's four villages it was found that 40 per cent of the households enumerated on the island in 1966 were absent in 1975. This seems to suggest that much of the migration involved whole family units, and therefore represented long-term rather than temporary movement from the island. In Qeleni only 28 per cent of the families resident in 1966 were wholly missing from the village in 1975. Emigration from Qeleni was more of a movement of individuals rather than entire families. Moreover, not all those who left were permanently lost to the village. Of the 43 Fijians who moved into the village during these nine years, 27 were members of families in the village.

This pattern of population circulation around a home base in the village was confirmed in the re-survey of Qeleni's population in July 1983. The total village population at this time was 300, a substantial increase over the number enumerated in 1975. Of those resident in 1975, 137 people were still there in 1983 (Fig. 9.3). Most of the other 163 people present had moved into the village (91), but there had also been substantial natural increase during the late 1970s and early 1980s (72 new births were recorded). Over half of the 'immigrants' had come into Qeleni from other communities on Taveuni, principally from Qeleni Road. The latter settlement seemed to have been almost completely abandoned by the middle of 1983, with only a few farms still active and fewer homes occupied.

Abandonment of the Qeleni Road settlement was a most unexpected discovery. In 1976 we had supposed that the settlement would continue to grow:

In villages such as Qeleni there is a move, among the younger farmers especially, towards using the *koro* [village] as a weekend residence and spending the bulk of the week in temporary housing on the block ... It is in this [settlement] community that there will be population growth; growth which will be increasingly at the expense of the village. (Bedford 1978: 188–9)

The predicted shift in population has not occurred, even though this process does continue elsewhere on the island, in the southern settlement

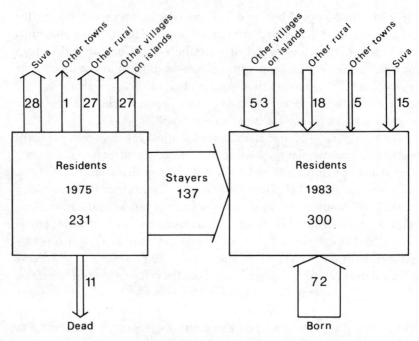

9.3 Changes in the population of Qeleni village, 1975–83

areas, around Vuna, and even in central-west Taveuni. The reasons for this setback in the process of 'individualisation' at Qeleni are instructive. Throughout Fiji there has been substantial turnover in settlement-block populations, especially in settlements based on nearby villages. Qeleni Road is perhaps an extreme case, but none the less significant.

New initiatives and old responses, 1975–83

In August 1975 twenty of the 68 blocks in the Qeleni Road subdivision had buildings on them, and fourteen of these were more or less permanently inhabited. Some of the residents who had been living in this area continuously for more than a decade were 'strangers' from outside Taveuni, mainly people from an area in Vanua Levu where there was a shortage of agricultural land. These immigrants had obtained access to land in the subdivision when government-sponsored land settlement schemes were very much in vogue in the early 1960s. The heads of six of the households surveyed in 1975 in Qeleni Road were from Vanua Levu. The rest of the residents were members of Qeleni's two *mataqali*, especially the smaller one called Nacivaciva. The head of this *mataqali* was keen to have the inland area of Nacivaciva land developed, especially after the demand for taro and *yaqona* stimulated considerable interest in cash cropping in the early 1970s.

It was the rapid growth in the *yaqona* trade within Fiji during the 1970s that transformed the rural economy of Taveuni, especially in the dispersed settlements. Thousands of *yaqona* plants were put into ground which had previously been either bush-covered, or was the site of abandoned cocoa and coconut groves – relics of the agricultural expansion programme of the 1960s. The *yaqona* economy boomed through the 1970s and in 1983 it was by far the major source of income in rural Taveuni. In Qeleni Road, however, several of the *yaqona* plantations were not well maintained. In some a disease was affecting the roots of the plants and was causing considerable concern to those who had invested their labour and land so heavily in this crop. Other plantations on the block looked as though they had been abandoned; secondary growth was choking the young plants. Taro, an important cash crop in the mid-1970s, had been virtually abandoned by 1983.

The decline of the Qeleni Road settlement was the result of many factors, some of which reflect the continuing ambivalence with which village resident Fijians have always regarded their 'independent' kin. As an example, it is instructive to consider the outcome of a timber project started in the mid-1970s by one of the early settlers. As Figure 9.2 shows, the Qeleni Road settlement extends quite deeply into 'Forest Reserve', and the Department of Forests at one stage proposed eviction of settlers from such land, but were over-ruled. The man concerned in the timber project had a clear title to his block of land and he attempted to establish a timber business with the support of the Ministry of Fijian Affairs. The project was designed to provide part-time employment for several of the younger men living in Qeleni Road while they were clearing the heavy bush on their blocks. Initially the project seems to have been successful but it was not long before the timber on land being developed by residents in the settlement was worked out. When the leader of the project attempted to get approval to extend logging onto blocks belonging to people resident in Qeleni village he ran into stiff opposition. Questions were being asked about the distribution of profits, especially as the entrepreneur had acquired a taxi, was getting loans from government agencies to start other businesses, and was an 'outsider' from Vanua Levu married to a Qeleni woman. Jealousy seems to have been an important motive for obstruction to this enterprise, and in 1981 the timber milling project was shelved indefinitely.

There were also direct conflicts of interest between residents on the block and their village-based kin. According to informants in the village in 1983 the initiative and enterprise of the Qeleni Road settlers was sapped continuously by the demand for produce (taro, copra, *yaqona*) and cash by kin in the village. Too much produce was 'pulled back' into the village rather than marketed, and the returns for hard physical labour on the block, in what were more difficult living conditions than those in the village, discouraged many young men. Initially successful attempts to establish a regular market for Qeleni Road fresh produce on the plantation island of Laucala to the east seem to have failed after the mid-1970s. When the demand for labour to work on sugar cane farms on Vanua Levu began to expand in the late 1970s many abandoned their land for seasonal wage employment. In July 1983 approximately 20 Qeleni men were absent cutting cane on Vanua Levu, mainly at Seaqaqa.

Another factor which seems to have played quite an important role in the depopulation of the Qeleni Road settlement is the desire of young couples to live in reasonably close proximity to the school attended by their children. The village school in Qeleni had been up-graded considerably between 1975 and 1983 and several former block dwellers said they had moved back to the village to take advantage of the school. Instead of commuting from the block to the village to use the latter's facilities, the movement was now in the opposite direction, from the village to the block to use the land. Given the distances involved, coupled with the fact that the trek to the blocks is over rough steep country, it is not surprising that land in Qeleni Road is not being farmed as intensively as it was in the mid-1970s, or, indeed, in the mid-1960s when cocoa and coconuts were being planted under government subsidy.

Not all of the former settlement residents moved to Qeleni village. Most of those had come from outside Taveuni either returned to their former homes, or moved on to a nearby coconut estate to work for wages, or went to Suva or Labasa in search of work. Those who had family in Qeleni village tended however to go back to the village. For Qeleni it certainly remains true that 'the village is still the focus of Fijian activity' (Lasaqa 1984: 57). But it must be stressed that within Taveuni the fate of Qeleni Road is unusual; many other settlements have prospered and grown during the same period.

There is indeed no strictly economic rationale behind the continuing strength of the Fijian village community. In many cases, as at Qeleni, villagers have not settled permanently on their own blocks of land, nor have they moved away in large numbers to seek regular wage employment. The community continues to offer greater security: it is a known world, and except for quarrels a fairly tranquil world. For older people it has been their home throughout their lives except for a few years working on estates or in town. For almost everyone over thirty the village is where they were born and where they went to school. Today access to retail shops, a hospital, secondary schools and government offices is not difficult from villages like Qeleni. All these services can be reached on a regular bus route which links all the larger rural communities on the island. Villagers on Taveuni are not isolated from the facilities in the urban centres. In this respect they are different from villagers on islands like Koro, Batiki and Kabara which do not have quasi-urban centres like Waiyevo-Somosomo on Taveuni or Tubou on Lakeba. Greater diversity in the rural economy, coupled with greater accessibility to urban amenities and a range of employment have kept a higher proportion of Taveuni's *mataqali* members on the island than is the case in most parts of the eastern periphery. For some the village way of life is still the strongest reason for choosing to remain.

Conclusion

The partial failure of the Qeleni Road settlement is not typical of the fate of independent farming in Fiji as a whole, now practised by as many as a quarter of all Fijian farmers. But while our selection of Qeleni may have proved, in retrospect, to have been unrepresentative, its failure illustrates weaknesses to which all of these initiatives are liable: the demands of village society, jealousies between individuals, the lack of follow-through on the part of Government agencies which promote or assist particular enterprises.

Although the Qeleni villagers have shown they are reluctant to become more fully individualised, the economy of the village has meanwhile undergone another and very signal form of transformation through its growing dependence on wages, earned either within Taveuni or through seasonal migration to the cane fields on Vanua Levu (Fig. 9.4). A growing dependence on wages is not perhaps a rural-based initiative – indeed it saps local initiative – but it represents a choice by villagers of a new role. By this means the village becomes, in part, a dormitory, and in addition must act as a nursery for the reproduction of labour serving the capitalised agricultural sector. In these circumstances, too, social support and economic support lose something of the close nexus which characterised the 'traditional' rural way of life. There are many villages like Qeleni in Fiji, though not many elsewhere in eastern Fiji. By virtue of the island's location and its diverse economy, the population of Taveuni is able to participate in wage-income activity much more than on the other islands which we studied, but people elsewhere would do the same if they could. Qeleni thus represents a growing trend toward proletarianisation of a voluntary kind, and if the trend is further advanced in this village than in others, the new approach to income-gaining exhibited there is none the

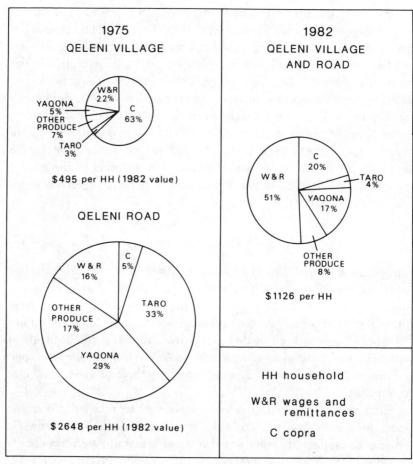

9.4 Sources of village income at Qeleni in 1982, by comparison with village and settlement incomes in 1975 (Data from Bedford (1978) and Siwatibau (1982))

less a widespread phenomenon of growing significance. We shall see below other evidence of such transformation.

Lakeba

Island of experiments

Lakeba too is distinctive in many ways, with an importance that far outweighs its modest size (56 km²). Historically, it became the key island in pre-colonial Lau and was the first base of the Tongan empire that extended over much of eastern Fiji during the third quarter of the nineteenth century. Its diverse resources, including important wetlands fed from permanent springs, had much to do with its focal position in intra-Lauan trade. It was the first place in which Christian missionaries were able to establish themselves in Fiji. As the residence of the paramount chief of Lau it has grown in national importance with the rise to power of the present holder of that title, Ratu Mara, who became Chief Minister in 1966, was Prime Minister from 1970 until 1987, and is now *de facto* Prime Minister again. Lakeba was the first island in eastern Fiji in which a telephone system was established (Spate 1959), even though it later fell into disuse. It was the first to be encircled by a motorable road. It was the third after Ovalau and Taveuni to receive an airstrip, and among the first to get a new jetty under a programme initiated in the 1970s. In 1983 it had the only full bank branch in the eastern region.

Lakeba's classic *talasiga* landscape, discussed in chapter 2, was the first area outside the two main islands to be reclaimed for plantations of *Pinus caribaea*, now producing small quantities of poles and other timber for construction in the islands and export to Suva. In 1980 it became the locus of an important innovation in decentralised copra milling, discussed in different contexts in this chapter and the next. Machinery from India, New Zealand and West Germany has been donated for forestry and for other purposes, and a 'China Friendship Road' across the island signals the international attention received, even though the Chinese mission's advice to plant rice in the wetlands was not heeded. Some Lakeba farmers had themselves taken up rice around 1970 and their paddy fields are clearly visible on the 1972 air photographs; however, this was an experiment that failed and by 1975 only the broken-down bunds remained.

The chiefly village of Tubou, where the first missionaries landed, where the Tongan ruler Ma'afu is buried and where the modern Tui Lau and Prime Minister resided, has increased in both local and national importance at the same time. This incipient urban centre in the south of the island, different though it is from the more multi-ethnic and commercial string of 'urban' villages and settlements in central-west Taveuni, is gradually having an effect on the life and structure of the six more traditional villages on the northern and eastern coasts of the island. The contrast between 'two Lakebas' was sharper when we first went to the island in 1975 than it is today.

Lakeba before 1975, and after

We went to Lakeba both because of the special problems of its landscape, and also because it had been severely smitten by Hurricane Val just four months before our preliminary visit there. We have reviewed the impact of storm and drought on the eastern islands in chapter 4, and aspects of the relief operations of modern times in chapter 6. It is interesting to compare the changing effect of major storms in Lakeba through recent years, as these events both punctuate and emphasise the changing structure of the island economy and society. In 1948 Lakeba was struck by a severe storm, but then not again until the major event in 1975, described above in chapter 4. Informants recall that recovery in 1948–9 was easier than in 1975–6. In the 1940s housing was still predominantly of local materials, and so was quickly replaceable. Emigration had not yet distorted the age-structure of the population to a significant degree, and extended-family working groups could more easily be assembled; moreover, modern individualism had not yet developed. The loss of cash income was less severe in 1948–9 than in 1975–6, partly because of good prices for such copra as remained in contrast to the low prices of the latter year, but also because dependence on imported foods was then much less than it later became; in 1974 each person was purchasing, on average, over $100 worth of imported goods from stores on the island, of which 46 per cent was foodstuffs (M. Brookfield 1979: 183). In 1948 the recommended supply of relief foodstuffs to Lakeba was only sufficient for 23 days at normal consumption (McLean 1976), whereas in 1975, and again after the much less severe storm of 1983, relief went on for months.

Changes in land use have contributed to this growing dependence. Often coconuts have been planted as part of the cultivation of food gardens, which they ultimately replace. The high per capita copra production which Lakeba achieved by the early 1970s was accompanied by a considerable loss of food-producing land. In the northern village of Yadrana, for instance, the valley flats just inland of the houses were formerly planted with irrigated taro, plantains and yams, but by the 1960s were devoted almost entirely to coconuts. The gardens have had to extend upslope and up-valley, into areas formerly regarded as too steep, difficult, poor or remote to be cultivated. Most of the inland gardens were for cassava, a crop readily damaged by high wind, and the shift to this crop advanced rapidly between 1948 and 1974. In 1948–9 the famine foods such as swamp taro (*Cyrtosperma chamissonis, pulaka*) and wild yams (*Dioscorea nummularia, tivoli*) were eaten as they were again in 1975–6, but whereas in 1948–9 the garden crops were soon back in full production, the same was not true twenty-seven years later.

The hurricane of January 1975 is an important event in the modern history of Lakeba, for most of the innovations that we describe below have taken place since this major shock to confidence. Although pine planting began earlier in the 1970s most of the trees were still small when the hurricane struck, and they yielded no income or production. Lakeba's

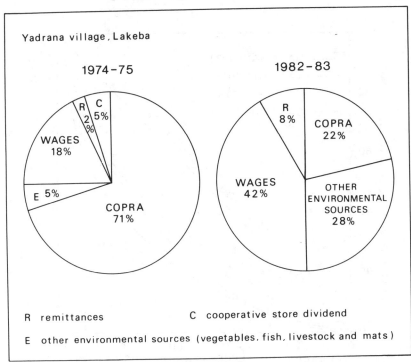

Yadrana village, Lakeba

1974-75

1982-83

R remittances   C cooperative store dividend

E other environmental sources (vegetables, fish, livestock and mats)

9.5 Sources of village income at Yadrana, 1974–5 compared to 1982–3 (Data from Table 9.3 and field surveys)

per capita production of copra was among the highest in Fiji, and the economy depended heavily on this crop, but in contrast to 1948, the market price of the small amount of copra that could still be produced in 1975 was declining month by month, to reach late in the year its lowest point in real terms for 40 years. The effect of copra dependence, when economic depression coincided with natural disaster, was what we observed when we first began work on this island.

The crisis at village level

The UNESCO/UNFPA project began its field work on Lakeba in July 1975, at a time when the fallen coconuts had been used up, ruined crops had been harvested and eaten, and savings had been spent. It was a time of crisis in a number of villages, particularly those in north Lakeba where damage had been quite severe and where supplementary earnings were available to very few households. A survey of 46 households in Yadrana village, north Lakeba, in July 1975, provides an indication of the degree of dependence on copra. With cash incomes averaging $848 per household, copra contributed 71 per cent of the total (Fig. 9.5).

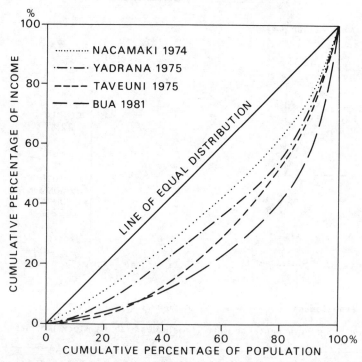

9.6 Lorenz curve showing distribution of cash income between households in four populations (Data from Nankivell (1978), Bayliss-Smith (1983b), and field surveys)

The survey also demonstrated the substantial variations that existed between households in their cash incomes (Fig. 9.6). The Lorenz curve for Yadrana is comparable to that of Batiki, both of which show less egalitarian income distributions than Nacamaki on Koro. On the other hand the inequality is even more marked in Taveuni district (1975 data) and in Bua Province (1981 data), where there are stark contrasts between households in access to resources because of social stratification and land tenure inequalities. These contrasts are less marked in Lakeba outside the Tubou area itself.

Per capita incomes for the twelve month period up to June 1975 averaged $124 at Yadrana, a level similar to Batiki (see Table 7.3), but a large proportion of this income derived from the second half of 1974 when copra returns were still quite substantial. In the aftermath of the hurricane, in July–September 1975, surveys of earnings during a seven-day period for a random sample of 22 households in Yadrana and Nasaqalau showed that household incomes had fallen to below $5 per week of which only 21 per cent derived from copra (Bayliss-Smith 1977a).

There is no doubt that this low income level, averaging on a per capita basis about $40 per year, persisted throughout the months that followed. Hurricane relief supplies alleviated the situation, but a number of households suffered real distress. Famine foods such as wild yams, swamp taro and various leaves were being consumed when available, and fish, shellfish and crabs were not only making a contribution to the diet (an estimated 13 per cent of food energy), but also had become important market items. Even so there were several reports of crops being stolen at night, and in some cases the abuse of *kerekere* (customary appropriation of a kinsman's property) began to place severe strains on inter-household relations. Both of the co-operative stores were under an obligation to supply store goods on credit because most society members were owed a dividend from the earlier period of high copra prices, but abuse of this practice lead to such indebtedness that within a year both stores were effectively bankrupt.

As a result of these strains on village society, new possibilities were being considered. Some emphasised the value of traditional forms of co-operation, as an insurance in times of trouble; others, probably the majority, saw increased individualism as a necessary step to safeguard the future prosperity of their families. New crops, the planting of pines, fishing companies, wage employment in Tubou and emigration to Suva – these were all topics which were widely discussed. In the short term, the necessary response in the villages was a return to the traditional subsistence economy, including the use of famine foods unfamiliar to the whole generation that had grown up since the 1948 hurricane. In the long term the 1975 crisis seems to have lead to a questioning of existing norms, and has thus been a catalyst for change. In particular, there have been innovations in the coconut economy, which could be as far-reaching as the switchover from village production of coconut oil to copra drying in the 1880s.

The two Lakebas

The first field work of the project, by Bayliss-Smith, was in 1975 and concentrated on the two northern villages of Yadrana and Nasaqalau, especially the former. In 1976, while the work discussed in chapter 2 was also in progress on the island, Muriel Brookfield resided for several months in the south of Lakeba, and carried out inquiries especially in Tubou, the adjacent village of Levuka, and in Waciwaci 5 km to the east. In what follows we first discuss change in the south of the island, then evaluate changes in the island as a whole mainly from the perspective of the northern village of Yadrana.

By the mid-1970s the scale of government and related activity had already led to a situation where 117 wage earners in Tubou, Levuka and the adjacent Government Station were receiving 82 per cent of the island's total wage income (M. Brookfield 1979: 177). Waciwaci received a further 8 per cent, and the remaining 10 per cent was scattered thinly among the five other villages. With agriculture in a state of crisis, a huge gap had opened up between the 'two Lakebas', differences characterised as follows:

> Lakeba has been dichotomized in different ways in the course of this discussion. A crop-dependent and a wage-dependent Lakeba emerge strongly ... while the distinction between Tubou and the rest of the island ... is of major importance in social terms, for all outer-villages interact more with Tubou than with each other, and are conscious of their subordination to Tubou and of the privileged status of the chiefly village.
>
> There are, nonetheless, sharp distinctions within Tubou, and in all parts of the island there are people who move between the crop-dependent and wage-dependent sectors; the greater part of the latter sector is made up of people who are also farmers. (M. Brookfield 1979: 194)

Tubou: the 'central place'

It will already be apparent that Tubou has become more than a village. For everyone on Lakeba it is the place of contact with the outside world, with visitors, goods or post arriving and departing almost every day by sea or by air. Ships call at Tubou and only at Tubou: the days when some ships circled the island are long past. All goods are landed here, and from here all exports leave. The sick from other islands in central and southern Lau are brought to the hospital at the Government Station by the medical ship, *Vuniwai-ni-Lau*. Children from the smaller islands are often sent to Lakeba rather than to Suva for their early post-primary schooling, and sometimes for their primary schooling as well. Government officials arrive frequently by air and sea, and more recently a series of official overseas visitors have come to the island through Tubou. There is a constant sense of activity, albeit low-key, and of comings and goings that is lacking in the quieter outlying villages. To all this is added not only meetings of the local Island Council, but also larger meetings of the Lau Provincial Council and occasionally even of the national Great Council of Chiefs. All villages in Lakeba are involved in these latter events, even though they take place in Tubou, since villagers are required to bring contributions to the feasts and often to take part in the entertainments provided. The largest churches and their associated youth groups are in Tubou, and more recently, since electrification of Tubou alone in the late 1970s, there has been added the more secular attraction of video. Awareness of the world beyond is high in Tubou, and opportunities to benefit from and to generate new ideas are many.

It is not surprising that Tubou, with its distinctive functions, also has a distinctive employment structure. In our survey in 1976 there were 99 households listed, but only 40 heads of household said they were full-time farmers. Almost all of the remaining households were headed by wage earners, and a few contained one or more other wage earners, in various types of employment ranging from managerial and governmental posts to clerical, mechanical and labouring work. The Roko, schoolteachers, business agents, Co-operative Society managers and their staffs, and the Public Works Department were all in Tubou; the non-Lakebans in the Government Station, and some others around in the village, were additional wage earners and spenders. There were already a few small entrepreneurs, a group substantially augmented by 1983. Many of these people could afford to pay for some of their farming work to be done for them, and a few relied entirely on employees if no relatives were available to undertake the work. The adjacent village of Levuka, which we discuss in more detail below, and Waciwaci to the east where several of the hospital nurses resided, walking each way to work, also participated in this substantial body of wage employment.

A distinctive feature of Tubou was the fact that by no means all women stayed and worked at home. About a third as many women as men were employed, mainly as schoolteachers, clerks and nurses, reflecting perhaps the value that Tubou people have long placed on educating all their children, and the ability of at least some members of this relatively wealthy village to meet the costs. The costs of education were sometimes shared between kin and affines belonging to different households. Disparities in income were, however, great, for Tubou was not the uniformly privileged community that some other Lauans often believed. Among a sample of 24 Tubou households drawn proportionately among the farming and non-farming population annual income in 1976 ranged from $131 to $7,988.

Tubou is part-village, part-town, and wholly neither. Unlike the quasi-urban centre in Taveuni, or any other quasi-town in Fiji, Tubou is entirely Fijian in population. In a sense it is a microcosm of the range of social conditions encountered in eastern Fiji all assembled in one place. As the village of a very high chief it is a place where traditional formalities are highly regarded; as a window on the world it is also a place beset by many social problems, including inter-generational conflicts of a wholly modern kind, and a considerable amount of petty crime. It is a place where small-scale entrepreneurship can flourish, but in which traditional organisational modes, or what are regarded as traditional modes, are employed to structure the larger economic activities. Since 1975 this set of contradictions has spread more widely in Lakeba, as we shall see below.

Levuka: a proletarian village

Within the larger fabric of Tubou, but not forming part of the village of Tubou in the perception of the people, is the distinctive small community of Levuka, located alongside the heavily silted Tubou creek. Unlike the Government station, and the forestry station and other new additions to the 'greater Tubou' complex, Levuka is a 'traditional' community dating from pre-colonial times. During the short period of our return to the field in 1983, work was concentrated on this smaller community with its more manageable population of only 132, rather than the 950 people of the whole complex.

Levuka is unlike any other of the villages studied by us in eastern Fiji. The Levukans, or 'Levukians', were described by Wilkes in 1841 (Wilkes 1952, vol. 2: 54) as trading specialists who had no fixed place of abode but resided principally at chiefly centres such as Lakeba, at Somosomo and Vuna on Taveuni, and in some other places. Settled late in Lakeba they were boat people who lived by fishing and trading. As was common in such cases they were given land on which to build shelters and to mend their boats and nets, but no more. As their trading function declined under the changes brought about by colonial rule, they established themselves in their settlement by the Tubou creek, and from this time on Lakeba had a settlement of proletarian rather than peasant people, a people who became used to making the most of any opportunities that were offered.

The landless Levukans quickly realised the need to have their own supplies of vegetables and fruit and by agreement, exchange and marriage eventually obtained leasing rights to a number of plots of land, including the northern part of Nabuni swamp from the people of Waciwaci, which gave them a valuable taro-growing block. By 1975 they, like other Lakebans, were interested in cash crops which would fetch a good price, and produced *yaqona* and copra from small blocks scattered over the southern part of the island. By the time Hurricane Val struck Lakeba over half the men in Levuka of working age gave their principal employment as farming. In May 1976, when Tubou, Levuka and Waciwaci were surveyed (M. Brookfield 1979), the population of Levuka totalled 132. There were 38 working males and of these 22 were 'farmers' (Table 9.1), though some of these also made extra money by selling such goods as 'Fiji' tobacco, handicrafts and fish. An estimate of the environmental income of Levuka for 1974–5 was $124 per capita, comparable with the whole income for Yadrana.

The remaining 16 males were all wage earners, ten of them in the Public Works Department either full- or part-time, work which they usually managed to combine with some early morning or weekend gardening.

Table 9.1 *Male occupations in Levuka*

	Males working	Farmers	Wage-earners
1976	38	22	16
1983	30	12	18

Source: Field data (M. Brookfield)

Others were employed in the local co-operative societies, in the hospital and the Tubou water-supply service – then the only one in Lakeba. Their wage earnings brought the average per capita income of Levuka up to $250–350 in 1974–6 (see Table 7.2), which explains why these almost landless people with their proximity to employment opportunities were the envy of the more distant villagers. In land opportunity terms, the Qeleni villagers in Taveuni were closest to the Levukans among those we studied, though there are quite a number of other small communities with very little land in the eastern islands. Few of them, however, had a nearby Tubou to provide alternative sources of income.

By 1983 the picture had changed dramatically. The lessons of Hurricane Val and the unstable and unsatisfactory price of copra had been learned. While the total population of Levuka remained unchanged at 132 the number of farmers had dropped from 22 to 12, and of these only seven remained from among the 'farmers' of 1976. Two of these seven had supplemented farming from other local opportunities, in one case fishing and in the other by brewing and selling a local intoxicating drink. Of those who had left farming, one had retired while six had gained employment in Lakeba; two in Tubou, three at the coconut-oil mill and one at the pine forestry station. The others had migrated, most of them to Suva.

The fact that five new 'farmers' were living in Levuka in 1983 deserves comment. One was a former public servant, retired from the Prison Service in Suva, two were young men formerly at school and two were former Public Works Department (PWD) workers. By 1983, however, wage earners outnumbered farmers in Levuka by three to two, while the total number of working males had dropped by 21 per cent since 1976 because of out-migration. The two female wage earners encountered in 1976 had married and moved to other parts of the island.

Levuka typifies the great desire of many island people for wage employment, wherever the wage is perceived as adequate. Since the Levukans have little tie to the land, though they are anxious to retain access to such as they have, they are quick to shift their labour input between activities when economic conditions change. They are willing proletarians if they are able to be, who are ready to pay for food, whether imported or locally produced, rather than produce it themselves. They are also prepared to adjust to the dietary changes – an increase in dependence on readily grown cassava rather than the preferred taro – that this frequently implies. Though there was no opportunity in 1983 to repeat the 1976 survey in the whole of Tubou and Waciwaci, there was no doubt that many others in the south of Lakeba had taken similar decisions. Levuka people exemplify in an extreme form the structural change that we also see in Qeleni and Yadrana, and which undoubtedly would take place in other 'traditionally-based' islands if the opportunity arose.

The wider changes in Lakeba

It will be apparent that in 1975–6 we encountered something of a centre–periphery structure at micro-level within Lakeba itself, a dichotomy strongly reinforced by the disastrous consequences of storm and economic depression for the agricultural communities. Before this event there was some marketing of produce from the other villages in Tubou, even though little transport was available other than canoes; this had ceased in 1975 and was barely resumed before we left the field in 1976. Since that time, however, Tubou has become an important market for village produce and a place of wage employment for village men. A regular bus service, instituted a few years ago, has done much to make this possible.

There are, however, larger changes in the island economy as a whole. Entrepreneurship, and the setting up of private small shops in competition with the Co-operative Societies, is not confined to Tubou but has also emerged in other villages. However the most important single factor in change has been the establishment of a small coconut oil mill at Wainiyabia, 8 km west of Lakeba on a former leasehold estate now held for the chiefly Vuanirewa *mataqali* by the Prime Minister. Together with the pine scheme, the plantings of which now cover more than half the interior of the island, this mill is a striking example of the use of Lakeba as a testing site for development initiatives thought to hold promise for Fiji's outer islands. We discuss the mill in some detail as a commercial innovation in chapter 10, since it forms part of a larger set of changes in the coconut industry as a whole. Here, however, we review the impact of this imaginative innovation on the island economy of 1983.

Revolution in the coconut economy

The coconut economy of Lakeba was a source of pride before 1975, since the island attained the highest yields in Lau and produced more copra

8 Making copra in Tubou, before the establishment of the coconut oil mill (TBS photograph, 1974). An employee of the Lakeba Co-operative Association is shovelling partially dried copra into racks, for stacking in the drier (right). When fully dry the copra is bagged and put into the store (left), prior to being shipped to Suva.

than the whole of the much larger island of Kadavu (Brookfield 1985). Following the major shock of that year production fell dramatically, and so did confidence in the future of the industry. New initiatives were needed, and they were taken in two stages, the first of which was centralised control over marketing replacing the voluntary partial centralisation that we encountered in the mid-1970s. At that time most villagers sold green coconut in small quantities to small village co-operative societies which then dried the copra, bagged it and sent it by lorry to the Lakeba Co-operative Association (LCA) in Tubou, which in turn organised shipping to Suva. In addition, however, there was a large minority of villagers who attempted to improve their returns by drying their own copra, and in some cases other people's through illegal purchases. There were 145 individual consigners of copra to Suva in 1974, accounting for one-third of the island's production (M. Brookfield 1979), but in 1976 this option was closed as a result of a move supported by the chiefs to improve and expand the LCA, which thus gained an effective monopoly in copra marketing. This control over an assured market was then followed by the establishment of the mill at Wainiyabia, which after 1980 accounted for almost the entire output of the island.

A few bold individuals resumed private shipping of dry copra in 1981, in protest at the poor prices offered by the mill. Occasionally whole nuts have also been sent to Suva for sale, even clandestinely, loaded aboard ship by night, but in general the voluntary embargo on private marketing arrangements has been respected.

The coconut oil mill began operation in 1980. Despite financial and technical difficulties, it has had a revolutionary effect on how the coconut industry on the island is organised. How far has this revolution in technology, and the element of coercion that its introduction has entailed, been of benefit to the villager?

Costs and benefits of centralised control

In Yadrana in 1983 there were complaints about the price offered by the mill, but in comparison with green copra prices offered elsewhere in eastern Fiji there seems to be no reason for discontent. The villagers on Koro, for example, received 7 cents per kg from the village co-operative stores, whereas the Lakeba price from the mill was 8.6 cents, the equivalent of 60 per cent of the Suva price for dry copra. On the other hand there is no doubt that private shipping of dry copra to Suva would be more rewarding, were this option still available. What also irked the villagers was losing the freedom to cut copra according to their own timetable rather than that of the factory, and the waste of time involved in travelling to Wainiyabia in order to receive cash payments. Most villagers would still prefer to dry their own copra in their own plantations (which are sometimes remote from the road), rather than having to conform to factory quotas and fixed rates of return.

An element of coercion is also present in the provision of wage labour for the mill. Initially each village on the island was allocated a proportional share of the labour force. There was free transport to and from Wainiya-bia, and with wage rates of 90 cents per hour for operators and 80 cents per hour for labourers, there was no shortage of willing hands, especially in the initial period when village economies had not fully recovered from localised damage caused by tropical storm Fay, which passed directly across the island in December 1979. However, after six months of operation the rates were reduced to 65 and 55 cents per hour respectively, which provides a weekly wage equivalent in value to only 250–300 kg of green copra. Under favourable conditions this amount of copra can be cut in about two days, particularly if family assistance is available. In 1983 two villages on the island refused to provide their quota of mill workers, ostensibly because there was such a shortage of labour in the village that both food crops and coconuts were being neglected, but in reality as a protest against the low wage rates offered by comparison with the more favourable returns and preferred life style in the village. This 'strike' led to a 10 per cent wage increase later in the year, as coconut oil prices improved.

Despite this unrest there is no doubt that the mill can continue to depend on a labour supply from Lakeba villages. Its success, and that of the LCA which runs it, are matters of particular concern to Ratu Sir Kamisese Mara, and in the villages his authority remains virtually unquestioned. Thirty-two people were employed at the mill (nine from Yadrana village), providing altogether $60,000 per year in wages to the island economy. At full capacity 72 people would be directly employed, or about 15 per cent of the adult male population of the island. This kind of scheme has the potential of transforming the economy of Pacific islands from casual cash cropping by subsistence-oriented farmers to industrial production by a rural proletariat under the quite rigid control of a centralised processing plant. It is significant, however, that this kind of revolutionary change has only occurred in the Fiji periphery by means of a pilot project that is subsidised, and through some measure of coercion within a patron–client relationship between the villagers and their traditional leaders. As such, it is doubtful if the Lakeba experience can be transposed to other islands in Fiji, where neither the social nor the political circumstances would be so favourable.

The changes in the Lakeba coconut economy in the 1980s are of the kind suggested as inevitable by Yen (1980), who reviewed the intractable problems that are faced by farmers in the Pacific islands in meeting the requirements of efficient commercial agriculture when operating within the mixed subsistence–cash crop mode. He concluded that 'production through larger-scale management systems seems likely to fill the role of the growth sector, if only by default'. The large-scale approach need not preclude smallholder land ownership, but 'success depends on correct decisions by the management, and the active acquiescence of all members of the group in planting plans, agronomic scheduling, and meeting quality standards' (Yen 1980: 99).[1]

Seen in this light the Lakeba coconut oil mill is an important social experiment. For copra it represents a radical attempt to improve productivity, and if successful it would lead to reform in what has been described as 'the almost medieval structure of the copra industry, with its low capitalisation, high labour coefficient, minimal R & D input, and archaic

---

[1] This 'plantation mode of management', strongly advocated by Ward and Proctor (1980) in the same report, has recently been criticised in a defence of the smallholder mode by Hardaker et al. (1984).

Table 9.2 *Energy output per hour of work, Lakeba*

Year	Food energy purchased per dollar spent (MJ)	Energy output (MJ) per person-hour of work			
		Subsistence agriculture	Fishing	Green copra cutting	Wage labour
1974	20.28	(11.0)	3.0	18.1	10.1 (PWD)
1975	28.36	6.0	3.0	7.4	15.6 (PWD)
1983	16.79	(11.0)	3.0	9.6	7.1– [a]10.1 (Mill)
					[b]26.2 (PWD)

Notes and sources: Subsistence agriculture: 1974 and 1983 are approximations based on estimated costs and returns at Nacamaki, Koro (see chapter 7). 1975 was a period of replanting after hurricane damage in January, and the productivity ratio is based on work during a survey of 40 person-weeks of activities in Yadrana (July) and Nasaqalau (September), and on food output assuming that the gardens will ultimately supply 62 per cent of the energy in the diet as in 1972 and 1973 (Bayliss-Smith 1977a: 90, 94, 95).

Fishing: 12 day survey of all fishing at Yadrana in 1975, covering 1,622 hours during which 861 kg of fish, 107 kg of shellfish, crustaceans, holothurians and octopus, and 22 kg of algae were obtained.

Copra, 1974: uses Nacamaki productivity data of 32,400 person-hours of work including travel per 215.5 tonnes green copra equivalent (i.e. 6.65 kg per hour – see chapter 7), converted to dollars using average Yadrana co-operative green price, July–December 1974, of $0.134 per kg, and then converted to local food energy equivalent using Nasaqalau store purchase data showing 20.28 MJ per dollar spent (Bayliss-Smith 1977a: 74–5, 81).

Copra, 1975: as above, but co-operative green copra price of $0.039 per kg for period March–December, yielding 28.36 MJ per dollar spent (a greater yield than the previous year because of concentration of expenditure on cheap starch and sugar foods during the post-hurricane crisis).

Copra, 1983: as above, but Wainiyabia mill price of $0.086 per kg of green copra, yielding 16.79 MJ food energy per dollar spent, based on data from two stores in Nasaqalau and Yadrana covering period 6/82–5/83.

Wages: weekly wage rates in 1974 of 50 cents, and in 1975 55 cents, per hour (PWD labourers, assuming 50 hour week including travel to and from village), and in 1983 44–60 cents per hour (Wainiyabia mill, 50 hour week, labourers and operators respectively), or $1.56 per hour (PWD labourers), in both cases converted to energy equivalent as for copra 1983 above.

systems of marketing and transportation' (Brookfield 1977: 136). However, the evidence so far does not suggest that productivity on Lakeba has been raised as a result of this experiment. Since the mill was established total output, assessed in terms of dry copra equivalent, has not reached 70 per cent of copra production in the pre-1975 period.[2] Hurricane damage and drought cannot account for more than a part of this decline. It is clear that many coconuts are not being collected, and as of 1983 the question must be raised as to whether there was sufficient economic incentive for villagers to do so at current prices.

Fluctuation in the village economy

Calculations showing the amount of energy gained per hour of work in various activities indicate how substantial have been the fluctuations in economic incentive over the past decade (Table 9.2). In 1974 copra cutting was twice as profitable as wage labour in average energy returns per hour of work. By 1975 the situation was reversed: labourers working for the Public Works Department were earning per hour twice as much as copra cutters. For persons receiving the minimum government wage, the gap between labourers and village copra cutters continued to widen in the following years. By 1983 PWD labourers were receiving the equivalent of 26 MJ food energy per hour, but the average return from copra, although somewhat better than in 1975, was now scarcely better than one-third of this level. For employees of the coconut oil mill the position was even less favourable. Mill earnings of only 7 MJ per hour represented an average return somewhat below that available from copra, and well below that to be gained from subsistence agriculture. Although the cash wage was popular, the discipline of the mill imposed severe constraints on individual freedom – especially for the technical and supervisory staff for whom breakdowns and other problems created frequent and unpredictable additional demands. Mill workers are compelled to reduce their own food production, unless their inputs can be substituted by family members or by paid labour; in any case an increase in store purchases is an almost inevitable consequence of their employment, and their dissatisfaction with the low wages paid gains force from this consideration.

The nature of village-based work has changed, however, with a substantial shift away from a dependence on copra (see Fig. 9.5). In Yadrana a random sample of 21 households (37 per cent of the total) was

---

[2] Total output for Lakeba in 1981 reached 770 tonnes of dry copra equivalent, well below the mid-1970s peak of over 1,000 tonnes (Brookfield 1985). The same is true of the particular village of Yadrana, where in 1974 total production reached 159 tonnes of which 51 tonnes were sold privately, in a period free from natural hazards and with record high prices (M. Brookfield 1979: 152, 172). In the twelve months July 1982–June 1983, according to LCA data, Yadrana residents sold 207 tonnes of green copra to the mill, worth almost $17,000 in net receipts. In dry copra equivalent this represents about 102 tonnes, to which should be added the output of one villager who bypassed the LCA with 2 tonnes of privately shipped copra. The total of 104 tonnes represents a substantial reduction since 1974.

Table 9.3 *Cash earnings of 21 households in Yadrana, July 1982–June 1983*

Source	Total income ($)	Number of households
Environmental		
Copra	6,350	18
Voivoi and mats	4,080	14
Fish	2,510	15
Crabs	590	4
Pigs	470	4
Taro	270	4
Pineapples	100	1
Cassava	20	1
Yaqona	20	1
Shell	20	1
Sweet potatoes	10	1
Non-environmental		
Regular wages	8,890	8
Remittances	2,370	11
Casual wages	110	3
Total	25,810	21
Average per household	1,229	–

Source: Field data

interviewed in 1983, and these data revealed a remarkable growth in informal marketing, particularly of handicrafts, fish, crabs, and vegetables (Table 9.3). Copra is now less important than all these other environmental sources of income, a situation inconceivable even ten years ago when 'the coconut overlay' was unquestioned, and when Tubou as a market barely existed and in any case was poorly integrated with its village hinterland.

At Yadrana, as at Qeleni, the other remarkable change is the growing predominance of wage-earning in the economy. Altogether one-third of Yadrana households now have at least one wage earner travelling daily to Tubou or Wainiyabia, and there are many households gaining income from casual labour, remittances and store profits. By comparison with 1975, when only two men had jobs outside the village and copra was still king, the village cash economy has been transformed. It is now based on linkages with a more diversified state-capitalist and petty-capitalist economy, and with markets no longer regulated by the village co-operative society. The influence of commerce is even extending to food crops, fishing and handicrafts, which can no longer be regarded as wholly subsistence activities.

Paradoxically, the position of the so-called subsistence sector has improved. For a while during the copra boom of 1974, the food energy from copra exceeded any likely to be obtainable from subsistence agriculture, but in the 1980s the average productivity of the two sectors has become very similar. Moreover, since yams, taro and fish now fetch good prices amongst the growing wage-earning population in Tubou, these items have gained in productivity beyond their purely subsistence value. One symptom of this change at Yadrana in 1983 was the construction in valley swamps of new taro irrigation systems, organised by small communal labour groups based on common *mataqali* affiliation. Once established the irrigated plots were being individually cultivated, with the intention that much of the taro produced would be sold.[3]

Conclusion: Towards kulaks and proletarians?

As well as the commercialisation of the subsistence sector, there are also growing tendencies on Lakeba for land and labour to become treated as commodities, and for a class of rich peasants, or kulaks, to emerge. Unlike Lomaiviti, in the Lau group land tenure has been partially individualised since the late nineteenth century (Walter 1978). No land market can exist amongst Fijians by law, but on Lakeba a number of informal arrangements exist (as mentioned for Levuka) whereby persons in need of land pay what is in effect a rent to the heads of land-owning *mataqali*. There were also signs in the 1970s of a casual labour market beginning to emerge amongst villagers. Those who could afford it were beginning to employ others to re-establish gardens, rebuild houses or dry copra. Already strongly developed in Tubou in the mid-1970s, this commercialisation of village labour continues and has extended to other parts of the island, reinforced by the emergence of a rural proletariat dependent on full-time wage labour and so having both the ability and the need to employ others to cultivate their food crop gardens. In Tubou, but not yet in other villages, there are also households partly dependent on purchasing locally produced foods, so that wage income is beginning to recirculate in the local economy rather than being channelled largely into store foods shipped into the islands from Suva and overseas.

[3] According to Yadrana villagers, water management in the valleys has become easier since the widespread afforestation of the *talasiga* catchments with *Pinus caribea*. Stream discharge has become more regulated, and flash floods after rain storms are less likely to occur. In the much larger Tubou valley, however, ground water flow has diminished especially in dry periods, causing problems for farmers (W. C. Clarke, personal communication).

On Lakeba the existence of a type of patron–client relationship between chiefs and commoners has certainly facilitated these changes, but elsewhere in the eastern islands, where the Fijian aristocracy plays a much less powerful role, we believe that the same tendencies exist but in a more latent form. What is happening on Lakeba is therefore an accelerated case of a general process of commercialisation of land and labour, a process happening at different rates on different islands, and taking different forms according to local opportunities. On Taveuni we see the emergence of seasonal wage-labourers still living in villages, alongside other villagers who are attempting to establish peasant farming enterprises. On Lakeba we see a more substantial transition to wage labour and petty market trading, in response to the establishment of centralised agri-business that now occupies a monopoly position in unskilled employment, copra marketing, and the pine industry.

Both of these kinds of change can be expected elsewhere in the Fijian periphery, particularly on the larger islands like Koro where similar innovations in technology are feasible. At the present the transition is being restrained only by traditional communal ideology, by the co-operative societies, and by a continuing rationale for a strong subsistence element in the household economy. On smaller and less favoured islands like Batiki and Kabara, probably the balance between costs and benefits will continue to favour adaptation within the traditional agrarian structure, at least for those – perhaps a minority – who choose not to emigrate.

In the past thirty years there have been numerous outside observers like ourselves who have predicted, and in some cases advocated, the structural transformations that we have identified in this chapter (Spate 1959; Ward 1964, 1965; Watters 1969; Fisk 1970; Ward & Proctor (eds.) 1980). The same social changes have occurred elsewhere in the world, and they were already underway thirty years ago in Fijian villages accessible to urban influences on the larger islands. To anticipate the extension of these trends to the whole of rural Fijian society was not, therefore, a very startling suggestion, particularly in view of the political pressures for rural (i.e. Fijian) 'development' within the late colonial state. To actually recommend such a process as a way of boosting agricultural production and raising rural living standards is, however, a much bolder step, and it is one we could not take without considering more explicitly the role of the state. Has government in Fiji demonstrated a capacity to intervene in the periphery in ways which can sustain villagers in their new projected role as peasant producers and wage labourers? It is to this question that we turn in the penultimate chapter, to consider what planning and policy measures are appropriate for an island periphery.

10

Regional development for an island periphery[1]

Issues and contradictions

The last four chapters have made clear that the island periphery is now heavily dependent on transfers of one kind or another from the national economy. The Government fleet exists largely to serve it; on a per capita basis its share of Government outlays is far higher than that of other regions; shipping freight costs, and some air fares and services are both controlled and subsidised; remittances from islanders working elsewhere are important sources of income. To all this has been added the copra price loans scheme which, though its outlays are recoupable in periods of high price, has represented a long-term interest-free subsidy to the producers in times of depression.[2]

Conditions at the end of 1982, when no less than 75 per cent of the price received by growers even in Vanua Levu and Taveuni consisted of subsidy (Brookfield 1985), gave rise to serious concern over the future of the coconut industry and of the whole region. The subsequent improvement, which continued up to 1985, eased immediate worries. None the less, external offers of World Bank and Asian Development Bank aid in the reconstruction of the industry were deferred, or were taken piecemeal without full consideration of their consequences. It is impossible not to see a grave want of confidence about the future in the 'planning' history of these years.

[1] This chapter draws heavily on a period of close observation, now ended, of the decision-making process in Fiji. References are therefore given only sparsely. It should therefore be said, however, that nothing that is written necessarily represents the collective view of the Fiji Employment and Development Mission (1982–4) or of the UNESCO/UNFPA Project (1974–6), still less of their sponsors.
[2] The loans scheme was in large measure backed by transfers from the EEC under the STABEX agreements negotiated within Lome I and Lome II. Fiji is somewhat unusual in that funds were applied directly to subsidy, and that repayments have been made promptly at a rate amounting to one per cent of current expenditure during the periods when repayment was being made. STABEX transfers are valuable sources of foreign exchange and some countries have used them to supplement general revenue, but in few (not including Fiji) they have been applied to generation of structural change in the afflicted economic sectors. A good review of the questions surrounding the STABEX programme is provided by Hewitt (1983).

Against this economic uncertainty has to be set a strengthening of the policy of sustaining the 'Fijian way of life' in the periphery, discussed in chapter 6 and exemplified in the village case studies. During the years of increasing gloom over the future of the basic coconut industry the rural development policy initiated in 1972 has continuously, though rather ineffectively, been applied through incorporation of Provincial, *Tikina* and island councils in the planning process at local level (Lasaqa 1984). This policy is to be pressed further with restoration of the small traditional *Tikina* which were combined into larger units by the colonial government in the 1940s (Cole et al. 1984) in order to give more effective voice to traditional Fijian forms of organisation than that provided by the colonial structure. These recommendations were given new force under the constitutional changes proposed after the coup. Emphasis is increasingly on the village and on groups of villages, and much less on the independent Fijian farmer on his own lease block, a policy initiated in an enthusiasm for new forms of organisation in the 1960s after the reports of Spate (1959), Burns et al. (1960) and Silsoe (1963), and discussed in chapters 5 and 6.

Yet as we have shown Fiji is a highly centralised country in which all real decisions are taken at the top. Vitally important decisions concerning the future of the agricultural economy and the transport system in the islands can only be taken at the top, and there was little indication that there had been much consultation with local Fijian authorities during a period of slow decision in 1983–5. The policy of moving increasingly toward 'conservation' in societal matters has been in potential contradiction with a mood threatening 'dissolution' in the economic sphere. It is necessary that this contradiction, which has now shifted from the regional level to the national, be understood and explained.

We must therefore take full account of the conditions of economic decision-making, for these are critical. There is a sense in which the situation in outlying Fiji represents an unresolved conflict between an ideology of village-based rural development and a weak national will to provide the means of achievement. While this is without the malign intent which Barkin and King (1970:77) attribute to a similar contradiction in Mexican rural planning, the general effect has been much the same. An official desire to improve conditions in the periphery has been conveyed with sufficient conviction, and supported with just sufficient action, to assuage discontent. Government meanwhile concentrated its real efforts on resource-development projects and on the promotion of manufacture and tourism located elsewhere.

A further important dimension in this contradiction is the prevailing economic philosophy of Fiji's rulers, which is non-interventionist with a strong preference for the free market. While practice has differed sharply from this philosophy there is great reluctance further to extend interventionism. It is as well therefore to begin this chapter by examining what would now be the economic condition of eastern Fiji had there been no subsidies or interventions beyond the level current at the time of Independence in 1970. At the same time, we shall use this opportunity to play devil's advocate and consider further the possible consequences of removing all constraints which render the factor market imperfect. In the view of committed free-market advocates this should lead to the maximisation of both the sum of profit and the sum of welfare, at least in the long term.[3] We shall, however, follow Adam Smith, whom such free-marketeers seem to revere almost as much as those of a different persuasion revere Karl Marx, and assume that Government provision of infrastructure rightly and properly remained as it has in fact been.

Eastern Fiji and the free market

The fate of enterprise

The evidence presented in chapter 4 suggests that if there had been no 'geographical distortion of the market' through the copra price loans scheme, direct and indirect shipping subsidies, and other forms of indirect aid since 1970, there might by now be no fully commercial producers of copra left in the eastern region. Independent producers would have been bankrupted, and cross-subsidisation within multi-enterprise corporations would not have survived the prolonged and repeated periods of depression. Mixed-farm small growers would have made and sold copra only during periods when the price was sufficiently high to offer them a reasonable return over the costs of freight and marketing, and these latter costs would have grown substantially for two reasons.

In the first place, sharp reduction in supply would probably have led both the coconut oil mills in Suva, which produced mainly for export, to shut down. Only the smaller mill at Lautoka, which serves mainly the domestic market, might have survived. Copra would therefore have had to be exported as copra to distant markets, at rising freight rates, as other Pacific islands have found.

---

[3] It is not our object to set up the free-marketeer as a 'straw man'. All that is presented here has actually been said within the context of the problems discussed in this chapter, though we refrain from offering sources. Our object is to relate these theoretical prescriptions to the reality which they would create. Many economists do not do this because, in Leontief's (1982: 104) words: 'Not having been subjected from the outset to the harsh discipline of systematic fact-finding, traditionally imposed on and accepted by their colleagues in the natural and historical sciences, economists developed a nearly irresistible predilection for deductive reasoning.' A useful discussion of the pros and cons of the free-market approach to regional problems is provided by Richardson (1969: 389–92). As will be seen, we·find the logic of the *laissez-faire* argument to have points in its favour,

Second, and more seriously for the islands, would have been the effect on internal shipping. Except on the services between Viti Levu and Vanua Levu, the main task of the internal fleet is the inward transport of copra. The outward task is much smaller, and the Government-subsidised 'Kaunitoni' often carries as little as 60 tonnes of cargo on its outward voyages to Lau, less than a fifth of capacity.[4] Between 1969 and 1974, before the present subsidy structure was fully established, the number of island calls by commercial vessels declined by 24 per cent (UNESCO/UNFPA Project 1977: 261). This decline would have accelerated as ships were withdrawn from service, and many islands would have found themselves deprived of shipping service altogether. For others, freight rates would have risen sharply in the absence of price control and subsidy, and the reduction in cargoes offering. For aircraft also, assuming that the airstrips would still have been built, there would in consequence of smaller incomes, have been fewer passengers other than one-way emigrants.

The places where a service would best have survived would have been those islands in which it was possible to develop alternative cash crops capable of bearing high freight rates and delays due to increasingly infrequent shipping. The obvious example is *yaqona*, which has flourished without benefit of subsidy or intervention of any kind. We may therefore assume that farmers all over the eastern islands would have switched massively into *yaqona* production, but this is ecologically almost impossible on dry and limestone islands, and the attempt on such islands would have failed. There would, however, have been major increases in production from favoured islands in Lomaiviti, Taveuni, parts of Lau and Kadavu, leading to a sustained excess of supply and hence to lower prices. Vegetable production would have failed, even more decisively than it has, both for want of reliable and suitable shipping, and also because of competition from producers in Viti Levu and northern Vanua Levu. Local fishery schemes have enjoyed little success even with substantial subsidy; in its absence we must assume that all would have failed. Handicraft production, depressed in the 1970s, could have enjoyed a recovery in the 1980s with improving fortunes for the tourist industry, but only if transport were available to shift produce to the market.

The last decade would therefore have seen a steep decline in regional

---

- given the premise that its consequences are socially and politically acceptable which they are not.
[4] In Fiji as a whole the outward cargo carried by inter-island shipping substantially exceeds inward cargo, by as much as 172 per cent in 1983. However, this excess consists almost entirely of petroleum products, together with general cargo carried on the Suva to Labasa (northern Vanua Levu) service. The opposite prevails in the eastern region.

income, the total elimination of cash income derived from local production in some islands, and increasing differentiation between and
within others. In these circumstances the opportunity cost of migration
would have declined sharply, leading to an increase in both permanent
and circular migration. For many, the alternative would have been a
return to a subsistence economy. Landless coconut workers would have
become destitute. Traders and co-operative societies would mostly have
been bankrupted as purchasing power declined. Even Government
employment would not have filled the gap since there would have been no
subsidy-related employment, and rationally other services would have
been reduced as population declined through emigration.

A brighter face to the coin?

Yet would all this have been wholly bad? Elements of this scenario have
indeed happened, especially on small islands which have lost direct
shipping service and where the costs of chartering small vessels have
become prohibitive. It could be argued that people unwilling to accept
reversion to a subsistence way of life could have been employed elsewhere,
and that the funds not spent on the islands could have been used to
provide much more rewarding employment. An incubus which absorbs
scarce national resources and diverts aid funds would have been removed,
and an unprofitable industry with bleak long-term prospects would have
been all but eliminated.

Even in 1980–5, when a general depression and rising unemployment
would have made impossible the absorption of displaced islanders in
other areas of the economy, these islanders would still have had their
'subsistence affluence' into which to retreat. The sum of national welfare
might well have been increased, and a necessary and ultimately inevitable
process of restructuring would merely have been accelerated. Moreover,
as a minor national benefit, the price of the popular *yaqona* beverage
might well have been reduced in consequence of the efforts of many more
islanders to switch into production of this crop!

If the free-market philosophy had been widely applied there might even
have been some direct benefits in the islands. Given zero opportunity cost
as copra estates, freehold land would have been offered for sale in greater
quantity and hence at lower prices. Some might have been taken up by
land-hungry Indo-Fijian entrepreneurs who might have found the means
to do something profitable with it. Other land would have been sold to
tourist developers and second-home buyers. For Fijians, it is likely that
leases would have been surrendered before the date of their expiry, thus
increasing land resources available for Fijian subsistence. If, moreover,

'imperfections' in the land market were to be relaxed sufficiently to permit the alienation of Fijian land, whole islands and parts of islands might have been sold or leased to developers. Especially in Lau, with its scenic and climatic advantages, we might by now have seen the genesis of a smaller version of the outer islands of the Bahamas, or the St Vincent Grenadines – the playground of wealthy tourists and yachtsmen, in which substantial incomes would flow to owners and to those islanders willing to transfer their income-getting enterprise from the unrewarding production of export crops to the provision of goods and services to wealthy visitors from the industrialised world.

Problems of the free-market solution

This vision, if such it be, of the effects of allowing the market to determine the use of human and natural resources in eastern Fiji carries the assumptions that the released resources could and would have been used to better effect in other economic sectors, and that relaxation of 'imperfections' in the land market would have found entrepreneurs willing and able to take advantage of the opportunities. If these assumptions are invalid then the outcome would be much more gloomy for the islanders. Moreover two other aspects are disregarded, and both have costs.

In the first place is the social cost of dislocation and adaptation, including the cost of relocation of migrants. Even the most doctrinaire of free-marketeers might regard their easement as a legitimate charge on public funds. The need for subsidy – and for Government intervention – would not so easily be eliminated. Second, and perhaps of greater economic significance, is the loss of investments that are far from fully amortised. In the case of coconut palms the amortisation period ranges from 50 to about 90 years. On the basis of a re-examination of the evidence Brookfield (1985) concluded that about 65 per cent of all Fiji's coconut palms were less than 45 years old in 1983. The proportion on Fijian land, and in all the eastern islands except Taveuni and on the Vanua Levu coast, would be higher than the average. Added to this is the investment represented by copra driers and coconut mills, other ancillary facilities, and in the form of learned skills. The lengthy amortisation period of investments in the coconut industry has long been, and remains, a major constraint to efforts at restructuring and even renewal.

The real and basic difficulty in the way of a free-market solution is not, however, economic. Its consequences, even if not exactly as outlined above, are in contradiction to some of the most dearly held objectives of those who hold power in Fiji. Paradoxically, it is only the more adverse effects of 'releasing' the market that are in any way compatible with these objectives – the preservation of a village-based subsistence economy in some islands, and the difficult creation of new forms of Fijian cash-producing activity in others, albeit at low levels of income. As we saw in chapter 6, migration and relocation of people are precisely what post-Independence policies have sought to avoid, while the probable effects of a freer market in land would be tolerable only in the much-tainted Northern Division; they are anathema in relation to Lomaiviti and especially Lau. Moreover, any relaxation of the conditions of tenure of Fijian land is politically impossible, and opposed by the great majority of Fijian commoners as well as chiefs.

Given that a full free-market solution to Fiji's problem in its eastern island periphery is politically unacceptable in view of its consequences, therefore, it is surprising that the alternative of taking greater central direction of affairs in the east seems almost equally unacceptable. We shall see examples below. The consequence has been a cumulative process of shoring-up that is not yet at an end, despite increasing disquiet concerning its cost. The need to resolve the contradiction in objectives is perceived, though the perception is clouded by an all too apparent reluctance to face all the evidence. This is the social and political environment within which any consideration of possible economic paths must be placed. Some discussion of the means available for decision-making is therefore a necessary next step in this argument.

The boundary conditions of planning

Ownership and control in eastern Fiji

We have seen in chapter 5 that large-scale capital is now almost absent from eastern Fiji, except on the corporate-held estates. It ceased to be involved in shipping more than a decade ago, and even air services are provided by a small locally-owned company. The structure of business comprises a number of small to medium entrepreneurs, mainly Indo-Fijian or Euro-Fijian, three small local shipping companies and a number of single-ship operators, the co-operative movement and a large body of Fijian farmers most of whom are smallholders and most of whom operate within the village system. A region in which significant trading houses arose in the late nineteenth and early twentieth centuries is now without any large private sector organisations other than the fast-vanishing branch operations of two Australian multi-nationals.

All else is government, but government is not a simple entity. There is the national government, represented through the Divisional and District administration, and there is the Fijian Administration represented through the Provinces, *Tikina* and island councils, and controlled by decisions of the Great Council of Chiefs. The local structure of national government, set up under colonial rule, never became strong in this area, and current trends will make it less so. The Provinces of the Fijian Administration vary greatly in effectiveness; the Lau Provincial Office on Lakeba has some of the functions of a District Office elsewhere, but this is unusual.

The developmental role of the Fijian Administration has been mentioned above but needs some elaboration. The Provincial Councils and the *Tikina* councils – properly *Bose Vanua* – have done little to initiate development planning and have mainly acted on 'advice' from above or directives from the Council of Chiefs. The Rural Development branch of the Fijian Administration set up in 1972, augmented soon after by the 'Business Opportunity and Management Advisory Service' has offered only weak direction to Provincial Councils and their staffs, which have embarked on ventures which have not proved to be commercial, or sometimes have apparently frittered away their funds (Qalo 1984). The linkages with the local officers of the specialist branches of national government have been, for the most part, poor.

Staffing is competent in some of the specialised branches such as Health and Agriculture, but the level of decision-making freedom is low, and in some cases the ability is also small. Local minor officials take their orders from Divisional headquarters or from Suva. The co-operative movement, which is controlled by government, has rather more local devolution of responsibility, but its chaotic financial condition has prompted a reconstruction in which greater centralisation of decision-making has an important part. Improved telecommunications, and the control of all sea transport in Suva, greatly facilitate the imposition of increasing central control notwithstanding the ideology of decentralisation.

Special features of the eastern region

Because of past emigration and for historical reasons related to the formerly much greater relative affluence of the eastern region, a significant proportion both of Ministers and of Permanant Heads and other senior officers of national Ministries are men from the eastern islands.[5] From

[5] Norton (1977: 62–3) provides important data on the rising importance of eastern islanders among Fijians in the Civil Service since 1950 and its basis in the strong educational advantage provided by higher education scholarship awards. During the period 1946–54, nearly half such awards went to eastern island students. In 1935–6 eastern islanders already predominated among medical officers and provided 42 per cent of all teachers; in 1950–2 and 1967–9 these two fields continued to be dominated by easterners, and in addition more than 40 per cent of the higher positions held by Fijians in the Civil Service were by then filled by men

1970 until 1982 the Governor-General, the Prime Minister and Deputy Prime Minister were respectively high chiefs of Bau (and hence Lomaiviti), Lau and Cakaudrove (Taveuni and southern Vanua Levu). Today Fiji's front men, the President and *de facto* Prime Minister, are still respectively the high chiefs of Cakaudrove and Lau, but the real power lies in the hands of a commoner, also from Cakaudrove. The nexus of traditional and modern authority is weakened but not yet broken. The modern history of eastern Fiji has been shaped by this nexus. The high chiefs' directives have had compelling force quite apart from their legal authority. By his national authority, the Prime Minister was able to attract public and even private sector services to Lau and especially to Lakeba. All this has been of major importance in making Lakeba an island of experiment for the eastern region, in ways that we discussed in chapter 9.

Proposals for change

Several reporters, including ourselves, have argued for greater government involvement in economic management. A Coconut Authority, with powers similar to those of the Pine Commission or the Fiji Sugar Corporation which succeeded the former Colonial Sugar Refining Company, has twice been proposed and twice rejected. It has been argued from within the private sector as well as by ourselves that the marine needs cannot effectively be served by the present mix of public and private ships, most of the latter being aged or unsuitable, or both, and in urgent need of replacement, and that a joint-venture company would better be able to raise and deploy the capital needed for re-equipment.[6] This too seems to have fallen on deaf ears. The situation is seen as less serious than that which prompted the government of Mauritius to set up its comprehensive Outer Islands Development Corporation in 1982. But the then govern-

from the east. In 1967–9 no fewer than 66 per cent of Fijian executive, clerical and professional officers aged under 26 years were from the eastern islands, indicating that the disproportionate share of power in the Civil Service held by easterners was likely to continue for much of the remainder of the century.

6 Such a proposal was advanced in about 1968 by the two multi-national companies then offering inter-island service, but was at the time rejected in favour of allowing the Co-operative Association to operate ships. Both these ships were lost, one of them in tragic circumstances. By that time, in 1973, the multi-national firms had withdrawn from inter-island service and the present small-company situation had become established. Writing of the first attempts to establish island-owned international shipping, Couper (1973: 245–6) remarked that: 'It is highly probable that these examples of state entrepreneurship in shipping will be emulated by others, for the state, able to call on national pride, and to separate management sufficiently from purely local interests to make possible 'efficient' operation, seems by far the most promising instrument with which to re-establish an island presence in the island trade; but careful planning is required to avoid over-tonnaging and duplication.' This seems equally applicable to internal services.

ment of Mauritius had an interventionist philosophy, while that in Fiji does not.

There are many who would agree with government in declining greater commercial involvement. The record of statutory authorities in Fiji is far from uniformly good, and some, such as the National Marketing Authority, have not only failed to live up to expectations but have had serious internal problems. Elsewhere in the world there is rising opposition to semi-government corporations on the ground of their bureaucracy, and management and financial inefficiencies. Moreover, in too many countries, their monopolistic and monopsonistic powers have yielded scope for corruption. But the need for organisations able to raise and deploy capital remains, and the private sector is not going to provide it.

The boundary conditions sharpened by events

The need to reduce subsidy levels, both direct and indirect, the impossibility of suddenly adopting a free-market policy, and the reluctance to embark on further intervention through semi-government authorities or corporations are all elements in the politics which surround planning. To these conditions are added the financial constraints of a national economy which, after a decade of remarkable success in the 1970s, fell on more difficult times in the 1980s. The basic problem is the persistently weak market for sugar, Fiji's major export, and this in turn is part of a serious weakness in many primary produce prices world-wide which remains disturbingly persistent in spite of general world economic recovery.

In terms of national revenues, the sugar-growing and tourist-attracting Western Division has provided net subsidies to the whole nation for many years, small in the Central Division, large in the Northern Division, and proportionately largest in the east. Following a 'resource-frontier' policy (Friedmann 1966) government has invested heavily in the expansion of sugar cultivation and the development of a softwood timber industry based on planting degraded *talasiga* land in the dry zones of both main islands with *Pinus caribaea*. Cane output increased by 46 per cent between 1970–2 and 1980–2 and would have increased further but for the devastating effect of hurricane and drought in 1983, and then of a further hurricane in 1985. Since 1981, however, the world price has been persistently weak, so that production above the quota provided in agreements with the EEC and others yields unfavourable returns. Such sugar as enters the free market was worth little more, weight for weight, than sand in early 1985. While it is the average price obtained that determines farmers' returns, this has lost its former buoyancy.

Up to 1980 earnings from sugar were increasing rapidly as production rose to 400,000 tonnes on the way to a targeted 550,000–600,000 tonnes by 1985. This remains the target for the late 1980s (Central Planning Office 1985) but the drop in price reduced sugar's share of domestic exports from 81 per cent in 1980 to 59 per cent in 1984, despite record production of cane in the latter year. The growers' price for cane, which rose from $10 to $35 per tonne during the 1970s, fell back to $19 per tonne in 1984. The effect of economic and natural events on the sugar industry, coupled with a weakening of manufacturing as a growth area in the early 1980s (Howard 1983) has left only tourism as a booming income earner, and the GDP of Fiji has oscillated wildly; the average annual growth in real GDP fell from 5.8 per cent in 1971–5 through 3.8 per cent in 1976–80 to only 2.0 per cent in 1981–5 (Central Planning Office 1985). A serious balance of payments problem emerged in 1983 leading to efforts to reduce imports and a bitterly contested wage freeze. Because of the substantial multiplier effect of sugar incomes on all parts of the Fiji economy the continuing weakness of the price of sugar is a constraint on all new initiatives. Despite hopes for improvement, conditions of world over-production in relation to present demand make it likely that the constraint will continue (*The Economist* 294 (7383), 2 March 1985).

The political events of 1987, coming at the same time as a new ENSO drought of some severity, wrought further damage. Cane farmers, over-whelmingly Indo-Fijian, delayed commencement of the harvest by two months before necessity overcame political protest, leading to inevitable reduction in the 1987 crop and in new planting for 1988. Moreover, uncertainty led many farmers to put cane land down to subsistence crops after harvest, reversing a fifteen-year trend away from mixed farming. With such dependency on sugar, the effect is more likely to be a static or declining GDP than the 5.0 per cent real annual growth between 1986 and 1990 which was targeted and which, before May 1987, looked like being exceeded in that year.

For the eastern region, with its heavy dependence on transfer payments of one kind or another, this is bad news. Moreover, while the regional economy was supported by a recovery in copra production to 25,000 tonnes and a two-year period of good prices between 1983 and 1985, the downturn of prices again affected copra in the latter year. The Suva price reached an all-time peak of $621/tonne in 1984, but the world price (based on the Philippines price) declined during 1985 from around US$500 at the beginning of the year to around US$260 by December, and continued to fall. Copra incomes in Fiji soon sank below mid-1983 levels, and further reductions in 1986 led to re-activation of the loans scheme. Meantime the drop in price triggered a major event, which we discuss below.

Some important initiatives were set in train in the coconut industry in the late 1970s, but there is no central design as has been the case with sugar, or the pine-timber industry. The immediate plan is only to sustain present production and continue the floor-price support scheme as necessary; longer term initiatives are put back into the 1990s. The period since 1980 could have seen much more active steps toward the revitali-sation of the coconut industry, but uncertainty over the future generated uncertainty in decision and action. Despite some piecemeal changes policy remained ambiguous. There have been unfortunate consequences of this indecisive approach.

Initiatives for change

More coconuts or not?

For more than twenty years reporter after reporter has pointed out that Fiji's copra yields are declining, and has attributed this primarily to the increasing average age of trees as replanting and new planting have failed to keep up with ageing of palms. While this is to some extent an artefact of the manner in which data have been collected and presented, thus concealing the effect of other factors such as declining standards of maintenance and soil exhaustion, the fact that about a third of Fiji's palms are now well into their period of declining yield is undoubtedly significant. The concern led to the successive and overlapping periods of subsidised replanting and new planting between 1963 and 1975 from which results were limited and disappointing, and this very fact has discouraged acceptance of newer proposals.

Such a major proposal was advanced in 1982 and 1983. After pro-longed investigation and discussion, the World Bank agreed to finance a $33 million Tree-Crops Development Project which involved the intro-duction and development of high-yielding palms from West Africa and the replanting or new planting of 4,800 ha over a five-year period as foundation for a complete replanting over about 25 years. It was also proposed to develop 4,000 ha of cocoa. Most of the area affected in the first stage was to be in Vanua Levu and Taveuni. It was expected that the high-yielding African palms would produce around 3.5 tonnes/ha of copra when fully bearing, over eight times the existing average yield. The area per family farm was to be limited to 2.0 ha of coconuts underplanted with cocoa, and a wage was to be paid during the establishment period as a loan recoverable from the seventh year onward together with other establishment advances.

To many this seemed like the last and best chance for the industry, but there were also serious doubts. The high-yielding varieties were untried in Fiji and the proposed initial replanting rate was inevitably slow. Demand placed on farmers' labour was high, amounting to 84 man weeks a year at full development, or the labour of 1.75 persons on the basis used for calculation (Brookfield 1985). Above all there would be a high debt burden, amounting to $3,300 per farm on average. All experience with earlier replanting schemes signalled caution over the ability and willingness of farmers to undertake repayment of so large a sum, especially in the light of an uncertain future for the copra market. Moreover, a considerable amount of central direction was necessarily involved, rather on the lines of the much-criticised 'plantation mode of management' urged for Pacific small farmers in a recent Asian Development Bank survey (Ward & Proctor (eds.) 1980). The organisational capacity of the co-operative movement and the Department of Agriculture would be, to say the least, strained.

The project was deferred, for reasons never made public. Some preparatory work was done, and a small seed garden for the development of new high-yielding varieties is now to be established. While this is coming into full production (not until 1993), nurseries will be established for the distribution of selected local seedlings the yield of which will be around 1.5–1.7 tonnes/ha. All this is several years behind the schedule of the original project.

The hesitations and changes in plan are revealing. No one doubts that if either the coconut industry or some replacement is to have a future there needs to be a major drive in setting up a new production base. Commitment, however, is very tardy in the greatest possible contrast to what has happened in sugar. Fiji's 1981–5 development plan was ambiguous, writing in one place of diversification out of coconuts and in another of undertaking new initiatives in the industry. The 1986–90 plan, written after the flirtations with major World Bank support, merely says that 'all possible sources of finance will be explored, including credit institutions, private sector support, farmers themselves and potential aid and loans from overseas' (Central Planning Office 1985: 51). While the new plan does offer some commitment to coconuts, in one sense it says even less than its predecessor; there is not one word about the large developments in coconut processing which have taken place and are continuing. No sense of a policy emerges. Extreme price instability underlies all this ambiguity. Only the World Bank (1983) retained sublime confidence. Both sugar and coconuts are said to be crops in which Fiji has a 'comparative advantage'; therefore Fiji should damn the torpedoes and press ahead with both.

Getting value out of the coconut

Before 1977 there had been virtually no technical developments in coconut processing for half a century or more, with the exception of hot-air driers designed for other crops but used in Fiji for copra drying. Even this innovation largely disappeared after the first oil-price shock in 1973. Minor improvements in the design of simple copra driers had been made from time to time but there was no fundamental technical change. The process remained labour-intensive, cutting the meat out of the nut by hand, collecting firewood and tending the drier. Estates, with division of labour, achieve only from 0.15 to 0.21 tonnes per man per week, and smallholders achieve much less. The mean Papua New Guinea smallholders' output of 0.03 to 0.04 tonnes per household per week (J. Guest, personal communication) is probably not much below the normal output of Fijian villagers.

In 1977 a Taveuni planter, who also runs a small abattoir, sought to reduce his costs by investigating a return to steam-heat drying. In 1981 he installed such a drier, fired by husk and shell, and also using the steam through a simple reciprocal steam engine to generate electricity. This innovation attracted much interest in the Pacific. The trial needs to be replicated, however, and adequately controlled before the economics can be established. Moreover it requires collection of whole nuts, expensive in terms of transport and probably feasible only where production is concentrated.[7]

A second innovation, introduced in 1983 on another estate, involved mechanical de-husking and splitting of the nuts, after which they are dried in the shell. The labour-intensive copra cutting stage would be eliminated. A third planter sought to produce frozen grated coconut for export mainly to Hawaii. With all machinery in operation his plant could make ten tonnes of grated coconut per day, employing 25 men and 70 women. However, after only a brief period of operation the estate went back to production of copra; marketing problems and lack of freezer space on shipping brought the experiment to a halt.

These innovations attracted interest, but not support. In 1982 plans were floated for a much more profound innovation at Savusavu on Vanua Levu, being an integrated mill designed to produce coconut oil, generate electricity, produce coir from the husk and activated carbon of high

---

[7] There needs to be imagination here. Whole nuts float high, and can readily be transported in flumes where water is available, as it is in much of the Northern Division coconut area. Nuts can also be collected in pods and towed behind outboard-powered boats within lagoons or even across sheltered sea. On one Taveuni estate a 'flying-fox' cableway has been contemplated. It is not necessary to think only in terms of road transport.

quality from the shell. The Asian Development Bank was behind this but initially the Government was doubtful because the technology was nowhere else used in combination, and because severe problems of both supply and marketing were foreseen. A proposed Bank feasibility mission was declined in early 1983, but later that year yet another external consultants' report repeated the arguments for decentralisation of milling from Suva to Savusavu (Atkins 1983).

Decentralisation of milling

One of government's reasons for declining the particular proposals of the Asian Development Bank was the failure elsewhere, on Taveuni and Lakeba, of two attempts to establish coir factories in the coconut districts. While there were technical problems the main problem was marketing, and in the case of Lakeba the factory was shut down only when its storage space was wholly filled with unsaleable coir. The Lakeba factory was a by-product of a pilot project in decentralised milling established in 1980 with the enthusiastic support of the then Prime Minister. This attempt to locate coconut-oil milling in the coconut growing areas is designed to add value and provide factory employment in the rural areas. Potentially it is an innovation with far-reaching consequences.

The move to decentralise milling has to be seen as a stage in a worldwide process of change. The colonial system of coconut oil production, set up in the hands of major international corporations such as Unilever and Proctor and Gamble in the early twentieth century, involved the shipment of copra from many sources to mills located in the metropolitan countries, where the oil could be blended with other oils in a wide variety of food and non-food end uses. It was comparable with the colonial system for processing a range of other crops, offering maximum opportunity to manipulate sources of supply, reduce costs, hold down raw material prices and appropriate surplus for investment or distribution under corporate control. It was supported by a range of technical arguments (Leubuscher 1951; Beckford 1972) all of which depended ultimately on low long-haul freight rates in shipping controlled by the metropolitan countries, and on the diversity of those countries' industrial systems.

These advantages were progressively eroded as local markets for oil and by-products emerged in the early stages of Third World industrialisation and as long-haul freight rates increased, at least in relation to the producer-price of raw materials even though they may have declined in real terms. In 1946 Carpenters set up a mill in Suva, and two others were later built in Suva and Lautoka. Western Samoa, Tonga and Vanuatu have all established mills since 1980, and although some economists assert that the value added is negative under current costs and returns and likely to remain so (Wall 1986), the trend continues throughout the Pacific.

For the outer islands the added cost of internal freight has also risen, even after subsidy. In 1982 it represented 12 and 15 per cent of the Suva price on copra from Taveuni and Lakeba respectively.[8] Added to the social need to provide factory employment in the islands there was therefore also an economic argument for greater decentralisation.

The Lakeba mill

We have discussed some of the local consequences of the Lakeba mill in chapter 9; here we view it as a commercial enterprise. M. Brookfield has provided most of the information. The mill commenced operation in 1980, and thereafter absorbed the whole Lakeba output. It was not constructed at market cost, but with substantial aid funds for buildings, equipment and the generator, low-cost transport by Marine Department ships, and absorption of losses on the attached coir factory for five years by the Ministry of Economic Planning and Development under an incentives scheme. The mill is designed for an output of 1,200 tonnes a year, but in 1982 only 364 tonnes of oil were produced together with 251 tonnes of meal. Extraction rates at 51.5 per cent were well below the normal 62–65 per cent range. Wages paid to a reduced workforce of 32 were only about half those paid in Suva, a cause of some discontent. Since 1983 supply has been augmented by copra from nearby Cicia and other islands, but transport problems arise from probable withdrawal of Marine Department service and the need to return drums empty since there is no bulk-loading. These led the operating Lakeba Co-operative Association to buy its own aged tug, a doubtful investment.

Assessment of mill accounts differs according to the source, but the Dickson Commission (1983) which created a new pricing formula for Fiji's copra believed that it operated at a profit. It seems unlikely that the subsidy elements were fully taken into account. The Lakeba Co-operative

---

8 The price of copra in Fiji has been determined according to formula since 1963. The formula price was based on the Philippines copra price less various deductions, including copra freight cost from Suva to London. Outstation buying prices are lower by approximately the freight cost between the outstation and Suva. This formula has been much criticised in the industry in recent years as offering a subsidy to the millers. Since no copra has been shipped from Suva to London since the mid-1960s a 'calculated' rate has been used in place of any real rate. In 1983 changes were made following the Dickson (1983) report. This used the real coconut-oil freight rate. Based on a 1983 Philippines price of $270 per tonne (Fijian), these changes brought the Suva price up from $145 to $187. The millers considered that this would deprive them of profit, but the growers still regarded the changes as inadequate.

Association manages a second small mill on Vanua Balavu as well as its own. Further mills were tentatively planned on Moala and Rotuma. This may be unwise until profitability can be more securely established, for the Lakeba Co-operative Association accounts for 1982 showed a significant loss, due almost entirely to the mill. In 1988 the mill was out of production.

The Savusavu mill and its consequences

With strong urging from the centre, the Fiji Development Bank and the Lautoka mill operator finally constructed the long discussed mill at Savusavu in Vanua Levu in 1984–5. The new mill, opened in August 1985, had an initial capacity of only 7,500–8,500 tonnes of copra, about the production of mainland Vanua Levu. A price advantage of $40 per tonne above the Suva price quickly garnered this supply.

The new mill came on stream, however, in a period when prices were already beginning to decline. Milling capacity in Fiji was raised to more than twice the national production, and the Suva mills, deprived of supply from the most productive area, faced an unpromising future. When the Dickson (1983) formula was adopted, both Suva mills threatened closure, but delayed action during a period of rising prices in 1983–84. The situation changed dramatically in 1985.

Consequences of a new depression

The price of copra and coconut oil declined rapidly through 1985 and remained very low through 1986. The 'loans scheme' for growers was revived, but with even less prospect of repayment, and to many even the subsidised price was unremunerative. The consequences for milling were, however, dramatic. Carpenters had already reduced the capacity of their Suva mill in the face of a reduction in their profit under the 1983 formula, shifting some of the aged but still-serviceable machinery to Papua New Guinea. Then in late 1985 they ceased buying copra on one day's notice and closed the mill; Burns Philp soon followed suit. The result was to leave no milling capacity in Suva, while in the country as a whole there was insufficient capacity to mill the whole crop, let alone the Tuvalu and Kiribati copra also formerly milled in Suva. Some of the machinery from Suva was removed to Punja's operation in Lautoka in northwestern Viti Levu, and other machinery was taken to Savusavu, thus again restoring milling capacity to around 40,000 tonnes by mid-1986. However, only Punja's mill at Lautoka remained as a private operation; the Savusavu mill is in effect owned by government, only managed on contract by Punja, and the small-island mills were run by the co-operatives. Punja's Lautoka operation itself enjoys certain of the benefits of a public enterprise.

Thus in a short space of time, private multinational enterprise disappeared altogether from the Fiji coconut industry, except as a producer on the few remaining estates in multinational hands, leaving all effective milling and buying in the public and semi-public sector. This is the product of policies designed supposedly to advance the role of private enterprise. At Savusavu, the coconut industry now does have a very efficient milling facility, one which has recaptured the advantage of bulk loading enjoyed by the former Suva mills through use of a flexible pipe floated out 400 m to ships. However, excess capacity remains and it is not clear how far the Savusavu operation as well as the small-island mills at Lakeba and Vanua Balavu, are in receipt of subsidy from public funds. All the hopes and plans for diversification of the product have made little impression, and failure to seize opportunities for a thoroughgoing reconstruction of the industry that were present in the early 1980s led to a situation in which future prospects are bleak. Moreover, there are consequences for the trading system of the islands which we examine more closely below.

The social consequences of innovation

It is important to draw together the threads of our 'external' view in this chapter and of the 'internal' view of the effect of the new mill on Lakeba, presented in chapter 9. There stress was placed on the assumption of central control over individual decision when to produce and where to deliver. While the Lakeba case is unusual, it does parallel in some measure the effect of contracting to agri-business buyers in Western farming, where

Once contracts are signed, processing companies usually make all the technical and marketing decisions about planting and harvesting, and provide the necessary farm supplies – fertilizers, pesticides and harvest machinery. (Vogeler 1981: 138)

It should also be noted that the new Savusavu mill is not intended to remain simply a commercial enterprise competing with other mills for supplies of copra; local growers are intended to buy the Fiji Development Bank shares. From the outset political pressure has been exerted on them to do so, but few have responded.

It would almost seem as though some of the social changes feared by certain opponents of the original Tree-Crops Development Project are entering through the back door of decentralised milling. Not only did these proposals require a large measure of direction over farmers' decision-making, but the large labour demand of two hectares of imported high-yielding palms made it never really likely that the selected block-holders would do all the work with family labour alone. It was always probable that they would become employers contracted to the scheme to which they were indebted, thus introducing a wider element of stratification into rural society. This is increasingly the model of the federal land development schemes of Malaysia, and it is the pattern in the Fiji sugar industry. Contracting, and wage labour, do not form part of the 'tradition' of Fijian village agriculture, but can we be sure that such arrangements would prove universally unpopular? There is already a sense in which they are not so different from the 'traditional' obligations to chiefs and there are, moreover, other straws in the wind.

There is evidence in these pages that the growing uncertainties of income from smallholder commodity production, since 1970, have weakened the will of villagers to remain independent producers. In chapter 9 we noted the failure of one of the settlement schemes in Taveuni, at Qeleni, and though the number of independent block-holders in Fiji as a whole continues to increase, a significant proportion of this increase is in the cane districts, and elsewhere – even in Taveuni – some of the most stable settlers are those with no easy village base to which to return. At Qeleni, we found block-holders from the village giving up their independence to work as seasonal cane-cutters in Vanua Levu or even to become resident workers on a Taveuni estate – the 'prison' from which aspiring block-holders were so readily drawn in the 1970s. Wage labour offers a secure and regular income, and wherever that income is perceived as adequate it is widely sought. With it has come the unofficial but clear beginnings of a 'market' in Fijian land, and the emergence of trade in food among rural Fijians. While there is still a long way to go before a clear division of labour becomes an established fact in rural Fiji, there is evidence of its emergence even in these peripheral islands. The formation of a class structure, such as we dismissed as a basis for contemporary analysis in chapter 5, would – perhaps will – be accelerated by such a trend.

Questions about export-based development

Export-base theory

Historically, the origin of regional development theory in colonised countries lies with the explorations of Harold Innis (1930; 1940) into the effect of fur and fish as staple export products on the economic and political history of Canada. As subsequently developed by North (1955),

Watkins (1963) and others, these ideas evolved into the 'export-base' theory of regional development in which the nature of the export staple, and the backward, forward and final-demand linkages which it generated determined many of the characteristics of the region.[9] For example, an export base productive of forward linkages localised in the area is more likely to generate a diversified economy than one in which forward linkages can best be developed in a remote market country. The exploitation of 'final-demand linkages', being investment in domestic industries producing consumer goods for factors in the export sector, is the measure of the success of an economy in developing away from its initial export orientation. In so far as this fails to happen, an inability to shift resources in response to dictates of the market, want of perception of local opportunities and an inhibiting 'export mentality' are likely to create persistent economic difficulties (Watkins 1963). We find this approach to regional economic analysis more fruitful than the various macro-level approaches.

While 'export base' theory is applicable mainly to lands of new settlement, closely associated from the outset with trade production for distant markets, it was usefully applied by Baldwin (1956; 1966) to the case of plantation and mining economies, where a skewed income distribution effectively limits the possibilities for development of final-demand linkages because of the low effective demand of the mass of the population. Significant rural diversification, then, must await the improvement of rural incomes by means specifically designed toward that end.

Alternative export staples in eastern Fiji

Eastern Fiji developed copra as its export base by 1880. For 50 years until the great depression, and again for about 20 years after 1946, copra served the region well though it generated few final-demand linkages since

---

[9] 'Linkages' are properly inducements to invest in activities supplying the industry in question (backward linkages), in activities using the product of the industry in question (forward linkages) or in activities producing consumer or intermediate goods for factors in the industry (final-demand linkages). They can also be conceived geographically, or in other forms of 'space', and this is the sense in which work on linkages has mainly been carried out in development inquiries. Where a 'web of linkages' has developed there is an integrated economy, potentially a 'growth pole' in the original sense postulated by Perroux (1955). However, linkages may 'jump space' so that the forward-linkage effects of an industry, and even the backward-linkages, may be physically located in remote areas either within the same country or overseas. Even final demand may largely be supplied by imports. This is the case in many colonial economies, where machinery and fuel (backward linkages) are imported, the processing and manufacturing industries using the product are overseas, and specialisation of production on an export crop (or mineral) results in large imports of consumer goods. In such cases there is no

the sum of effective demand was small. However, until the 1960s the people of eastern Fiji were among the best-housed Fijians in the country, and the best able to afford travel and education, and it is in part this legacy that gave them their still-dominant place in Fijian politics and Government. By the 1960s, however, copra was already beginning to fail as an export staple and in the 1970s it crumbled. In the 1960s the search for an alternative or additional export staple began in earnest, and prevailing official wisdom offered cocoa.

The initial efforts with cocoa were unfortunate. The introduction was badly managed, the wrong variety was planted, and government-controlled marketing led to capricious changes in buying practice that alienated farmers. An attempt to create a population of coconut/cocoa block-holders within the Land Development Authority settlement schemes failed when the block-holders chose instead to produce for the domestic market. At the end of the 1970s, however, a new drive began with new varieties of cocoa. Government was again the buyer, and serious attempts were made not only to develop underplanting of coconuts but also to develop cocoa monoculture settlements in inland areas of Vanua Levu. As in the 1960s, however, performance fell far behind plans, so that in 1985 only 40 per cent of a planned 9,300 ha had been planted. It was then realised that with substantial new planting in other countries world over-production was likely, and the price began to fall in 1985. Revised plans concentrate on improvements in quality and yield, rather than on rapid extension of planting (Central Planning Office 1985).

A second possibility is coffee, almost wholly confined to Taveuni where Carpenters planted about 200 ha on their estates in a strange experiment said in some quarters to be a 'last chance' for their plantation enterprises in Fiji. Perhaps because of such an approach, Carpenters declined to act as the 'nucleus estate' for smallholder production which they were expected to become. A coffee-planting drive among Taveuni farmers was therefore halted, but not before 100 ha were planted, the produce of which had to be bought and processed by government at an exiguous margin.

A fundamental question

These attempts to generate new export tree crops suffer from their smallness, and they would not exist at all were government not ready to act as buyer, albeit at prices which tend to be sticky upward as well as

local 'web of linkages' and each unit of production (plantation or mine) is linked with overseas suppliers and markets. The model of 'plantation economy' is based on this situation. For a discussion see Beckford (1972) and Brookfield (1975c).

downward in response to variations in the world price. Both crops suffer quite severely from international price fluctuations and hence are not much better than copra. Much is hoped for from special provisions for sale in Australia and New Zealand under preferential arrangements that are a form of aid, but this is no secure basis for a new major export industry.[10] The 'export mentality' is of little help if all it can produce is small businesses no more productive of forward linkages than copra, if as much, and in which the overhead costs, borne by government, almost inevitably contain yet more hidden subsidies from the very outset.

There is a more fundamental question to be asked, and it needs to be asked more widely than in eastern Fiji (Brookfield 1986a). Is an 'export-base' approach any longer viable in the absence of a 'resource frontier' situation and in the presence of constraints of small scale and a high cost penalty deriving from peripheral hinterland location? Fiji's agricultural and other planners do not seem to have faced this question squarely, although we posed it in a more tentative manner than we do now in an earlier publication (UNESCO/UNFPA Project 1977). Is not the real weakness of the coconut industry the growing unsuitability of an export-base approach to development under changing conditions of production, market and transport? If so, is there any point in trying to replace one export base with another? Might not any real hope for future economic growth in the eastern region lie in another direction altogether?

Diversification and the home market

Although specialisation for the home market has never enjoyed a prominent place in the minds of Fiji's colonial and post-colonial agricultural planners, there is nothing whatever new about such specialisation in eastern Fiji. Indeed, as we have shown in earlier chapters, one of the most effective economic consequences of colonialism was the almost total destruction of an active and well-developed inter-island specialisation in

---

10 These arrangements under the South Pacific Regional Trade and Economic Co-operation Agreement (SPARTECA) came into effect in 1979 and offer duty-free quotas on a range of primary and manufactured products of island countries into the Australian and New Zealand markets. Soap, made in Fiji from coconut oil and imported tallow, is one such product. The Agreement represents a positive response by Australia and New Zealand to the 'trade rather than aid' (or as well as aid) pleas voiced by island countries in the annual South Pacific Forum meetings. Such arrangements, like the more recent U.S. Caribbean Basin Economic Recovery Act, represent regional foreign policy measures in violation of the General Agreement on Tariffs and Trade (GATT), and as such tend to arouse the hostility of other trade partners, especially those offering similar products and running trade deficits with the importing countries concerned. In the Australian case there has been an equally strong plea from the Southeast Asian (ASEAN) group of countries, and the future of a regional preferential arrangement must be regarded as only doubtfully secure.

production that had evolved over a period of several hundred years before the nineteenth century. Anthropological accounts of eastern Fiji written between the 1920s and 1940s, already partly reconstructions of the past, are full of accounts of inter-island specialisation and trade (e.g. Hocart 1929; 1952; Thompson 1938; 1940a; 1940b). All this is now almost dead, but new opportunities were grasped early to enter the local trade created by colonialism. Locally owned schooners continued until the 1940s to carry produce among the islands and to Levuka, until the last were driven from the sea by old age and indebtedness (Couper 1973; Knapman 1975). In the 1940s sporadic attempts to market *yaqona* and vegetables in Suva and Labasa were recorded in the Taveuni District files and in 1935 there was already substantial commercial production of *yaqona* on Kadavu (Parham 1935). In the 1950s O'Loughlin (1956: 69) recorded that:

The islands of Koro and Beqa send vegetables to market in Levuka and Suva. The sight of a Fijian canoe crossing a lively sea, laden down with vegetables, melons, paw-paw, bananas, fish, mats and perhaps a couple of well-built Fijian women as well as their menfolk convinces one that the lure of the market is strong to the Fijian people in spite of their apathetic approach to economic activity.

In the 1960s and 1970s, as we have seen in earlier chapters, the 'lure of the market' and 'apathetic approach' were revealed to be a strong preference for the most rewarding activities, and these were found in the supply of *yaqona*, fruit and vegetables rather than in the cultivation of export crops.

This remained equally true in 1983 when, on the basis of rather spotty input data, it could be calculated that an average full week's work in *yaqona* production might yield in Taveuni $231 for 58 kg of the best parts of the root, cut and dried, and that for taro, when it could be sold, a mean week's work might yield $169 for 565 kg of trimmed roots (Brookfield 1985). These returns are much better than that from any export crop, and they have risen roughly in line with the rate of inflation, but the work of final *yaqona* preparation is demanding and that of taro cultivation arduous. Moreover, the persistent difficulties in getting taro to market have been compounded by the problem of corm rot, sometimes leading to the almost total loss of a shipment before it could be sold in Suva.

The crippling problem in marketing island produce has been transport. In modern times it is only the inner islands which have been able to sustain supply of fresh produce, using small owner-operated cutters. In 1971 the National Marketing Authority was set up and one of its objectives was to extend marketing opportunity to growers in places not adequately reached by the commercial system; only Lau was excluded, being too remote. With local support from the Department of Agriculture, purchasing quotas were set in such islands as Koro and Taveuni and farmers were given planting quotas. The system did not work for want of shipping, and also because the Authority quickly encountered problems of over-supply. In Taveuni the annual buying quota for taro was 610 tonnes a year but only 31 and 48 per cent respectively was bought in 1975 and 1976. The islands were increasingly treated only as a reserve source of supply, and by 1979 buying had ceased. In 1982 a Peace Corps Volunteer in Taveuni set up a Taveuni Marketing Association, co-ordinating supply and organising transport, including even use of empty space on small tourist aircraft flying to Nadi in western Viti Levu where prices are highest. The initiative did not long survive the departure of its founder.

With so lengthy a record of failure, except only in the *yaqona* trade, the discouragement of further initiatives is perhaps understandable. Yet the failures have been human more than material. The latest Taveuni failure seems to have owed much to inter-departmental rivalries. Food prices in Viti Levu and northern Vanua Levu remain high, and the islands can still grow abundant crops of a range of fresh fruit and vegetables. Moreover, they can also supply the whole coconuts used in almost every meal in traditional Fijian cooking, the price of which ran as high as 15–20 cents each in Suva and Lautoka and 8–10 cents in Labasa in 1983. Domestic consumption of coconuts in Fiji is unknown, but older estimates of the annual equivalent of 5–8,000 tonnes of copra have recently been revised upward to 12–15,000 tonnes, or up to 75 million coconuts, about 120 nuts per person per year (Coconut Board *Reports*). A Food and Agriculture Organisation team cited a projection of the equivalent of 24,000 tonnes of copra in 2006, equal to the whole 1986 production of copra (FAO 1980). While this may be an over-estimate it prompts a different approach to the question of diversification from that which has hitherto been current.

Market diversification and the outer islands

In sending produce to Suva and western Viti Levu the eastern islands are in disadvantageous competition with the south and east of Viti Levu, where producers have access to the city by the extensive and improving road network. In the smaller supply of Labasa and the cane districts of Vanua Levu they are in disadvantageous competition with producers in touch with the growing Vanua Levu road system. Against this some islands have soil and climatic advantages in the production of *yaqona*, and the whole region has a comparative advantage in the production of coconuts, in which there is substantial and still-continuing investment with a long amortisation period. Fiji as a whole has a comparative advantage in the south Pacific region based on the scale – small in a global context but substantial in a regional context – of its manufacturing and tourism sectors. Can we envisage a scenario in which the advantages can be brought together and used to outweigh the disadvantages of an island periphery? Moreover, can we envisage a scenario which can come about with the minimum of government intervention and subsidy that is clearly desired?

The question can be put another way. If we are right in believing that the export-base approach to development is, and has for some years been of declining utility in the peripheral eastern islands, how far and how rapidly can the regional economy shift to an emphasis on supply of its potential forward and final-demand linkages within the Fiji economy as a whole, together with the backward linkages of tourism? In other words, how far and how fast can *linkage* diversification be achieved?

One aspect is the growing size of the urban market. If the urban proportion had risen only marginally from its 37.2 per cent by the 1976 census, the urban population of Fiji would comprise 260,000 people of the 670,000 national total estimated for 1986. The urban population in Suva-Nausori, alone, must now be 150,000, compared with only some 50,000 people in all the eastern islands plus southern Vanua Levu. But this is not the whole of the potential market. Since much of the production increase in the cane areas has taken place through the elimination of rotational food crops from cane-farmers' land, a greater proportion of the food of the 100,000 or so in cane-growing families is now purchased. The hotel industry, serving a mean daily population of about 5,000 overseas visitors, also purchases all its food. Although as a proportion of total imports Fiji's food imports have declined from the 20 per cent level attained in the late 1970s, they are still uncomfortably high, fluctuating between 14 and 16 per cent in the early 1980s. An important element in recent government agricultural policy is a reduction in this bill through the rehabilitation and extension of rice-growing areas on the two main islands. Up to now, however, the larger part of the fruit and vegetable needs of the food-buying population has been satisfied by growers in Viti Levu, where there has been major expansion of market-garden production in recent years.

Fiji's industries using edible and non-edible oil as input are of limited scale and most are located in Suva and Lautoka. However, lack of capacity to produce refined oil of sufficient quality restricts the range of products, and foodstuffs based on edible oil continue to be imported, together with animal and vegetable oils in refined state. A confectionery industry scarcely exists.

Prospects for change are perhaps of more significance. It now seems more than likely that the urban population of Fiji will reach 300,000 by

1990 and may reach 400,000 before 2000. Fiji is now beginning to run out of usable land, and future expansion will have to rely on greater intensification of land use (Ward 1985). This has implications in terms of more specialised production. Moreover, an increasing proportion of the remaining unused land will in future lie in Vanua Levu and on the larger eastern islands.

Prospects for enlargement of the edible oil-using industry depend not only on population growth but also on investment. There is scope not only for import-replacement but also for regional export (UNDP 1977). Edible oil-using industries have scope for export expansion in Australia and New Zealand under the South Pacific Regional Trade and Economic Co-operation Agreement (SPARTECA) arrangements, and in this area the higher quality of Pacific than of Asian coconut oil does offer a comparative advantage. The key need is for better refining capacity, but no steps have been taken in this direction. In the West Indies a scattered coconut industry linked forward to more centralised food-processing industries supplies a very high proportion of regional needs, and moreover offers the Caribbean coconut growers a stable market largely insulated from international price fluctuations.

If the whole-coconut and *yaqona* demand is added to this it would seem possible to envisage a scenario in which an increasing proportion of total marketable rural production in the east can be taken up within Fiji, including use in forward-linkage industry geared to export. Expansion of handicraft production depends mainly on further growth in the tourist industry although products of local use such as mats could well be encouraged. But it is likely to be some time before the production of perishable fruit and vegetables can compete in the urban market with more advantageously-located production. Moreover, new ships are a prerequisite of any new efforts at competition.

A spatial view of the problem

In so far as Von Thünen's classic analysis (Hall 1966) is relevant to conditions in Fiji, the problems of sea transport and break of bulk would seem to place most of the eastern region into the outer rings around the 'isolated state'. In this analogy the weight-reduction involved in further processing of coconuts to yield oil in the outer islands for refining in Suva would seem to have much sense, while one would expect the whole-coconut trade to be drawn principally from the inner islands. *Yaqona*, also a weight-reduced crop of high relative value, is clearly a suitable product for an outer-ring region, while fresh vegetables are highly marginal. These spatial variations disregard ecological differences, and their effective operation depends heavily on the actual conditions of transport. Before reaching a conclusion to this examination of possibilities, therefore, a closer look at the transport stranglehold is necessary. It has arisen as a major constraint throughout the foregoing discussion.

Easing the transport stranglehold

Transport and a maritime periphery

Any form of commercial activity in a peripheral area suffers a transport-cost penalty by comparison with activities that are centrally located. We have seen the measure of this for eastern Fiji in chapter 4, and have referred to it frequently. The nature of this penalty varies greatly, however, according a number of variables among which the state of technology and the cost of operating that technology are of major importance. Thus if all movement is by foot across that featureless plain beloved of an earlier generation of geographers we would expect a steep and uniform cost-surface to emerge, but if natural barriers are interposed then there is immediately a need for technology to overcome them. For a long period of time overland transport was much more costly than waterborne transport because of superior technology in the latter field. In Fiji this was still the situation at the time of colonisation in the nineteenth century, but modern developments have inverted this pattern so that the former locational advantage of maritime areas within an archipelago of large and small islands has now become a disadvantage.

The importance of road construction and up-grading in regional development has been appreciated for many years. It is not uncommon in areas newly penetrated by roads that the value of the new business generated exceeds the cost of construction of the road in only a few years, and in addition there are substantial social benefits.[11] At sea, however, the road already exists and to become effective requires only terminal facilities which can, where traffic is light, be nothing more than those provided by nature. Sea transport, however, involves costly and time-consuming break of bulk at each end of the voyage and sea vehicles are more costly to build and operate than road vehicles. Modern freight-forwarding technology overcomes the break-bulk problem, but at high capital cost.

There is a fundamental question to be asked about the role of

[11] This is not, however, universal. There are areas along greatly improved roads in Papua New Guinea where the production of export crops is in decline. The opportunity cost of labour input into this production is apparently perceived as below that of occasional wage employment and other alternative income sources. Other elements than the road are also necessary.

government in sea transport, and it is one on which views differ sharply. Other than railways and many airlines, transport in the market-economy world is mainly in the hands of private operators subject to varying degrees of regulation in which safety is the minimum criterion for intervention. The advantages of private operation are fundamentally those stated for a *laissez-faire* approach to regional problems as a whole by Lösch (1954: 333):

Every individual faces spatial geographic differences whose controlling influence is attuned to his exact location more finely than any planning could be … if geographic price differences were to be abolished, or even merely frozen, they would soon have to be replaced by *complete* spatial planning which would face the enormous task of taking into account the effects of thousands of locations upon one another – something that only the play of changing prices has so far been able to do successfully for any length of time.

This rather idealistic statement ignores the real-world complexities of freight-rate and fares distortion, generally downward by governments and upward by cartels of private operators, but it none the less reflects the fact that innovations can more readily be adopted by a market economy in which the successful reap rewards while the failures go to the wall. In an age of rapid technological change in transport, absence of competition commonly leads to persistence with outdated modes. However, there are exceptions to the value of market forces where the scale or value of business are insufficient, in competition with other opportunities, to attract innovating entrepreneurs or the necessary risk-capital. One of these areas is eastern Fiji, but it is not alone.

The accepted principle is none the less that operation of the vehicles of road and sea transport alike is best left to the private sector. The large burden of building, maintaining and up-grading roads is accepted by the state. The cost of terminal facilities at sea is comparatively small, but the capital cost of suitable vehicles is much greater than on land, and their operating costs are high.[12] Where service is desired for public reasons governments have subsidised its costs for centuries with lucrative mail contracts and by more direct means. Moreover, the sea as a road offers special problems which the state cannot possibly resolve for the operators.

12 The problems of the sea arise in no small measure from its natural variability as a 'road'. Except in sheltered waters small craft can operate safely only in fair weather so that larger 'vehicles' are necessary. This is the case in eastern Fiji although small ships do serve surprising places. The risk of major hazards from storm raises the need not only for safer and more powerful ships but also for marked and lighted harbours of refuge in the few sheltered natural havens of the region. Government has done nothing about this, and ships running long distances to shelter suffer a severe cost penalty. There are also unexpected hazards. In 1984, for example, rafts of pumice floated into Fijian waters from a submarine volcano in Tonga. Entering ships' engines through intake ports the pumice did severe damage. This type of problem does not occur on land.

Should not government therefore provide its aid to transport in other ways, where this is needed?

The unsatisfactory mix in Fiji

As we have seen above, Government has entered the field of commercial sea transport in Fiji by a variety of means, but has declined to go further. Freight rates are regulated and in part subsidised, substantial sums have been spent on terminal facilities of a rather basic order, and Government ships have not only carried cargo and passengers, but also provide without cost a number of supplementary services such as carriage of water during periods of drought.

The total commercial fleet, government and private, included 58 ships of very varied size, type and age in 1983. Most of the smaller private vessels serve the inner islands and all the larger private vessels serve the trade between Viti Levu, Vanua Levu and Taveuni, where 51 per cent of the total traffic of 140,000 tonnes in 1980 was carried. The northernmost route between the two main islands is profitable and has attracted innovators. A subsidiary of the Inchcape group has operated a tug-and-barge service between Suva and Labasa since the early 1970s, and occasionally it serves other places in the north. Since 1983 private local companies have initiated 'roll-on roll-off' services between Viti Levu and Vanua Levu, extending these services to other large islands – Taveuni, Koro, Gau and Kadavu. Since they form part of the reconstruction of the transport system following the cessation of copra milling in Suva they require closer examination.

A crisis in transport

There are occasions in the economic history of countries and regions when fortunate coincidences do take place, and for the western part of the eastern islands of Fiji the period 1983–5 was such an occasion. The idea of 'roll-on roll-off' (Ro-Ro) service between the main islands of Fiji has been around for some time; we advocated it as part of the proposals made from our 1974–6 project (UNESCO/UNFPA Project 1977). Government did not itself take up the idea, and did not even provide ramps at most of the new island jetties constructed between 1974 and 1982 – a programme based on partial implementation of a much older report (Couper 1965). But in 1983 one of the larger private local shipping companies that had emerged in the wake of withdrawal from shipping by the multinational island trading companies in the early 1970s initiated a service between the landing at Natovi, on the east coast of Viti Levu opposite Ovalau, and

Nabouwalu at the southwestern tip of Vanua Levu. They used a well-found second-hand ship of 900 tons brought from the Inland Sea of Japan. It became possible to make the road journey from Suva to Labasa within 12 hours using this ship, even though the Natovi terminal left much to be desired, as it still does.[13] This company later added a second and smaller ship. Then another company was formed to operate a Ro-Ro vessel between Suva and Savusavu, a longer sea journey but with shorter road connections.

It was around this time that the Suva coconut-oil mill were closed, and all capacity except for the outer-island mills became concentrated at Savusavu and Lautoka. In a rather striking example of the adaptability of private operation the companies put both the two larger Ro-Ro ships on the Suva–Savusavu run, calling at Koro, Ovalau and Gau on certain voyages, and extending to Taveuni from Savusavu and to Kadavu from Suva. Much copra is carried on these ships, in trucks, to the Savusavu factory, which is 8 km from the wharf there. Only a smaller ship maintained the Natovi–Nabouwalu connection. In 1986 a third company was formed to operate a larger Ro-Ro vessel, over 1,500 tons and with considerably superior passenger accommodation, along the run between Suva and Savusavu through Lomaiviti, with extension to Taveuni expected late in 1987. Older conventional ships serving the north, including Rotuma, now call at Savusavu inward with copra. Thus the Savusavu mill obtains all the copra of northern Fiji and Lomaiviti, about three-quarters of the crop, while there is an actual improvement in service as the Ro-Ro ships are also popular with passengers, and are quite heavily used by trucks carrying general cargo. Freight rates are not cheap, but absence of break-of-bulk does much to offset the cost. Even during the severe downturn in Fiji's economy in the months after the coup, when the main roads of both large islands were almost eerily empty of their usual traffic, vehicle space on several of these Ro-Ro services remained fully taken up.

For the smaller Lomaiviti islands, and for Lau, the situation was less happy. Ships serving these islands with general cargo outward from Suva, including the 'Kaunitoni', must either call inward at Savusavu – a considerable diversion – and then proceed light to Suva, or else adjust their Lauan itineraries so that copra can be collected from Lakeba and Vanua

---

[13] Bird's (1971: 94) 'first law' should operate here: 'If you improve a stage in the process of cargo handling you will immediately have to improve the stage before and after that one'. But this assumes there is one authority. The minor country roads which run to the terminals of the Ro-Ro ferry are not the responsibility of the marine authorities. An interesting question arises in this case: should government provide necessary support infrastructure to a commercial venture that is in competition with other commercial ventures? In Fiji there would seem to be doubts; the shipping company had itself to pay for dredging at one of its terminals.

Balavu, and carry coconut oil in drums back to Suva. Otherwise, if copra is brought to Suva it must be loaded on trucks and either driven 140 km to Lautoka or put on board one of the Ro-Ro ships to Savusavu. By mid-1987 the operation of ships to the small islands and the production of copra on those islands had become unprofitable. The outlying mills ceased production, and many islanders ceased to make copra. Nor, until Savu-savu is declared a port-of-entry – a desirable move delayed now for many years – can the Tuvalu copra that used to come to Suva find a milling outlet in Fiji; reportedly, it goes to Tonga instead.

Nor is this the end of the problem. While the new milling situation was coming about, Fiji's authorities were actively into doctrinaire plans to fully privatise inter-island shipping, selling off the commercially usable vessels of the Government fleet. Though these ships are far better found and maintained than most private ships, having been built new for Fiji rather than bought second-hand, they were not built for low-cost operation; the private sector did not want them. Of the four Ro-Ro vessels from Japan, two are low, open, and so ill-maintained as to be unsafe in open-sea conditions in the view of one expert we refrain from naming, a view which we strongly support after sailing in them. Only one ship is really capable of carrying container traffic, yet the advantages of making possible through container traffic throughout the road system of the larger islands is clearly evident (Brookfield 1984b). The capital-cost problem of fleet replacement with suitable ships is *not* resolved by leaving the problem to under-capitalised private companies. Moreover – and despite the considerable enterprise demonstrated by these companies – changing the locational distribution of an agro-industry with strong government intervention is *not* compatible with a policy of leaving the transport system serving that industry to be sorted out by the economists' famous 'hidden hand'. The 'hidden hand' is there, but it can strike as well as serve, and its victims are – and one dark and stormy night may more directly be – the islanders, as well as some of the goals of government social policy.

Wider implications of the argument

Islands and the export-base economy

It seems now to be accepted that peripheral island and archipelagic regions constitute at least a special case in the problems of economic development (Dommen (ed.) 1980; Shand (ed.) 1980; Jalan (ed.) 1982). Contrary to some prevailing wisdom we have suggested that an export-base approach, which was successful when sea transport was the highest transport technology available, and when small scale was not a crippling disadvantage, is increasingly inappropriate. The problem of eastern Fiji is also that of all the smaller island countries of the Pacific; their economies are not export-led, but are driven by current-account invisible flows (Bertram & Watters 1984). Prospects for commodity production are limited except where the land resource is substantial, and in Fiji this effectively means only the two larger islands, and Taveuni if its transport disadvantages can be overcome. For the peripheral islands, export-commodity production offers only the possibility of limited returns except where high-value commodities can be developed. Their vulnerability to market fluctuations is compounded by small scale which limits the possibilities of adding value through forward-linkage processing, and by the transport disadvantage which they inevitably suffer. Their vulnerability to external decisions affecting their livelihood has been strikingly demonstrated by the events since 1985.

We do not however agree with some pessimists that subsidisation of acceptable standards of consumption and welfare is the only viable goal of policy. Eastern Fiji has certain special advantages arising from its incorporation within a nation that has a diversified economy with a large urban sector relative to its size. It seems to us that it is possible, by judicious investment in transport, and in forward-linkage industry that will use island products, to create the means of economic revival in at least a major part of this island region. The possibilities of the regional market in surrounding island countries with fewer resources cannot be said to have been fully explored, so dominant is the export mentality and, as in the Caribbean, so damaging to regional co-operation (Beckford 1972; Girvan 1973). Contrary to Bertram and Watters (1984), but with Ward and Proctor (1980) and Jackson et al. (1984), we believe that there is substantial scope for productive development in many small-island parts of the South Pacific region, provided that the institutional constraints can be overcome, provided too that new technologies can be introduced, and also that problems of transport and development can be tackled regionally and not only nationally. The atolls and more crowded countries such as Tonga and Samoa excepted, most Pacific islands have substantial resources in relation to their population. Their peasantry does not suffer the ills of share-cropping tenantry, though various forms of tenancy-at-will offer only insecure access to land for a significant proportion of Fiji's farmers, mainly but not only Indo-Fijians. Though there is a landless rural population in several countries, it is not on the Asian or Latin American scale. Rapacious control over market and finance linkages by middlemen and moneylenders is only locally a problem. Perhaps most important, and a consequence of the small scale of their economies, the inroads of exploitative private capitalism have withdrawn from most of them to the degree that they – or their governments – enjoy an unusual degree of control over local resource-allocation decisions. At least in rural areas there is little grinding poverty. By comparison with, say, the South Asian or Latin American peasantry, the people of the Pacific islands are, or should be, fortunate indeed.

What sort of future?

We agree in principle with Hau'ofa (1980: 487) that the most basic decision concerns the kind of life that Pacific islanders want in the future:

If what has been said is alarming, the Pacific Islanders must face the question of what kinds of society they want for the year 2000 and beyond. If they want a capitalist society and further westernisation, then they have to take the risks required and adjust accordingly. Otherwise, they must reduce their aspirations and devise other alternatives, for the present situation is untenable.

The 'present situation' can be described, however, in very different ways according to the standpoint of the observer. By some measures, including their role as takers of prices and decisions made elsewhere and the locational disadvantages from which they suffer in the modern spatial system, the islanders are marginalised and deprived. Yet if one looks at the level of services and support which they enjoy, beyond the wildest dreams of any Asian peasant, they are 'fat cats of a seventh world'. Both these views of the 'present situation' have elements of truth, and both are part of the context in which islanders might try to 'decide' what kind of future they want. Yet, as we have seen, this basic decision is hardly theirs any more.

Nor is the situation static. One clear conclusion is that islanders value security, and that the combined insecurities of natural and economic hazard have generated very varied responses. Since one of these responses has been heavy emigration, and this runs counter to government policy, the external response has been one of protection in order to ease the consequences of risk and uncertainty, and to stress the partly lost securities of the old village system which some of the most recent measures are designed to bolster. The alternative response, that of putting support behind greater individual effort, so that a minority can stand a better chance of success in their enterprises, has been adopted only in a half-hearted manner characterised by failure to offer support in some of the most critical areas. The consequence is that real opportunities are not being seized.

Yet there is a discernible trend toward the separation of an enterprising and successful minority, who are willing to take risks, from a majority which values the village as a socially satisfying base from which they seek their personal securities in the search for paid employment, at home or elsewhere. The natural and economic disasters of the post-Independence years, however, much eased by intervention from the centre, have been profoundly unsettling. Traditionalist approaches to the future, despite strong backing by the still-respected – though much criticised – chiefs, will not succeed in halting trends toward greater differentiation within and between places, trends which will lead toward a separation between individual farmers and entrepreneurs, wage and salary earners of varying levels, and a protected village society which is not independent because it relies so heavily on support and decision-making from without. Even a modest degree of withdrawal of such support, such as might be made by a future government not heavily dominated by eastern chiefs, would certainly accelerate the differentiating trends, and our conclusion has to be that greater class stratification will emerge whatever set of policies are applied. Notwithstanding the appearance of calm, the charm of ceremony and the soothing daily and weekly round, the eastern islands are now far removed from any traditional past and are well on the way to becoming part of a modern and much harder world. It may be less hard for them if this fact is recognised, and if some productive investments are made in time.

The Pacific is undergoing a remarkable wave of political change, not confined to Fiji though the recent events there are – in 1987 – the most dramatic. The future economies of Fiji and other island countries, themselves subject to changes in the global economic and strategic system, will create different conditions of life in the islands from those inherited from colonialism through the first generation of independent modern existence. Local decision-making has proved adaptable in the past, and ability to adapt will certainly be required in the future. The unforeseen events of 1987 in Fiji have spread shock-waves throughout the Pacific, possibly presaging the end of the Western democratic systems no longer seen as appropriate by many people in several Pacific countries. The effect future political changes will have on the livelihood and welfare of people in peripheral regions such as the one we have studied cannot be foreseen, and we should not try to foresee it. But the need to bring informed analysis to bear on these places and people in the world periphery moves much higher up the scale of priorities than it has been in the past.

There is one final aspect of the islanders' problems that we should not ignore, and it harks back to our discussion of the changing physical environment in chapter 2. It now seems reasonably certain that global warming is not only a reality, but that it will have a significant effect on the level of the sea. Some authorities believe that this effect will become apparent within the lifetime of people now living. Higher tides, greater beach erosion, more frequent sea flooding of villages and of low-lying gardens and coconut groves, and greater risk from sea surge in cyclonic storms may also form part of the future environment of the islanders. Although these are high islands, less at risk than atolls, most of the life of the islanders is lived around the shore. A deep dependence on external economic, social and political forces may be augmented by recrudescence of a much earlier set of problems, those of change in the shape and conditions of the islands themselves.

II

Island studies and geography

In 1809 William Lockerby, a sailor from Liverpool, England, was marooned by his captain on the Fijian island of Vanua Levu. In his words, 'by this accident I was left ... far from every object that was near and dear to me, and possessing but very faint hopes of a vessel calling at such a simply dismal corner of the Globe that might carry me and my unfortunate comrades again into civilised society' (Lockerby 1925: 19).

Almost 180 years later we found ourselves in a similar position to William Lockerby: marooned, so to speak, through various accidents of our respective careers, far from academic origins, and in the same isolated (but surely not 'simply dismal') corner of the globe. If this book represents a vessel through which we can communicate once more with 'civilised society', what news can we bring back from the island world? What relevance has academic geography for the study of islands? And what relevance can island studies have to the wider (or perhaps narrower) field of academic geography?

In fact during the Fiji research we never lost sight of these questions despite, on occasion, the more pressing claims of soil science, economics, anthropology, demography, and other disciplines. Indeed, since our work in eastern Fiji was conceived, in part, as an exploration of appropriate methodology for UNESCO's MAB Project 7, the Ecology and Rational Use of Island Ecosystems (see Foreword), it would have been hard for us to escape altogether from questions of wider relevance. In this chapter a selective assessment is made of what our experience in studying eastern Fiji can contribute to certain debates within geography.

We consider first the proposal that island biogeography and the human geography of islanders can make a special contribution to general theory concerning the relationship of human populations to their environment. We go on to examine the particular claims of time geography and energy analysis as ways of elucidating that relationship. Finally we critically examine our own role as foreigners conducting island research, and potentially having some influence on state policy for intervention in islands and in the lives of islanders.

Underlying this whole discussion is the vexed question of ideology and its distorting effect upon the perceptions of both the researcher and the consumer of research findings.[1] Geographers have long wanted to establish their expertise in the integrated study of population–environment problems, and have therefore been tempted to make the implicit claim that their work produces 'value-free' insights that possess universal 'scientific' status (Anderson 1973; Harvey 1974; Slater 1975; Gregory 1978; Monk & Hanson 1982). This assumption of 'neutral' research is made less frequently in geographic inquiry in the mid-1980s than it was in the mid-1970s when we carried out our substantive field research in Fiji. However, even at that time it was an issue that we felt must be faced: does the freedom to carry out such research in the Third World merely serve the professional interests of First World researchers, while at the same time legitimising the actions of exploitative interest groups? In this respect as in others, the island world can perhaps provide a useful microcosm in which to examine an issue that calls into question the whole rationale for geographical research.

Islands in geography

Island ecosystems: stasis or crisis?

Twenty-five years ago, at a time of some ferment in the social sciences, a number of workers began to question the validity of the traditional lines of demarcation between disciplines, and to search for ways in which links could be established across these boundaries. Systems theory was seen by some as a useful means by which a more integrated view of reality could be constructed.[2] For geography the notion of 'ecosystem' was particularly attractive, especially for those who still viewed the subject, despite its cartographic origins and 1960s preoccupation with landscape

---

[1] For two extreme examples of contrasting ideology in Fiji, see Spate's (1961) lucid satire 'On being an expert', and his (1960) account of Ratu Emosi's millenarian vision of the ideal island polity. The former includes advice that the four authors of this book hope to have heeded: 'If you (as visiting Experts) have really passed yourself off as all things to all men,... you cannot justly complain if at one and the same time you are written off as a long-haired very brash young man, a balding middle-aged fossil, a violent reactionary, and a violent revolutionary' (Spate 1961: 9). (Readers can supply their own identifications). The latter account includes the acute observation that uneducated but literate Fijians have little information upon which to base a sociology beyond the Bible and first-hand observation of very small sectors of European and Indian culture, in an island context 'where the scale of things inhibits any effective display of the real spiritual and intellectual achievements of Western [and Eastern?] civilisation' (Spate 1960: 61).

[2] No attempt is made in this section to review the literature on systems theory, islands and geography, since much more extensive treatments are already available (e.g. Stoddart 1967; Langton 1972; Chorley 1973; Bennett & Chorley 1977; Bayliss-Smith 1977c; Gregory 1980; Ellen 1982).

geometry, as essentially the study of people's relationship to their environment. It thus became possible to argue that 'man's place in the ecosystem' was an entirely reasonable surrogate definition for the discipline, and from here it was a short step to the suggestion that to study 'man's place in the island ecosystem' would provide valuable insights of some general interest (Fosberg 1963; Stoddart 1967).

This is a highly condensed version of a particular strand in the recent history of Anglo-American geography, but it does help to explain why studies of small-scale societies in bounded or insular environments have remained prominent (Ellen 1982; Carlstein 1982). In the 1960s and 1970s these small 'island' specialists might not have felt they were exactly in the mainstream, but they could still claim to be swimming with the intellectual tide, even though their fieldwork destinations were almost invisible on the map. Moreover, this period also saw a proliferation of small independent states, many of them island groups. Even in large countries like India it began to be realised that 'macro-scale planning of agricultural development spreads far too coarse a net over the landscape, given the great variations between areas and, within areas, between villages' (Farmer 1977: 205). All these arguments contributed to the case, strongly argued in 1973 in a UNESCO Expert Panel in which two of us participated, for the inclusion of Island Ecosystems as a project in the Man and the Biosphere programme (UNESCO 1973), and from this impetus the UNESCO/UNFPA Eastern Fiji project evolved.

The project departed in some significant ways from the then current concepts of the MAB programme, and as Glaser (1980: 10) noted, 'the main emphasis is on man and change, rather than on inventories and conservation, with the ultimate aim of providing information for management purposes'. An emphasis on history – both physical and human – was introduced from the outset, and it provided us years later with the means of writing this book. In a broad review of MAB projects in the tropics, Golley (1984: 49) remarked that:

The Fiji study is especially important to MAB since it raised questions about static concepts within MAB planning, especially about the analogy of social stability and the stability of natural systems, and concluded that MAB should focus on process rather than structure. The Fiji studies of island communities illustrate the diversity of human response to environment. There is great difficulty in applying a concept of "standard" man and nature in the real world, and especially of identifying a "standard" response from man faced with environmental opportunity.

In the context of islands, we further differed in our approach from the standard wisdom of the day, as incorporated in the early programmatic statements of MAB, by focussing our attention on two misconceptions about islands. The first concerns the supposed vulnerability of islands to external impacts. In fact, when viewed as *societies* rather than as *ecosystems*, the small islands of eastern Fiji have shown themselves to be exceptionally resilient. Their cultures are much less transformed by the exchange economy that the larger populations of the main islands. We have come to realise that in the post-colonial context eastern Fiji differs only in degree, and not in kind, from other rural parts of the developing world (see chapter 1). The 'impact' of the colonial period can also be interpreted in terms no different from those applicable elsewhere (see chapter 3).

We would also point, secondly, to a related misconception about the 'adaptive' nature of the pre-colonial relationship of populations to island ecosystems. There has been a tendency for this relationship to be conceptualised, perhaps romanticised, as involving homeostatic mechanisms which maintained a dynamic equilibrium between population and resources, and which did not jeopardise the underlying productivity and diversity of the ecosystem. In Fiji, as elsewhere in the Pacific, there is now increasingly persuasive evidence for a destructive use of resources in prehistory (see chapter 2), so that crisis rather than stasis may be a more relevant focus of study.

We therefore conclude that social and economic processes on islands are not distinctively different, and in the Pacific at least the management of island environments has not necessarily deteriorated from a more ecologically 'rational' pattern that evolved during some golden age, towards the modern, materialistic, and more damaging relationship. In some ways this is reassuring, since it keeps island research within the mainstream of geography, but conversely the smallness of the island world means that unless we can claim some depth of insight not easily obtainable on the mainland then we risk being ignored on the grounds of global irrelevance.

It is here that we can point not only to what we hope we have achieved in this study, but also to some more general arguments. The revolution in biology that stemmed from Charles Darwin's observation, that in the Galapagos Islands 'here both in space and time we seem to be brought somewhat nearer to that great fact – that mystery of mysteries – the first appearance of new beings on this earth', is paralleled in ecology by the stimulus provided by the more recent Equilibrium Theory of Island Biogeography (Stoddart 1983; MacArthur & Wilson 1967). For human geography, as for biogeography, we still support the claim made in our first project report (UNESCO/UNFPA Project 1977: 1):

Islands offer an exceptional opportunity to study, under relatively controlled conditions, the entire spectrum of ecological, demographic, economic and social factors that influence population–environment relationships. This is particularly true as population/environment systems on islands are small and easily modelled, and can at the same time be representative of larger systems.

Herein lies the value of islands for geography. It is not the unique characteristics of their ecosystems, nor the special adjustments to resource limitations that their inhabitants are supposed to have made, nor their particular vulnerability to external impacts. They are not essentially different, but merely more extreme, and conveniently replicated versions, of what is found in the more familiar continental world of conventional geographical study.[3]

Islands as geographical objects

An unresolved issue in geography is the identification of a specially geographical 'object' of study. All the sciences have tended to identify and concentrate their efforts upon a structurally integrated object of study existing at a particular spatial scale (Rowe 1961; Chapman 1977). A whole hierarchy of such objects can be visualised, ranging from sub-atomic and atomic particles upwards to the levels of molecule, cell, organ and organism. Explanation is achieved in a particular science by relating one's observations to the levels of inquiry immediately above or below one's own, but without the need to range further in the microscopic or macroscopic direction. For example, botanists and zoologists study *organisms*, individual plants and animals, and the 'environment' of their object is what is now generally termed the *ecosystem*. For an ecologist the ecosystem itself is the object of study. If the geographer studies human beings in relation to their 'ecosystem', should we be defining these *human use systems* as constituting our structurally integrated objects of study? More to the point, in island studies does the island itself constitute such an object?

The answer that emerges from this book is that such a view is simplistic in the extreme, since human use systems do not exist at a particular level in some neat hierarchy of spatial scales. Instead there is a nested hierarchy of 'objects' in which men and women individually or collectively participate, ranging from household units and villages at the micro-scale, to island ecosystems and core-periphery systems of regional interaction at the macro-scale. Mobility, trade and exchange enable people to interact at

---

[3] In reaching this conclusion we seem to have advanced not a single step further than Lucien Febvre seventy years ago, in his masterly review (written in 1918) of the geographical significance of isolation: 'What value, then, have these [naturally bounded regions] ... which we have been successively reviewing? ... Their value for us is only of a practical kind. They are convenient for study. That is the only way in which they interest us and in which they can help us to discover a series of less superficial and better established relations between the possibilities of an environment and the societies exploiting them' (Febvre 1932: 235).

these various scales, and although we find that for certain purposes the island is a convenient and appropriate unit for analysis, a more complete explanation has demanded both a more micro-scale (see chapters 7, 8 and 9) and a more macro-scale (see chapters 3, 4 and 10) perspective.

Nor is this problem of interlocking spatial scales of interaction an artefact of the modern political economy of the Fiji islands. Sahlins' (1962) classic account of traditional society in Moala (Lau group) necessitated a consideration of economy and polity at family, kindred, village, island, and eastern Fiji regional scales, with the previous linkages of Moalans extending over a somewhat wider geographical region than the range of interaction at the time of his fieldwork in the mid-1950s. In aboriginal times double canoes were constructed, and until the 1940s schooners were plied by the islanders to neighbouring islands in Lomaiviti and to Viti Levu, but 'the schooners are now all sunk or in ruins, and no vestige remains of a double canoe' (Sahlins 1962: 82). Decision-making was becoming more and more concentrated at the scale of the nuclear family, and power over external linkages and the terms of trade had passed from the islanders into the hands of agencies beyond the island world. The island itself was the scale to which the Moalans themselves had become restricted, a situation only mitigated since that period by the increased freedom provided by migration. Perhaps only very isolated oceanic islands and atolls functioned as discrete human use systems in pre-colonial times, and here colonial contact could enhance rather than diminish the range of geographical systems with which the population itself could interact.[4]

We would suggest, therefore, that geographers should avoid becoming locked into the study of some 'structurally integrated object' existing at a particular spatial scale. The relationships between social, economic and ecological phenomena can certainly be modelled in the simplistic terms implied by such a straitjacket, but in reality the relationships are more complex. Because of the discipline's insistence on a search for linkages between phenomena, geographers are in a good position to avoid pushing the square pegs of the real world into the round holes of preconceived models. Our own study confirms that the interconnectedness of people and places does not take place within neatly bounded spatial units; in other words, islands do not enable the investigator to escape from the rigour of a full geographical analysis.

---

[4] As examples, in the Solomon Islands the outlying islands of Tikopia and Ontong Java had only intermittent contact with neighbouring islands in pre-colonial times, but they are now firmly located as outer islands within a trade and migration system centred on Honiara (Kirch & Yen 1982; Bayliss-Smith 1974, 1978b).

The time geography of islanders

Time resources

An assumption underlying MAB Project 7, and one reflected in other geographers' concepts of insularity (see chapter 2), is that on islands resources are limited. It was for this reason that islands played a particular role in the 1970s in writings on human ecology, since they appeared to provide a clear microcosm of the 'spaceship earth' concept of finite resources and limits to growth (e.g. Billings 1970; Odum 1971; Fosberg 1972; Hardin 1972; Hardin & Baden (eds.) 1977). Real islands, however, are not like spaceships. Islanders relate to a much wider range of resources than those of their island ecosystem, and in eastern Fiji, as we have shown (chapter 6), the net out-migration of islanders has left a large part of this region with static or declining population numbers.

It became clear at an early stage of our work that aggregate land resources could not be regarded as an important constraint on island populations or economies, since island 'carrying capacity' was in no danger of being exceeded (UNESCO/UNFPA 1977; Bayliss-Smith 1980). On the other hand, as we showed in chapter 5, land resources are distributed unevenly among island populations, and for some social groups problems of *access* to land (rather than land shortage *per se*) are indeed constraining their economic progress. For many other people, however, space is arguably less of a constraint than is time. Our concern in the project with the time resources of islanders, and with energy analysis as a way of expressing the relative value of time, followed the stimulus of Rappaport (1968), Sahlins (1974) and others, rather than the emerging 'time-geography school'.[5] Nevertheless we find ourselves basically in agreement with the principles of time geography as outlined by Carlstein, Parkes and Thrift (1978: 120):

The fact that activities, tasks and projects consume time and that space has a limited packing capacity led to a general packing problem both in a population time budget and in the space-time budget of a given area, domain or region. Given a population with its distribution of capabilities and qualities, only a certain volume of time-demanding activities can be packed into it.

Our study could easily be expressed in this sort of terminology, since it is clear that the progressive integration of eastern Fiji into the exchange economy and into a core-periphery regional system has added to the

[5] Time geography, although mapped out by Torsten Hagerstrand in the early 1970s, had not in fact achieved its full expression by Carlstein, Parkes and Thrift (1978; Parkes & Thrift 1980; Carlstein 1982) until long after the time-and-motion studies, activity surveys and migration history surveys that we carried out, particularly on Koro, Batiki, Lakeba and Kabara, as integral parts of our initial fieldwork strategy.

'time-demanding activities' of islanders very considerably. This is exemplified firstly in the new opportunities for mobility, which in serving the interests of the individual also diminish the aggregate resources of labour available in the islands through absenteeism; and secondly in the increased diversity of activities within the rural economy, in productive, domestic and recreational spheres. New machines, new skills, new crop and new leisure pursuits have been superimposed on a base load of 'traditional' social and economic activities, few of which have actually disappeared despite almost 150 years of exposure to alternatives.

The net result is that whereas for some islanders competition for space is not particularly important, competition for time is increasingly prominent. Consciousness of time has been transformed by the daily and weekly rhythms of church and school activities, by the periodicity of marketing opportunities, and through the introduction by return migrants of clock-time attitudes. In our activity surveys only the older informants had difficulty in relating their daily experience to our own concept of hours of input into work or leisure. As illustrated in chapter 7 (see Fig. 7.7), the totality of the active pursuits of villagers is both varied and substantial, occupying on average blocks of time fully equivalent to the Western norm of a 40-hour working week.

For many tasks decisions about the use of time resided in colonial times with the chief or senior man of *yavusa* or *mataqali* (Ward 1964). Today these decisions are very largely in the hands of individual men and women operating on an autonomous basis within nuclear-family household units. Communal labour, which despite increasing resistance occupied villagers for at least one day a week until the 1960s, is now rarely mobilised. On more traditional islands, for example Koro, heavy tasks like bush clearance and housebuilding sometimes still take place on a collective basis. Free *yaqona* and social pressure (plus the promise of ultimate reciprocity) is sufficient to persuade individuals willingly to abandon themselves for a time to the direction of others. But elsewhere in the eastern islands, for example Taveuni and Lakeba (chapter 9), even this relic of a more communal pattern of time use has disappeared. Individuals must rely on their own efforts, with corresponding gains in both incentive and social vulnerability (see chapter 5).

Time costs and energy benefits

Of course much decision-making that affects the islands has been taken over by the bureaucracy, by the business community and by other agents of the capitalist economy (see chapter 3), but what capacity for independent choice remains with the islanders is now being exercised by them in a greatly altered social context. Decision-making is increasingly centred on individuals, takes place across a widening range of both options and constraints, and must be guided by costs and benefits some of which are imperfectly known. Constraints and imperfect knowledge must not be forgotten, but even so we are impressed by the match between the observed behaviour of islanders on the one hand, and on the other hand our assessment of what constitutes 'rational' behaviour in the light of the calculated benefit/cost ratio of various activities (see chapters 7, 8 and 9).

We have found it useful to calculate such a ratio using techniques from ecological energetics, whereby the food energy gained or potentially gained per hour of work is compared for different activities, to determine which choice would optimise output (if labour input is held constant) or leisure (if not). For example, the comparison between copra and food crops is revealing. Copra provides returns that have generally been low, fluctuating, and outside the control of individual farmers, whereas the subsistence sector is more dependable and usually more rewarding. In this case energy analysis has revealed the good economic reasons for a continuing self-sufficiency in food production on Koro (see Table 8.3), and for dissatisfaction with the wage levels available to the new rural proletariat of Lakeba (see Table 9.2).

This approach means we can assess the costs and benefits of decisions in a way that we believe is consistent with villagers' own perceptions. It also enables us to characterise 'conservative' farmers in the Fiji periphery as being 'rational' decision-makers, but rational in a sense different from that used by 'rational' development planners, or by the architects of Man and the Biosphere and other such projects for ecologically 'rational' management.

The data required for energy analysis are not obtainable except through painstaking and prolonged fieldwork at micro-scale. The relatively self-contained nature of the villages and islands in eastern Fiji certainly facilitated this procedure, demonstrating again the special value of insularity. We would, however, claim that the value of energy analysis transcends the island world, and can contribute in an important way to any geographical research in which the social value of time as well as space is given an appropriate emphasis.

The rational management of islands

Pampered periphery?

Our focus on the decision-making behaviour of individuals did not distract us from the broader socio-political context within which these decisions are made. It is becoming fashionable to talk of 'marginalised' rural peoples in the Pacific (see, for example, Hau'ofa 1985). The argument is that as small countries become integrated more firmly into regional and global economic structures, there is a tendency for the gaps in life style, power and privilege between urban-based bureaucrats, business-men and politicians and rural-based farmers to widen. The urban élites have more in common with each other, and increasingly more trans-national interaction with each other, than they do with their rural kin. In the process it is said that rural people become progressively more marginalised both in terms of real access to the material and welfare benefits of economic growth, and in terms of political power to influence the course of events within their own countries and islands.

Yet, as we have shown in several chapters, the reality is much more complex. Urban élites in many parts of the Pacific, especially the poli-ticians, have a vested interest in ensuring marginalisation of their rural kin does not reach levels which encourage wholesale depopulation of the periphery. Small island peripheries throughout the Pacific remain impor-tant power bases legitimating the authority of indigenous chiefs. Retain-ing a population in the periphery with a lifestyle in the 1980s which conforms reasonably well to the neo-traditional stereotype created by European colonialism and supported by the post-colonial élites, requires a structure of state-directed subsidies – a transfer of value from core to periphery. In this regard, it is more appropriate to talk of 'pampered peripheries' in some areas, rather than 'depressed dependencies'. The small islands on the spatial peripheries of Pacific countries are not necessarily the homes of marginalised village communities in any real welfare or even economic sense, especially where an important com-ponent of the state's ideology is to preserve a viable village livelihood. The really 'marginalised' people in many Pacific countries are often in the cores; the unemployed, landless people who have no village to which they can return.

Concepts of 'rational' management

In this book we have considered the island world in terms of ecosystems, externalities, capitalist penetration, dependency and energy analysis, and as such we have clearly adopted world views that are far removed from those of the islanders themselves. It is therefore worth considering how successful we have been in bridging the gap between our ideologies and those of our informants.[6] All of us have the experience of repeated visits

---

[6] We define ideology, following Anderson (1973), as 'those systems of ideas which give distorted and partial accounts of reality, with the objective and often unintended consequences of serving the interests of a particular group or class'.

for fieldwork in eastern Fiji over the last decade, but despite the free and open dialogue with individuals that was provided by Fijian hospitality, by the government, and by most of the business community, there remain some formidable barriers of language, gender and cultural values. Given our own diversity of views, it is difficult to generalise about reflections of ideology in our various accounts of reality.[7] What we can say is that we have at least benefited from exposure of our preliminary versions of 'reality' to critical comment both within Fiji and in the wider academic world, and we hope this has eliminated some of the more obvious shortcomings.

Whose interests are served by geographical research of the kind that we have carried out? Have we at least fulfilled our initial assignment, and provided data and ideas of use for the 'rational management of island ecosystems'? Such questions are worth asking, since there is a presumption of ultimate and general benefit which lies behind the ideology of Man and the Biosphere's 'rationality' and that of other environmentalist programmes.

Rationality in this sense, termed *substantive rationality* by Simon (1976), refers to human behaviour within a specified structure of rules, and describes the response which will be appropriate, or rational, if these rules are followed. For the natural sciences and for the MAB programme, a rational management of environmental resources is one that is ecologically optimum in some specified sense, and it is assumed this objective is both desirable and feasible. Ways for achieving this objective can be defined by the researcher using the methodology of normal science, and can be applied to the real world by any 'rational' decision-maker.

Our project included a substantial 'normal science' component of this kind, covering marine resources (Salvat 1980) as well as soils and landforms (see chapter 2). It quickly became clear that the island ecosystems in eastern Fiji are not fundamentally threatened by current management practices, although there is evidence of mismanagement in the past leading, for example, to land degradation only recently checked by reafforestation. On the other hand the human resources of the islands do show evidence of suboptimal 'management', if we broaden that term to include the unwillingness or incapacity of governments to counteract many symptoms of eastern Fiji's peripheral location and marginal status

---

[7] Within the project there was continual discussion and common objectives, joint fieldwork and collective reports, but at no time did we attempt to establish a common viewpoint. Indeed, our individual ideas and values have probably shifted over the period of involvement with eastern Fiji. This diversity of views is reflected in the earlier publications of the project, and it is one reason for our wish to make clear that the various chapters of this book are written by different principal authors (see Editorial note).

in relation to capitalism. It is ironic that a relatively 'rational' ecological adjustment should be the unintended side-effect of regional and structural imbalances that are widely regarded as being undesirable, and which are now identified as elements that central planners should strive to eliminate.

We are forced to conclude that a worthwhile investigation into island problems cannot be conducted within the confines of the particular substantive rationality that is implied by the term 'rational management of island ecosystems'. To understand what has happened and is happening in eastern Fiji requires a wider definition of what constitutes 'rational management'. It also requires that we consider a different concept of rationality altogether. We were constantly faced in the field with islanders making decisions that were clearly 'irrational' from the point of view of optimising land use, income or environmental conservation, but which were nevertheless thoroughly rational in another sense.

There is indeed a second concept of rationality (*procedural rationality*) which describes how decisions are actually made (Simon 1976). For a psychologist a person can be regarded as making a 'rational' decision if he has given appropriate thought and consideration to a problem with which he is faced. These thought processes must obviously be carried out by the decision-maker in the light of his particular needs and prejudices, and in the context of his ability to cope with the complexities and contradictions of the particular problem. The concept of procedural rationality accurately describes the basis for most decisions concerning the exploitation of the environment. Villagers in eastern Fiji, for example, are clearly not equipped with the linear programming techniques, market forecasts, probability models of hazard recurrence, etc., which might enable an agricultural economist to define what is the most substantively rational decision. Instead, islanders must draw upon their own past experience and knowledge, in order to make decisions that will produce an adequate livelihood for themselves and their families but will not jeopardise cherished social values. As our village studies have shown (chapters 7–9), the decisions made by islanders are wholly rational in this sense, but do not lead to an aggregate pattern of resource use which is rational from the planner's point of view.[8]

It is foolish to apply substantively rational solutions to real world problems, because decisions in the real world are not, and usually cannot, be made in a situation of purely substantive rationality. Just as their respective interests may not coincide, so the world view of islanders is not

[8] An attempted expansion of this theme by Bayliss-Smith was used by UNESCO to strengthen the role of the social sciences in MAB research (UNESCO 1977), and the current concept of 'rational management' within the MAB programme is undoubtedly less narrow than that which we have criticised here.

the same as that of mainlanders, and not at all the same as that of rational managers or their academic advisers. An awareness of this fact is, we hope, one of the strengths of this book. We believe that a sound geographical synthesis requires not only a full analysis of the interwoven relationships of people and environment at all relevant spatial scales, but also an integration of the 'top-down' view of rational resource analysis with the 'bottom-up' view of farmers, fishermen, copra-cutters and wage labourers. Only by explicitly examining these contrasting perceptions and ideologies can we establish the true nature of conflicts and contradictions, and so achieve a more complete synthesis of the relationships between islands, islanders and the world.

Appendix

PUBLICATIONS OF THE UNESCO/UNFPA EASTERN FIJI PROJECT

The Project Working Papers

These papers were prepared in mid-1976, and were printed for Unesco by the Australian National University, Canberra. Nos. 1 and 2, and Nos. 4, 5 and 6 were bound together, though separately paginated, so that there is a total of only four volumes.

1 DENIS, B. 1976. *The soils of Lakeba and Taveuni*. Project Working Paper No. 1.
2 SALVAT, B.; RICARD, M.; RICHARD, G.; GALZIN, R.; TOFFART, J. L. 1976. *The ecology of the reef-lagoon complex of some islands in the Lau group: preliminary report*. Project Working Paper No. 2.
3 BEDFORD, R. D. 1976. *Kabara in the 1970s*. Project Working Paper No. 3.
4 HAYNES, P. H. 1976. *Some aspects of agriculture in Taveuni and Lakeba*. Project Working Paper No. 4.
5 BROOKFIELD, H. C. 1976. *The Taveuni farmers*. Project Working Paper No. 5.
6 HARDAKER, J. B. 1976. *Economic aspects of agriculture and marketing in Taveuni*. Project Working Paper No. 6.
7 BAYLISS-SMITH, T. P. 1976. *Koro in the 1970s: prosperity through diversity?* Project Working Paper No. 7.

The Island Reports

UNESCO/UNFPA Island Reports 1. 1977. *The hurricane hazard: natural disaster and small populations*. Australian National University for Unesco, Canberra.

BROOKFIELD, H. C. Editorial introduction, pp. 1–8.
McLEAN, R. F. The hurricane hazard in the eastern islands of Fiji: an historical analysis, pp. 9–63.
BAYLISS-SMITH, T. P. Hurricane Val in north Lakeba: the view from 1975, pp. 65–97.
BROOKFIELD, M. Hurricane Val and its aftermath: report on an inquiry among the people of Lakeba in 1976, pp. 99–147.
CAMPBELL, J. R. Hurricanes in Kabara, pp. 149–75.

UNESCO/UNFPA Island Reports 2. 1977. *Koro in the 1970s: prosperity through diversity?* Australian National University for Unesco, Canberra.

BAYLISS-SMITH, T. P. Koro in the 1970s: prosperity through diversity? pp. 1–97.

UNESCO/UNFPA Island Reports 3. 1978. *Taveuni: land, population and production*. Australian National University for Unesco, Canberra.

BROOKFIELD, H. C. Editorial introduction: unweeded garden island? pp. 1–11.
DENIS, B. A descriptive note on the soils of Taveuni, pp. 13–20.
BROOKFIELD, H. C. Land holding and land use on Taveuni island, pp. 21–84.
BEDFORD, R. D. Rural Taveuni: perspectives on population change, pp. 85–244.
NANKIVELL, P. S. Income inequality in Taveuni: a statistical analysis of data from the Resource Base Survey, pp. 245–98.
BROOKFIELD, H. C.; HARDAKER, J. B. A preliminary note on copra production in Taveuni District and adjacent areas, pp. 299–309.

UNESCO/UNFPA Island Reports 4. 1978. *The small islands and the reefs*. Australian National University for Unesco, Canberra.

BROOKFIELD, H. C. Editorial introduction: small is beautiful? pp. 1–8.
BEDFORD, R. D.; McCLEAN, R. F.; MACPHERSON, J. Kabara in the 1970s: home in spite of hazards, pp. 9–66.
BAYLISS-SMITH, T. P. Batiki in the 1970s: satellite of Suva, pp. 67–128.
SALVAT, B.; RICARD, M.; RICHARD, G.; GALZIN, R.; TOFFART, J. L. A summary review of the reef-lagoon economy of Lau, pp. 129–45.

UNESCO/UNFPA Island Reports 5. 1979. *Lakeba: Environmental change, population dynamics and resource use*. Australian National University for Unesco, Canberra.

BROOKFIELD, H. C. Editorial introduction, pp. 1–2
BROOKFIELD, M. Introduction to Lakeba, pp. 3–12.
LATHAM, M. The natural environment of Lakeba, pp. 13–64.
McLEAN, R. F. The coast of Lakeba: a geomorphological reconnaissance, pp. 65–82.
SALVAT, B.; RICHARD, G.; TOFFART, J. L.; RICARD, M.; GALZIN, R. The reef-lagoon complex: geomorphology, biotic associations and socio-ecology, pp. 83–92.
HUGHES, P. J.; HOPE, G.; LATHAM, M.; BROOKFIELD, M. Prehistoric man-induced degradation of the Lakeba landscape: evidence from two island swamps, pp. 93–110.
LATHAM, M. Land resource potential, pp. 111–26.
BROOKFIELD, M. Resource use, economy and society: island at the crossroads, pp. 127–98.
BEDFORD, R. D.; BROOKFIELD, M. Population change in Lakeba 1946–76: perspective on fertility and migration, pp. 199–216.
BROOKFIELD, H. C. Lakeba, the eastern islands and the work of the project in retrospect, pp. 217–41.

The General Reports

1 UNESCO/UNFPA. 1977. *Population, resources and development in the eastern islands of Fiji: information for decision-making*. Australian National University for Unesco, Canberra, 407 pp.

2 BROOKFIELD, H. C. (ed.). 1980. *Population–environment relations in tropical islands: the case of eastern Fiji.* MAB Technical Notes 13. Unesco, Paris.

BROOKFIELD, H. C. Introduction: the conduct and findings of the interdisciplinary Fiji project, pp. 13–28.

BEDFORD, R. D. Demographic processes in small islands: the case of internal migration, pp. 29–60.

BAYLISS-SMITH, T. P. Population pressure, resources and welfare: towards a more realistic measure of carrying capacity, pp. 61–94.

HARDAKER, J. B. Modelling the Taveuni island economy: a preliminary study, pp. 95–112.

LATHAM, M.; DENIS, B. The study of land potential: an open-ended inquiry, pp. 113–24.

McLEAN, R. F. The land-sea interface of small tropical islands: morphodynamics and man, pp. 125–30.

SALVAT, B. The living marine resources of the South Pacific – past, present and future, pp. 131–48.

McLEAN, R. F. Spatial and temporal variability of external physical controls on small island ecosystems, pp. 149–76.

BROOKFIELD, H. C. The Fiji Study: testing the MAB approach, pp. 177–204.

BROOKFIELD, H. C.; BEDFORD, R. D. Formulating guidelines for population programmes and environmental management in small island regions, pp. 205–23.

3 OFFICE DE LA RECHERCHE SCIENTIFIQUE ET TECHNIQUE OUTRE-MER (ORSTOM). 1983.
Îles Fidji Orientales: Étude du milieu naturel, de son utilisation et de son évolution sous l'influence humaine/The Eastern Islands of Fiji: A Study of the Natural Environment, its Use and Man's Influence on its Evolution, edited by M. Latham With H. C. Brookfield, Travaux et Documents de l'ORSTOM No. 162, Paris, 184 pp.

LATHAM, M., Introduction: La contribution ORSTOM/ORSTOM's contribution, pp. 5–210.

LATHAM, M., McLEAN, R. F.; BROOKFIELD, M. Lakeba, pp. 13–61.

DENIS, B.; BROOKFIELD, H. C. Taveuni, pp. 63–82.

LATHAM, M.; CAMPBELL, J. Kabara, pp. 83–92.

LATHAM, M.; BAYLISS-SMITH, T. P. Nairai et/and Batiki, pp. 93–100.

LATHAM, M.; HUGHES, P. J.; HOPE, G.; BROOKFIELD, M. Sedimentation dans les zones marécageuses de Lakeba: conséquences sur l'érosion et l'occupation humaine de l'île/Sedimentation in the swamps of Lakeba and its implications for erosion and human occupation of the island, pp. 103–19.

BAYLISS-SMITH, T. P. Pluviométrie, infiltration et ruissellement a Lakeba/Rainfall, infiltration and runoff on Lakeba, pp. 121–7.

LATHAM, M. Origine de la formation a talasiga/Origin of the talasiga formation, pp. 129–41.

LATHAM, M. Evolution des charactéristiques du milieu après reforestation de zones a talasiga/Evolution of the environment after the reafforestation of talasiga areas, pp. 143–51.

DENIS, B.; BROOKFIELD, H. C. Evolution des sols et des rendements en culture semi-continue de taro/Evolution of soils and yields under the semi-continuous cultivation of taro, pp. 153–60.

LATHAM, M. Conclusion: Ecologie et developpement/Ecology and development, pp. 161–6.

References

Aharon, P. & Veeh, H. H. (1984) Isotope studies of insular phosphates explain atoll phosphatization. *Nature*, 309, 614–17

Ali, A. (1980), *Plantation to politics: studies on Fiji Indians*. University of the South Pacific and Fiji Times and Herald Ltd, Suva

Anderson, J. (1973) Ideology in geography: an introduction. *Antipode*, 5 (3), 1–6

Anderson, J. W. (1880) *Notes on travel in Fiji and New Caledonia*. Ellissen and Co., London

Anon. (1834) Voyage of the ship Emerald 1899 to 1836. Pacific Manuscripts Bureau, ANU, Canberra, Film PMB 205

  (1880) Minutes of the Executive Council sitting for the hearing of claims to land, 1879–80. Pacific Manuscripts Bureau, Australian National University, Film PMB DOC 206

Atkins (1983) *Western Vanua Levu Regional Plan, vol. 2: Growth Centres.* Atkins Land and Water Management, Cambridge, for CPO, Suva

Baker, A. R. H. (1984) Reflections on the relations of historical geography and the Annales school of history. In A. R. H. Baker and D. Gregory, eds., *Explorations in Historical Geography*, 1–27. Cambridge University Press

Baldwin, R. E. (1956) Patterns of development in newly settled regions. *The Manchester School of Economic and Social Studies*, 24: 161–79

  (1966) *Economic development and export growth: a study of Northern Rhodesia 1920–1960.* University of California Press, Berkeley and Los Angeles

Barkin, D. & King, T. (1970) *Regional economic development: the river basin approach in Mexico.* Cambridge University Press, London and New York

Barnett, T. P. (1981) Statistical relations between ocean/atmosphere fluctuations in the tropical Pacific. *Journal of Physical Oceanography*, 11, 1043–58

Bates, M. (1963) Nature's effect on and control of Man. In F. R. Fosberg, ed., *Man's place in the island ecosystem*, 101–16. Bishop Museum Press, Honolulu

Baxter, M. W. P. (1980) *Food in Fiji: the produce and processed foods distribution systems.* Development Studies Centre Monograph No. 22, ANU, Canberra

Bayliss-Smith, T. P. (1974) Constraints on population growth: the case of the Polynesian outlier atolls in the pre-contact period. *Human Ecology*, 2, 259–96

  (1977a) Hurricane Val in north Lakeba: the view from 1975. In H. C. Brookfield, (ed.) *The hurricane hazard: natural disaster and small populations*, 65–97, UNESCO/UNFPA Island Reports 1, Australian National University for UNESCO, Canberra

(1977b) *Koro in the 1970s: prosperity through diversity?*, UNESCO/UNFPA Fiji Project Reports, No. 2, ANU Press for UNESCO, Canberra

(1977c) Human ecology and island populations: the problems of change. In T. P. Bayliss-Smith and R. G. A. Feachem, eds. *Subsistence and survival*, 11–20. Academic Press, London

(1978a) Batiki in the 1970s: satellite of Suva. In H. C. Brookfield (ed.) *The small islands and the reefs*, 67–128, UNESCO/UNFPA Island Reports 4, Australian National University for UNESCO, Canberra

(1978b) Changing patterns of inter-island mobility on Ontong Java atoll. *Archaeology and Physical Anthropology in Oceania*, 13, 41–73

(1980) Population pressure, resources and welfare: towards a more realistic measure of carrying capacity. In H. C. Brookfield, ed., *Population, environment and resources in tropical islands: the case of eastern Fiji*, 61–93 MAB Technical Notes No. 13, UNESCO, Paris

(1982) *The ecology of agricultural systems*. Cambridge University Press

(1983a) Pluviométrie, infiltration et ruissellement a Lakeba/Rainfall, infiltration and runoff on Lakeba. In M. Latham & H. C. Brookfield (eds.) *Iles Fidji orientales/The Eastern Islands of Fiji*. Travaux et Documents de l'ORSTOM. No. 162, 121–7. Paris

(1983b) A household survey of villages in Bua Province. In *Western Vanua Levu Regional Plan*, vol. 4, Technical Papers. Atkins Land and Water Management, Cambridge, for Central Planning Office, Suva, 32pp.

(1984) Energy flows and agrarian change in Karnataka: the Green Revolution at micro-scale. In T. Bayliss-Smith and S. Wanmali eds., *Understanding green revolutions*, 153–72. Cambridge University Press

Beckford, G. L. (1972) *Persistent poverty: underdevelopment in plantation economies of the Third World*. Oxford University Press, New York

Bedford, R. D. (1976) Kabara in the 1970s: dimensions of dependence in a contemporary Lauan society. UNESCO/UNFPA Project Working Paper, No. 3, Canberra, 92pp.

(1978) Rural Taveuni: perspectives on population change. In H. C. Brookfield, ed., *Taveuni: land, population and production*, 85–224. UNESCO/UNFPA Fiji Project Reports, No. 3, ANU Press for UNESCO, Canberra

(1980a) Demographic processes in small islands: the case of internal migration. In H. C. Brookfield, ed., *Population–environment relations in tropical islands: the case of eastern Fiji*, 29–60. UNESCO Press, Paris

(1980b) The depopulation debate. In R. D. Bedford, *Perceptions, past and present, of a future for Melanesia*, 1979 Macmillan Brown Lectures, University of Canterbury

(1981) Melanesian internal migration: recent evidence from eastern Fiji. *New Zealand Journal of Geography*, No. 71, 2–6

(1984) Population movement and the articulation of modes of production in eastern Fiji: a comment. In D. K. Forbes and P. J. Rimmer, eds. *Uneven development and the geographical transfer of value*, 199–206. Human Geography Monograph No. 16, The Australian National University, Canberra

(1985) Population movement in a small island periphery: the case of eastern Fiji. In M. Chapman and R. M. Prothero, eds., *Circulation in population movement: substance and concepts from the Melanesian case*, 333–59. Routledge and Kegan Paul, London

Bedford, R. D. & Brookfield, H. C. (1974) Report on aspects of the Eastern Division Resource Base Survey 1974, Ministry of Fijian Affairs and Rural Development, 17 pp. (mimeo)

Bedford, R. D. & Brookfield, M. (1979) Fertility, migration and population change. In H. C. Brookfield, ed., *Lakeba: environmental change, population dynamics and resource use*, 199–215. UNESCO/UNFPA Fiji Island Reports, No. 5, Australian National University for Unesco, Canberra

Bedford, R. D., McLean, R. F. & Macpherson, J. (1978) Kabara in the 1970s: home in spite of hazards. In H. C. Brookfield, ed., *The small islands and reefs*, 9–65. UNESCO/UNFPA Fiji Island Reports, No. 4, Australian National University for Unesco, Canberra

Bellwood, P. (1978) *Man's conquest of the Pacific*. Collins, London

Belshaw, C. S. (1964) *Under the ivi tree: society and economic growth in rural Fiji*. Routledge and Kegan Paul, London

Bennett, R. J. & Chorley R. J. (1977) *Environmental systems: philosophy, analysis, control*. Methuen, London

Berryman, K. (1979) *Seismotectonic zoning study of the Fiji islands*. New Zealand Geological Survey, EDS Report No. 70

Bertram, L. G. & Watters, R. F. (1984) *New Zealand and its small island neighbours: a review of New Zealand policy toward the Cook Islands, Niue, Tokelau, Kiribati and Tuvalu*. Institute of Policy Studies, Victoria University of Wellington, Wellington, New Zealand

(1985) The MIRAB economy in South Pacific microstates. *Pacific Viewpoint*, 26, 497–520

Best, S. (1977) Archaeological investigations on Lakeba, Lau Group, Fiji. *New Zealand Archaeological Association Newsletter*, 20(1), 28–38

Bienefeld, M. A. (1982) *A note on the consumer price index*. Fiji Employment and Development Mission, WP 1, (mimeo), Suva

(1984) *Work and income for the people of Fiji: a strategy for more than just survival*. Final Report of the Fiji Employment and Development Mission. Government Printer, Suva

Billings, W. D. (1970) *Plants, man and the ecosystem*, 2nd edn. Macmillan, London

Bird, J. (1971) *Seaports and seaport terminals*. Hutchinson, London

Birks, L. (1973) *Archaeological excavations at Sigatoka dune site, Fiji*. Bulletin of the Fiji Museum, No. 1, Suva

Bjerknes, J. (1969) Atmospheric teleconnections from the equatorial Pacific. *Monthly Weather Review*, 97, 163–72

Bloom, A. L. (1980) Late Quaternary sea level change on South Pacific coasts: a study in tectonic diversity. In N. A. Morner, ed., *Earth rheology, isostasy and eustasy*, 505–16. Wiley-Interscience, Chichester

Boyan, R. H. (1961) Koro: Fiji island of progress. *South Pacific Bulletin*, 11(1), 37–8

Boyd, R. (1911) *Report of the census taken on the night of 2 April 1911*. Legislative Council of Fiji, Council Paper No. 44 of 1911, Suva

Boyd, R. & Stewart, D. R. (1922) *Report of the census taken on the night of 24 April 1921*. Legislative Council of Fiji, Council Paper No. 2 of 1922, Suva

Bridgeman, H. A. (1983) Could climatic change have had an influence on the Polynesian migrations? *Palaeogeography, Palaeoclimatology, Palaeoecology*, 41, 193–206

Britton, H. (1870) *Fiji in 1870: being the letters of the Argus special correspondent*. Samuel Mullen, Melbourne

Britton, S. G. (1980) The evolution of a colonial space economy: the case of Fiji, *Journal of Historical Geography*, vol. 6, no. 3, 251–74

Brookfield, H. C. (1969) On the environment as perceived. In C. Board, R. J. Chorley, P. Haggett and D. R. Stoddart, eds., *Progress in Geography*, vol. 1 52–80. Arnold, London

(1952) *Colonialism, development and independence: the case of the Melanesian islands of the South Pacific*. Cambridge University Press

(1975a) Multum in parvo: questions about diversity and diversification in small developing countries. In P. Selwyn, ed., *Development policy in small countries*, 54–76. Croom Helm in association with the Institute of Development Studies, Sussex, London

(1975b) *Preliminary Report on the Taveuni Resource Base Survey*. Report to the Permanent Secretary for Fijian Affairs and Rural Development (mimeo), Suva

(1975c) *Interdependent development*. Methuen, London

(1977) Constraints to agrarian change. In J. H. Winslow, ed., *The Melanesian environment*, 133–8. Australian National University Press, Canberra

(1978) Land holding and land use on Taveuni island. In H. C. Brookfield, ed. *Taveuni: land, population and production*, 21–84, UNESCO/UNFPA Island Reports 3, Australian National University for UNESCO, Canberra

(1979) Land reform, efficiency and rural income distribution: contributions to an argument. *Pacific Viewpoint*, 20, 33–52

(1980) The Fiji study: testing the MAB approach. In H. C. Brookfield, ed., *Population–environment relations in tropical islands: the case of eastern Fiji*, 177–204. MAB Technical Notes 13, UNESCO, Paris

(1981) Man, environment and development in the Outer Islands of Fiji. *Ambio*, 10 (2–3), 59–67

(1984a) Intensification revisited. *Pacific Viewpoint*, 25, 15–44

(1984b) Boxes, ports and places without ports. In B. S. Hoyle and D. Hilling, eds., *Seaports systems and spatial change*, 61–79. John Wiley and Sons Ltd. Chichester

(1985) An historical and prospective analysis of the coconut economy and the coconut districts. In H. C. Brookfield, F. Ellis and R. G. Ward, *Land, cane and coconuts: papers on the rural economy of Fiji*, 111–247. Department of Human Geography Publication 17, Australian National University, Canberra

(1986a) Export or perish: commercial agriculture in Fiji. In M. J. Taylor, ed., *Fiji: issues in island development*. Allen and Unwin, Sydney (in press)

(1986b) Frost, drought and human occupation. In B. J. Allen, ed., *Child of El Niño: frost and drought in Papua New Guinea*. Publication HG/20, Department of Human Geography, Research School of Pacific Studies, Australian National University, Canberra

(1988) Fijian farmers each on their own land: the triumph of experience over hope. *Journal of Pacific History*, 23, 15–35

(forthcoming) The behavioural environment: how? what for? and whose? In F. Foal and D. Livingstone, eds., *The behavioural environment*. Croom Helm, London

Brookfield, H. C. & Bedford, R. D. (1980) Formulating guidelines for population programmes and environmental management in small island regions. In

H. C. Brookfield, ed., *Population–environment relations in tropical islands: the case of eastern Fiji*, 205–23. MAB Technical Notes, no. 13, UNESCO Press, Paris

Brookfield, M. (1977) Hurricane Val and its aftermath: report of an inquiry among the people of Lakeba in 1976. In H. C. Brookfield, ed. *The hurricane hazard: natural disaster and small populations*, 99–147, UNESCO/UNFPA Island Reports 1, Australian National University for UNESCO, Canberra

(1979) Resource use, economy and society: island at the cross-roads. In H. C. Brookfield, ed. *Lakeba: Environmental Change, Population Dynamics and Resource Use*, 127–97, UNESCO/UNFPA Island Reports 5, Australian National University for UNESCO, Canberra

Bureau of Statistics (1977) *Vital statistics in Fiji: a report for the year 1976*. Government Printer, Suva

(1981) *Household income and expenditure survey 1977*. Government Printer, Suva

(1984) *Current economic statistics, January 1984*. Government Printer, Suva

Burns, A., Watson, T. Y. & Peacock, A. T. (1960) *Report of the commission of inquiry into the natural resources and population trends of the Colony of Fiji, 1959*. Legislative Council of Fiji, Council Paper No. 1 of 1960, Suva

Burns Philp (1929) Burns Philp (South Sea) Company Ltd., Levuka Branch, Fiji. Managers' Reports on Annual Balances 1920–1952. Pacific Manuscripts Bureau, ANU, Canberra, Film PMB 151.

Burrows, W. (1936) *A Report on the Fiji census 1936 (26 April)*. Legislative Council of Fiji, Council Paper No. 42 of 1936, Suva

Calvert, J. & Williams, T. (1858) *Fiji and the Fijians*, (2 vols.). Alexander Heylin, London

Cameron, J. (1983a) *The extent and structure of poverty in Fiji and possible elements of a government anti-poverty strategy in the 1980s*. Fiji Employment and Development Mission, WP 19, (mimeo), Suva

(1983b) *Development dilemmas in Fiji*. School of Development Studies, University of East Anglia, Discussion Paper No. 137

Campbell J. R. (1977) Hurricanes in Kabara. In H. C. Brookfield, (ed.) *The hurricane hazard: natural disaster and small populations*, 149–75, UNESCO/UNFPA Island Reports 1, Australian National University for UNESCO, Canberra

(1984) *Dealing with disaster: hurricane response in Fiji*. Government of Fiji and Pacific Islands Development Program, Honolulu

Carlstein, T. (1982) *Time resources, society and ecology. Vol. 1: Pre-industrial societies*. Allen & Unwin, London

Carlstein, T., D. Parkes & N. Thrift (eds.) (1978) *Timing space and spacing time*, 3 vols. Arnold, London

Catala, R. (1957) Report on the Gilbert Islands: some aspects of human ecology, *Atoll Research Bulletin* 59, Pacific Science Board, Washington, DC

Central Planning Office (1966) *Fiji development plan 1966–1970: development planning review*. Legislative Council Paper No. 11 of 1966. Government Printer, Suva

(1970) *Fiji's sixth development plan, 1971–1975*. Government Printer, Suva

(1975) *Fiji's seventh development plan, 1976–1980*. Government Printer, Suva

(1980a) *Fiji's eighth development plan, 1981–1985, Vol. 1: policies and programmes for social and economic development*. Government Printer, Suva

(1980b) *Fiji's eighth development plan, 1981–85. Vol. 2: policies and programmes for regional development*. Government Printer, Suva

(1983) Draft regional plan for Koro. CPO, Suva (MS)

(1985) *Fiji's Ninth Development Plan 1986–1990*. Parliament of Fiji, Parliamentary Paper No. 69 of 1985, Government Printer, Suva

Chandra, R. (1986) Internal migration. In J. Bryant, ed., *The population of Fiji*. South Pacific Commission, Noumea (in press)

Chandra, R. C. (1981) Rural-urban population movement in Fiji 1966–1976: a macro-analysis. In G. W. Jones and H. V. Richter, eds., *Population mobility and development: Southeast Asia and the Pacific*, 329–54. Development Studies Centre Monograph No. 27, Australian National University, Canberra

Chapelle, T. (1978) Customary land tenure in Fiji: old truths and middle-aged myths. *Journal of the Polynesian Society*, vol. 87, no. 2, 71–88

Chapman, G. P. (1977) *Human and environmental systems: a geographer's appraisal*. Academic Press, London

Chapman, M. & Prothero, R. M. eds. (1985) *Circulation in population movement: substance and concepts from the Melanesian case*. Routledge and Kegan Paul, London

Child, R. (1974) *Coconuts* (2nd edn.). Longman, London

Chorley, R. J. (1973) Geography as human ecology. In R. J. Chorley, ed., *Directions in Geography*, 153–70. Methuen, London

Christiansen, S. (1975) *Subsistence on Bellona Island (Mungiki)*. Folia Geographica Danica, vol. 13, Copenhagen

Clammer, J. (1975) Colonialism and the perception of tradition in Fiji. In Talal Asad, ed., *Anthropology and the colonial encounter*, 199–220. Ithaca Publishers, London

Clark, J. A. (1980) A numerical model of worldwide sea level changes on a viscoelastic earth. In N. A. Norner, ed., *Earth rheology, isostasy and eustasy*, 525–34. Wiley-Interscience, Chichester

Cliff, A. D. & Haggett P. (1985) *The spread of measles in Fiji and the Pacific*. Department of Human Geography Publication HG/18, Research School of Pacific Studies, Australian National University

Climate Analysis Center (1982–3) *Special Climate Diagnostics Bulletin*. NOAA, Washington, DC

Cole, R. V., Levins, S. I. & Matahau, A. V. (1984) *The Fijian Provincial Administration: a review*. Pacific Islands Development Program, East-West Center, Honolulu

Connell, J. C. (1985) *Migration, employment and development in the South Pacific: Fiji*. Country Report No. 3, South Pacific Commission and International Labour Organisation, Noumea

Corney, B. G., Stewart, J., & Thomson, B. (1896) *Report of the commission appointed to inquire into the decrease of the native population, 1893*. Government Printer, Suva

Couper, A. D. (1965) *Report on the inter-insular shipping and trade of Fiji*. Canberra, Australian National University, Department of Geography (mimeo)

(1973) Islanders at sea: change, and the maritime economies of the Pacific. In H. C. Brookfield, ed., *The Pacific in transition: geographical perspectives on adaptation and change*, 229–48. Edward Arnold, London

Crocombe, R. (1971) Social aspects of cooperative and other corporate land-holding in the Pacific Islands. In P. Worsley, ed., *Two blades of grass: rural cooperatives in agricultural modernization*, 159–98. Manchester University Press

Crotty, R. (1979) Capitalist colonialism and peripheralisation: the Irish case. In D. Seers, B. Schaffer and M-L. Liljunen, eds., *Underdeveloped Europe: studies in core-periphery relations*, 225–35. Harvester Press, Hassocks, Sussex

Cumming-Gordon, C. F. (1882) *At home in Fiji*. A. C. Armstrong, New York

Cumpston, I. M. (1956) Sir Arthur Gordon and the introduction of Indians into the Pacific: the West Indian system in Fiji. *Pacific Historical Review*, 25, 369–88

Darby, H. C. (1951) The changing landscape. *Geographical Journal*, 117, 377–94

Davidson, J. M. (1977) Western Polynesia and Fiji: prehistoric contact, diffusion and differentiation in adjacent archipelagos. *World Archaeology*, 9, 82–94

Denis, B. (1983) Taveuni. In *Iles Fidji Orientales/The eastern islands of Fiji*, 63–79. Travaux et Documents de l'ORSTOM no. 162, Paris

de Ricci, J. H. (1875) *Fiji: our new province in the South Seas*. Edward Stanford, London

Derrick, R. A. (1945) Fijian reaction to trade and industry in the early days. *Transactions and proceedings of the Fiji Society of Science and Industry*, vol. 3

(1950) *A history of Fiji*. Government Printer, Suva

Dickinson, W. R. (1967) Tectonic development of Fiji. *Tectonophysics*, 4, 543–53

(1968) Sigatoka dune sands, Viti Levu (Fiji). *Sedimentary Geology*, 2, 115–24

Dickson Commission (1983) *Report of the commission of inquiry into the coconut industry*. Coopers and Lybrand, Suva

Dods, M. T. (1891) *Report of the Registrar General on the census taken on 5 April 1891*. Minute Paper CSO No. 2121 of 1891, Suva

(1901) *A report on the census of 31 March 1901*. Minute Paper 2919 of 1901, Suva

Dommen, E. C. ed. (1980) Islands (special issue), *World Development* 8: 929–1059

Eagleston, J. H. (1831) Logbook of Barque 'Peru', 1830–1833. Pacific Manuscripts Bureau, ANU, Canberra, Film PMB 205

Eastern Division (1980) File 18/4, Hurricane relief and damage. Divisional Commissioners Office, Levuka.

(1983) *Handbook of government work programme*. Divisional Commissioner, Levuka

Ellen, R. (1982) *Environment, subsistence and system. The ecology of small-scale social formations*. Cambridge University Press

Ellis, F. (1984) Relative agricultural prices and the urban bias model: a comparative analysis of Tanzania and Fiji. *Journal of Development Studies*, vol. 20, no. 3, 28–51

(1985) Employment and incomes in the Fiji sugar economy. In H. C. Brookfield, F. Ellis and R. G. Ward, *Land, cane and coconuts: papers on the rural economy of Fiji*, 65–110. Department of Human Geography Publication 17, Australian National University, Canberra

Emberson, H. J. (1881) *Report of the Registrar General upon a census taken on 4 April 1881*. Enclosure to Despatch No. 183 of 29 December 1881, Suva

F.A.O. (1980) *Coconut Industry of Fiji*. TCP/FIJ/8901 (1). FAO, Rome

Farmer, B. H. (1977) Geography and agrarian research: experience from Tamil Nadu and Sri Lanka. In Indian Geographical Society, *The Golden Jubilee Volume 1976*, 198–206. IGS, Madras

Febvre, L. (1932) *A geographical introduction to history*. Kegan Paul, London and Knopf, New York

Finney, B. R. (1985) Anomalous westerlies, El Niño and the colonisation of Polynesia. *American Anthropologist*, 87, 9–26

Fisk, E. K. (1970) *The political economy of independent Fiji*. ANU Press, Canberra

Fison, L. (1881) Land tenure in Fiji. *Journal of the Royal Anthropological Institute*, vol. 10, 332–52

Fontes, J. C., Launay J., Monzier M. & Recy J. (1977) Genetic hypothesis on the ancient and recent reef complexes in New Caledonia. In ORSTOM, *Geodynamics in the South-West Pacific/Geodynamique du Sud-Ouest Pacifique*, 289–99. Editions Technip, Paris

Fosberg, F. R. (ed.) (1963) *Man's place in the island ecosystem*. Bishop Museum Press, Honolulu

(1972) Man's effects on island ecosystems. In M. T. Farvar and J. P. Milton, eds., *The careless technology*, 869–80. Natural History Press, Garden City, New York

France, P. (1968) The founding of an orthodoxy: Sir Arthur Gordon and the doctrine of the Fijian way of life. *Journal of the Polynesian Society*, 77, 6–32

(1969) *The charter of the land: custom and colonisation in Fiji*. Oxford University Press, Melbourne

Frazer, R. (1973) The Fijian village and the independent farmer. In H. C. Brookfield, ed. *The Pacific in transition: geographical perspectives on adaptation and change*, 75–96. Edward Arnold, London

(1982) Interprovincial migration and urbanisation of indigenous Fijians, 1956–76: a study of age and sex preferences using the census survival technique, 28 pp. (mimeo)

Friedmann, J. (1966) *Regional development policy: a case study of Venezuela*. MIT Press, Boston, Mass.

Frost, E. L. (1969) *Archaeological excavations of fortified sites on Taveuni, Fiji*. University Press of Hawaii, Honolulu

(1979) Fiji. In J. D. Jennings, ed., *The prehistory of Polynesia*, 61–81. ANU Press, Canberra

Gailey, C. W. (1987) State, class and conversion in commodity production: gender and changing value in the Tongan islands. *Journal of the Polynesian Society*, 96, 67–80.

Garnock-Jones, P. J. (1978) Plant communities on Lakeba and Southern Vanua Balavu, Lau Group. In *Lau-Tonga 1977*, 95–117. Royal Society of New Zealand Bulletin 17, Wellington

Geddes, W. R. (1945) *Deuba: a study of a Fijian village*. Memoirs of the Polynesian Society, Wellington

(1956) Acceleration of social change in a Fijian community. *Oceania*, vol. 16, no. 1, 1–14

Gill, J. B. (1976) Composition and age of Lau Basin and Ridge volcanic rocks: implication for evaluation of an inter-arc basic and remnant arc. *Geological Society of America Bulletin*, 87, 1384–95

Gillion, K. L. (1962) *Fiji's Indian migrants: a history to the end of indenture in 1920*. Oxford University Press, Melbourne

Girvan, N. (1973) The development of dependency economics in the Caribbean and Latin America: review and comparison. *Social and Economic Studies* 22: 1–33

Gittins, J. W. (1947) *A report on the results of the census of the population 1946 (3 October)*. Legislative Council of Fiji, Council Paper No. 35 of 1947, Suva

Glacken, C. J. (1963) This growing second world within the world of nature. In F. R. Fosberg, ed., *Man's place in the island ecosystem*, 75–100. Bishop Museum Press, Honolulu

Gladwin, T. (1970) *East is a big bird*. Harvard University Press, Cambridge, Mass.

Glaser, G. (1980) Foreword. In H. C. Brookfield, ed., *Population and environment in tropical islands: the case of eastern Fiji*, 9–12. MAB Technical Notes No. 13, UNESCO, Paris

Golley, F. (1984) Land management strategies in the humid and subhumid tropics. In F. di Castri, F. W. G. Baker and M. Hadley, eds., *Ecology in practice, Part I: ecosystem management*, 29–96. Tycooly International and UNESCO, Dublin and Paris

Golson, J. (1977) No room at the top: agricultural intensification in the New Guinea Highlands. In J. Allen, J. Golson and R. Jones, eds., *Sunda and Sahul*, 601–38. Academic Press, London

  (1982) The Ipomoean Revolution revisited: society and the sweet potato in the Upper Wahgi Valley. In A. Strathern, ed., *Inequality in New Guinea Highlands societies*, 109–36. Cambridge University Press

Goneyali, E. (1975) Who wants to stay on the farm? In S. Tupouniua et al., *The Pacific way: social issues in national development*, pp. 58–62. South Pacific Social Sciences Association, Suva

Goodman, R., Lepani, C., & Morewetz, D. (1985) *The economy of Papua New Guinea: an independent review*. Development Studies Centre, Australian National University, Canberra

Gordon, A. H. (1879) *Paper on the system of taxation in force in Fiji*, Harrison, London

Gourou, P. (1963) Pressure on island environment. In F. R. Fosberg, ed., *Man's place in the island ecosystem*, 207–25. Bishop Museum Press, Honolulu

Green, R. C. (1976) Lapita sites in the Santa Cruz Group. In R. C. Green and M. M. Cresswell, eds., *Southeast Solomon Islands cultural history*, 245–65. Royal Society of New Zealand Bulletin 11

  (1979) Lapita. In J. D. Jennings, ed., *The prehistory of Polynesia*, 27–60. ANU Press, Canberra

Gregory, D. (1978) *Ideology, science and human geography*. Hutchinson, London

  (1980) The ideology of control: systems theory and geography. *Tijdschrift economische en sociale Geographie*, 71, 327–42

Groube, L. M. (1971) Tonga, Lapita pottery, and Polynesian origins. *Journal of the Polynesian Society*, 80, 278–316

Groves, M. (1963) The nature of Fijian society. *Journal of the Polynesian Society*, vol. 62, 272–91

Hall, P. (1966) *Von Thunen's isolated state*. English trans. of *Der isolierte Staat* by C. M. Wartenberg, edited with an introduction. Pergamon, Oxford

Hardaker, J. B. (1976) Economic aspects of agriculture and marketing in Taveuni. Project Working Paper No. 6, UNESCO/UNDP Project on Population and

Environment in the Eastern Islands of Fiji. Development Studies Centre, ANU, Canberra

Hardaker, J. B., Fleming, E. M., & Harris, G. T. (1984) Smallholder modes of production in the South Pacific: prospects for development. *Pacific Viewpoint*, 25, 196–211

Hardin, G. (1972) The tragedy of the commons. *Science*, 162, 1243–8

Hardin, F. & Baden, J., eds. (1977) *Managing the commons*. Freeman, San Francisco

Harris, M. (1968) *The rise of anthropological theory*. Routledge and Kegan Paul, London

Harvey, D. (1974) Population, resources and the ideology of science. *Economic Geography*, 50, 256–77

Hau'ofa, E. (1980) A Pacific islander's view. In R. G. Ward and A. Proctor, eds., *South Pacific agriculture: choices and constraints*. Asian Development Bank and Australian National University, Canberra: 484–7

(1985) The new South Pacific society: integration and independence. Opening Address at the Auckland Conference on Pacific Studies, University of Auckland, 19–22 August, 1985. mimeo. 18pp.

Heath, I. (1974) Towards a reassessment of Gordon in Fiji. *Journal of Pacific History*, vol. 9, 81–92

Heddinghaus, T. R. & Krueger, A. F. (1981) Annual and interannual variations in outgoing longwave radiation over the tropics. *Monthly Weather Review*, 109, 1208–18

Henderson, G. C. (1931) *Fiji and the Fijians, 1836–1856*. Angus and Robertson, Sydney

Hewitt, A. (1983) Stabex: analysing the effectiveness of an innovation. In C. Stevens, ed., *E.E.C. and the Third World: a survey 3, The Atlantic rift*, 152–65. Hodder and Stoughton, London

Hocart, A. M. (1929) *Lau Islands, Fiji*. Bernice P. Bishop Museum Bulletin No. 62, Honolulu

(1952) *The Northern States of Fiji*. Royal Anthropological Institute of Great Britain and Ireland. Occasional Paper No. 11, Aleuin Press, Herts, UK

Holmes, R. L. (1887) Hurricane in Fiji. *Quarterly Journal Royal Meteorological Society*, 13, 37–45

Hooper, S. J. P. (1982) A study of valuables in the Chiefdom of Lau, Fiji. Unpublished PhD thesis, University of Cambridge

Hopley, D. (1982) *The geomorphology of the Great Barrier Reef: Quaternary development of coral reefs*. Wiley, New York

Horne, J. (1881) *A year in Fiji*. Eyre and Spottiswoode, London

Howard, M. C. (1983) *Export processing zone advocacy and the evolution of development strategies and investment policies in the South Pacific*. Paper presented to one day seminar on Export Processing Zones in Asia. University of Sydney, Centre for Asian Studies (mimeo)

Howe, K. R. (1984) *Where the waves fall: a new South Sea islands history from first settlement to colonial rule*. George Allen and Unwin, Sydney

Hughes, P. J., Hope, G., Latham M. & Brookfield M. (1979) Prehistoric man-induced degradation of the Lakeba landscape: evidence from two island swamps. *UNESCO/UNFPA Fiji Island Reports* 5. Australian National University for UNESCO, 93–110

Hull, T. & Hull, V. (1973) Fiji: a study of ethnic plurality and family planning. In

T. E. Smith, ed., *The politics of family planning in the Third World*, 168–216. George Allen and Unwin, London

Hunt, T. L. (1981) New evidence for early horticulture in Fiji. *Journal of the Polynesian Society*, 90, 259–66

(1986) Conceptual and substantive issues in Fijian prehistory. In P. Kirch, ed., *Island societies: archaeological approaches to evolution and transformation*, 20–32. Cambridge University Press

Innis, H. A. (1930) *The fur trade in Canada: an introduction to Canadian economic history*. University of Toronto Press

(1940) *The cod fisheries: the history of an international economy*. University of Toronto Press

Isdale, P. (1984) Fluorescent bands in massive corals record centuries of coastal rainfall. *Nature*, 310, 578

Jackson, J. (1835) Appendix. In J. E. Erskine, *Journal of a cruise among the islands of the Western Pacific*. J. Murray, London

Jackson, R. G. et al. (1984) *Report of the committee to review the Australian overseas aid program*. Australian Government Publishing Service, Canberra

Jalan, B. (ed.) (1982) *Problems and policies in small economies*. Croom Helm and St Martin's Press, London and New York

Jarre, R. (1955) Notes sur les changements survenus dans les coutumes Fidjiennes depuis l'occupation Européens. *Journal de la Société des Océanistes*, vol. 11, 15–36

Jarvie, I. C. (1970a) Understanding and explanation in sociology and social anthropology. In R. Borger and F. Cioffi, eds., *Explanation in the behavioural sciences*, 231–48. Cambridge University Press

(1970b) Reply (to Winch, 1970). In R. Borger and F. Cioffi, eds., *Explanation in the behavioural sciences*, 260–9. Cambridge University Press

Johannes, R. E. (1981) *Words of the lagoon: fishing and marine lore in the Palau district of Minonesia*. University of California Press, Berkeley

Johnson, J. S. & Lambert J. N. (1982) *The national food and nutrition survey of Fiji*. National Food and Nutrition Committee, UNDP and FAO, Suva

Jones, C. (1976) Emigration from Fiji. Unpublished thesis, School of Social and Economic Development, University of the South Pacific, Suva

Jones, R. (1978) Why did the Tasmanians stop eating fish? In R. A. Gould, ed., *Explorations in ethno-archaeology*, 11–47. University of New Mexico Press, Albuquerque

Kirch, P. V. (1976) Ethno archaeological investigations in Futuna and Uvea (Western Polynesia): a preliminary report. *Journal of the Polynesian Society*, 85, 27–70

(1981) Lapitoid settlements of Futuna and Alofi, Western Polynesia. *Archaeology in Oceania,*, 16, 127–43

(1982a) A version of the Anuta sequence. *Journal of the Polynesian Society*, 91, 245–54

(1982b) Ecology and the adaptation of Polynesian agricultural systems. *Archaeology in Oceania*, 17, 1–6

(1983) Man's role in modifying tropical and subtropical Polynesian ecosystems. *Archaeology in Oceania*, 18, 26–31

Kirch, P. V. & Yen D. E. (1982) *Tikopia. The prehistory and ecology of a Polynesian Outlier*. Bishop Museum Bulletin No. 238, Honolulu

Kirk, W. (1952) Historical geography and the concept of the behavioural environment. In Indian Geographical Society, *Silver Jubilee Souvenir and N. Subrahmanyam Memorial Volume*, 152–60

Knapman, B. (1975) Economic change and organizational innovation: the example of Mavana Village and Tota Co-operative Plantation, Vanua Baluva, Fiji. Unpublished MA thesis in Social Sciences, Flinders University, Adelaide

(1976a) Indigenous involvement in the cash economy of Lau, Fiji, 1840–1946. *Journal of Pacific History*, vol. 11, no. 3, 167–88

(1976b) Pushing out to windward: aspects of European plantation enterprise in northern Lau, Fiji, 1870–1971. *Journal of Pacific Studies* (University of the South Pacific), vol. 2, 25–40

(1984) Capitalism and colonial development: studies in the economic history of Fiji. Unpublished Ph.D. thesis, The Australian National University, Canberra

(1985) Capitalism's economic impact in colonial Fiji 1874–1939: development or underdevelopment? *Journal of Pacific History*, vol. 20, no. 2, 66–83

Knapman, B. & Walter, M. A. H. B. (1980) The way of the land and the path of money: the generation of economic inequality in eastern Fiji. *Journal of Developing Areas*, vol. 14, 201–22

Ladd, H. S. & Hoffmeister J. F. (1945) *Geology of Lau, Fiji*. Bernice P. Bishop Museum Bulletin 181, Honolulu

Lal, B. V. (1980) Approaches to the study of Fijian indentured emigration with special reference to Fiji. *Journal of Pacific History*, vol. 15, no. 1–2, 52–70

(1984a) Labouring men and nothing more: some problems of Indian indenture in Fiji. In K. Saunders, ed., *Indentured labour in the British Empire 1834–1920*, 126–57. Croom Helm, London

(1984b) *Girmitiyas: the origins of the Fiji Indians*. Journal of Pacific History (monograph), Canberra

Lambert, S. M. (1938) *East Indian and Fijian in Fiji: their changing numerical relation*. Special Publications 32, Bernice P. Bishop Museum, Honolulu

Langdon, R. A. (1975) *The lost caravel*. Pacific Publications, Sydney

Langton, J. (1972) Potentialities and problems of adopting a systems approach to the study of change in human geography. In C. Board et al. eds., *Progress in Geography*, vol. 4, 125–80. Methuen, London

Lasaqa, I. Q. (1973) Geography and geographers in the changing Pacific: an islander's view. In H. Brookfield, ed., *The Pacific in transition: geographical perspectives on adaptation and change*, 299–311. Edward Arnold, London

(1984) *The Fijian people before and after Independence, 1959–1977*. Australian National University Press, Canberra

Latham, M. (1979) The natural environment of Lakeba. *UNESCO/UNFPA Fiji Island Reports* No. 5, Australian National University for UNESCO, 13–64

(1983a) Le milieu naturel et son utilisation sur les îles/The characteristics and use of the natural environment of the islands. In *Iles Fidji Orientales/The eastern Islands of Fiji*, 13–97. Travaux et Documents de l'ORSTOM, no. 162. Paris

(1983b) Origine de la formation à talasiga/Origin of the talasiga formation. In Iles Fidji Orientales/The eastern Islands of Fiji, 129–41. Travaux et Documents de l'ORSTOM, no. 162, Paris

Latham, M. & Brookfield H. C. (eds.) (1983) *Iles Fidji Orientales. Etude du milieu naturel, de son utilisation et de son évolution sous l'influence humaine/The eastern Islands of Fiji. A study of the natural environment, its use and man's influence on its evolution*. Travaux et Documents de l'ORSTOM, no. 162, Paris

Latham, M., Hughes, P. J., Hope, G., & Brookfield, M. (1983) Sedimentation dans les zones marécageuse de Lakeba: conséquences sur l'érosion et l'occupation humaine de l'île/Sedimentation in the swamps of Lakeba and its implications for erosion and human occupation of the island. In *Iles Fidji Orientales/The Eastern Islands of Fiji*, 103–20. Travaux et Documents de l'ORSTOM, no. 162, Paris

Lau Provincial Council (1912) Minutes of meetings, National Archives of Fiji, Suva

Leach, E. R. (1961) *Pul Eliya, a village in Ceylon*. Cambridge University Press (1984) Ocean of opportunity? In *XV Pacific Science Congress 1983, Formal Proceedings*, 97–103. Royal Society of New Zealand, Dunedin

Legge, J. D. (1958) *Britain in Fiji, 1868–1880*. Macmillan, London

Leontief, W. (1982) Academic economics. Letter in *Science*, 217: 104–7

Leslie, D. M. & Blakemore L. C. (1978) Properties and classification of the soils from Lakeba, Lau Group, Fiji. In *Lau-Tonga 1977*, 165–90. Royal Society of New Zealand Bulletin 17, Wellington

Lessin, A. P. & P. J. (1970) *Village of the conquerors, Sawana: a Tongan village in Fiji*. Eugene, Oregon

Leubuscher, C. (1951) *The processing of colonial raw materials: a study in location*. HMSO, London

Lloyd, D. T. (1982) *Land policy in Fiji*. Occasional Paper No. 14, Department of Land Economy, University of Cambridge

Lockerby, W. (1925) *The Journal of William Lockerby, sandalwood trader in the Fijian islands during the years 1808–1809*. In E. Thurm and L. C. Wharton, The Hakluyt Society, London. Reprinted 1982, Fiji Times & Herald, Suva

Lodhia, R. N. (1978) *Report on the census of the population, 1976 (13 September) Vol. 1: basic tables*. Parliament of Fiji, Parliamentary Paper No. 13 of 1978, Suva

Lösch, A. (1954) *The economics of location*, trans. from the 2nd rev. edn. by W. H. Woglom with assistance of W. F. Stolper, Yale University Press, New Haven

McAlpine, J. R. & Kreig, G. with Falls, R. (1983) *Climate of Papua New Guinea*. CSIRO and Australian National University Press, Canberra

McArthur, N. (1958) *Report on the census of the population, 1956 (26 September)*. Legislative Council of Fiji, Council Paper No. 1 of 1958, Suva (1967) *Island populations of the Pacific*. ANU Press, Canberra (1971) Fertility and marriage in Fiji. *Human Biology in Oceania*, vol. 1, no.1, 10–22

MacArthur, R. H. & Wilson E. O. (1967) *The theory of island biogeography*. Princeton University Press

McLean, R. F. (1976) Notes on tropical storms and hurricanes in the eastern islands of Fiji. UNESCO/UNFPA Population and Environment Project (mimeo) (1977) The hurricane hazard in the eastern islands of Fiji: an historical analysis. In H. C. Brookfield, ed. *The hurricane hazard: natural disaster and small populations*, 9–64. UNESCO/UNFPA Island Reports 1, Australian National University for UNESCO, Canberra (1979) The coast of Lakeba: a geomorphological reconnaissance. *UNESCO/*

UNFPA Fiji Islands Reports, 5, 65–82. Australian National University for UNESCO

(1980a) The land–sea interface of small tropical islands: morphodynamics and man. In H. C. Brookfield, ed., *Population–environment relations in tropical islands: the case of eastern Fiji*, 125–30. MAB Technical Notes 123, UNESCO/UNFPA, Paris

(1980b) Spatial and temporal variability of external physical controls on small island ecosystems. In H. C. Brookfield, ed., *Population–environment relations in tropical islands: the case of eastern Fiji*, 149–75. MAB Technical Notes 13, UNESCO/UNFPA, Paris

(1983) Géomorphologie cotière/Coastal geomorphology. In *Iles Fidji Orientales/The Eastern Islands of Fiji*, 23–7. Travaux et Documents de l'ORSTOM, no. 162, Paris

McLean, R. F., Stoddart, D. R., Hopley, D. & Polach, H. (1978) Sea level change in the Holocene on the northern Great Barrier Reef. *Philosophical Transactions of the Royal Society of London*, A 291, 167–86

Macnaught, T. J. (1974) Chiefly civil servants. Ambiguity in district administration and the preservation of a Fijian way of life. *Journal of Pacific History*, vol. 9, 3–20

(1977) "We seem no longer to be Fijians": some perceptions of social change in Fijian history. *Pacific Studies*, vol. 1, no. 1, 15–24

(1982) *The Fijian colonial experience a study of the neo-traditional order under British colonial rule prior to World War II*. Pacific Research Monograph No. 7, Development Studies Centre, ANU Press, Canberra

Marx, K. (1867) *Capital*, vol. 1. Otto Meissner, Hamburg

May, J. F. (1985) Perspectives démographiques régionales auz îles Fidji pour la période 1976–2001. Unpublished thesis submitted in the Department of Demography, Université Catholique de Louvain, Belgium

Meillassoux, C. (1972) From reproduction to production: a Marxist approach to economic anthropology. *Economy and Society*, vol. 1, 93–105

(1975) *Femmes, greniers et capitaux*, Maspero, Paris (published in English in 1981 as *Women, meal and money: capitalism and the domestic community*. Cambridge University Press

Monk, J. & Hanson, S. (1982) On not excluding half of the human in human geography. *Professional Geographer*, 34, 11–23

Moynagh, M. (1981) *Brown or white? a history of the Fiji sugar industry, 1873–1973*. Pacific Research Monograph No. 5, Development Studies Centre, ANU Press, Canberra

Nair, S. (1980) *Rural-born Fijians and Indo-Fijians in Suva: a study of movements and linkages*. Development Studies Centre Monograph No. 24, Australian National University, Canberra

(1985) Fijians and Indo-Fijians in Suva: rural–urban movements and linkages. In M. Chapman and R. M. Prothero, eds, *Circulation in population movement: substance and concepts from the Melanesian case*, 306–30. Routledge and Kegan Paul, London

Nankivell, P. S. (1978) Income inequality in Taveuni: a statistical analysis of data from the Resource Base Survey. In H. C. Brookfield, ed., *Taveuni: Land, Population and Production*, 245–97. UNESCO/UNFPA Island Reports 3, Australian National University for UNESCO, Canberra

Narayan, J. (1984) *The political economy of Fiji*. South Pacific Review Press, Suva

Narsey, W. (1979) Monopoly capital, white racism and superprofits in Fiji: a case study of CSR. *The Journal of Pacific Studies*, no. 5

Nation, J. (1978) *Customs of respect: the traditional basis of Fijian communal politics*. Development Studies Centre Monograph, No. 14, ANU Press, Canberra

Nayacakalou, R. R. (1964) Traditional and modern types of leadership and economic development among the Fijians. *International Social Science Journal*, vol. 16, no. 2, 261–72

(1971) Manipulating the system. In R. G. Crocombe, ed., *Land tenure in the Pacific*, 206–26. Oxford University Press, Melbourne

(1975) *Leadership in Fiji*. Oxford University Press, Melbourne

(1978) *Tradition and change in the Fijian village*. South Pacific Social Sciences Association and the Institute of Pacific Studies, University of the South Pacific, Suva

North, D. C. (1955) Location theory and regional economic growth. *Journal of Political Economy*, 63: 243–58

Norton, R. (1977) *Race and politics in Fiji*. Queensland University Press, St Lucia

Odum, H. T. (1971) *Environment, power and society*. Wiley-Interscience, New York and London

O'Laughlin, B. (1977) Production and reproduction: Meillassoux's Femmes, Greniers et Capitaux. *Critique of Anthropology*, No. 8, 3–32

O'Loughlin, C. (1956) *The Pattern of the Fiji Economy*. Legislative Council Paper No. 44, Government Printer, Suva

Palmer, J. B. (1965) Excavations at Karobo, Viti Levu. *New Zealand Archaeological Association Newsletter*, 8(2), 26–34

Parham, B. E. V. (1935) Wilt disease of the "Yangona". *Agricultural Journal of Fiji*, 8: 2–8

Parkes, D. & Thrift, N. (1980) *Times, spaces and places*. Wiley, Chichester

Peet, R. (1980) The consciousness dimension to Fiji's integration into world capitalism. *Pacific Viewpoint*, 21, 91–115

Pereira, H. C. (1973) *Land Use and Water Resources*. Cambridge University Press

Perroux, F. (1955) Note sur la notion de pole de croissance. *Economie Appliquée*, 8: 307–20

Philander, S. G. H. (1981) The response of equatorial oceans to a relaxation of the trade winds. *Journal of Physical Oceanography*, 11, 176–89

Polanyi, K. (1944) *The great transformation*. Reinhart, New York

Poulsen, J. (1968) Archaeological excavations on Tongatapu. In I. Yawata and Y. H. Sinoto, eds., *Prehistoric culture in Oceania*, 85–92. Bishop Museum Press, Honolulu

Prescott, J. R., Robertson, G. B. & Green, R. C. (1982) Thermoluminescence dating of Pacific Island pottery: successes and failures. *Archaeology in Oceania*, 17, 142–7

Qalo, R. P. (1984) *Divided we stand: local government in Fiji*. Institute of Pacific Studies, University of the South Pacific, Suva

Quain, B. (1948) *Fijian village*. University of Chicago Press

Quinn, W. H., Zopf, D. O., Short, K. S. & Kuo Yang, R. T. W. (1978) Historical trends and statistics of the Southern Oscillation, El Niño and Indonesian droughts. *Fishery Bulletin*, 76, 663–78

Racule, R. K. (1985) Doctor in the Fijian islands: F. B. Vulaono 1924–76. In M. Chapman and R. M. Prothero, eds., *Circulation in population movement:*

substance and concepts from the Melanesian case, 149–72. Routledge and Kegan Paul, London

Ramage, C. S. (1968) Role of a tropical 'maritime continent' in the atmospheric circulation. *Monthly Weather Review*, 96, 365–70

Rappaport, R. A. (1963) Aspects of man's influence upon island ecosystems: alteration and control. In F. R. Fosberg, ed., *Man's place in the island ecosystem*, 155–70. Bishop Museum Press, Honolulu

(1968) *Pigs for the ancestors: ritual in the ecology of a New Guinea people*. Yale University Press, New Haven

Rasmusson, E. M. & Carpenter, T. H. (1982) Variations in tropical sea surface temperature and surface wind fields associated with the Southern Oscillation/El Niño. *Monthly Weather Review*, 110, 354–84

Rasmusson, E. M. & Hall, J. M. (1983) El Niño, the great equatorial Pacific Ocean warming event of 1982–1983. *Weatherwise*, 36, 166–75

Ravuvu, A. (1983) *Vaka itaukei: the Fijian way of life*. Institute of Pacific Studies, University of the South Pacific, Suva

Reid, A. C. (1977) The fruit of Rewa: oral traditions and the growth of the pre-Christian Lakeba state. *Journal of Pacific History*, 12, 2–24

(1979) The view from Vatuwaqa: the role of Lakeba's leading lineage in the introduction and establishment of Christianity. *Journal of Pacific History*, 14, 154–67

(1981) Crusaders: the religious and relationship background to Lakeban expansion in the 1850s. *Journal of Pacific History*, 16, 59–69

(1983) The chiefdom of Lau: a new Fijian state built upon Lakeban foundations. *Journal of Pacific History*, 18, 183–97

Reiter, E. R. (1978) Long-term wind variability in the tropical Pacific, its possible causes and effects. *Monthly Weather Review*, 106, 324–30

Richardson, H. W. (1969) *Regional economics: location theory, urban structure and regional change*. Weidenfeld and Nicolson, London

Roe, K. K., Burnett, W. C. & Lee, A. I. N. (1983) Uranium disequilibrium dating of phosphate deposits from the Lau group, Fiji. *Nature*, 302, 603–6

Roger Williams Technical Services Ltd. (1966) *Survey of the United States and Canadian non-food uses of coconut oil. Prepared for the Food and Agriculture Organization of the United Nations*. Roger Williams, Princeton, NJ

Rogers, G. (1974) Archaeological discoveries on Niuatoputapu Island, Tonga. *Journal of the Polynesian Society*, 83, 308–48

Ross, H. M. (1973) *Baegu. Social and ecological organisation in Malaita, Solomon Islands*. University of Illinois Press, Urbana

Roth, G. K. (1951) *Native administration in Fiji during the past seventyfive years*. Occasional Paper No. 10, Royal Anthropological Institute, London

(1953) *Fijian way of life*. Oxford University Press, Melbourne

Rothfield, R. & Kumar, B. (1980) *Report on the census of agriculture 1978*. Parliamentary Paper No. 28 of 1980. Government Printer, Suva

Routledge, D. (1978) American influence on the politics of Fiji, 1849–1874. *Journal of Pacific Studies*, vol. 4, 66–88

Rowe, J. S. (1961) The level-of-integration concept and ecology. *Ecology* 42, 420–7

Rowland, M. J. & Best, S. (1980) Survey and excavation on the Kedekede hillfort Lakeba Island, Lau Group, Fiji. *Archaeology and Physical Anthropology in Oceania*, 15, 29–50

Rutz, H. J. (1982) Bureaucracy and brokerage: Fijian villages and public goods. In W. L. Rodman and D. A. Counts, eds., *Middlemen and brokers in Oceania*, 149–86. University of Michigan Press, Ann Arbor (ASAO Monograph No. 9)

Sahlins, M. D. (1958) *Social stratification in Polynesia*. University of Washington Press, Seattle

  (1962) *Moala: culture and nature on a Fijian island*. University of Michigan Press, Ann Arbor

  (1974) *Stone age economics*. Tavistock, London

  (1983) Other times, other customs: the anthropology of history. *American Anthropologist*, 85, 517–44. Reprinted in *Islands of History*, University of Chicago Press (1985)

Salvat, B. (1980) The living marine resources of the South Pacific–past, present and future. In H. C. Brookfield, ed., *Population and environment in tropical islands: the case of eastern Fiji*, 131–48. MAB Technical Notes 13, UNESCO/UNFPA, Paris

Salvat, B., Ricard, M., Richard, G., Galzin, R. & Toffart, J. L. (1976). The ecology of the reef-lagoon complex of some islands in the Lau group. UNESCO/UNFPA Project, Working Paper No. 2. Development Studies Centre, Canberra

Sayes, S. A. (1984) Changing paths of the land: early political hierarchies in Cakaudrove, Fiji. *Journal of Pacific History*, 19, 3–20

Scarr, D. (1965) John Bates Thurston, Commodore J. G. Goodenough, and rampant Anglo Saxons in Fiji. *Historical Studies, Australia and New Zealand*, 11, no. 43, 361–82

  (1967) *Fragments of empire: a history of the Western Pacific High Commission 1877–1914*. Australian National University Press, Canberra

  (1970) A Roko Tui for Lomaiviti: the question of legitimacy in Fijian administration, 1874–1900. *Journal of Pacific History*, 5, 3–31

  (1972) Creditors and the house of Hennings: an elegy from the social and economic history of Fiji. *Journal of Pacific History*, 8, 104–23

  (1973a) Cakobau and Ma'afu: contenders for pre-eminence in Fiji. In J. W. Davidson and D. Scarr, eds., *Pacific Island Portraits*, (revised edition), 95–126. Australian National University Press, Canberra

  (1973b) *I, the very Bayonet. The majesty of colour, (Vol. 1)*. Australian National University Press, Canberra

  (1979) John Bates Thurston: grand panjandrum of the Pacific. In D. Scarr, ed., *More Pacific Island portraits*. Australian National University Press, Canberra

  (1980a) *Viceroy of the Pacific. The majesty of colour, (Vol. 2)*. Pacific-Research Monograph No. 4, Australian National University Press, Canberra

  (1980b) *Ratu Sukuna: soldier, statesman, man of two worlds*. Macmillan Education Ltd, London

  (ed.) (1983) *Fiji: the three-legged stool. Selected writings of Ratu Sir Lala Sukuna*. Macmillan Education Ltd, London

  (1984) *Fiji: a short history*. Allen and Unwin, Sydney and London

Schofield, J. C. (1977a) Late Holocene sea level, Gilbert and Ellice Islands, West Central Pacific Ocean. *New Zealand Journal of Geology and Geophysics*, 20, 503–30

  (1977b) Effect of late Holocene sea-level fall on atoll development. *New Zealand Journal of Geology and Geophysics*, 20, 531–6

(1979) Effects on sea level change on human migration in the Pacific Ocean. Paper presented at XIV Pacific Science Congress, Khabarovsk

(1980) Postglacial transgressive maxima and second-order transgressions of the Southwest Pacific Ocean. In N. A. Morner, ed., *Earth Rheology, Isostasy and Eustasy*, 517–21. Wiley-Interscience, Chichester

Schultz, T. W. (1964) *Transforming traditional agriculture.* Yale University Press, New Haven, Connecticut

Schutz, A. J. (ed.) (1977) *The diaries and correspondence of David Cargill, 1832–1843.* ANU Press, Canberra

Seeman, B. (1862) *Viti: an account of a government mission to the Vitian or Fijian Islands in the years 1860–61.* Macmillan, Cambridge

Shand, R. T. (ed.) (1980) *The island states of the Pacific and Indian oceans: anatomy of development.* Development Studies Centre Monograph 23, Australian National University, Canberra

Sillitoe, P. (1983) *Roots in the earth: crops in the Highlands of Papua New Guinea.* Manchester University Press

Silsoe, Lord (1963) *Report on the Fiji coconut industry survey.* Crown Agents, London

Simon, H. A. (1976) From substantive to procedural rationality. In S. J. Latsis, ed., *Method and appraisal in economics*, 129–48. Cambridge University Press

Simpson, R. H. & Riehl, H. (1981) *The hurricane and its impact.* Blackwell, Oxford

Siwatibau, S. (1981) *Rural energy in Fiji: a survey of domestic rural energy use and potential.* International Development Research Centre, Ottawa

(1982) *A report on the resurvey of 10 Fijian villages.* Fiji Employment and Development Mission, WP (mimeo), Suva

Slater, D. (1975) The poverty of modern geographical enquiry. *Pacific Viewpoint*, 16, 159–76

Smart, C. D. (1965) An outline of Kabara prehistory. *New Zealand Archaeological Association Newsletter*, 8(21), 43–52

Smythe, W. J. (1864) *Ten months in the Fiji Islands.* Henry and Parker, Oxford and London

Sofer, M. (1985) Yaqona and the peripheral economy. *Pacific Viewpoint*, vol. 26, no. 2, 415–36

Southern, W. (1986) The Late Quaternary environmental history of Fiji. Unpublished PhD thesis in Geography, Australian National University, Canberra

Spate, O.H.K. (1959) *The Fijian people: economic problems and prospects.* Legislative Council of Fiji, Council Paper No. 13 of 1959, Suva

(1960) Under two laws: the Fijian dilemma. *Meanjin Quarterly* (Melbourne), 19 (2). Reprinted in Spate, O.H.K., 1966, *Let me enjoy*, 46–65. Methuen, London.

(1961) On being an expert. *Quadrant*, Reprinted in *Let Me Enjoy*, 3–14. 1966, Methuen, London.

(1979) *The Spanish Lake*, vol. 1 of *The Pacific since Magellan*. ANU Press, Canberra

Specht, J. & White, J.P. (eds.) (1978) *Trade and exchange in Oceania and Australia.* Sydney University Press, and *Mankind*, 11(3)

Spriggs, M. J. T. (1981) *Vegetable kingdoms: taro irrigation and Pacific prehistory.* Department of Prehistory, Research School of Pacific Studies, Australian National University, Canberra

(1983) Mungo's echo? Pleistocene terrace formation in the western Pacific. *Quaternary Australasia*, 1(1–2), 42–4

(1985) Prehistoric man-induced landscape enhancement in the Pacific: examples and implications. In I. S. Farrington, ed., *Prehistoric intensive agriculture in the Tropics*, 409–34. British Archaeological Reports, Oxford

(1986) Landscape, land use and political transformation in southern Melanesia. In P. V. Kirch, ed., *Island societies: archaeological approaches to evolution and transformation*, 6–19. Cambridge University Press

Stanner, W. E. H. (1953) *The south seas in transition: a study of post-war rehabilitation and reconstruction in three British dependencies*. Australian Publishing Company, Sydney

Stoddart, D. R. (1967) Organism and ecosystem as geographical models. In R. J. Chorley and P. Haggett, eds., *Models in Geography*, 511–48

(1971) Coral reefs and islands and catastrophic storms. In J. A. Steers, ed., *Readings in applied coastal geomorphology*, 155–97. Macmillan, London

(1983) Grandeur in this view of life: Darwin and the ocean world. *Bulletin of Marine Science*, 33, 521–7, reprinted in *On Geography* (1986) 219–29. Blackwell, Oxford

Stoddart, D. R., Spencer, T. & Scoffin, T. P. (1985) Reef growth and karst erosion on Mangaia, Cook Islands: a reinterpretation. *Zeitschrift für Geomorphologie*, NF suppl. 57, 121–40

Stokes, E. (1968) The Fiji cotton boom in the eighteen sixties. *New Zealand Journal of History*, 2, no. 2

Subramani (ed.) (1979) *The Indo-Fijian experience*. University of Queensland Press, St Lucia

Sutherland, W. M. (1901) *A report on the Fijian population census of 31 March 1901*. Minute Paper 2919 of 1901, Suva

Tarte, J. V. (n.d.) Remittances of James Valentine Tarte (1837–1918). Pacific Manuscripts Bureau Microfilm PMB 431, Menzies Library, Australian National University, Canberra

Taylor, F. W. & Bloom, A. L. (1977) Coral reefs on tectonic blocks, Tonga island arc. *Proceedings 3rd International Coral Reef Symposium*, 2, 675–281, Miami

Taylor, M. J. (1984) Business organisations and transfer of value: examples from Fiji. In D. K. Forbes and P. J. Rimmer, eds., *Uneven development and the geographical transfer of value*. Department of Human Geography Publication 16, Australian National University, Canberra: 175–97

Thompson, L. (1938) The culture history of the Lau islands, Fiji. *American Anthropologist*, 40, 181–97

(1940a) *Southern Lau, Fiji: an ethnography*. Bernice P. Bishop Museum Bulletin, No. 162, Honolulu

(1940b) *Fijian frontier*. Octagon Books, New York

(1949) The culture history of the Lau islands, Fiji. *American Anthropologist*, 40, 181–97

Thomson, B. (1908) *The Fijians: a study of the decay of custom*. Heinemann, London

Thornley, A. W. (1977) The vakamisoneri in Lau, Fiji: some comments. *Journal of Pacific History*, 12, 107–12

Titley, A. L. (1976) The future population carrying capacity of the smaller islands. Background Paper, United Nations Fiji Regional Planning Project, 10pp. (mimeo)

Titley, A. L. & McKee, S. I. D. (1976) Population estimates. Background Paper, United Nations Fiji Regional Planning Project, 18pp. (mimeo)

Tubuna, S. (1985) Patterns of return migration in the Wainbuka River valley: Viti Levu, Fiji. In M. Chapman and R. M. Prothero, eds., *Circulation in population movement: substance and concepts from the Melanesian case*, 213–24. Routledge and Kegan Paul, London

Twyford, J. T. & Wright A. C. S. (1965) *The soil resources of the Fiji islands*, 2 vols. Government Printer, Suva

UNDP (1977) *Regional Planning Project, Fiji. Project findings and recommendations*. United Nations Development Programme, Suva, for UNDP, New York

UNESCO (1973) *Programme on Man and the Biosphere (MAB) Expert panel on project 7: ecology and rational use of island ecosystems. Final report.* MAB Report series No. 11, Paris

(1977) The social science component of MAB research. MAB/1CC–5/1NF 3, Paris (mimeo)

UNESCO/UNFPA Project (1977) *Population, resources and development in the eastern Islands of Fiji: information for decision-making.* Australian National University for UNESCO, Canberra

Vayda, A. P. & Rappaport R. A. (1963) Island Cultures. In F. R. Fosberg, ed., *Man's place in the island ecosystems*, 133–42. Bishop Museum Press, Honolulu

Vogeler, I. (1981) *The myth of the family farm: agribusiness dominance of U.S. agriculture.* Westview Press, Boulder (Col.)

Vusoniwailala, L. (1985) Communication, social identity, and the rising cost of Fijian communalism. *Pacific Perspective*, 12, no. 2, 1–7

Wairiki Mission (n.d.) Pamphlet on Wairiki Mission. Pacific Manuscripts Bureau Microfilm PMB 467, Item 3, Menzies Library, Australian National University, Canberra

Wall, D. (1986) *Coconut processing in the Pacific Islands.* Canberra, Australian National University, National Centre for Development Studies, Islands/Australia Working Paper 86/18

Walsh, A. C. (1978) The urban squatter question: squatting, housing and urbanisation in Suva, Fiji. Unpublished PhD dissertation, Massey University, Palmerston North

(1982) *Migration, urbanization and development in South Pacific countries.* ESCAP Comparative Study on Migration, Urbanization and Development, Country Report No. 6, New York

(1984) The search for an appropriate housing policy in Fiji. *Third World Planning Review*, 6, no. 2, 185–200

Walter, M. A. H. B. (1978) The conflict of the traditional and the traditionalised: an analysis of Fijian land tenure. *Journal of the Polynesian Society*, 87, no. 2, 89–108

(1983) Strategic gardening. *Oceania*, 53, 389–99

Ward, G. F. A. (1971) *The growth of tropical cyclones in the Southwest Pacific.* NZ Met. Service Tech. Note No. 201, Wellington

Ward, R. G. (1961) Internal migration in Fiji. *Journal of the Polynesian Society*, 10, no. 3, 257–71

(1964) Cash cropping and the Fijian village. *Geographical Journal*, 130, 484–506

(1965) *Land use and population in Fiji: a geographical study.* HMSO, London

(1967) The consequences of smallness in Polynesia. In B. Benedict, ed., *Problems of smaller territories*, 81–96. Institute of Commonwealth Studies, Commonwealth Papers, No. 10, University of London, London

(1969) Land use and land alienation in Fiji to 1885. *Journal of Pacific History*, 4, 3–25

(1972) The Pacific bêche-de-mer trade with special reference to Fiji. In R. G. Ward, ed., *Man in the Pacific Islands: essays on geographical change*, 91–123. Oxford University Press

(1985) Land, land use and land availability. In H. C. Brookfield, F. Ellis and R. G. Ward, *Land, cane and coconuts: papers on the rural economy of Fiji*, 15–64. Department of Human Geography Publication 17, Australian National University, Canberra

Ward, R. G. & Proctor, A. (eds.) (1980) *South Pacific agriculture: choices and constraints.* Asian Development Bank and Australian National University, Canberra

Watkins, M. (1963) A staple theory of economic growth. *Canadian Journal of Economics and Political Science*, 29, 141–58

Watters, R. F. (1965) The development of agricultural enterprise in Fiji. *Journal of the Polynesian Society*, 74, 490–502

Watters, R. F. (1969) *Koro: economic and social change in Fiji.* Clarendon Press, Oxford

Watts, M. (1983) On the poverty of theory: natural hazards research in context. In K. Hewitt, ed., *Interpretations of Calamity*, 231–62. Allen and Unwin, Boston

Whitehead, C. (1981) *Education in Fiji: policy, problems and progress in primary and secondary education, 1939–1973.* Pacific Research Monograph No. 6, The Australian National University, Canberra

Wilkes, C. (1852) *Narrative of the United States Exploring Expedition during the years 1838, 1839, 1840, 1841, 1842*, vol. 2. Ingram Cooke, London

Williams, T. (1858) *Fiji and the Fijians. Vol. 1 The islands and their inhabitants.* Alexander Heylin, London (reprinted 1982, Fiji Museum, Suva)

Winch, P. (1964) Understanding a primitive society. *American Philosophical Quarterly*, 1, 307–24

(1970) Comment (on Jarvie, 1970a). In R. Borger and F. Cioffi, eds., *Explanation in the behavioural sciences.* Cambridge University Press, 249–59

Wittfogel, K. A. (1957) *Oriental despotism.* Yale University Press, New Haven

Wooster, W. S. & Guillen, O. (1974) Characteristics of El Niño in 1972. *Journal of Marine Research*, 32, 387–404

World Bank (1983) *Economic situation and prospects of Fiji.* World Bank, Washington, DC

World Fertility Survey (1976), *Fiji fertility survey 1974. Principal report.* Government Printer, Suva

Wyrtki, K. (1975) El Niño – the dynamic response of the equatorial Pacific Ocean to atmospheric forcing. *Journal of Physical Oceanography*, 5, 572–84

Yen, D. E. (1980) Pacific production systems. In R. G. Ward and A. Proctor, eds., *South Pacific agriculture: choice and constraints*, 73–106. Australian National University Press, Canberra, for Asian Development Bank, Manila

Young, J. M. R. (1970) Evanescent ascendancy: the planter community in Fiji. In

J. W. Davidson and D. Scarr, eds., *Pacific Islands portraits*, 147–75. Australian National University Press, Canberra

(1982) The response of Lau to foreign contact: an interdisciplinary reconstruction. *Journal of Pacific History*, 17, 29–50

Zwart, F. H. A. G. (1968) *Report on the census of the population, 1966 (12 September)*. Legislative Council of Fiji, Council Paper No. 9 of 1968, Suva

(1979) *Report on the census of the population, 1976 (13 September) Vol. 2: Demographic characteristics*. Parliament of Fiji, Parliamentary Paper No. 43 of 1979, Suva

Index